# SUNDIAL

Theoretical Relationships Between Psychological Type, Talent and Disease

Barbara E. Bryden, Ph.D.

Center for Applications of Psychological Type, Inc.
Gainesville, Florida

Published by
Center for Applications of Psychological Type, Inc.
2815 NW 13th Street, Suite 401
Gainesville FL 32609
352.375.0160
www.capt.org

CAPT, the CAPT logo, and Center for Applications of Psychological Type are trademarks of Center for Applications of Psychological Type Inc. in the United States and other countries.

Introduction to Type is a trademark or registered trademark of CPP, Inc. in the United States and other countries.

Myers-Briggs Type Indicator, Myers-Briggs, and MBTI are trademarks or registered trademarks of the Myers-Briggs Type Indicator Trust in the United States and other countries.

Printed in the United States of America.

Library of Congress Cataloging-in-Publications Data
Bryden, Barbara E., 1954–
Sundial: theoretical relationships between psychological type,
talent, and disease/Barbara E. Bryden
p. cm.
Includes bibliographical references.
ISBN 0-935652-46-9
1. Typology (Psychology). 2. Mind and Body. 3.Ability. 4.Personality—
Physiological aspects. 5. Medicine and psychology. 6. Holistic medicine.
I. Title.

BF698.3.B79 2003
155.2'6—dc21
2003046203

*For my family and friends, with love.*

# TABLE OF CONTENTS

# TABLE OF CONTENTS

# FIGURES

✳ ✳ ✳

'In the beginning was the dream and the dream was with God and the dream was God.' How do we live God's dream for us? God's dream for us is like a great underground river that calls to its heart. When we go with its flow, we are centered. But we must let go before we can dive into it, unlearn so much before we swim. Our place is in the water, not on the riverbank. God is already at our center. Centering is more about letting go of the wrong maps than about drawing new ones. Our estranged hearts will find their own way home once we set them free. They were created with their own compasses already in place. Why are we so slow to trust them? (O'Leary, 1991)

✳ ✳ ✳

# ✳ ACKNOWLEDGMENTS ✳

In reflecting on her 1994 recording "The Visit," Loreena McKennitt, Canadian harpist and songwriter, had these thoughts on creativity:

> I have long considered the creative impulse to be a visit—a thing of grace, not commanded or owned so much as awaited, prepared for. A thing, also, of mystery . . .

Surely, *Sundial* was an incredible "visit." I had experienced nothing like it—the dreams, the strange occurrences associated with it, the synchronicities that seemed to support its direction, and the marvelous personalities I came to know because of it. It was a wondrous and tremendously meaningful personal experience for me that is as much a story in my life as the book itself. I am not the same person because of it.

The text is in two parts, in two hemispheres as it were, much like the human brain. On the face of it, the first part is perhaps more scientific, more logical and sequentially ordered; the second part more creative, non-linear and interconnected. It evolves, hopefully, with the reader, from halves into wholes.

*Sundial* began to take shape conceptually about 1986, during my dissertation years, and I owe its metamorphosis to book form to family and friends, notably Romie Christie, and my father and mentor, Dick Bryden. Ideas were shared only at home until Romie convinced me to put them to paper during a long drive home from the north in January 1993. Later, my patient and wise father became chief reviewer, and the first draft went to the publisher in 1997. My mother, Shirley Bryden, and my children, Jaime, Jennifer and Jill, gave endless love and support through this process, and Dolly Brownell Hussey was instrumental in formatting the material. The ideas have grown and grown since the early days, as I hope I have, and I thank the people closest to me, from the bottom of my heart, for their tireless, selfless and caring contributions to this evolution. I am very grateful to Bery Juschka for reading and discussing earlier drafts.

The writing of *Sundial* and the time it has taken to get it to print have caused me to think deeply about what matters, about the life that is all around me, and the love and respect I feel for the important individuals who are a part of it. It is *because* of these people, and *for* these people, that I write down these ideas: for my beautiful and amazing children; for my always devoted parents; for my sisters Joan and Lisa; for my grandchildren Aiden and Chloe, and for Kevin Luykenaar, Wayne Kondro, Guy Bourget, Marlon Smith, and Romie and Jim. For other friends who have "been there" over the years—Pearl Tomey, Ellie and Stan Goodwin, Phyllis and Stan Schreiter, Barbara Ratz, Julia Herscovitch, Jan and Joey Brown, Wendy Wildeman, Nancy and Don Dempson, Dolly and Derek. I thank Tory who walked with me as I thought, and Peyto who has continued in this role.

I would also like to take this opportunity to thank friends and colleagues at the University of Calgary, such as Dr. Marilyn Samuels, Division of Applied Psychology, for their support over time, and five who have had a lasting impact on me: Dr. Robert F. Lawson of Ohio State University; Dr. H. Z. Darwish of the University of Calgary Departments of Paediatrics and Clinical Neurosciences, and the Alberta Children's Hospital; Christine E. Silverberg, Gowlings LLP; Dr. Patricia S. Cowings and Dr. William B. Toscano, Psychophysiological Research Laboratory, NASA Ames Research Center.

I am indebted to people at the Center for Applications of Psychological Type for working to get *Sundial* ready for publication—Jerry Macdaid, Margaret Fields, Keven Ward, Keith McCormick, Christy Freeman, Heather Curry, Eleanor Sommer, Elayna Rexrode, and Dr. Charles Martin. I am particularly grateful to Dr. Mary McCaulley, who supported my work and made publication possible.

Finally, I would like to pay special tribute to someone whose soul is somewhere else now, but whose memory nevertheless continues to affect me, Ruth Bryden, who will always be "Sam" to me.

My deepest, heart-felt thanks to you all.

Barbara E. Bryden
Calgary, Canada
November, 2004

This book is about some relationships that might exist between psychological type, talent and disease that, for reasons about to be discussed, may follow an oddly circular model of cognitive development in the brain, roughly analogous to the movement of light around a sundial. The relationships have not been proven conclusively in most instances, are inductively reasoned from a variety of old and new perspectives, and are highly uncertain at best, as these connections are only recently being explored by the psychological type community. Nevertheless, there are valid purposes to such a preliminary attempt, which are namely *to enhance our limited understanding of the role of cognition in disease processes, and to create a researchable model of psychological type, talent and health that has heretofore been lacking in the typological literature.* It is hoped that by first examining pathological patterns that may or may not be present in the different types and talents, we might better understand the conscious conditions for health in each of these various categories.

Why the connection to talent? Because, as will become apparent, talent, like personality, represents an adaptive pattern of cognition in an individual that is repeatedly engaged over the course of a lifetime, and one which can be successfully traced to some areas of the brain more than others in the execution of the talent. To link disease with a particular talent, therefore, and with the types most often recognized as having that talent, is to link disease to repetitious patterns of cognitive activity in certain quadrants of the brain. The link is, of course, associative rather than causal, which means that Type X, Talent Y and Disease Z, for example, may present together in the same physical package, as do blue eyes and blonde hair, but it does not mean that Type X or Talent Y causes Disease Z any more than blue eyes cause blonde hair. A major thesis of the book is that, if disease-related cognition can be localized in this way, it follows that health might be maintained, or perhaps even achieved in some instances, by a purposeful shifting of one's thinking and feeling to areas of the brain not so related. A given type may be able to modify his preferences, in other words, in a desired direction, to reduce his identified health risks.

It is not our intention to provide an in-depth discussion of the theory of psychological type as this text is an advanced conjectural application of type theory and dynamics for readers reasonably fluent in their complexities. Other investigators have done a superb job of explaining type theory and its many other practical uses, and to attempt to revisit those here would be vexatiously redundant and divergent from *our main purpose of applying type to issues within health.*

Readers new to a concept of type are referred to the seminal writings of Carl Gustav Jung, Katharine Briggs, Isabel Briggs Myers, and Mary McCaulley, and to the excellent work of present-day members of the type community including Naomi Quenk, Alex Quenk, Sandra Krebs Hirsch, Jean Kummerow, Nancy Barger, Linda Kirby, Judith Provost, Scott Anchors, Gordon Lawrence, John DiTiberio, Eleanor Corlett and Nancy Millner, David Keirsey and Marilyn Bates, Olaf Isachsen and Linda Berens, Paul Tieger and Barbara Barron-Tieger. A complete list of titles is available from the Center for Applications of Psychological Type (CAPT) of Gainesville, Florida; from the Association for Psychological Type (APT) of Kansas City, Missouri; from CPP, Inc. of Palo Alto, California; and from Psychometrics Canada of Edmonton, Alberta. Readers new to the field are also advised to first take the personality inventory which measures psychological type—the *Myers-Briggs Type Indicator*® (*MBTI*®) instrument—and to have a thorough understanding of their own particular preferences before reading this text.

It must be said that it is also not our purpose to provide a complete review of the other ancient perspectives and modern schools of thought presented in this book: the neuro-psychology of talent; neurologist Norman Geschwind's talent-deficit theory; Hindu chakra theory; Chinese medicine; native medicine wheels; the physics of chaos theory; relativity; and spirituality. Rather, this is an eclectic look at a number of unusual and seemingly disparate approaches to health, and a tentative interrelating of ideas within them to build new insights for applications of type theory to the body. At no point along the way is this undertaking an exact and technical science, but rather an artistic science, or a technical art—an active, evolving process of piecing together isolated bits of a very large and ancient puzzle.

Close up, the outcome of this endeavor is a rather enormous collection of complex facts from a number of very diverse fields, in any one of which it is easy to get lost. Viewed from "above," from the vantage point of the gestalt, it appears as an exquisite tapestry of unified form and simpler purpose that is difficult to miss. And so, while the puzzle-solving process may be inward-turning, analytic and scientific to some limited degree—at the level of deducing and reducing intricate detail—the product is nevertheless art in some sense, an inductive, imperfect, perhaps aesthetically pleasing, outward-looking, holistic model for prediction and change that may turn out to encompass the health of the globe as much as the individual.

The result, it is hoped, is an unusual union of contemporary Western psychology and ancient, Eastern and indigenous traditions, with which to better explore the health needs of a New Age. It is, therefore, an example of the new psychology—something we might call "bioenergetic psychology" or "spiritual psychology"—a blend of conventional science of mind and the wisdom of the ancients, for new synergistic applications to the health of the body. The goal, of course, is the understanding and integration of mind, body, heart and soul (spirit), for the development of the "whole" person.

We begin our cumulative journey through the perspectives with a refresher of relevant type concepts.

# PART ONE

# CHAPTER ONE

## A BRIEF DISCUSSION OF PSYCHOLOGICAL TYPE THEORY

✳ ✳ ✳

Readers new to a concept of type will learn about ideas crucial to theoretical arguments presented throughout this book including the following:

* ✳ A history of Jungian psychological type, and the instrument for measuring it, the *Myers-Briggs Type Indicator® (MBTI®)*
* ✳ Definitions for the four *MBTI* scales: Extraversion–Introversion, Sensing–Intuition, Thinking–Feeling, and Judging–Perceiving
* ✳ Talent domains to which different psychological types appear to be drawn
* ✳ The circular process of type development through life, known as *individuation*
* ✳ Behavioral consequences of a "one-sided" personality, as described by Carl Jung and Naomi Quenk
* ✳ The role of psychic energy and energy flow in psychological and disease processes
* ✳ Energic differences between Extraverts and Introverts
* ✳ The Jungian notion of *compensation,* in which a one-sided personality psychologically compensates for his or her own personality excesses, in order to achieve an innate sense of balance.

These concepts are related to theories of brain organization and talent in chapter 2, on the assumption that these more traditional ideas about psychological type are seen again, described in different language, in the modern-day science of neuropsychology.

Each chapter throughout *Sundial* is preceded by an introduction like this one and is followed by a brief summary to help readers focus on the salient points essential to later arguments.

✳ ✳ ✳

**About the time of the First World War**, the great Swiss psychoanalyst Carl Jung (1971) developed a three-scale theory of psychological type involving what he called *attitudes* and *functions* of thought. The attitudes are two general orientations in personality within which the individual relates to the world. One of these was thought to be inward toward the inner thought and feeling world of the individual (introversion), and the other outward toward the action, people and things in a person's external environment (extraversion). The four functions of thought, on the other hand, affect how an individual perceives the world and deals with information and experience. The functions were considered to be polar opposites of each other—thinking and feeling, and sensing and intuiting—and Jung grouped them with the two attitudes to form eight different psychological types. Jung himself had preferences for introversion, intuition and thinking.

Beginning in the 1920s, two American women, Katharine Cook Briggs and her daughter Isabel Briggs Myers, formalized Jung's work by creating a forced-choice personality inventory known as the *Myers-Briggs Type Indicator (MBTI)* instrument, which measured Jung's three bipolar scales, plus a fourth one of their own invention that aimed to assess the individual's lifestyle preferences for organization (Myers & McCaulley, 1985). The scales became known as Extraversion (E) versus Introversion (I), Sensing (S) versus Intuition (N), Thinking (T) versus Feeling (F), and the fourth scale, Judging (J) versus Perceiving (P).

When responses to the *MBTI* instrument are scored, an individual's dominant preference on each of the bipolar scales—E or I, S or N, T or F, J or P—is obtained. There are no right or wrong answers on this inventory, the results are personally affirming, and the correctness, strength and variability of the preferences are often compared to preferences for handedness (Myers, 1987). Some people are strongly right-handed, others moderately left-handed, and still others inhabit the "ambi-handed" state in between, yet no one preference can be judged functionally better or worse than another because the "best" preference for a person is simply the one that the individual decides works most effectively for him. So it is with psychological type.

The scale preferences obtained through the inventory are combined into a four-letter acronym for the person, such as ESTP or INFJ, which corresponds to a psychological type profile that holistically describes the traits associated with that type. Katharine Briggs had preferences for INFJ, Isabel Myers for INFP, Jung for INTP, meaning all three original type theorists had in common the reflective theory-making inclinations of Introverts with Intuition (IN). Because of the addition of the J–P scale in the *Myers-Briggs®* conception of the traits, sixteen surprisingly accurate psychological type profiles are generated by *MBTI* results, each of them correlated in over fifty years of rigorous research with various cognitive talents and vocational choices (Table 1). Isabel Myers, quoting a verse in the Book of Romans, called these "gifts differing" and wrote a theoretical text by the same name on the subject (Myers & Myers, 1980). Distributions of the qualities and cognitive interests on the sixteen squares of the type table create a matrix of patterns that has been shown, over the years, to have the wide applications of a human periodic table of elements.

Myers and McCaulley (1985) clearly defined the qualities assessed by each of the four *MBTI* scales. The Extraversion–Introversion scale measures the ways in which a person is energized, the Extravert drawing his energy from his surroundings, the Introvert from within himself. The Sensing–Intuition scale measures the ways in which a person receives information, the Sensing type using his sensory modalities to collect detailed factual information, the Intuitive type using his intuition to see possible relationships between larger chunks of information, or wholes. The Thinking–Feeling scale refers to how a person makes a decision, the Thinking type using logic to study alternatives in an analytical and objective manner, the Feeling type to make decisions with other people in mind and in a values-oriented way. The fourth scale, Judging–Perceiving, refers to an individual's lifestyle orientation to the world, the Judging person preferring to live in a more decisive, planned and organized way, the Perceiving person in a more spontaneous, flexible and process-oriented way.

Overall, the inventory has been found to be quite reliable—the type categories have a test-retest reliability of .62 to .90, and a split-half reliability of low .50s to high .70s (Sewell, 1986)—but more recently there has been some statistically demonstrated doubt as to the validity of the fourth scale added by Myers (Bokoros et al., 1992; Harasym et al., 1995. Complex factor analysis in three independent studies shows that J actually collapses into S,

**Table 1.** Type Table of Academic Subjects Significantly Preferred by Each Type, from Choices on the *MBTI* Form G (Myers & McCaulley, 1985)

| ISTJ<br>**Mathematics<br>Practical Skills** | ISFJ<br>**Practical Skills** | INFJ<br>**Art<br>English<br>Music** | INTJ<br>**Science** |
|---|---|---|---|
| ISTP<br>**Mathematics<br>Practical Skills** | ISFP<br>**Practical Skills** | INFP<br>**Art<br>English<br>Music** | INTP<br>**Art<br>Science** |
| ESTP<br>**History<br>Mathematics<br>Practical Skills** | ESFP<br>**History** | ENFP<br>**Art<br>English<br>Music** | ENTP<br>**Art<br>Science** |
| ESTJ<br>**Mathematics<br>Practical Skills** | ESFJ<br>**Mathematics<br>Music** | ENFJ<br>**Art<br>English<br>Music** | ENTJ<br>**English<br>Science** |

and P into N, which means, in English, that if we have preferences for S, we also very likely have preferences for the linear, structured organization of J. Similarly, if we have preferences for N, this work suggests we also very likely have preferences for the unfettered, non-linear freedom of P. When all the research on this question is in, we may find we eventually arrive at a compromise position between the Jungian and *Myers and Briggs* concepts of personality measurement, one which includes two attitudes, four functions and *three* scales represented by E–I, SJ–NP, and T–F.

In any event, despite the clarity of Myers' and McCaulley's definitions, Jung's original names for the attitudes and functions are often confusing to readers in that the terms do not mean what we might normally expect them to mean. For instance, Extraversion can connote an active and outgoing personality, and Introversion reserved and reflective tendencies, but not always. Sensing can signify realistic, down-to-earth and perhaps physical inclinations, and Intuition abstract, imaginative and perhaps theoretical leanings, neither of which may sound like things sensory or intuitive in the normal usage of the words. Thinking can mean objective, logical and impersonal, and Feeling subjective, values-oriented and personal. Judging can mean planful and structured, and Perceiving, adaptable and easygoing. But again, not always.

Thankfully, there are countless degrees, permutations and combinations of traits and abilities in a person, the sum of which is wide variability in personalities and talents, the "gifts differing," that accompany them. Again and again in the typological literature, we are cautioned that Introverts are not necessarily quiet or reclusive, that Intuition is not just about gut hunches, that Thinking types feel and Feeling types think, that Judging types are not necessarily judgmental, nor Perceiving types necessarily perceptive, and that type does not explain everything about a person. In short, we are reminded that, while any two people may have similar preferences, they are anything but clones.

Nevertheless, some generalizations across types are possible. Jung and Myers assumed we are born with our preferences and that these innate tendencies, which are eminently dynamic and energetic, develop and reach their fullest potential over the course of a lifetime. The preferences are hierarchical within a person, and probably within society, such that the dominant preference is what is conscious, the auxiliary and tertiary preferences are somewhat conscious, and the least preferred fourth function, the inferior function, is unconscious (Quenk, 1993). Thus, an INTP, like Jung, is said to have a dominant Thinking process and an auxiliary Intuition process in which he operates most of the time, and a tertiary Sensing function and an inferior Feeling function of which he is much less aware. An INFP like Myers, on the other hand, is said to have a dominant Feeling process, auxiliary Intuition, tertiary Sensing, and inferior Thinking. The less conscious processes of the third and fourth functions begin to access what the individual regards as the negative or unacceptable part of his psyche, which Jung called the *"Shadow."* The Shadow is said to be the repository of the personal unconscious, housing all those things a person doesn't want to acknowledge about himself.

Jung believed we spend the first half of life developing our dominant and auxiliary functions as we strive to accomplish our major life goals concerning love and work. After midlife, we begin to give more weight to our less preferred functions as the life goal changes to become one of striving to be the best version of ourselves we can be. Jung thought it is the flow of psychic energy between and among the opposite functions that creates this dynamic character of type. Throughout life, however, we still retain our essential type because it is experientially most adaptive for us.

## Energy and Jung's Notion of the One-Sided Personality

Key to later discussions in this book is the Jungian notion that *the self evolves through life, not in a linear pattern as the hierarchy of preferences implies or as historical timelines normally depict, but in a circular or spiral pattern towards a center that represents the balance of opposite preferences.* This process, known as *individuation,* was thought to occur throughout life, but increasingly so at midlife when the person begins to experiment with new versions of himself that were previously less important or even hidden. That personality development repeatedly moves, over time, around an individual's *mandala* (Sanskrit for *"circle"*) of preferences means development of the individual is fluid, not stuck in one place, and is truly a life cycle.

Sometimes we act on our preferences a little too much though, and we become what Jung called a "one-sided" personality. His clinical work with emotionally debilitated patients demonstrated to him just how maladaptive this could be. Even in non-pathological instances:

> When a person devotes excessive energy to one thing, she ignores, rejects, or devalues its opposite. If one of the attitudes or functions embodied in psychological type theory is overemphasized, the opposite attitude or function will be neglected. When this happens, a person may risk having inappropriate perceptions or making poor judgments, since only one aspect of a situation is allowed into awareness . . . As a general rule, when we overdo one function or attitude to the exclusion of its opposite, our use of it tends to become rigid, automatic, and stereotypical. Its exaggerated form appears as a caricature of a normal effective mental process (Quenk, 1993: 5–6).

In her important book *Beside Ourselves,* Naomi Quenk (1993) describes the exaggerations of traits that can occur when personality becomes overly one-sided (Table 2, page 11), and suggests that we actually experience the unconscious inferior function when we are fatigued, stressed, ill, or otherwise "beside ourselves." In Quenk's view, then, illness involves acting out our opposites and not being ourselves. An eruption of the inferior function is thus a *reaction* to illness, or part of being ill, but we do not know, typologically speaking, what precipitates illness in the first place. Could physical disease result, in part, from a simple overemphasis of some preferences and an underemphasis of others, as does mental illness, or might some other type-related processes be at work?

Neither Jung nor Quenk dealt specifically with typological aspects of disease of the body—nor would we imply that they should have, given the psychological focus of their work—yet there are some incidental clues about the nature of physical disease in their views of the surfacing of the inferior function. For example, Quenk writes:

**Table 2. Adaptive Versus One-Sided Type Preferences (Quenk, 1993)**

| Preference | Adaptive Form | One-Sided Form |
|---|---|---|
| Extraversion | Charming<br>Enthusiastic<br>Sociable | Boastful<br>Intrusive<br>Loud |
| Introversion | Deep<br>Discreet<br>Tranquil | Aloof<br>Inhibited<br>Withdrawn |
| Sensing | Pragmatic<br>Precise<br>Detailed | Dull<br>Fussy<br>Obsessive |
| Intuitive | Imaginative<br>Ingenious<br>Insightful | Eccentric<br>Erratic<br>Unrealistic |
| Thinking | Lucid<br>Objective<br>Succinct | Argumentative<br>Intolerant<br>Coarse |
| Feeling | Appreciative<br>Considerate<br>Tactful | Evasive<br>Hypersensitive<br>Vague |
| Judging | Efficient<br>Planful<br>Responsible | Compulsive<br>Impatient<br>Rigid |
| Perceiving | Adaptable<br>Easygoing<br>Flexible | Procrastinating<br>Unreliable<br>Scattered |

The general precondition for eruption of the inferior function is a lowering of our general level of consciousness. Jung referred to this as an *abaissement du niveau mental . . . It permits a transfer of energy from the more conscious and developed functions to the relatively unconscious tertiary and inferior functions.* Several circumstances encourage this transfer of energy; the most common ones are fatigue, illness, and stress (Quenk 1993: 48, emphasis added).

Jung himself writes:

Psychic processes which under normal circumstances are functions of the will, and thus entirely under conscious control, can, in abnormal circumstances, become instinctive processes when supplied with unconscious energy. This phenomenon occurs . . . as a result of fatigue, intoxication, or morbid cerebral conditions in general, an abaissement du niveau mental ensues—when, in a word, the most strongly feeling-toned processes are no longer, or not yet, under conscious control . . . They do so only when supplied with an energy which is foreign to them (Jung, 1971: 451, emphasis added).

Both authors suggest that *energy* plays a role in psychological and disease processes. In the early twenty-first century, such an idea is gaining ever-increasing support, but is still regarded with utmost skepticism by a great many of us schooled in traditional Western science. As in Jung's day, a notion of energy in the body is considered questionable by many, altogether "flaky" by some, because it is difficult to prove and impossible to see with the naked eye, criticisms Jung countered with pragmatic arguments like the following:

> Now though the idea of energy is admittedly a mere verbal concept, it is nevertheless so extraordinarily real that your electricity company pays dividends out of it. The board of directors would certainly allow no metaphysical argument to convince them of the unreality of energy. *'Energy' designates simply the conformity of the phenomena of force*—a conformity that cannot be denied and that daily gives striking proof of its existence (Jung, 1971: 33, emphasis added).

Today, of course, we can also point out that MRI scans, X-ray equipment, ultrasound, electroencephalograms (EEG), electrocardiograms (ECG), polygraph, Kirlian photography and cameras detect and measure this "invisible" activity through us and all around us. Even without such hi-tech evidence, Jung felt psychic energy, the energy of the mind, is probably no different in operating principles than any other form of energy these tools might pick up—light energy, chemical energy, electrical energy, heat energy, mechanical energy, etc.—and that psychic energy should therefore be subject to the same laws of energy governing Newtonian physics that they are. Two such laws are that all energy is "interconvertible" from one form into another (the second law of thermodynamics) and that the movement of such energy is dependent on positively and negatively charged poles:

> The concept of energy implies that of polarity, since a current of energy necessarily presupposes two different states, or poles, without which there can be no current. Every energic phenomenon (and there is no phenomenon that is not energic) consists of pairs of opposites: beginning and end, above and below, hot and cold, earlier and later, cause and effect, etc. (Jung, 1971: 202).

The parallels he was drawing to the contradictory nature of type preferences are clear. Jung went on to describe how both instincts of a given bipolarity, such as Sensing–Intuition, want to exist, and quotes Schiller in identifying the reciprocity of these opposing functions:

'We have now reached the conception of a reciprocal action between the two instincts, of such a kind that the operation of the one at the same time establishes and restricts the operation of the other, and each reaches its highest manifestation precisely through the activity of the other.' Hence, if we follow out this idea, *their opposition must not be done away with, but on the contrary is something useful and life-promoting that should be preserved and strengthened* (Jung, 1971: 103–104, emphasis added).

As in the stretching of a rubber band, there can be no kinetic energy, no creative tension, no movement of one end, without the very existence and opposition of the other end. Energy is bound in their opposition. Thus one type preference acts as a necessary psychological bulwark against which the opposing preference is stabilized, both are needed for energetic homeostasis, and one is thought to have greater energy potential than the other, very likely related, Jung thought, to brain functions, though he didn't indicate which ones:

> The lack of differentiation in the unconscious arises in the first place from the *almost direct association of all the brain centers with each other, and in the second from the relatively weak energic value of the unconscious elements.* That they possess relatively little energy is clear from the fact that an unconscious element at once ceases to be subliminal as soon as it acquires a stronger accent of value; it then rises above the threshold of consciousness, and it can do this only by virtue of the energy accruing to it . . . The *strong energic value of the conscious contents* has the effect of intense illumination, whereby their differences become clearly perceptible and any confusion between them is ruled out. In the unconscious, on the contrary, the most heterogeneous elements possessing only a vague analogy can be substituted for one another, just because of their *low luminosity and weak energic value* (Jung, 1971: 112–113, emphasis added).

As energies, psychological polar opposites need and demand a "depotentiation," a resolution, not unlike that required by the tension built up in a stretched rubber band, between two magnets approaching each other, or in a build-up of static electricity. Restrained, the potential increases until an artifact of it explodes through the barriers into consciousness. Unconscious processes, such as a creative idea, thus lie concealed in the mind until such time as an energy "boost" of this kind, or some other kind, allows them to surface. He speaks of the creative idea as a "jewel" which "contains possibilities for a new release of energy," repressed, bound and literally escaping from the unconscious side of the self when it is sufficiently energized (Jung, 1971: 259). He conceives of inspiration and the inferior function rising in the same way:

> . . . impetus to action [or] inspiration that transcends conscious understanding has its source in an accumulation of energy in the unconscious (Jung, 1971: 243).

Under normal conditions, therefore, energy must be artificially supplied to the unconscious symbol in order to increase its value and bring it to consciousness . . . the disposable energy is withdrawn into the self—in other words, it is *introverted* (Jung, 1971: 114).

Pursuing the possibility that type functions are controlled by "brain centers," Jung theorized about two essential energic processes in the brain, primary and secondary, that have since been likened to right and left hemisphere functioning, respectively (Galin, 1974). Jung thought primary and secondary processes characterize Extraversion and Introversion:

The primary [cerebral cell] function would correspond to the actual performance of the cell, namely the production of a positive psychic process, for example an idea. This performance is an energic process, presumably a discharge of chemical tension; in other words it is a process of chemical decomposition. After this acute discharge . . . the secondary function comes into action. It is a process of recovery, a rebuilding through assimilation.

It is therefore only natural to ask whether there may not be individuals, or even types, in whom the period of recovery, the secondary function, lasts longer than in others, and if so, whether certain characteristic psychologies may be traceable to this. A short secondary function, clearly, will influence far fewer consecutive associations in a given period of time than a long one. Hence the primary function can operate much more frequently [in the extraverted type]. The psychological picture in such a case would show a constant and rapidly renewed readiness for *action and reaction*, a kind of *distractibility* . . . The rapid recovery of the primary function produces a higher reactivity, *extensive* rather than intensive . . . .

[In the introverted type] the secondary function is particularly *intense* and prolonged . . . The idea has a lasting influence, the impression goes deep. One disadvantage of this is that the associations are restricted to a *narrow* range, so that thinking loses much of its variety and richness. Nevertheless, the contractive effect aids synthesis, since the elements that have to be combined remain constellated long enough to make their abstraction possible. This restriction to one theme enriches the associations that cluster round it and consolidates one particular complex of ideas, but at the same time the complex is shut off from everything extraneous and finds itself in isolation . . .

Hence it may easily happen that a particularly strong and therefore particularly isolated and uninfluenceable complex becomes an 'overvalued idea,' a dominant that defies all criticism and enjoys complete autonomy, until it finally becomes an all-controlling factor manifesting itself as 'spleen.' In pathological cases it turns into an obsessive or paranoid idea, absolutely unshakable, that rules the individual's entire life . . .

Hence we regularly find an extraordinary concentration on *inner processes*, either on physical sensations or on intellectual processes, depending on whether the subject belongs to the sensation or to the thinking type. The personality seems *inhibited, absorbed or distracted, 'sunk in thought,' intellectually lopsided, or hypochondriacal*. In every case there is only a meager participation in external life and a distinct tendency to solitude and fear of other people . . . Accordingly this type has a decided tendency to fight shy of external stimuli, to keep out of the way of change, to stop the steady flow of life until all is amalgamated within . . . When a stimulus hits on a complex, the result is either a violent explosion of affect, or, if the isolation of the complex is complete, it is entirely negative (Jung, 1971: 273–278, emphasis added).

The brain state of Extraversion (right hemisphere functioning?) thus emerges as relatively tolerant, expansive, distractible, active, reactive and generally faster at recovering from energy expenditure, perhaps because it draws its energy from limitless reserves outside the person. The brain state of Introversion (left hemisphere functioning?), meanwhile, is intensely, narrowly and rigidly focused, critical, and having a prolonged recovery from energy expenditure, perhaps because it strives to find the healing energy it needs mostly from the limited reserves within.

Although Jung did not pursue it, we might extrapolate from these distinctions and say that the Extravert has less cause for stockpiling his own internal energy reserves because he relies on absorbing the energy he needs from others. The Introvert, on the other hand, having fewer such associations, collects, stores and conserves his energy—the energy is "introverted"—knowing he will choose to rely on himself when his reserves are depleted. As a result, using a molecular analogy, Extraversion (right hemisphericity) is effectively a positively charged energy pole which risks energy deficiencies that require replenishment from without, while Introversion (left hemisphericity) is in a sense a negatively charged pole which risks energy build-ups that must be released to the environment from within.

According to this new hypothesis, then, Extraversion should have an especially weak positive "charge"—"low luminosity and weak energic value"—when it is not the person's preference, where Introversion should have an especially strong negative "charge" when it is. The converse, of course, should be true for Extraverts—strong positive "charge," weak negative "charge"—and neither state, in its one-sided form, can be said to be more or less physically advantageous than the other. As with a cell membrane, striated muscle tissue, a battery, or any other charged cell, both poles are necessary for the effective movement of energy through the whole. To use an analogy from elsewhere in nature, the Extravert is the buffalo, a social animal whose health is helped by the collective strength of the herd. The Introvert is the bear who saves his energy for regular periods of self-imposed isolation and self-sufficiency. And both are, of course, necessary to the balanced functioning of the individual as well as the personality ecosystem. Sometimes, however, when we are one-sided, we are more buffalo-like or bear-like than we care to admit!

Jung saw the human psyche as being capable of growing, adapting and healing itself, and believed that people are capable of learning from life experiences and directing their own personality development through the various voluntary and involuntary periods of one-sidedness. One way of correcting for an imbalance was through *projection*, a mechanism in which a person unknowingly attributes his least preferred or unconscious attributes to another person. While in the "grip" of the inferior function, as Quenk puts it, when one-sidedness has gone too far, the person finds fault with these attributes in others, unaware that he is actually acting out a poor version of them himself. When *not* in the grip, the mildly one-sided person may experience projection as an *attraction* to these same traits, perhaps even finding a partner of opposite type. In doing so, the person integrates his psyche by bonding with others who emphasize the very same traits he tends to neglect. Projection is thus the Jungian magnet where one-sided poles of like charge repel, and opposite poles attract.

Another way of correcting for a personality imbalance, in Jung's view, is through *compensation*, a mechanism he basically borrowed from Newton's third law of motion, which said that every action force has a reaction force equal in magnitude and opposite in direction. In the psychological context, this means that the individual himself (not to mention the people around him) reacts in resistance to his own excesses in an unwitting attempt to restore his own equilibrium:

> A one-sided ("typical") attitude leaves a deficiency in the adaptive performance which accumulates during the course of life, and sooner or later this will produce a disturbance of adaptation that drives the subject toward some kind of compensation. But the compensation can be obtained only by means of an amputation (sacrifice) of the hitherto one-sided atti-tude. This results in a temporary accumulation of energy and an overflow into channels not used consciously before though lying ready uncon-sciously. The adaptive deficiency, which is the *causa efficiens* of the process of conversion, is subjectively felt as a vague sense of dissatisfaction. Such an atmosphere prevailed at the turning-point of our era (Jung, 1971: 19).

Jung recognized the ramifications of man's psychic activity for the larger context of the world, and often speculated on its meaning globally, culturally and historically. For instance, he writes:

> From all this it is abundantly clear that any attempt to equalize the one-sided differentiation of the man of our times has to reckon very seriously

with an acceptance of the inferior, because undifferentiated, functions. No attempt at mediation will be successful if it does not understand how to *release the energies of the inferior functions and lead them towards differentiation. This process can take place only in accordance with the laws of energy, that is, a gradient must be created which offers the latent energies a chance to come into play* (Jung, 1971: 86, emphasis added).

The idea of an energy transfer, involving typology and the body—which we will refer to as the process of *cognitive shifting*, or change in thinking through learning, intention and other influences—is the subject of this book. We will also consider an extension of compensation-projection models of the mind for diseases of the body, the language of communication between the two being "interconvertible" forms of energy. Finally, like Jung, we will offer a global interpretation of these processes, which, as Jung had hoped for, may be a theoretical gradient along which the energies of all types may actually reside.

First, however, we will examine some of the "brain centers" and processes that might be responsible for some of our many gifts differing. As we do so, Jungian concepts will occupy the shadows between the lines.

✳ ✳ ✳

**Chapter 1 serves as a review of** relevant type concepts for readers new to the field. From this review, it is apparent that psychological type is a Jungian concept that has been in existence since the 1920s. It is assessed with a popular instrument known as the *Myers-Briggs Type Indicator (MBTI)* instrument, which has itself been researched and tested for reliability and validity since the 1950s. The *MBTI* scales measure individual stylistic *preferences* and have been shown to correlate with a great many variables including cognitive style and vocational interests such as those found in practical skills, the arts and science. It is this connection that forms the basis of a consideration of type and talent domain.

Three Jungian notions described in this chapter are central to later discussions in this book: (1) the circular process of type development through life, known as *individuation*; (2) the role of psychic *energy* and energy flow in fueling this process; and (3) the one-sided personality which may have deleterious effects on well-being before eventually undergoing *compensation* to right itself and regain balance. The four preference scales in psychological type—E–I, S–N, T–F, and J–P—are bipolar and fluid, and are comparable in that sense to right and left-handedness. While we all possess both options for a given construct, each of us will naturally emphasize one side more than the other in the expression of our preferences. *Cognitive shifting*, which is about changes in thinking that occur as a result of learning and other influences, may be the mechanism by which these things are capable of "moving" to some extent.

# CHAPTER TWO
## A NEUROPSYCHOLOGY OF TALENT

✴ ✴ ✴

Neuropsychological principles and evidence will be reviewed for a general sense of the origins of type and talent in the human brain. Topics include the following:

* ✴ Definitions of common terms and methods for studying brain function
* ✴ Theories of talent development in the brain
* ✴ The laterality hypothesis: the sidedness of cognitive functions and talent areas
* ✴ The localization of psychological type functions in the brain

Chapter 2 is an overview of these concepts from which chapter 3 later provides specific examples in writing, music and visual art. From this discussion, it becomes apparent that psychological type and its associated cognitive preferences are brain-based to a large extent, and may therefore be subject to additional interpretations and applications stemming from that premise. In other words, by integrating these two fields—psychological type and the neuropsychology of talent—we may stand to learn more than we would learn from the study of either field alone. Because neuropsychology gets its evidence largely from the study of diseased and injured patients, the mixing of these two disciplines is automatically the beginnings of a study of type and disease. It also becomes clear that Jung's notion of compensation of the one-sided personality may really be about laterality of brain functions and, as we shall see in chapter 3, the cognitive shift.

✴ ✴ ✴

**Neuropsychology is the fascinating** and rapidly growing study of the relationship between brain and behavior—in essence, the study of what the brain is or does on the inside in order to affect what the person thinks, feels and does on the outside. As a tool, it is of tremendous value in the assessment of impairments caused by stroke, epilepsy and head injuries, and it is extremely useful in the monitoring of deterioration and improvement. Practicing neuropsychology normally involves a lot of testing—including intelligence testing, memory testing and the like—which assesses a person's abilities in various regions of the brain to see if things are functioning as they should be. Such information is invaluable to the health professional trying to ascertain whether a reading difficulty is due to brain damage, whether an epileptic is a suitable candidate for surgery to end his seizures, or whether a stroke patient is likely ever to speak again.

Most of neuropsychology's emphasis is on cognitive dysfunction or hypofunction or deficit—what is *wrong* with a person's thought processes relative to some established and accepted test norms. Not surprisingly, therefore, it is more often carried out in a health setting. A neuropsychology of talent, on the other hand, is of greater interest to educators in school settings since it is a science of cognitive function and hyperfunction and abilities—what is *right* with a person's thought processes, or even super-right, compared to most people. It is the study of the brain regions and processes underlying giftedness, and is in effect the healthful side of the same disciplinary coin.

## Definitions and Tools

Definitions abound as to what constitutes "giftedness," which is usually associated with verbal skills like writing, or "talent," which is usually associated with nonverbal skills like dance, and they invariably contain cut-off points in achievement, frequency or potential (such as an IQ above 130) which are supposed to help us determine what is gifted or talented behavior and what is not. For some of us, however, this debate would appear to be rather pointless since we feel we can recognize giftedness and talent all around us, in all the shades and degrees of the colors of the rainbow, without any help, if the truth be known, from all the various available definitions.

As the *Myers-Briggs*® typology teaches us, each of us is gifted or talented (hereafter these terms to be considered one and the same) in ways that are peculiar to our own particular preferences. Howard Gardner (1983) at Harvard Project Zero posited the existence of numerous kinds of intelligence—linguistic, spatial, mathematical, musical, kinesthetic and personal. From the *Myers-Briggs* perspective, there may be at least as many as sixteen intelligences when we also include the non-academic talents of the various types—social skill, theatrical ability, comedic talent, physical or mechanical ability and so forth. An ESTP may be an athlete, an ESFJ a social genius, an INFP a writer, an INTP a mathematician, and none, we would argue, is a more preferable or valuable form of talent than any other, because the world needs all of them in order to function. We would probably also agree that the gift must be *used* in order to be a gift. Unlike the unproven potential of a tested IQ, the sixteen types not only use their talents, but also hopefully *live* them in some way, every day.

Leaving behind the tricky and value-laden issue of what talents are rarer or more important, there is the more interesting question of what is underneath talent, specifically the talents that comprise an individual type. What are the internal patterns governing the external patterns we see in types and temperaments across the type table? And if we can identify the patterns, what are the implications of the trends for type researchers and individuals? These questions, stemming from a need to understand *why* type patterns exist, guide the inception and plan of the neuropsychological discussion to follow. Because it is impossible to do justice to all talents in these respects, concepts will be illustrated by concentrating on some artistic talents, which appear to be especially prevalent on the right side of the type table, those being the abilities involved in writing, music and drawing. The theory linking these talents will evolve slowly and additively from there.

In the artistic realm, as in other talent domains, a number of central questions and hypotheses about the talented brain have been, and are being, investigated.

1. **Is there a neurological substrate for talent?**

   The hypothesis is clearly yes because we know that talent is lost when the brain is damaged or diseased, and that the development of talent is critically tied to hormonal development of the normal brain, especially at puberty. These things would likely not occur if talent resided ephemerally somewhere else.

2. **Where is the neurological substrate for talent?**

   Many authors have concluded that, for at least some talents—music, savant talents, pattern recognition, artistic design, and the spatial aspects of chess—exceptional ability is related to superior or unusual functioning of the right hemisphere. Others propose that specific sites, on one or both sides, are responsible. For example, two functions often said to be part of Intuition (N), seeing connections and recognizing patterns, may be localized in the association areas and the parietal lobes, roughly above and behind the ears on both sides (Waterhouse, 1988).

3. **What caused the neurological substrate to be different?**

   It is generally agreed that practice alone is not enough to make a brain talented. Neither can genetic factors by themselves account for it, since some talents, albeit few (such as chess skill) show no family history of exceptionality in the domain. In most cases, there would seem to be some genetic predisposition to learn or excel in a particular field, on top of which practice is overlaid (Fein & Obler, 1988).

With this general rule as the backdrop, there are a number of hypotheses attempting to explain the existence of a talented brain. Some investigators think that injury and other factors cause a displacement and re-organization of the cortical architecture. Others think there are chemical and electrical triggers of hyperfunction—such as excess neurotransmitter (a kind of conduction fluid, it might be said) in savant talent, and excess calcium in exceptional memory—which serve to benefit cognition just as other elements, such as aluminum or lead, act so as to detract from it. Connections have been drawn between schizophrenia or epileptic misfiring and creativity, and between fetal hormones and the cognitive shifts so often observed in the performing of various talents. There are theories of hypercomplex cells and more neural, alternate, or better conducting pathways. And there are theories about the duplication of tissue in critical centers, and of exceptional centers actually crowding out other functions and giving themselves more room to grow unimpeded.

While our discussion will ultimately draw on all these views to some very limited degree, there are two Jungian-like neuropsychological concepts that will stand out above the rest. One is the *compensation hypothesis*, that talented centers have evolved in the brain so as to compensate for weaknesses in other areas of the brain, weaknesses that may have resulted from a simple under-emphasis in most cases, but perhaps also from sensory deprivation, arrested growth or injury in extreme cases. And the other hypothesis, the *laterality hypothesis*, is that talent involves the unusual or heightened laterality (one-sidedness) of abilities that may result from any number of internal or external influences.

### 4. What common components of talented abilities make them outstanding?

Most special talents are characterized by a prodigious memory for images or sounds, and an exceptional ability to recognize patterns in them and generate new ones (Waterhouse, 1988). Concepts of information "chunking" and pattern recognition appear again and again in the neuropsychological literature on talent.

### 5. How does one go about studying these behaviors?

The most common method for studying brain-behavior relationships has been to examine the deficient abilities of the brain-damaged patient and draw conclusions about normal activity. More recently, exceptional abilities in the gifted are being compared to normal abilities, or exceptional abilities in the savant (such as that so convincingly portrayed by Dustin Hoffman in *Rain Man*, and in the film starring Richard Dreyfuss entitled *Silent Fall*) are compared to the abilities of non-savants with mental retardation, normal people, or prodigies (Fein & Obler, 1988). Case studies are often used to examine isolated abilities, as group studies are used to demonstrate associations between abilities such as those between drawing skills and handedness.

A very common investigative tool in neuropsychology is the lesion study, where activity in damaged or diseased brains is used to make inferences about function in the intact brain. If an injured region on the left side of the brain cannot do calculations that the same region in a normal brain can, it is logically inferred that that particular region is responsible for calculation activity. Lost functions can be compared to the abilities of healthy people or to the abilities of the lesion group prior to disability, which has made this method particularly useful to the study of literary and graphic skills.

CT scans, paper-and-pencil tests and object-manipulation tests are also very common. If a person can't find his way around his own house and a CT picture of the brain reveals a damaged region on the right side, this is a very good indication that the right side is involved in this kind of orientation in space. Drawing tests, and tests using building blocks or maps, will further localize where the trouble spot is, allowing investigators to reach conclusions about what areas of the brain are involved in spatial abilities. Psychometric testing of this kind is used in the study of all the various talents.

A thoroughly fascinating though invasive means of studying abilities is through intracarotid sodium Amytal injection. This method, which was first developed at the Montreal Neurological Institute, is actually a presurgical procedure that is used to help locate speech in a patient's brain so that a surgeon doesn't later cut into it. The method is especially helpful in the surgical treatment of left-handed patients in whom laterality for speech can be rather variable.

At the start of this procedure, the left hemisphere is very carefully anaesthetized using the Amytal, causing temporary paralysis on the right side of the body but leaving the right side of the brain, and the left side of the body, wide awake for ability testing. One function after another (e.g., naming objects, counting, etc.) is tested in the awake right hemisphere while the left hemisphere is fast asleep. The drug wears off, the patient returns to normal, and a few days later the right hemisphere is anaesthetized and tests are done on the side that was first sedated so as to compare the functions in the two awake hemispheres. The patient, often an epileptic who wants his epileptogenic sites (seizure-triggering areas) surgically removed, seldom remembers any of the experience.

The drug used to accomplish this feat wears off in a matter of minutes, but the effects before it does wear off can be astonishing for the observer interested in split-brain psychology or in behavior in general. Two very different people can emerge from the same individual— the left-hemisphere "person" rather talkative, pleasant and cooperative, the right-hemisphere "person" quiet, pouty and difficult. The sidedness of abilities also becomes very obvious as one hemisphere performs things the other cannot—the awake left hemisphere speaking but without the usual "ring" and inflection to the voice, and the awake right hemisphere humming songs without using any of the words! The message to the surgeon in such cases is clear: make incisions in the right side of the person's brain, only after it has been demonstrated that speech doesn't reside there. The message to the rest of us is that the cognitive and emotive differences in the hemispheres are a very observable reality.

Studying commissurotomized patients can also reveal a great deal about the sidedness of abilities and behavior. The commissures are those parts of the brain that connect the two hemispheres. When they are severed through surgery, again to relieve a chronic condition such as epilepsy, the hemispheres no longer "talk" to each other and carry on as if the other side of the brain, and the side of the body it controls, aren't even there. Thus there are tales of the patient whose left hemisphere understood the words of the no-smoking policy in the hospital, but whose right hemisphere couldn't have cared less, the left hand that consequently took the cigarettes out of his pocket, and the right hand that put them back in! Another story involves the woman whose right hand would do up the buttons on her dress, just to be followed immediately behind by the left hand which would undo them all. She eventually learned to sit on her left hand when she dressed.

The trouble with all these various methods of studying the brain, as is probably very apparent, is that they all rely on damaged or diseased brains for inferences about the healthy brain. And unfortunately, the subjects under study are often far from normal. What's more, these methods don't tell us much about abilities in the developing child's brain, or about changing neurological processes in brains of any age, since what these tools provide is basically a photograph in time of activities which ideally require a video.

For these reasons, many investigators, particularly those examining musical abilities, prefer process measures of normal functioning, "process" meaning that the investigator watches brain activity that is currently in progress. The various physiological methods of this kind include measures of handedness, lateral eye gaze (looking right or left, up or down, during a particular cognitive activity), regional blood flow, MRI scans, PET scans, evoked potential recordings, and EEG.

Where the CT scan (computerized transaxial tomography) is essentially a three-dimensional x-ray of the brain, the PET scan (positron emission tomography) is an expensive scan that provides a colored biochemical map of where glucose is being metabolized during a particular activity the person is doing; hot spots show up as red or yellow areas on a monitor and less involved regions as shades of blue. Another less publicized tool, the evoked potential, is a recording of the neural response that results when the brain is stimulated in certain ways, and EEG is a more general reflection of all neural activity in resting or active states. These kinds of techniques are always impressive in talent studies, but they are often criticized for the limited number of subjects they can examine because of the cost.

Yet another process measure of normal functioning, which manages to get around some of these concerns, is the competitive input method. These techniques examine brain laterality by presenting contrived and competing information—sounds or images—to both hemispheres to discover which hemisphere is better suited to process it.

In dichotic listening experiments, for example, tones are simultaneously presented to each ear, through headphones, to determine the ear (hemisphere) that best processes them (Kimura, 1964). The ear has crossed connections to the opposite hemisphere (the sense of smell is actually the only sensory modality that is not crossed), so a right-ear superiority for remembering words, and a left-ear superiority for recognizing music, is the typical finding in right-handed adults. What this means, in English, is that the brain prefers to do auditory word processing in its left hemisphere, and music processing in its right hemisphere.

The same kind of test for the visual modality, something called the tachistoscopic technique, has been much used by investigators, like the late Philip Bryden at the University of Waterloo, in seeking out laterality for vision. In these experiments, which help us to understand the foundations of graphic skills, a tachistoscope (projector, viewer, screen) flashes visual stimuli to the left and right visual fields of each eye, while the subject focuses on a fixation point. The processing accuracy of one side relative to the other again indicates hemisphere superiority for the task. As before, a right-field advantage for words tells us that there is greater left-hemisphere involvement in visual language processing. A left-field advantage for spatial arrays implies greater participation by the right hemisphere in visuospatial activity.

Each of the various methods of studying the brain is flawed in some way, and the competitive input techniques are no exception. The complaints leveled at these methods are that tones and lines are very far removed from the larger artistic wholes of phrases or design. Furthermore, the results can change in some instances according to an individual's problem-solving strategy or training. To these criticisms, regardless of method, can also be added the problems associated with studying artistic subjects. In music especially, investigators have to consider many different kinds and degrees of innate ability, training, anatomy (lips, fingers, voice) and roles (listener, performer, composer), each of which can affect the brain organization of musical skills.

Despite the failings of individual methods, some generalizations about brain-behavior relationships in talent are possible when the findings of diverse methods corroborate each other (Gardner, 1982). To illustrate, in 1874, lesion studies first identified the right posterior region of the brain as having a special role in visual thinking, as people with damage to this area could no longer perform it. In the 1950s, lesion studies linked the parietal lobe in the right posterior area with visual imagery, dreaming, visual memory and other visuospatial abilities (Humphrey & Zangwill, 1951). In the 1970s, there was EEG evidence that spatial and color imagery are also right-hemisphere functions in people who are not artists (Robbins & McAdam, 1974). Finally, in the 1980s, PET scans demonstrated that visual hallucinations are a right-parietal function, and lesion studies comparing artists and non-artists showed that artists rely on the right hemisphere for artistic skills more than do non-artists (Gardner & Winner, 1981).

In this instance, then, the combination of findings is rather convincing evidence of the right-sidedness of visual ideation generally, and of visual artistic abilities specifically, despite the limitations of any one method standing alone. Since visual art is often an academic preference of Intuitive Feeling (NF) types and to a lesser extent Intuitive Thinking (NT) types, the findings that these tools have made possible would appear to suggest some distinctive right-hemisphere emphasis on the right side of the psychological type table (Table 3).

## Laterality: The One-Sidedness of Talent

It has been said that functional asymmetries are more the rule than the exception in the human body (Weinstein, 1978). One foot, one gland, one organ, one eye is larger, more capable, and more sensitive than the other, despite outward appearances of overall symmetry. The fact that

**Table 3. Fine Artists (n = 114; Macdaid et al., 1986)**

| ISTJ | ISFJ | INFJ | INTJ |
|---|---|---|---|
| n = 2 | n = 3 | n = 19 | n = 8 |
| 1.75% | 2.63% | 16.67% | 7.02% |
| **ISTP** | **ISFP** | **INFP** | **INTP** |
| n = 0 | n = 1 | n = 25 | n = 12 |
| 0.00% | 0.88% | 21.93% | 10.53% |
| **ESTP** | **ESFP** | **ENFP** | **ENTP** |
| n = 1 | n = 0 | n = 16 | n = 0 |
| 0.88% | 0.00% | 14.04% | 0.00% |
| **ESTJ** | **ESFJ** | **ENFJ** | **ENTJ** |
| n = 1 | n = 2 | n = 14 | n = 10 |
| 0.88% | 1.75% | 12.28% | 8.77% |

some 90–95 percent of people are right-handed is, of course, the strongest testament to the body's tendency to slight, healthy imbalances in structure and function and, in some cases, overt one-sidedness (Kinsbourne, 1978).

The same oblique morphological pattern is found in the head. Select areas of the right hemisphere, and portions of the skull covering them, are larger than corresponding areas of the left, yet the entire left hemisphere is usually larger than the right in most right-handed people (Rubens, 1977; Weinstein, 1978). While size rarely determines skill, it is hard not to think such things when we observe that the planum temporale region, the neural substrate for speech, is larger in the left hemisphere in most people (Geschwind & Levitsky, 1968; Kolb & Whishaw, 1985). There are biochemical asymmetries as well—higher levels of norepinephrine in sub-cortical areas of the left hemisphere, lower levels of dopamine in the right (Glick et al., 1977)—the net effect of which is an expectation of side-to-side variations in behavior.

Behavioral differences do, of course, occur and have been formally documented for 5,000 years, probably beginning with the writing of the Chinese *I Ching* and, in the last 100 years, with lesion studies and experiments using the various non-invasive techniques described earlier (Table 4, page 28). Unfortunately, popular psychology has done much to mar the credibility of these distinctions, rendering hemisphericity something of a passing fad with short roots on the West Coast. Popular enthusiasms may have changed, but the brain has not. The hemispheres are indeed differentially organized (Figure 1, page 29) and it is important for us as students of psychological type to acknowledge this very significant contributor to human behavior.

Muriel Lezak (1976) gives an excellent short summary of the higher functions controlled by the two sides:

The left hemisphere mediates all verbal transformations including reading and writing, understanding and speaking, verbal ideation, and even comprehension of verbal symbols traced on the skin . . . Moreover, left hemisphere lateralization of verbal functions extends to the musculature of speech, which appears to be under its sole control even though bilateral structures are involved. Yet it has relatively minor involvement in the perception of shapes, forms, and patterns whether by sight, sound, or touch, and in copying and drawing nonverbal figures . . . The same studies show that the right hemisphere dominates nonverbal visual-spatial transformations, including the processing and storage of visual information, tactile and visual recognition of shapes and forms, perception of directional orienta-

**Table 4. Parallel Ways of Knowing: Roles and Means of Processing in the Hemispheres**

| Left Hemisphere | Right Hemisphere | Source |
|---|---|---|
| Yang (Positive, Conscious, Aggressive, Masculine) | Yin (Negative, Unconscious, Emotional, Feminine) | *I Ching*, Ritsema & Karcher, 1994 |
| Temporal | Spatial | Lashley, 1960 |
| Sequential | Simultaneous | Luria, 1966 |
| Intellect, Reason | Intuition (Hunches) | Levy-Agresti & Sperry, 1968 |
| Propositional, Conceptual | Appositional, Structural | Bogen, 1969b |
| Secondary Process | Primary Process | Galin, 1974 |
| Directed | Free | Bogen, 1975 |
| Convergent | Divergent, Imaginative | |
| Objective | Subjective | |
| Abstract | Concrete | |
| Digital | Analogic | |
| Verbal | Nonverbal | |
| Logic | Inspirational Hunches | Lezak, 1976 |
| Critical Science-Mindedness | Artistic-Mindedness | |
| Analysis, Details | Relational, Wholes, Synthesis | Edwards, 1979 |
| Linear | Nonlinear | |
| Relational | Unitary | Bever, 1983 |

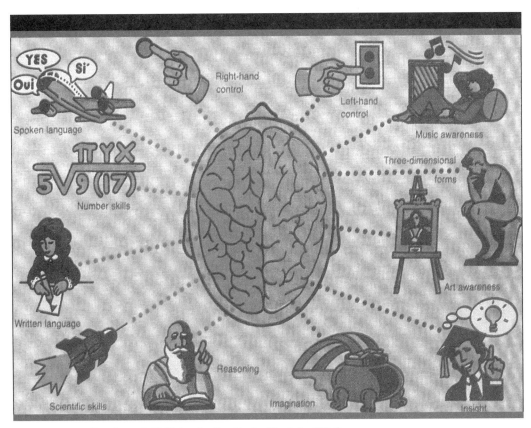

**Figure 1. Localization of Abilities in the Brain (Restak, 1984)**

tion and perspective, and copying and drawing geometric and representational designs and pictures. Native musical ability is also localized on the right. Under special test conditions, a few commissurotomized patients have demonstrated some limited verbal recognition and monosyllabic utterances associated with right hemisphere activity (43).

The most important distinction here, that of the left hemisphere being verbal and the right hemisphere being nonverbal, is incontestable in most instances and is therefore of great importance in theorizing about the brain foundations of psychological type. For example, the ENFJ who reminds herself not to "let sociability slow her down on the job" (Myers, 1987: 15), might have an expressive left-hemisphere facility that is not found in the more right-sided ISFP who "sees much but shares little" (Kroeger & Thuesen, 1988: 234).

But we must be careful about what we mean here. At the height of the hemisphericity craze, it was commonly held that science takes place in the left hemisphere, and art in the right, which was really a rather ridiculous idea for at least three reasons. First, it suggested that one hemisphere contains complete functions that the other does not have, which we now know is not the case. Second, it reduced all cognitive activity to two disciplines, science and art, to say nothing of the brain organization required for working construction or running for political office. And third, it implied that if Fred was a scientist, Fred lived in the left side of the neuropsychological duplex, with no one next door!

It is true, as we shall see, that there are many more music- and art-related functions subserved by the right side of the normal brain, although the functions are not exclusive to the right. Rather, each function may be predominant on the right with lesser degrees of capability on the left. This conception of the brain, the *laterality hypothesis*, has, in many circles, come to replace the dominance theory that once prevailed in the scientific community and popular culture (Milner, 1980).

Where dominance theory said that one whole hemisphere rules the other in every department, giving a person a distinctive left- or right-sided personality and the scientific or artistic abilities that go with it, the laterality hypothesis sees the hemispheres as housing discrete, paired functions which share responsibilities for the same task. They can be of equal strength and kind in both hemispheres, dominant on one side, or different in character in each hemisphere (Milner, 1973). Thus, for example, the function of musical memory is equally represented and equally strong in both hemispheres (Deutsch, 1977). So is the ability to recognize harmony changes (Gates & Bradshaw, 1977). Timbre (tone) processing, on the other hand, is more prevalent on the right side, with simple timbre problems being processed on the left side and complex ones on the right (Sidtis, 1980). In speech, it is the reverse, with complex language normally happening on the left side and simple, monosyllabic words, such as curses, happening on the right (Lezak, 1976).

To simplify this collection of possibilities, we can imagine cognitive functions as a row of seesaws tipping left or right, or balancing, across a playground. Sometimes we might see a group of them tilting in the same direction, other times not, but they are always moving with the moods and strengths of various participants. This analogy, weighted *for each skill* in differing amounts from side to side, seems a fair representation of the laterality concept. We no longer conceive of the brain as just one seesaw with an overweight bully sitting heavily on one end.

So to return to our original statement about psychological type and language, about an ENFJ having some verbal tendencies an ISFP may not have, this is not to say that an ENFJ talks and an ISFP doesn't, or that an ENFJ lives in the left hemisphere and an ISFP in the right. On the contrary, it says only that the ENFJ may be "weighted" toward the left, and the ISFP toward the right, on this one function that is speech. It makes no comment on the sidedness of any other function—which could be the reverse, or equal in both directions—and, as in type theory, it makes no judgment as to whether the verbal or the nonverbal preference is the more valued state.

Indeed, as concepts, there are several parallels between brain laterality and the polarity of type preferences. In *Introduction to Type*, Myers (1987) makes two unintentional references to the sidedness of brain functions:

> All of us use both hands all of the time, but we tend to prefer one to the other. It's the same with your preferences: for each of the four scales, all of us use both preferences at different times, but not both at once and not, in most cases, with equal confidence. So when asked to choose, most people can and do indicate a preference (4).

All of us use all of the functions and attitudes at different times. Our type is made up of those we prefer most (31).

Extraversion–Introversion, Sensing–Intuition, Thinking–Feeling, Judging–Perceiving—like the simple and complex components of timbre processing, these would all appear to be paired functions, seesaws, sharing responsibilities for their respective tasks. Like other paired cognitive functions, one of the pair is usually preferred over the other, though both may be used, and both are necessary for optimal functioning of the individual. In neuropsychological terms, E and I would seem to oversee the *direction of focus* in the person (outward or inward), S and N to determine the *focus in time and space* for the person (the details of what was, or what is, versus what could be in the big-picture world of the imagined future), T and F to monitor the *directional path of thought processes* (linear or nonlinear), and J and P to decide the *presentation or form* of all of the above (structured or unstructured). Thus an ENTJ is outwardly focused toward possibilities not yet realized and proceeds in a linear and structured fashion to make them happen, where the ISFP is inwardly focused on what is happening right now and reacts to it in a nonlinear and unstructured fashion. In this way, type represents the weighting of four distinct functional seesaws, tilting in response to that individual's preferences.

Direct physical evidence of a laterality of type preferences for the attitudes comes from Martha Wilson and Marlin Languis (1989) at Ohio State University. Using electrophysiological brain mapping techniques, they have demonstrated that Introversion "leans" toward the left side and appears to be localized in the left temporal-parietal area (above and behind the left ear) which is known for its convergent, inward-focused processing of symbolic-analytic information like written language, arithmetic and other abstractions. Two other studies (James, 1986; Crossman & Polich, 1989) confirm this left-right distinction. Newman (1989), however, has theorized that Extraversion is mediated in part by the brainstem, in the vicinity of an arousal center known as the reticular activating system, which might suggest that Extraversion is lowermost in the brain of the E–I scale, while Introversion is uppermost. If our paired-function hypothesis is correct, the outward-focused, more distractible function of Extraversion should reside in the right hemisphere where processes are divergent and less focused than in the left hemisphere, as well as closer to the front end of the brain where social behavior and expressive speech are more prevalent than at the back end.

Studies employing brain mapping techniques, the Herrmann Brain Dominance Instrument (HBDI), the Brain Preference Indicator (BPI), the Hemispheric Mode Indicator (HMI), and various hemisphericity tasks (e.g., verbal versus spatial tachistoscopic tasks), add to our limited knowledge of typology and the brain. James (1986) and Crossman and Polich (1989) found that Introversion, Sensing, Thinking and Judging tend to be lateralized in the direction of the left hemisphere, while Extraversion, Intuition, Feeling and Perceiving tend to be lateralized in the direction of the right hemisphere. Sensing, Thinking and Judging appear to be strongly associated with left hemisphere function, perhaps in particular left limbic function. Feeling may be associated with the limbic system, perhaps particularly on the right side. Intuition and Perceiving appear to be more anterior than posterior. Ford (1988), too, found that Sensing and Judging were related to analytical and logical preferences in the left hemisphere, while Intuition and Feeling were related to creative, holistic preferences and a sense of intuitive knowing in the right hemisphere. Laposky et al. (1991) found left-right distinctions for Sensing and Intuition, and other researchers (1997) found left-right distinctions for SJ and NP.

Other links between laterality and the preferences, though, can only be inferred, guessed at, and implied at this point, from lesion studies, competitive input studies, a knowledge of type, and the mere observation of people. At this place in time, it looks as if the Intuition–Sensing function might one day be shown to be lateralized from front to back, as well as from side to side, as hypothesized in Figure 2. For example, using electrophysiological correlates, Newman (1989) found that Intuition is left anterior, Thinking is left posterior, Sensing is right anterior, and Feeling is right posterior.

The major functional distinctions in the brain, between verbal-mathematical processes in the left hemisphere and nonverbal-spatial-emotional processes in the right, surely sound very much like the impersonal logic of the Thinking function and the more subjective human approach of the Feeling function, respectively. Many of us will also know that the anterior end of the brain—the frontal lobes just behind the forehead—is the motor unit that formulates intentions, organizes plans of action, and executes the plans, which sounds like the future orientation and imaginary aspects of Intuition, especially Intuitive Thinking (NT). The posterior end of the brain, meanwhile—the temporal lobes in the vicinity of the ears, the parietal lobes above and behind the ears, and the occipital lobes at the back of the head—is

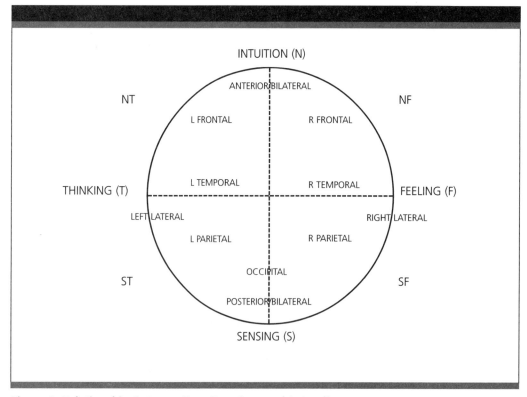

**Figure 2. Relationship Between Type Functions and Laterality**

the sensory unit that receives, processes and stores sensory detail in visual, auditory and somatosensory modalities (Kolb & Whishaw, 1985), all of which is unmistakably reminiscent of the Sensing function.

More specifically, we know that the occipital lobes are S-like in their processing of primary sensory information that is visual. The parietal lobes are also S-like in their processing of somatic sensations and perceptions, and are N-like in their integration of sensory information from somatic, visual and auditory regions in places called association areas. Consequently, the parietal lobes are important to cognition in the visual arts and other activities requiring a relating of facts and ideas. The temporal lobes, meanwhile, are S-like in that they process auditory sensations and auditory and visual perceptions, as well as long-term memory of past events, and they are F-like in that they have an emotional component which has been shown to be important for learning, particularly in music, language and other fields dependent on communication by sound. Finally, the frontal lobes seem to possess N, F and P characteristics in that these areas are responsible for intellectual synthesis, associative learning and foresight (N), ethical behavior, affect, self-awareness, social behavior, the fine motor movement of expressive speech and facial gestures (F), and behavioral spontaneity (P).

*Without a doubt, all types possess all qualities and abilities and use all parts of the brain at all times. However, it is clear some types will stress some functions more often or more intensively than others in the expression of their preferences.* If it were possible to follow the different types over the course of a lifetime, through PET scanning or some other such tool, we could well expect the images for the preferences to light up accordingly. A dominant Intuitive type might be found to spend relatively more time or metabolic energy towards the front end of the normal brain, or on the right side, where N-like processes seem to proliferate. Similarly, a dominant Sensor might be found to stress the back end of the brain or the left side, where S-like processes seem to predominate, a dominant Thinker the left side, a dominant Feeler the right side, and so forth. But we cannot know any of this for certain at this stage, and can only infer these things by piecing together the very disjointed and tiny bits of information we do have.

To illustrate the role of inference in formulating our conception, we can consider the localization of emotion in the cortex (acknowledging, however, that much emotional processing happens below the cortex at the level of the limbic system). Most of us tend to be well versed on the laterality of intellectual abilities. Thanks to dominance theory, we know that math has a strong left-hemisphere presence and poetry some right-hemisphere involvement. What may be less clear to us is the sidedness of mood and personality traits. This is a complicated matter, far from the comparatively neat left-right distinctions that are sometimes possible with cognition. With these variables, laterality seems to go left and right, front and back, and up and down.

To begin with, and very much in keeping with the Jungian ideas of compensation and depotentiation, the hemispheres tend to act as counterbalances to each other, keeping the extremes of mood and personality in check. If the balance is tampered with, as in the case of injury, disease or sedation of one side, the other side is released, or "disinhibited" as it is called, to do pretty much as it likes. For a variety of functions, the effect might be likened to one person jumping off the seesaw, much to the great consternation and shock of the person still on it. For instance, when the right hemisphere is suppressed, the left hemisphere responds with surprising indifference—the person ignores the left side of his own body, failing to put his left arm in a sleeve, for example (a phenomenon called contralateral neglect), he talks a lot, and he may be euphoric, even maniacal. When the left hemisphere is suppressed, a catastrophic reaction follows in which the person is aphasic (unable to speak), fearful and depressed. Bryan Kolb and Ian Whishaw (1985), at the University of Lethbridge, have described this kind of emotion under carotid sodium Amytal:

> Injections of the left hemisphere [release of the right hemisphere] indeed provoke a catastrophic reaction as the drug wears off. The patient despairs and expresses a sense of guilt, of nothingness, of indignity, and worries about his own future or that of his relatives, without referring to the language disturbances overcome and to the hemiplegia just resolved and ignored. As the drug wore off after injection of the right hemisphere [release of the left hemisphere], a 'euphorical' reaction was reported, as the patient appears without apprehension, smiles and laughs and both with mimicry and words expresses considerable liveliness and sense of well-being (553).

Stunning observations like these, in the same individual, have led to claims that the left hemisphere is involved in positive affect, and the right in negative affect (Kolb & Whishaw, 1985; Ley & Bryden, 1976). From a typological perspective, this would seem to suggest a certain left-sided emphasis (and right-sided under-emphasis) in types that are characteristically upbeat, and a right-sided emphasis (left-sided under-emphasis) in types experiencing emotional difficulties.

Front-to-back site of function is as important as side of function in the production of behaviors and, in many cases, it is not hard to imagine the possible connections to type. For example, the spontaneous talking in the account above is especially noticeable following right-frontal lobe lesions (the area roughly behind the right side of the forehead). Injury to this area produces, in addition to talkativeness, poor jokes and puns, pointless stories, profanity, and a patient amused and indifferent to the reaction of listeners. This area also controls expressions on the left side of the face, such as the wink, and the emotional tone of speech, which becomes flattened with such an injury, as in tone-deafness (Kolb & Whishaw, 1985).

We can imagine these same traits on a much less exaggerated scale, in a healthy person who has no injury whatsoever in the right-frontal area but who for some reason de-emphasizes this region in favor of some other area. Is it possible that such an under-emphasis in this area contributes to the development of a type whose strengths do not lie in quiet reflection, inspired pun-making, toneful speech, or interpersonal sensitivity? Could it be that underactivity in this area accounts, at least in part, for a type who likes to chat (E), who doesn't list lyrical speech or creative word play among his strong suits but who might very well use colorful "physical" language in its place (S), who can be a bit blunt or insensitive if the situation requires it (T), and who may wander when telling stories, following his interests (P)? Conversely, perhaps heightened activity in this area produces a type who is quiet (I), is good at pun-making and creating story-cohesiveness (N), is sensitive to the needs and reactions of listeners (F), and who prefers to come to closure and make some kind of point when she tells these stories (J).

In effect, the typological opposites that are the sports-minded ESTP and the literary INFJ might really be lateral opposites in which one type emphasizes an area of the brain that the other does not. To be attracted to one's opposite, in that event, would be to project and compensate for one's neuropsychological weaknesses by adopting the cognitive, personality and learning style strengths of another person—to fill up one's neuropsychological "holes," as it were, in the creation of a whole. Given the brain also takes this compensatory kind of action within itself, Jung's notions of compensation and projection, and Myers' view of the "mutual usefulness of opposite types" (read: mutual usefulness of opposite functions) almost certainly have some bases in underlying neuropsychological processes.

Moving backwards from these more anterior regions of the brain to the temporal and parietal lobes above and behind the ear, we find other interesting personality and emotional traits of relevance to psychological type. Fear, obsession, organizational ability, and attention to detail happen here, as we learn from lesion studies and psychiatric studies.

For example, right-temporal and right-parietal patients exhibit paranoia and excessive concern for their personal lives, which would seem to suggest a release of such fears in the left hemisphere. Temporal-lobe epileptics suffer from intense bipolar disease characterized by humorlessness, obsessional behavior, orderliness, compulsive attention to detail, dependence, repetitiveness, religiosity, hypermoralism, philosophical interests and other personality changes. Right-temporal patients with this affliction tend to be more obsessional, and left-temporal patients more concerned with personal destiny, which appears to suggest that a certain obsessive concern for matters of the present naturally occurs on the left side of the brain, while a future-oriented concern for personal destiny is more naturally endemic to the right side (Kolb & Whishaw, 1985; Flor-Henry, 1976).

This is the diseased state, to be sure, but again it seems possible that healthy, much less extreme versions of these same qualities are visible every day in some types more than others. If this were so, stress-induced exaggerations of Judging (J) would appear to be alive and well and living in the temporal lobes! We might also speculate, based on these lesion studies, that paranoia, obsessive behavior and concern for matters of the present will be more prevalent in types which emphasize the left-temporal areas and underutilize the right, and that existential worries and concern for the future will be more the case for types who emphasize the right-temporal areas to the relative neglect of the left. In support of our brain-map hypotheses (Figure 2, page 32), Huot et al. (1989) have found more temporal lobe indicators (i.e., problems causing less-than-optimal temporal-lobe functioning) in Intuitive types, Feeling types and Perceiving types, than in Sensing types, Thinking types and Judging types, which might make sense if Intuitive types, Feeling types and Perceiving types are indeed focusing more of their energies towards the front end.

By and large, the study of emotional asymmetry in healthy people supports the findings of lesion studies. EEG recordings, for example, show that the normal right hemisphere is involved in emotions generally, and in negative affect specifically (Tucker, 1981; Tucker et al., 1981). Depression, especially, seems to "reside" there. As an interesting personal test of these claims, we can examine the right and left sides of our own face. The right side, which is controlled by the more upbeat left hemisphere, has been described as being "full of vitality, smiling, social." The left side of the face, controlled by the more upset right hemisphere, has been described as "dead, concentrated, passive, demoniac, solitary" (Wolff, 1933:175). Examination of the left and right sides of people's faces in a magazine reveals how positively negative most left sides look!

There is lesion-study and tachistoscopic evidence that recognition of faces and facial expressions is also more of a right-hemisphere task (Ley & Bryden, 1976). Mary McCaulley (1981) found that EF types outperform IT types on the nonverbal recall of faces, but that IT types outperform EF types on a test of numerical memory. Having already noted that Introversion seems to be localized in the left temporal-parietal area (Wilson & Languis, 1989), the same region that is heavily involved in reading and math, it is apparent we are suggesting that IT is a leftward-leaning preference and EF a rightward-leaning preference that is asymmetric in the same direction as some artistic abilities. Emotion and personality, it would seem, are very likely co-lateralized in the same direction as some cognitive functions.

Lest we think we are beginning to see a general plan to the brain not unlike the left brain-right brain dichotomy of old, we will now confound and confuse that impression by noting that the left-right distinctions to this point are the "typical" case most representative of *right-handed adult males who, as a group, exhibit a high degree of laterality. Brain organization can be even more one-sided for certain functions in people with special training, high intelligence, mental illness, or certain kinds of talent (Bever & Chiarello, 1974; Shagass et al., 1978; Thatcher et al., 1983). It can also be less one-sided and more balanced in females, children under six years of age, and non-right-handers who write with their left hand or with both hands equally well (Bogen, 1969b; Hardyk & Petrinovich, 1977; Milner, 1973).* So, while the typical model of hemispheric asymmetries is of great value in theorizing about the brain, it is well to remember these and other individual differences when comparing the data on talent.

For example, in the case of handedness, sodium Amytal studies show that 96 percent of right-handed people and 70 percent of left-handed people have speech on the left side. Of remaining non-right-handers, 15 percent have speech on the right side, and 15 percent have it on both sides, meaning other functions, like drawing, can be similarly reorganized (Rasmussen & Milner, 1977). These muddled possibilities make things difficult for the surgeon trying to avoid speech centers, and for the student trying to understand talent. But a distinctive advantage of more bilateral representation for the person herself is that she is more likely to recover from damage or inadequacies on one side of the brain by compensating for the functions, even speech, on the other side. In other words, where the lateral state rigidly puts all its cognitive eggs in one basket, the bilateral condition adaptively spreads them around. As we shall see, there are pluses and minuses both ways.

In light of this connection between handedness and the hemispheres, it is worth harking back to the comments in *Introduction to Type:*

> All of us use both hands all of the time, but we tend to prefer one over the other. It's the same with your preferences (Myers, 1987: 4).

If IT is left-sided and more numerical, and EF right-sided and more artistic, we might well expect to find more right-handers among ITs and more left-handers among EFs. This is only the beginning of what could be a system of physiological correlates connecting psychological type and various kinds of talent.

---

✳ ✳ ✳

---

**Much can be learned about the functioning** of normal, healthy brains by studying the effects on this functioning of damage or disease; an appreciation of what is normal, or even gifted, is discovered through an examination of its absence. As a result, the science of neuropsychology has typically focused on lesion studies and various other invasive and non-invasive techniques in its attempts to understand the relationships between brain and behavior, including the relationships between brain and personality, and between brain and cognition. A neuropsychology of talent uses these same methods to infer the origins of talent in the brain.

One of the findings of this discipline is that *abilities within a talent*, and traits within a personality, like handedness, tend to be bipolar and lateralized in the brain in one particular direction more than another. Type preferences, of course, appear to exhibit the same thing. To the extent that some kinds of cognitive deficit and disease may also be so characterized, all of this sounds very much like Jung's conception of the state and consequences of the one-sided personality.

It needs to be emphasized that all types possess all qualities and abilities and use all parts of the brain at all times. However, it is clear some types will stress some functions more often or more intensively than others in the expression of their preferences.

# CHAPTER THREE

## A NEUROPSYCHOLOGICAL APPROACH TO ABILITIES IN WRITING, MUSIC AND VISUAL ART

*✳ ✳ ✳*

In this chapter the principles described in chapter 2 are illustrated for just three talent areas—writing, music and visual art—because it is clearly impossible to do this for *all* talent domains. Detailed examples provide a sense of the volume of data on this subject from which we can induce grounded principles of theory for relationships between type, talent and disease. Topics include the following:

* Psychological type profiles of writers, musicians and visual artists
* The *cognitive shift*, as applied to literary and musical abilities, in which sidedness of function changes as a result of learning and other influences
* The bilateral nature of writing talent
* The right-sided nature of musical and artistic talents
* Individual differences in laterality of cognitive functions, by gender and handedness
* Cognitive style as a reflection of laterality
* Developmental shifts in laterality
* Genius as an expression of laterality
* The compensatory model in talent development and psychopathology

Having looked at the principles in detail as they apply to writing, music and visual art, we will attempt to explain *why* these observations occur with a talent-deficit theory of giftedness in chapter 4.

*✳ ✳ ✳*

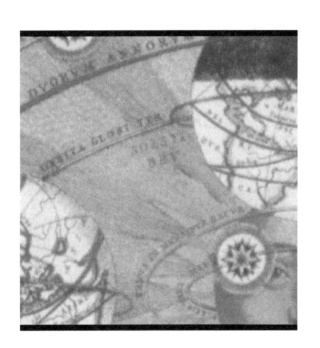

**Looking more closely now at the** "brain centers" involved in some artistic talents, a review of the literature shows that almost nobody purposely set out to study brain-behavior relationships in the arts until the 1970s. Neurologists and neurosurgeons documented interesting arts-related observations on an isolated basis since the early twentieth century, usually accidentally as they watched key functions like speech or computation. But in the 1970s there was a contagious realization that the findings made by these specialists hold great promise for the study of all behavior, even artistic behavior (Levy, 1976).

In that decade, and through the early 1980s, investigators like Thomas Bever, Karl Pribram, and especially Howard Gardner and Ellen Winner argued for the existence of a kind of artistic literacy—an ability to encode and read verbal, pictorial, musical or gestural symbols—asserting that it is really as cognitively demanding as literacy in any other domain (Gardner & Winner, 1981). No debate came from anyone who has ever painted a landscape or sight-read a new piece of music! A neuropsychological approach to the arts emerged and was swept along by the renaissance in split-brain research, the result being that we now have some understanding of where artistic skill, motivation and style originate in the brain.

The sections to follow take a brief look at some of the findings in this perspective for three art forms—writing, music and particularly drawing because it is easier to study on paper—talents that are often found, though certainly not exclusively so, as vocational preferences on the right side of the psychological type table (Tables 5–7, pages 42–43).

## Literary and Musical Abilities, and the Cognitive Shift

While verbal functions generally have been explored a great deal, the higher functions involved in creative writing have not been examined much, making writing the least understood of these three art forms. One thing is certain: strong linguistic competence is crucially tied to left-hemisphere function. Yet creativity in writing also makes demands on the right hemisphere, for sensitivity to context, figurative and emotional language, distinctions between reality and fantasy, and grasping the point and structure of stories (Gardner & Winner, 1981).

Writers and poets—who are very often NT or NF, as we know from the type literature (Macdaid et al., 1986)—are ruined by left-hemisphere brain damage. The poet Charles Baudelaire, for example, used to write lines like this:

**Table 5. Writers and Journalists (n = 517; Macdaid et al., 1986)**

| ISTJ | ISFJ | INFJ | INTJ |
|---|---|---|---|
| n = 23 | n = 21 | n = 23 | n = 45 |
| 4.34% | 3.96% | 4.34% | 8.49% |
| **ISTP** | **ISFP** | **INFP** | **INTP** |
| n = 7 | n = 12 | n = 72 | n = 46 |
| 1.32% | 2.26% | 13.58% | 8.68% |
| **ESTP** | **ESFP** | **ENFP** | **ENTP** |
| n = 1 | n = 19 | n = 91 | n = 39 |
| 0.88% | 3.58% | 17.17% | 7.36% |
| **ESTJ** | **ESFJ** | **ENFJ** | **ENTJ** |
| n = 26 | n = 18 | n = 46 | n = 28 |
| 4.91% | 3.40% | 8.68% | 5.28% |

**Table 6. Musicians and Composers (n = 136; Macdaid et al., 1986)**

| ISTJ | ISFJ | INFJ | INTJ |
|---|---|---|---|
| n = 4 | n = 7 | n = 6 | n = 12 |
| 2.94% | 5.15% | 4.41% | 8.82% |
| **ISTP** | **ISFP** | **INFP** | **INTP** |
| n = 3 | n = 2 | n = 13 | n = 7 |
| 2.21% | 1.47% | 9.56% | 5.15% |
| **ESTP** | **ESFP** | **ENFP** | **ENTP** |
| n = 3 | n = 6 | n = 23 | n = 8 |
| 2.21% | 4.41% | 16.91% | 5.88% |
| **ESTJ** | **ESFJ** | **ENFJ** | **ENTJ** |
| n = 8 | n = 14 | n = 15 | n = 5 |
| 5.88% | 10.29% | 11.03% | 3.68% |

The poet is like the prince of clouds, who rides out the tempest and laughs at the archer. But when he is exiled on the ground, amidst the clamor, his giant's wings prevent him from walking (Darwin, 1979:35).

We notice the metaphorical language he uses and the vivid word-picture he paints. Unfortunately, Baudelaire suffered a left-sided stroke after which he could only utter an oath, *cré nom*, his more emotional forms of speech—swearing, and pause words like "um" and "ah"—having been spared in the unaffected right hemisphere. Expressive aphasics like Baudelaire, who have experienced damage at the anterior end of the left hemisphere, tend to

**Table 7. Fine Arts Seniors (n = 33; Myers & Myers, 1980)**

| ISTJ<br>n = 0<br>0.00% | ISFJ<br>n = 0<br>0.00% | INFJ<br>n = 3<br>9.09% | INTJ<br>n = 4<br>12.12% |
|---|---|---|---|
| ISTP<br>n = 1<br>3.03% | ISFP<br>n = 1<br>3.03% | INFP<br>n = 10<br>30.30% | INTP<br>n = 6<br>18.18% |
| ESTP<br>n = 0<br>0.00% | ESFP<br>n = 0<br>0.00% | ENFP<br>n = 4<br>12.12% | ENTP<br>n = 0<br>0.00% |
| ESTJ<br>n = 0<br>0.00% | ESFJ<br>n = 1<br>3.03% | ENFJ<br>n = 1<br>3.03% | ENTJ<br>n = 2<br>6.06% |

lose their synthetic and sequential planning skills in writing and their verbal fluency—the ability to shift flexibly from one verbal idea or possibility to another—which would seem to place these functions, when intact, more to the front end of the normal brain.

Receptive aphasics, meanwhile, who have suffered damage further back on the left side, in the temporal-parietal area, the "Introversion" area we might say, can become oddly more fluent as a result of the damage, yet less meaningful. A Russian novelist by the name of Uspensky, who had this latter problem, wrote sentences like this:

> From underneath an ancient straw cap with a bleak spot on its shield there peeked two braids resembling the tusks of the wild boar; a chin grown fat and pendulous definitely spread over the greasy collars of a calico dicky and in thick layer lay on the coarse collar of the canvas coat, firmly buttoned on the neck (Gardner, 1982: 331–32).

Some of us might find ourselves sufficiently overwhelmed by the descriptive detail on first reading that we can't grasp the central thrust of the sentence, or the meaning of the whole. We can compare Uspensky's sentence to a passage of a speech written by William Faulkner for his acceptance of the Nobel Prize in 1950:

> [The writer] must teach himself that the basest of all things is to be afraid; and, teaching himself that, forget it forever leaving no room in his workshop for anything but the old verities and truths of the heart, the old universal truths lacking which any story is ephemeral and doomed—love and honor and pity and pride and compassion and sacrifice (Darwin, 1979: 210).

Again, some of us find ourselves rereading a line or two in order to be sure of the message. For some of us, only on rereading and sifting the detail is it possible to make sense of it.

In blunt contrast to both these passages is a line by Ernest Hemingway (1940) in *For Whom the Bell Tolls:* "But did thee feel the earth move?" No detail here, only a solitary metaphor that is literature's answer to the picture that is worth a thousand words.

Howard Gardner (1982), of Harvard Project Zero, thinks the writing styles of Faulkner and Hemingway—one elaborate, the other quite sparse—are reminiscent of the two aphasic styles, and has proposed a connection, therefore, between literary style and pathology. Another possibility he considers is that verbose writing and reductionist writing are healthy, much less exaggerated forms of aphasic styles, brought on by different strengths and weaknesses within the normal brain.

Gardner did not draw any connections to type, but we can imagine that a wordy *rococo* style, for instance, with lots of descriptive detail and embellishment, is the more likely writing style of a Sensing writer, and may possibly result from some normal under-emphasis of the left temporal-parietal area. A reductionist writer, who truly gets lost in detail, leaps over it, and removes as much of it as he can in favor of generalizations, is more likely an Intuitive writer who would appear to be influenced by some relative degree of underactivity in the left-frontal area. And the fact that both verbal fluency and synthetic planning skills tend to disappear in expressive aphasia suggests that at least some creative writing skills, perhaps those involving Intuition, are localized more to the front end of the normal brain.

When Sensing types and Intuitive types must work together in joint authorship—to write a report, say—we might be wise to remember these differences and anticipate the conflicts that may result from pitting one writing style that likes and needs detail against another that can't abide it. For to force brevity on a Sensing type is to frustrate his need to include all necessary pieces of the whole. And to force detail on an Intuitive is to exile him on the ground, amidst the clamor, where his wings can't walk. Nevertheless, both types are often faced with the difficult task of having to walk and fly together in the same piece of writing, both types always amazed by the natural abilities and opposite-pulling tendencies of the other.

Beyond this question of details versus wholes, there is the matter of comprehension, lessons on which can be learned from lesion studies. In people who are not professional writers, right-sided brain damage produces a set of literary deficits quite distinct from those caused by damage to the left side. A superficial command of language remains intact, but there are often severe literary impairments, such as a failure to appreciate irony, jokes, proverbs and metaphors so crucial to the very existence of literature. Instead, these patients rely on literal interpretations of these vehicles, and think "heavy heart," for instance, is an expression of weight rather than sadness (Winner & Gardner, 1977). They may be unable to connect details of a story to make sense of the whole, or to accept fantasy as anything other than literal and humorless reality. And when they do find something funny, it is usually inappropriate. Aphasics, on the other hand, while certainly less able to generate language, are remarkably sensitive to all these aspects of literary form and purpose.

There are other hints here of possible left-right differences in normal, healthy Sensing and Intuitive types. A Sensing type prefers literal, practical and down-to-earth interpretations of reality, may eschew fantasy as "flaky" and metaphorical language as "flowery," and sometimes miss the big picture for concentrating on its component parts. The Sensing writer might therefore appear to be operating in a leftward or posterior-leaning mode. An Intuitive, in contrast, is drawn to fantasy, theory, metaphor and puns, dismisses practicality as "boring" and factual detail as pedantic, and sometimes makes mistakes of accuracy in spelling, arithmetic, dates, times, names or quantities, because he is so busy concentrating on the bigger picture. The writer with a preference for Intuition is operating in a rightward or anterior-leaning frame of mind. Both types will write, but one may produce "know that" or "know how" books of factual and useful realism (S), and the other may create "know why" books about human or conceptual intangibles (N).

The pattern here, in short, is a right hemisphere that is needed for a global sense of what is going on in writing and why, and a left hemisphere that is needed for the mechanics of writing, and for greater involvement in the writing process overall (Gardner, 1982). *Accordingly, we might call writing, in any type, a bilateral art form, which "leans" in a leftward direction.*

Music, on the other hand, which is strongly over-represented by Intuitive Feeling (NF) types, is in some ways writing's neuropsychological mirror image. Here, both hemispheres are certainly engaged but the right hemisphere appears to play the more important role, especially for technical skill and for the emotional aspects of actually performing music (Gardner & Winner, 1981). Perhaps because music is easier to assess, or because many researchers working in this area are also amateur musicians, this art form is much studied.

Studies of people with no musical training who have suffered brain injury show us that tone processing and tonal memory are localized in the right-temporal area, and that pitch, melody production and instrumental performance are also housed on the right side, particularly in the frontal area (Shapiro et al., 1981). When sodium Amytal is used to sedate the right hemisphere, singing is reduced to a monotone, but when it sedates the left side, it produces melody without words, which clearly demonstrates the role of the right hemisphere in creating musical sound (Bogen & Gordon, 1971). Rhythm, on the other hand, appears to live a more egalitarian existence, being more equally represented in both hemispheres.

Studies of healthy people who have no musical training tend to confirm these trends. Dichotic listening experiments demonstrate the right-sidedness of tone and timbre processing, melody, pitch, whistling and harmony (Bradshaw et al., 1972; Gordon, 1970; Kimura, 1973; Pribram, 1982; Sidtis, 1980). The left hemisphere participates equally with the right for a very few tasks (like musical memory and recognition of harmony changes) and appears just slightly dominant in rhythm processing (Deutsch, 1977; Gates & Bradshaw, 1977), but generally plays a secondary role for most other musical functions.

Figure 3 (page 46) summarizes the rather unequal distribution of musical functions in the normal brain. In symbolic terms, it shows that the audible and expressive components of

| | Left | Relative Sidedness Of Activity (L) --------------------------- (R) | Right |
|---|---|---|---|
| Pitch | High | --------------------- | Low |
| Range | High | --------------------- | Low |
| Timbre | Simple | --------------------- | Complex |
| Intervals, Scales | High | --------------------- | Low |
| Melody | Unfamiliar | --------------------- | Familiar |
| Singing | Words | --------------------- | Humming |
| Whistling | Whistling | --------------------- | Whistling |
| Instrumentation | Instrumentation | --------------------- | Instrumentation |
| Harmony, Chords | Simple | --------------------- | Complex |
| Analysis Strategy | Sequential | --------------------- | Holistic |
| Musical Affect | Musical Affect | --------------------- | Musical Affect |
| Harmony Changes | Harmony Changes | --------------------- | Harmony Changes |
| Musical Memory | Musical Memory | --------------------- | Musical Memory |
| Rhythm, Pulse | Complex | --------------------------------- | Simple |
| Rhythm Changes | More | --------------------------------- | Less |
| | Accurate | | Accurate |

**Figure 3. Relative Control of Native Musical Abilities in the Hemispheres (Right-Handers)**

music (i.e., the spatial aspects of music) are disproportionately right-sided, while the rhythmic components (the linear, time aspects) are more bilateral with some leanings toward the left. Interestingly, conductors use the right hand (left hemisphere) to indicate meter and tempo, and the left hand (right hemisphere) to convey expressive style, emotion, intonation and dynamics.

For our purposes, the most fascinating observation within the study of musical abilities is the finding that *left-hemisphere brain activity increases with musical training. A phenomenon known as a cognitive shift occurs with the environmental influence of education.* Beginning with Bever and Chiarello's (1974) dichotic study of musicians and non-musicians—in which right-ear (left-hemisphere) superiorities for sound recognition were discovered in the musicians—numerous experiments in musical functioning have demonstrated that there is a leftward shift in musical abilities as a result of training. Pitch discrimination, melody processing, perception of octave patterns, and complex musical decision-making have all been shown to happen more on the left side of the brain in musically experienced people (Craig, 1979; Johnson, 1977; Oscar-Berman et al, 1974; Shanon, 1980). Females and left-handers show less of this effect, though, and sometimes even a reversed effect as we might anticipate given a brain organization which is often more bilateral than that of males or right-handers (Gordon, 1975).

For those skeptical of the contrived nature of dichotic listening experiments, John Mazziotta and Michael Phelps (1985) have taken biochemical pictures, through PET scanning, of right-temporal tone-processing in musically untrained people, and left-temporal activity in trained people performing the same task (Figure 4). In fact, the pictures are so convincing as to make the cognitive shift phenomenon in music, at least, a nearly unassailable reality.

It is not that musical functions suddenly get tired of living right of center and actively

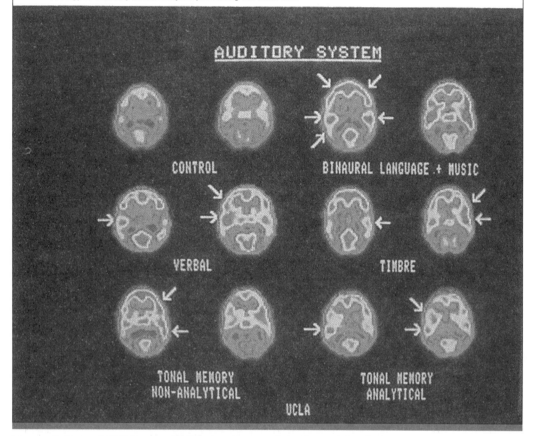

**Figure 4. Normal PET Scans of Different States of Auditory Stimulation (Mazziotta & Phelps, 1985)**

defect across the corpus callosum to the other side, but rather that the owner of these abilities, as a result of training, now has a verbal, time-oriented, analytic processing strategy which cues the left side and enables him to "read" the complexities of music in a way he never could as a non-musician. The right hemisphere, meanwhile, continues to do the more holistic, general attending to sound that is characteristic of the untrained (Thomas & Shucard, 1983). The trained musician therefore names, reads, counts and analyzes music where the non-musician merely absorbs and appreciates what he hears, uncritically.

The process is apparently not unique to music. Shifting is believed to occur with any highly developed skill as verbal labels are attached to nonverbal information, leaving the right hemisphere free for the processing of novel, not-yet-coded information in a variety of modalities (Bever, 1983; Gardner, 1982). In learning to speak a language, for example, the right hemisphere is thought to play a prominent role in the initial acquisition of language, while the left hemisphere plays a larger role in storing and operating the systems and strategies so learned. As Schneiderman and Desmarais (1988) write:

> There is both clinical and experimental evidence of greater *right-*hemisphere processing of language in bilinguals and second-language acquirers than in monolinguals [but bilinguals are] more left-lateralized in their first language than in their second . . . Other studies report proficient bilinguals to be more left-lateralized in their second language than were nonproficient bilinguals. All of the preceding findings suggest that the right hemisphere plays a major role in the acquisition of various skills and knowledge, including language, which are then organized into left-hemisphere-based descriptive systems (115).

Camilla Benbow (1988), who studies gifted math students, accounts for improvements in math scores from grade seven to grade twelve in the same way. She too says training produces a leftward "shift in the relative activation of the two hemispheres" (63) and that such a shift may have something to do with the fact that most important contributions to mathematics are made at a young age when the math is still new (read: right-sided) to the learner. Clearly, at least for some cognitive functions involved in math, language and music, the learner appears to "move" from a state of right-sided novelty to left-sided familiarity with experience.

To the extent that type preferences and talent preferences are related, meaningful lessons for type are embedded in this phenomenon of cognitive shifting in talent. Type preferences in the individual are quite stable over time and will test out more or less the same each time a person completes the *Myers-Briggs Type Indicator®* (*MBTI®*) instrument, as indicated in the relatively high test-retest reliability of the inventory (Sewell, 1986). One presumes this is because the neuropsychological foundations underlying the preferences are also very stable. Once an Extravert, always an Extravert, very likely because the person's basic tendency toward right hemisphericity (or some other activation pattern) isn't alterable through mere exposure to opposite influences. Nevertheless, some people's score on *MBTI* retest can shift slightly under stressful circumstances or during transitional periods, which reminds us of the cognitive shift phenomenon.

What we are suggesting here is that *even though a person's type is basically unchanging, as handedness or the natural right-sidedness of musical cognition is basically unchanging, there is at least some fluidity in the laterality of type preferences that hinges on choice.* It may be possible to learn to adapt some aspects of a preference to the needs of one's experience, environment and education, just as the musician adapts to formal training. The TF scale in particular, which the literature documents as the most variable and unstable of the scales (Myers & McCaulley, 1985), would seem to be the scale on which behavioral shifting is most possible. Perhaps even JP allows some flexibility for learning and change, though EI and SN are likely much less malleable due to the comparative rigidity of their underlying neuropsychological structures.

As a result, a right-lateralized Extravert in a relative state of brainstem-activated arousal has great difficulty making a social butterfly out of a left-lateralized and energy-conserving Introvert. And an Intuitive type, also very possibly right-lateralized or anterior-lateralized, has an arduous task making an abstract physicist or painter out of a Sensing mechanic or librarian.

Why? Because the teacher is effectively asking that the student transform his laterality for arousal and focus functions, which is about as reasonable and probable as getting him to suddenly become left-handed. But a Thinking type and a Feeling type who live together for many years do seem to teach each other to move toward the middle of the scale—the Thinking type to be somewhat more considerate, the Feeling type to be somewhat more objective—in response to the needs and moderating influences of the partner. It may well be just such a movement toward bilaterality that makes couples more alike over time. Indeed, a failure to shift must account for many a divorce.

A person in transition might also make a cognitive and typological move in response to the changing needs of his environment, learning to function with his left hand, as it were, while his right hand is hurting. In doing so, he emphasizes areas of the brain he is not accustomed to emphasizing, and appears justifiably awkward because they are not his true, "fixed" preferences. The Introverted divorcee, for example, goes to a singles' dance to meet people (E) and feels socially clumsy and out of place. The Intuitive Perceiving type, perhaps forced by circumstances to be financially practical and organized (SJ) for the first time in her life, doesn't know where to begin. With time, both will likely revert to their genuine preferences or some balance of the extremes, but not without the experimental, even radical, trial-and-error period characteristic of an adaptation to change.

Studies of cognitive shifting in music tell us that new learning experiences are often under the temporary control of right-hemisphere processing which later move left with familiarity. This would seem to suggest that any transition in life, much of which is simply an adaptation to something new, might spark temporary right-sided activation and an accompanying swing toward right-sided type preferences, such as Feeling and Perceiving perhaps, which will later shift left as the person adapts to the situation and organizes it in his own mind. It also suggests that people in transition might actually be helped through difficult times by encouragement of the Feeling and open Perceiving necessary to the first stage of familiarization. By first allowing themselves to experience the relative chaos of right-sided activity—just as the musician must first allow himself to listen to music—they can then proceed to the more ordered left-sided existence of analysis, familiarity and acceptance. Which is to say, the act of simply tolerating chaos may be a first step to regaining psychic order.

What happens to musical strategies after "migration?" Does music somehow become tied to language as it shifts leftward, given the left hemisphere is clearly the language hemisphere in most people? No, it turns out. In fact, music and language are quite dissociated, even in the reading of music, which is quite odd considering the apparent overlap of the functions. In the literature there are tales of a Wernicke's aphasic who couldn't read text but who could read music at the piano, and a musician who couldn't read music but who could read text, and dozens of other case studies since the early twentieth century which demonstrate the disconnectedness of music and language (Soukes & Baruk, 1930; Gardner & Winner, 1981). Even severe language disorders don't seem to have much of an effect on musical competence, just as musical disorders such as tone deafness have very little impact on language skills, apparently because music and language are controlled by quite different mechanisms. Country singer Mel Tillis stuttered badly when he spoke, yet his singing was flawless and fluid. Countless early jazz personalities couldn't read a note and were very often linguistically illiterate as well, but neither disability affected their stature as great musical talents of the period. Though they can and often do exist together in the same individual, musical talents do not appear to require verbal talents, or vice versa.

Instead, music is tied more to emotion than to language, more to the right hemisphere than to the left, despite any strategy shifts in sound analysis that may occur as a result of training. In fact, lesion studies of *gifted musicians* suggest that very little of the left hemisphere is used in the highest forms of the art. A Russian composer, Shebalin, had severe brain damage on the left side, but continued to teach and compose; Dmitri Shostakovich said of the man's fifth symphony, "a brilliant creative work, filled with highest emotions, optimistic and full of life" (Gardner, 1982). A Swiss pianist suffered severe Wernicke's aphasia, couldn't understand speech or speak himself, yet his recognition of music and his ability to perform remained intact. An American choral composer with the same problems couldn't read words but continued to compose (Gardner, 1982). And clearly to top them all, Handel may have suffered a left-sided stroke which paralyzed his right arm, yet he went on to write *Messiah* a couple of years later, in just twenty-one days.

Little is known about the effects of right-sided damage on gifted musicians because there are so very few reports of it in the neuropsychological literature. Of course, the easiest explanation for this situation is that, for whatever reasons, the effects of such damage have seldom been formally documented for musicians. An alternative, if initially outrageous hypothesis—which will be further explored in chapter 5—is that gifted musicians, on the whole, have simply had fewer strokes on the right side of the brain, possibly resulting in fewer right-damaged musicians for investigators to write about.

Among famous musicians in the right-damaged category, there is Igor Stravinsky who may have sustained a right-sided stroke later in life but for whom no cognitive deficits were ever recorded. Among lesser-known artists, there is one young composer, studied by Gardner (1982), who managed to retain his musical knowledge and continued to teach and write books about music after the stroke. Despite these abilities, the man was unfortunately no longer motivated to compose and couldn't conjure up the appropriate emotional atmosphere or conceive of the whole piece. Neither did he listen to music for enjoyment anymore, finding he no longer experienced the wonderful associations he once did. His attempts at composition were likewise uninspired and uninspiring.

That this man retained high-order language and technical skills, yet lost the "mood" of music and the urge to compose, dramatizes the hemispheric distinctions between playing music and creating it—all that remained was the composer's left-sided technique, the tools of the trade without any of the passion. This case and those preceding it therefore suggest that *music is, for the most part, a rightward-leaning art form*. The claim is qualified, however, in that there is much individual variation stemming from the many roles a musician might play—

listener, composer, singer, instrumentalist, teacher—and the various degrees of formal (read: leftward) training a musician might have.

## Graphic Skills in Non-Artists and Artists

A spatial ability was once defined as a cognitive combination of mental imagery and movement, form and time (Harris, 1978). Music fits this description—in requiring that the music maker recognize tonal distance (pitch) and dance nimbly along keys and conceptual fences in the creation of a structural form—but these more spatial aspects of music are usually overlooked because of our insistent preoccupation with the "linguistic" features of music, namely notation and counting. Indeed, we even speak of the "language of music," as if to drive home the point.

Graphic skills, for some reason, are allowed to be purely spatial, being more hemispherically aligned with musical functions than with language functions, and being predominantly right-sided in nature. The use of imagery, movement, form and perspective in time and space is more immediately obvious for graphic skills than it is for musical skills, and the lion's share of information on them, for our purposes, comes from lesion studies of artistic and particularly non-artistic populations. Once again, this is an art form that is strongly over-represented by Intuitive Feeling (NF) types and Intuitive Thinking (NT) types, especially Introverts (Myers & McCaulley, 1985).

To start with, we can examine the graphic functions of people who do not draw, paint or sculpt for a living, people who may be talented in some other area, even an artistic area, but who are not as a rule noted for exceptional graphic abilities. Investigations of the *graphically untalented* brain, as we might call it, show that, as for music, the left hemisphere plays an important, yet secondary role (Table 8, page 52). Beginning with Elizabeth Warrington's (1966) now classic study of drawing disabilities—in which right-damaged patients were found to perform consistently poorer than left-damaged patients in the copying of drawings—numerous studies have demonstrated that right-hemisphere patients, especially those with posterior injuries, have very different remaining drawing abilities than do left-hemisphere patients. What follows are just some of the multitude of distinctions that have been identified.

Right-damaged patients tend to underestimate distance, angles and symmetry, and fail to improve no matter how much they practice. Better at free drawing, they have a great deal of difficulty copying things, and make incorrect asymmetric versions of a model, with gross spatial alterations. The overall appearance of their creations is lopsided, disorganized and fragmented. They pay more attention to detail than to form, add much more detail than is necessary, and produce bizarre unrecognizable objects that incorporate very extraneous bits of information, such as a stem on a potato. Most noteworthy, they ignore the left side of the page in their own drawings, just leaving it blank, which is part of the phenomenon of contralateral neglect. Leaving out one side of a picture naturally creates very odd drawings such as half a bicycle wheel on the right side of the page or half a portrait which, incidentally, usually seems to display negative facial affect such as sadness or anger (Gardner, 1982; Gianotti & Tiacci,

**Table 8. Relative Art-Related Deficits Resulting From Unilateral Lesion**

| Left | Right | Likely Site | Source |
|---|---|---|---|
| Visual scanning, search | Visual scanning, search | Frontal | Lezak, 1976 |
| Visual flexibility (holding a perception during a distraction), disembedding figures | | Frontal | Lezak, 1976 |
| | Spatial perception, space-form abilities | Parietal*, temporal, occipital | Critchley, 1953 |
| | Spatial point localization | Posterior | DeRenzie, 1978 |
| | Slope Identification | Occipital | Hubel & Wiesel, 1963 |
| | Estimation of distance, angles, symmetry | | Warrington et. al., 1966; Gazzaniga & LeDoux, 1978 |
| | Depth perception, spatial relations | Parieto-occipital | DeRenzie, 1978 |
| | Tactile shape discrimination | | DeRenzie, 1978 |
| | Visual discrimination and recognition of simple figures and designs | Posterior | Milner, 1980 |
| | Visual organization of fragmented or ambiguous information | Parieto-temporal | Lezak, 1976 |
| | Sense of direction | Temporal, parieto-occipital | Milner, 1980 |
| Analysis of spatial orientation | Detection of spatial orientation | | DeRenzie, 1978 |
| Visual memory of spatial position | Tactile memory of spatial position | Posterior | DeRenzie, 1978 |

**Table 8. (Continued)**

| Left | Right | Likely Site | Source |
|---|---|---|---|
| Memory for figures and drawing | Copying simple geometric designs, memory for design | Parietal | Piercy et al., 1960<br>Boller & DeRenzie, 1967<br>DeRenzie, 1978<br>Hier et al, 1983 |
| Free drawing | Free drawing | Parietal | Piercy et al., 1960 |
|  | Color perception, color memory, color drawing |  | DeRenzie & Spinnler, 1967 |
| Planning and sequencing of drawing movements |  | Frontal | Piercy et al., 1960<br>Warrington et al., 1966 |
| Detailed drawing (oversimplification) | Simple drawing (overelaboration) |  | Piercy et al., 1960 |
| Analysis of mental rotation of images | Block design, object assembly mental rotation of images | Parietal | DeRenzie, 1978<br>Hier et al., 1983a |
| Design fluency | Design fluency* | Frontal*, frontocentral* temporal, left frontal | Jones-Gotman & Milner, 1977 |

*Predominant

1970; Jones-Gotman & Milner, 1977; Kaplan, 1980; Piercy et al., 1960; Warrington et al., 1966). Figure 5 (page 54) gives some idea of the magnitude and kinds of drawing disabilities seen in these patients.

Left-hemisphere patients, on the other hand, have a very different set of drawing problems. Just the opposite of right-hemisphere patients, these people are better at copying than free drawing, because free drawing requires that they plan what to draw and then arrange the plans in a sequence, which they have difficulty doing. They reproduce models fairly well though, even internal lines, and while they may draw more curved angles or more angles in general than are necessary, the final product is really quite acceptable. Also in total contrast to right-hemisphere patients, they pay more attention to form than to detail, and oversimplify details or leave them out altogether, the overall effect of which is simplicity, clarity, even child-like qualities, which pay attention to contours and overall composition (Gardner, 1982; Gazzaniga & Le Doux, 1978; Gianotti & Tiacci, 1970; Grossman, 1980; Jones-Gotman & Milner, 1977; Kaplan, 1980; Piercy et al., 1960; Warrington et al., 1966).

Figure 6 (page 55) gives examples of left-damaged work, which are similar to that of normal elementary school students—poor technical quality, symmetrical objects, and quite recognizable subject matter displaying positive facial affect. Considering most non-artistic

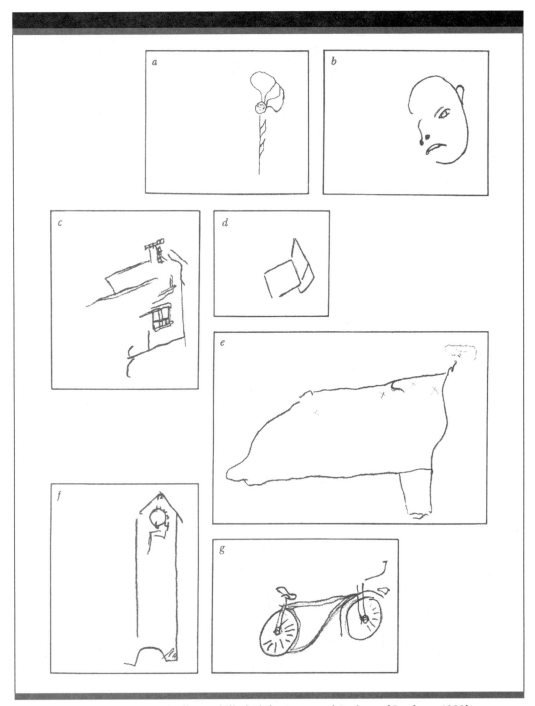

**Figure 5. Drawings by Artistically Unskilled Right-Damaged Patients (Gardner, 1982)**

From *Art, Mind, and Brain: A Cognitive Approach to Creativity* by Howard Gardner.

adults draw much like this anyway, we can see that left-hemisphere damage (release of the right hemisphere) doesn't have nearly the same profound impact on drawing abilities that right-hemisphere damage does—because many of the skills that are absolutely essential to drawing are still intact in the undamaged right hemisphere. Left-damage may have disastrous consequences, however, for other kinds of abilities such as speech.

Combined, these findings implicate the posterior right hemisphere in the non-artist's

**Figure 6. Drawings by Artistically Unskilled Left-Damaged Patients (Gardner, 1982)**

From *Art, Mind, and Brain: A Cognitive Approach to Creativity* by Howard Gardner.

estimation of distance, angles and symmetry, in learning to copy designs, in doing simple free drawings, and in putting it all together to make a coherent spatial whole. The left hemisphere would appear to play the greater role in detailed free drawing, and in the planning and sequencing of actual drawing movements. Although these inferences come from lesion studies, we also have EEG evidence that the same patterns occur in healthy subjects (Clare & Suter, 1983). *Drawing in normal, non-artistic people is a bilateral activity with rightward tendencies.*

In people who are not artists then, we see again that the left hemisphere controls the intricacies, or perhaps embellishments of design—the detail, as we said—while the right hemisphere monitors the artistically more important functions of fluency, form and appropriateness. In writing, we likened the ornamental rococo style of left-hemisphere functioning to the Sensing preference, and the simpler, barer, reductionist style of right-hemisphere operation to Intuition. It seems reasonable to suppose that the same distinctions might also hold true for visual art, that ornate calligraphy or intricate needlepoint, for example, are left-sided and perhaps more Sensing on balance, than minimalist cartoon caricatures or large, unadorned sculptures which are right-sided and perhaps more Intuitive, even in people who aren't professional artists.

To this point, we have mentioned only the left-to-right differences in graphic functions, but there are also some very important front-to-back differences to consider. Within the right hemisphere, for example, the posterior end of it (right rear quarter of the brain) seems to perform the basic mechanics of design, while the anterior end (right front quarter) looks after the more creative aspects. Constructional capacities, drawing and memory for design have all been localized in the right parietal region (Hier et al., 1983a, 1983b), just as design fluency, which is defined as planning and inventiveness in drawing, has been found to be controlled in large part by the right frontal area (Jones-Gotman & Milner, 1977).

Very significant for the localization of Intuition, the frontal lobes on both sides of the brain appear to be involved in creativity generally. Zangwill (1966) was among the first to propose this connection, noting that some aspects of intelligence—namely, divergent and ideational thinking, spontaneity, imagination, verbal fluency, and putting plans into action—suffer with injury to this region. The right frontal area has since been linked with emotionality (which is defined as motivation, inspiration and gratification sustained), proverb interpretation, the motor components of block construction and design copying (Benton, 1968), pitch and musical error detection (Shapiro et al., 1981), melody production, memory for rhythm and melody, and the ability to play a musical instrument (Botez & Wertheim, 1959). Given this right frontal area, even in children, is the right hemisphere's anatomical answer to the large speech-related zones of the left hemisphere (Rourke et al., 1983), it seems that artistic abilities are an inborn adjunct to verbal abilities in the brain, if to a lesser degree in the social spheres outside it.

Non-artistic people appear to have a relatively even distribution of artistic abilities across the hemispheres—hence the many very rational claims that competent art requires the integrated use of both sides—but *gifted artists* rely heavily on the right hemisphere, especially for coherence, style and emotionality. For them, Gardner and Winner (1981) have found that *"the left hemisphere seems to play little or no role"* (376). This suggests that a shift has happened, with training or other influences, to an asymmetric representation that is really uncommon among the unskilled. As we have seen, left-sided damage will disrupt the drawing abilities of lay people, but it seems *not* to affect gifted painters in terms of their productivity, technique or tone, because much of their artistic skill is concentrated on the right side.

It is as if left-damaged painters actually have two selves—a non-artistic, linguistic self that can suffer substantially from the damage, and an artistic self that does not. In this regard, the post-traumatic notes of a French painter, described by Alajouanine (1948), are revealing:

> There are in me two men, the one who paints, who is normal while he is painting, and the other one who is lost in the mist, who does not stick to life—I am saying very poorly what I mean—There are inside me the one who grasps reality, life; and there is the other one who has lost his regard for abstract thinking . . . these are two men, the one grasped by reality to paint, the other one, the fool, who cannot manage words anymore (238).

This sorrowful passage attests to the fact that high-level thought, in visual art as in music, can occur quite independently of language and other left-hemisphere skills. In fact, some severely left-damaged painters not only retain their artistic abilities, learning how to do things again with the non-paralyzed left hand, but also are actually said to *improve* following loss of language (Gardner, 1982; Schweiger, 1985). Improvement in art, of course, is a personal judgment so we will not make much of the point, except to say that the underlying message is important: *the separation of art and language is pronounced in the talented,* probably so that one process cannot interfere with the other.

 A number of authors believe that the use of language actually inhibits art. The case of the talented child Nadia, in the literature, is one of many pieces of evidence for this. Autistic and left-handed, this little girl produced truly astonishing drawings (Figure 7, page 58) until age ten when speech therapy helped her to talk and be more sociable. After that, her drawings declined sharply in quantity, quality and spontaneity (Gardner, 1982). Gardner also reported the case of an artist who couldn't name objects he saw—a problem known as visual agnosia— whose drawing accuracy actually got worse the more he learned to recognize objects and call them by name. Moreover, Betty Edwards (1979), an accomplished American art educator, has described how art students cannot talk and draw at the same time, and how drawings improve when the students cannot talk about, symbolize or schematize a model in verbal ways (e.g., "That's a bowl of fruit"). Finally, there is the common observation that artistic productivity and quality in children tend to disappear the more we develop their language skills. Most young people basically stop drawing—with the exception of doodling—before they ever reach high school.

One explanation often given for these observations is that there is competitive bilateral interference between verbal and nonverbal processing in which one form suffers with disruption by the other. Like the old trick of patting the head while rubbing the belly, it is very difficult for the brain to perform verbal and visual processes at the same time:

> There is already evidence that visualizing and verbalizing are two naturally interfering ways of representing stimulation or memory at all ages and that the degree of interference does not change much with age or cognitive style. The interference of the two modes has been amply demonstrated in adults . . . for several kinds of simultaneously performed tasks, and it

appears as a basic opposition in the literature on lateralization of cerebral hemispheric function (Haber & Haber, 1988: 236).

Competition effects and the ensuing cognitive inefficiencies are believed to occur in any instance where there is "crowding" or overlap of functions, which is often the case in the bilateral condition where abilities are effectively duplicated on both sides of the brain. The bilateral condition, as we have mentioned, is more common among left-handers and females (Kinsbourne, 1972; McGlone & Davidson, 1973; Milner, 1973). In left-handers, especially boys, language is particularly vulnerable to verbal-nonverbal competition effects that in some instances can produce dyslexia, stuttering or other verbal deficits. In girls and women, however, nonverbal skills such as spatial abilities (e.g., directional orientation in a building or city) are thought to be more susceptible to the interference (Lansdell, 1962; Witelson, 1974, 1977).

Since bilateral development and overlap of functions can be a counterproductive state for some thought processes, Moscovitch (1977) has proposed that one hemisphere actively inhibits processes in the other so as to prevent this situation from occurring. It is, in part, the job of the corpus callosum—one of the structures connecting the two hemispheres—to act as border guard and to inhibit and restrict the flow of information between them. Congenital

**Figure 7. Drawings by Nadia, Age 5 1/2, of a Rooster, and a Horse and Rider, (Gardner, 1982)**
From *Art, Mind, and Brain: A Cognitive Approach to Creativity* by Howard Gardner.

absence of a corpus callosum acts to inhibit nothing and the result is little or no functional asymmetry in the hemispheres. But in normal children, beginning about the age of five, the corpus callosum becomes operational, and a series of changes occurs: the flow of information is restricted; handedness becomes fixed; competition effects become noticeable; reading readiness is observed; and the functions of the two hemispheres begin to become more and more distinct, more and more asymmetric.

In the gifted, then, in whom verbal or nonverbal performance is exceptional, it is very likely that verbal and nonverbal processes are even more separate, more lateralized, more insulated against competition effects, and that superior nonverbal competence exists at the expense of verbal competence, and vice versa, to reduce competitive interference. An incidental educational implication of this is that, as in the brain, separation of verbal and nonverbal skills, and not integration, may be needed for optimum development of either. Of larger meaning for the question of type, talent and disease, however, is that *the brain naturally lends itself to one-sidedness (left or right) in some people (e.g., right-handers, left-handers, males, artists), and to a more balanced state of bilaterality in others (e.g., ambi-handers, females, writers).* As we shall see, uninterrupted laterality may be very advantageous to the expression of some talents, but perhaps risky for the continued health of the talented.

## Shifting and Graphic Style

In keeping with this theme of inhibition and separation of verbal and nonverbal processes, we note that a Bulgarian painter written up in the literature, called Z. B. to protect his identity, suffered a *left-sided* stroke, which caused him to lose his speech but not his artistic fluency. His painting style, however, was changed from a straightforward narrative depiction of events to "strange and fantastic dreamlike images, clear colors, and symmetrical patterns" indicating that a shift had occurred to a right-hemisphere presence (Gardner & Winner, 1981: 374). But the stylistic transformation that happened in Z. B. is slight compared to what happens in *right-damaged* artists who are especially dependent on right-hemisphere functioning for what they do. German neurologist Richard Jung (of no relation to C. G. Jung) collected the work of four such painters and found in it the unilateral neglect, disrupted contours and lack of organization we saw earlier, in Figure 5 (page 54), in lay people with similar injuries.

The change in style in Jung's artists is dramatic. After the damage, the work becomes more expressive, bizarre and emotional, as if "an inhibitory mechanism has been released and the patients can now give freer vent to their most primitive, least disguised feelings" (Gardner, 1982: 323). Similar to left-sided damage that releases artistic abilities on the other side, right-sided damage can release emotional sensitivity and sense of thematic appropriateness on the same side. Freud, and others of psychoanalytic bent, might liken this transformation to expression by the *id* (Galin, 1974).

Self-portraits by Anton Räderscheidt and Lovis Corinth (Figures 8–9, pages 60–61), typify the right-damaged style. Corinth, for instance, sustained a right-hemisphere stroke and the changes that followed in his art were often discussed by art critics of the 1920s. Many of

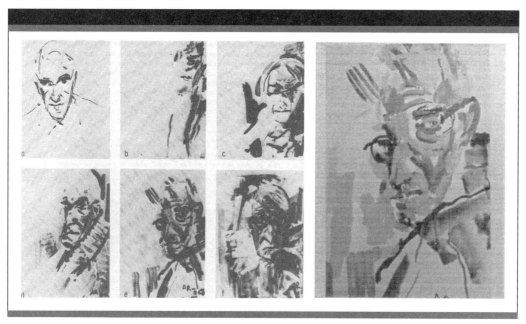

**Figure 8. Right-Damaged Style in a Skilled Artist: Self-Portraits by Anton Räderscheidt,
Before and at Two-Month Intervals After a Right-Hemisphere Stroke (Gardner, 1982)**

From *Art, Mind, and Brain: A Cognitive Approach to Creativity* by Howard Gardner.

us might want to challenge that it could have been the sheer psychological trauma of brain damage that caused the changes, but we can disprove to ourselves the likelihood of this explanation by noting that the same changes don't happen after left-damage (see Figure 6, page 55). As we have seen, left-damage effects on drawing are not only less severe, they are also quite different in character.

Making the leap to healthy artists, it seems quite probable that, as in writers and musicians, *particular styles reflect much more subtle degrees of laterality,* and that comparable styles among many artists of a period might reflect similar patterns of brain organization across a group. Impressionists and expressionists, for example, actively sought the impassioned and sometimes outlandish coarseness that Corinth and Räderscheidt managed to achieve with right-sided brain damage. This is not to say that the lot of them were brain-injured, of course, only that they may have had in common a certain normal preference for under-emphasis of the right side.

Corinth's work is also stylistically similar to that of Vincent Van Gogh who, in the last year of his life, experienced a depression so severe that it eventually led to his suicide. Depression, too, appears to behave as a right-sided problem, though PET scanning has suggested it may actually originate with underactivity of the left side, particularly in frontal areas, effecting a rightward shift (Tucker et al., 1981; Phelps et al., 1983). Earlier we suggested potential links between underactivity of the left frontal area, reductionism, stylistic simplicity, and Intuition. With all of these factors being associated with right laterality, depressive tendencies could be yet another piece of the quadrangle—which should not surprise us, given the recognized changeability of mood and "divine discontent" in Intuitive types (Thorne & Gough, 1991). At

**Figure 9. Right-Damaged Style in a Skilled Artist: Self-Portraits by Lovis Corinth, Before (1911) and After (1921) a Right-Hemisphere Stroke (Gardner, 1982)**

From *Art, Mind, and Brain: A Cognitive Approach to Creativity* by Howard Gardner.

any rate, there would appear to be enough stylistic contrasts here between left- and right-damaged abilities for us to suggest that the same directional emphases probably occur in the normal population, only on a much smaller and less obvious scale.

Aesthetic meaning and aesthetic preferences—which are defined as the reading of and liking for composition, balance and expressiveness in art—may also have a hemispheric basis. Gardner (1975a) has shown that left-damaged patients have no problem whatsoever grouping paintings by style. They can even exceed normal control subjects at the task, which would appear to be another example of the benefits to art of constraining or suppressing language. In contrast, right-damaged patients have very little style sensitivity, and are overwhelmed by the subject matter, which they can only classify by content. So, at least some issues in aesthetics and style would appear to be under right-hemisphere jurisdiction. In healthy people, the right hemisphere is also better equipped to recognize faces, facial expressions and body contours (Harris, 1986; Ley & Bryden, 1976) perhaps explaining why artists, whose drawing abilities are chiefly right-activated, take great interest in portraiture and the human form.

As many of us will remember from our kindergarten years, children tend to draw unusually balanced pictures, full of symmetrical objects such as box houses, round suns and elliptical clouds, usually placed squarely in the center of the page. For artistic adults, however, *asymmetric* design is often preferred, and this is readily seen in statues that are heavier on one side, or in great paintings that focus attention left or right of center. Incredulously, even this

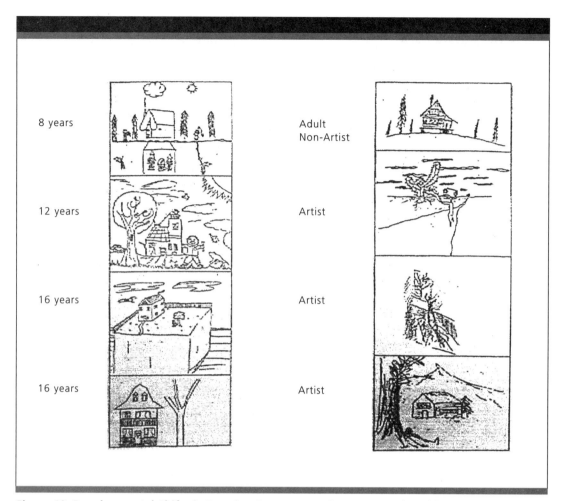

**Figure 10. Developmental Shifts in Drawing Symmetry and Asymmetry (Juschka, 1990)**

preference has a hemispheric foundation and it has been localized in the male right hemisphere and the female left hemisphere (Lansdell, 1962). *Asymmetry of design is usually more prevalent in males, strong right-handers, strong left-handers, and those with art training or exceptional drawing abilities (Levy, 1976; Juschka, 1990)—in other words, people with a high relative degree of laterality*—which is a good indication that the strength and direction of the asymmetry on paper might actually parallel the asymmetry of abilities in the brain.

In support of this claim, a blind study found a developmental effect, a gender-handedness effect, and a training effect on the positioning and balance of drawings on a page (Juschka, 1990). Drawing tests of eight-year-olds, twelve-year-olds, sixteen-year-olds, non-artistic adults and senior art students showed that placement on a page moves from a state of centered symmetry in children, to asymmetry in adolescents, and back again to symmetry in adults, with the exception of talented art students who tend to draw way over to the left side of a page (Figure 10).

In groups composed of different combinations of gender and handedness, placement was also found to move from centered symmetry in female ambi-handers to slightly greater asymmetry in right-handers of both sexes (Figure 11), and finally to marked left-asymmetry

**Figure 11. Sex-Handedness Variations in Drawing Symmetry and Asymmetry (Juschka, 1990)**

in male left-handers. And this is rather amazing given the current thinking is that ambi-handers have relatively bilaterally organized "symmetrical" brains, and strong right-handers and left-handers more laterally organized "asymmetric" brains. In a sense, placement of drawings on a page mirrors laterality in the brain. What's more, drawing scores were found to increase the further left a person drew (r>.46 for all groups, p<.05). That is, drawing scores were higher in people presumed to have greater laterality, which we might have predicted assuming the lateralized condition is relatively free of verbal-nonverbal competition effects.

*Asymmetry in drawing therefore seems to reflect not only the amount of brain asymmetry in a person, but also his drawing talent,* the very extremes of which we see in the one-sided neglect of brain-damaged works. *Right-damaged artists ignore the left side of space, where healthy artists emphasize it—clear evidence that much of an artist's kind of talent has its origins in the right hemisphere.* Because placement on a page seems to "move" with age and the amount of training a person has had, symmetry and asymmetry in drawing is apparently a fluid process, rather than a static feature of design, and in that sense appears to be visual art's version of the cognitive shift.

Two early historical studies by Gaffron (1950) and Levy (1976) proffered that right-handers and whole Western cultures tend to like art whose content is mainly on the right side, while true left-handers favor the reverse, apparently reflecting their scanning biases when they look across something. The drawing study mentioned previously disputes that claim with limited empirical evidence that right-handers tend to choose as their focus the center of a page, or just left of center, while left-handers draw even further to the left, perhaps because their drawing abilities are more exclusively right-lateralized.

However, this finding doesn't dismiss the possibility that left-sided asymmetry is *culturally* less valued—though that is probably unlikely where the majority of people in a culture have the same handedness (right). This raises the question of whether nonconformity in art might occasionally stem from a reversal of "normal" asymmetry. Facial profiles by the left-handed Leonardo, for example, all face right, contrary to the profiles drawn by the vast majority of right-handers (Di Leo, 1983). Raphael, too, is said to have placed figures on the left side of paintings simply to shock anybody who looked at them. In fact, a very early study by Wolff (1933), in which large volumes of great art and children's art were examined, revealed that left-sided expressions and symbols are common in the work of people considered to be "social deviants and persons of high talents" (175). Wolff says the left side contains the more abstract and "collective" expressions of these people—following Carl Jung's notion of the collective unconscious in art—while the right side contains their more individualistic expressions.

Centers of interest, asymmetry and balance have long been discussed as elements of art. In music, too, attention is directed, mostly to higher-pitched melody (processed by the left hemisphere), which might be analogous to important content on one side of pictures. There are also asymmetries of form, rhythm, meter, and so forth, which are usually counterbalanced so as to please an audience. Levy (1976) says, "the human aesthetic sense is profoundly affected by the fact that the human brain is laterally differentiated" (443). And since that sense appears to vary with handedness, gender and training, it would seem that laterality plays at least part of a role in determining the wide variety of artistic tastes.

## Shifting in Genius, "Insanity" and Cognitive Development

Direction and extent of laterality may also be crucial factors in intelligence, creativity and psychopathology. An important case in point is a tissue study of Albert Einstein's brain which found that Einstein's preserved left hemisphere has about 75 percent more glial (conduction) cells per neuron than the control brains to which it was compared (Diamond & Scheibel, 1985). The density of glial cells in Brodmann area 39—a posterior part of the left parietal lobe involved in reading, speech, calculation and most importantly, processes involved in making associations and leaps—is nearly *twice* that of controls, which suggests that Einstein was very strongly left-lateralized for the verbal-analytic functions that made him famous.

Another tissue study, this time of the brain of a Japanese composer, found disproportionate cell density on the *right* side (Laytner, 1985), which leads to the speculation that musicians and visual artists, as compared to creators in linguistic and numerical fields, might exhibit greater pockets of right-hemisphere abilities such as those measured by the subtests of performance IQs. Some evidence for this in healthy people comes from the finding that art students score higher than other students on drawing tests that tap right frontal, temporal and parietal lobe function (Juschka, 1990). We also have the work of Thatcher et al. (1983) who looked at the direction of asymmetry in gifted children. By correlating IQ and EEG asymmetries in these children, Thatcher's team found that IQ increases the more *dissimilar* the waves are in the two hemispheres—larger wave amplitudes on the left or larger wave amplitudes on the right depending on whether the talent is generally verbal-analytic like an Einstein, or nonverbal-spatial like a composer or a painter. The pattern seems to be that *talented people in some diverse fields live with a relatively high degree of laterality.*

It is often said, though, that high intelligence and creativity are essentially distinct, and so they shouldn't be talked about in the same breath like this in any conception of talent (Getzels & Jackson, 1962; Zangwill, 1966). What this complaint might really be saying is that whatever aspects of IQ conventional psychometric techniques actually manage to measure, these tests don't adequately pick up right-hemisphere functions critical to intelligence in the arts. Why? Because the tests often tap left-hemisphere processes even when they're trying very hard not to. For example, a test is intended to be spatial but is perhaps introduced with written instructions explaining how to do it, or is solved using verbal cues such as multiple choice answers, the net effect being that the "nonverbal-spatial" test really draws upon verbal-analytic functions prevalent on the left side. It is difficult to envision how else an examiner can state the question and score the answer, if not through written or spoken speech, but that is the kind of problem confronting test-writers. Imagining how we would ask a person to describe where he lives, without anyone using words, or even symbols representing words, gives us a fair idea of the predicament in which test-writers find themselves.

Because of the dilemma of how to assess nonverbal processes in nonverbal ways, and in spite of reported test validities, IQ tests may inadvertently concentrate on left-hemisphere activity to the relative disadvantage of processes on the right side. A bit of physiological evidence for this comes from the observation that more oxygen is taken up on the left side of the brain during intelligence testing, than on the right (Feinberg et al., 1960). Considering most tests of academic potential and achievement face the same problem of how to assess nonverbal skills—whether in exams, or IQ tests, or things like SATs—it should not surprise us to learn that artists and architects may not score as high on tests like these than do talented people in purely verbal spheres (MacKinnon, 1970; Peterson & Lansky, 1977; Roe, 1975).

Standard tests of potential and achievement just don't seem to measure the kinds of intelligence possessed by nonverbally, physically or gesturally talented people, whether they are artists, musicians, athletes, actors or gifted mimics like Robin Williams. In response, Gardner (1983) has aptly proposed a theory of multiple intelligences in which spatial intelligence is distinct from linguistic, musical, logical-mathematical, bodily-kinesthetic, and personal types of intelligence. IQ and achievement tests are probably only best at measuring the verbal-analytic kinds we see in writers, scientists and mathematicians. So, if a person doesn't do so well on such a test, we probably shouldn't conclude he isn't talented, just that he probably isn't *as* talented in verbal-analytic areas as he is in other areas. In most instances, given half a chance, we will find that the person shines in his own chosen nonverbal sphere because that is the direction of his laterality, and more philosophically, because perhaps that is what he was put on this planet to do.

Here again is evidence of a competitive dissociation between language and art, and the notion that *a person may excel in one domain at the expense of another*—this time in the artistic person who doesn't do as well on verbal tests biased in favor of left-sided processes. To underscore the point, there are lesion studies which show that artistic judgment in lay people actually increases as verbal intelligence decreases following brain damage (Lansdell, 1962), and a study of architects (right-handers) which finds negative correlations between their design skills and their academic achievement; design abilities were actually better in the architects with lower academic grades (Peterson & Lansky, 1977)! People with mental retardation who are artistically talented—savants like the English painter Bryan Pearce, or Japanese artists Yamashita and Yamamura—would seem to be rather final proof that artistic creativity and artistic intelligence can be quite separate from traditional conceptions and assessment of intelligence.

A clear trend emerges in Thatcher's (1983) work with the EEG asymmetries in children—from little EEG asymmetry in low IQ/low achievers, to greater asymmetry in gifted children, to very lopsided asymmetry (a ratio of 2:1) in pathology. Which is to say, *electrical activity in the brain becomes more one-sided in a person the more talented he is, and the more brain-injured he is*. And since psychopathology often produces hemisphere deficits quite indistinguishable from those of brain damage (Tucker et al., 1981), the question leaps out at us as to whether the infamous "fine line" between genius and insanity couldn't be that line between adaptive and maladaptive asymmetry. Is it possible that "insanity" is just another unfortunate step beyond the productive asymmetric state we call "genius?"

Greater laterality and sometimes reversed laterality, compared to normal control subjects, have been reported for schizophrenia, affective (mood) disorders such as depression, and developmental disorders such as dyslexia and autism (Tanguay, 1985). Harris (1986) says that, "all individuals show a predilection for one or the other of the hemispheric modes of consciousness. This probably genetic tendency accounts for predilections in psychopathology, character and style" (24). In this light, it is interesting that our very limited empirical evidence on type and psychopathology shows that the incidence of schizophrenia and unipolar depression may tend toward the left side of the type chart, particularly I, S, F and J (Tables 9–10). On the other hand, the incidence of bipolar disorder and substance abuse—in women at any rate—may tend toward Intuition (N) on the right side (Tables 11–13, pages 68 and 69; Bisbee et al., 1982; Luzader, 1984). For mental illness, it may eventually turn out that Jung's one-sidedness in the individual will extend to one-sidedness on the psychological type table.

It is the belief of Harris and others that faulty neurotransmitter action in the *left* hemisphere—*high* levels of dopamine—triggers pre-frontal lobe disorders in the predisposed individual, disorders such as schizophrenia, hysteria, narcissism and paranoia. *Low* norepinephrine and serotonin (a dopamine relative) in the prone *right* hemisphere also acts on the pre-frontal area, but here it contributes to the expression of bipolar disorder, depression, agoraphobia, masochism, obsessive-compulsive disorder, dependent and anti-social behavior. The condensed version of the hypothesis is that a person's anxiety over something gradually exhausts the serotonin supply—his "battery" runs down, as it were—and produces disinhibition of the left hemisphere, and an all out shift to right-hemisphere processing when things reach the psychosis stage (Shagass et al., 1978). The chemical imbalance we hear so much about in psychiatric disorders essentially creates a laterality imbalance, and probably vice versa.

**Table 9. Schizophrenic Psychiatric Patients (n = 110; Bisbee et al., 1982)**

| ISTJ | ISFJ | INFJ | INTJ |
|---|---|---|---|
| n = 16 | n = 27 | n = 2 | n = 2 |
| 14.55% | 24.55% | 1.82% | 1.82% |
| **ISTP** | **ISFP** | **INFP** | **INTP** |
| n = 5 | n = 11 | n = 2 | n = 1 |
| 4.55% | 10.00% | 1.82% | 0.91% |
| **ESTP** | **ESFP** | **ENFP** | **ENTP** |
| n = 4 | n = 3 | n = 2 | n = 3 |
| 3.64% | 2.73% | 1.82% | 2.73% |
| **ESTJ** | **ESFJ** | **ENFJ** | **ENTJ** |
| n = 13 | n = 15 | n = 3 | n = 1 |
| 11.82% | 13.64% | 2.73% | 0.91% |

**Table 10. Depressed Psychiatric Patients (n = 198; Bisbee et al., 1982)**

| ISTJ | ISFJ | INFJ | INTJ |
|---|---|---|---|
| n = 33 | n = 46 | n = 4 | n = 4 |
| 16.67% | 23.23% | 2.02% | 2.02% |
| **ISTP** | **ISFP** | **INFP** | **INTP** |
| n = 10 | n = 37 | n = 5 | n = 0 |
| 5.05% | 18.69% | 2.53% | 0.00% |
| **ESTP** | **ESFP** | **ENFP** | **ENTP** |
| n = 2 | n = 12 | n = 5 | n = 2 |
| 1.01% | 6.06% | 2.53% | 1.01% |
| **ESTJ** | **ESFJ** | **ENFJ** | **ENTJ** |
| n = 16 | n = 22 | n = 0 | n = 0 |
| 8.08% | 11.11% | 0.00% | 0.00% |

PET scans show us that psychiatric problems often underactivate or overactivate one or more areas of the brain. For example, in depression, there is underactivity in the left frontal area, and in schizophrenia there is underactivity mainly in left frontal and temporal areas (Kolb & Whishaw, 1985; Phelps et al., 1983; Restak, 1984), both of which may actively induce a rightward shift of the kind Harris suggests. More recent work implicates miscommunication in the limbic system and underactivity in frontal areas. EEG studies also show us that there is excessive electrical activity going on in the right hemispheres of people suffering from panic disorder and obsessive-compulsive disorder (Rapoport, 1989). Indeed, at their worst, it is as

**Table 11. Bipolar Psychiatric Patients (n = 29; Bisbee et al., 1982)**

| ISTJ | ISFJ | INFJ | INTJ |
|---|---|---|---|
| n = 1 | n = 2 | n = 2 | n = 1 |
| 3.45% | 6.90% | 6.90% | 3.45% |
| **ISTP** | **ISFP** | **INFP** | **INTP** |
| n = 1 | n = 1 | n = 3 | n = 0 |
| 3.45% | 3.45% | 10.34% | 0.00% |
| **ESTP** | **ESFP** | **ENFP** | **ENTP** |
| n = 0 | n = 1 | n = 0 | n = 4 |
| 0.00% | 3.45% | 0.00% | 13.79% |
| **ESTJ** | **ESFJ** | **ENFJ** | **ENTJ** |
| n = 2 | n = 8 | n = 2 | n = 1 |
| 6.90% | 27.59% | 6.90% | 3.45% |

**Table 12. Male Substance Abusers (n = 244; Luzader, 1984)**

| ISTJ | ISFJ | INFJ | INTJ |
|---|---|---|---|
| n = 49 | n = 20 | n = 9 | n = 19 |
| 20.08% | 8.20% | 3.69% | 7.79% |
| **ISTP** | **ISFP** | **INFP** | **INTP** |
| n = 26 | n = 9 | n = 29 | n = 18 |
| 10.66% | 3.69% | 11.89% | 7.38% |
| **ESTP** | **ESFP** | **ENFP** | **ENTP** |
| n = 12 | n = 3 | n = 18 | n = 8 |
| 4.92% | 1.23% | 7.38% | 3.28% |
| **ESTJ** | **ESFJ** | **ENFJ** | **ENTJ** |
| n = 12 | n = 5 | n = 2 | n = 5 |
| 4.92% | 2.05% | 0.82% | 2.05% |

**Table 13. Female Substance Abusers (n = 115; Luzader, 1984)**

| ISTJ | ISFJ | INFJ | INTJ |
|---|---|---|---|
| n = 9 | n = 8 | n = 4 | n = 1 |
| 7.83% | 6.96% | 3.48% | 0.87% |
| **ISTP** | **ISFP** | **INFP** | **INTP** |
| n = 2 | n = 10 | n = 25 | n = 12 |
| 1.74% | 8.70% | 21.74% | 10.43% |
| **ESTP** | **ESFP** | **ENFP** | **ENTP** |
| n = 0 | n = 5 | n = 14 | n = 10 |
| 0.00% | 4.35% | 12.17% | 8.70% |
| **ESTJ** | **ESFJ** | **ENFJ** | **ENTJ** |
| n = 4 | n = 3 | n = 7 | n = 1 |
| 3.48% | 2.61% | 6.09% | 0.87% |

if the whole right hemisphere is ablaze with overfiring, a kind of miniature, counterfeit version of a complex partial seizure.

If this is what these disorders can do to people, it is not unreasonable to expect that the stylistic features of any art they produce in these states might reflect not only the side, but also perhaps even the site, of the dysfunction. We can observe what rightward-pushing depression might have done to Van Gogh's work, and even more vividly to Edvard Munch's tortured expressions in *The Scream* (Figure 12). In contrast, Di Leo (1983) shows us how "leftward" psychosis might affect style. He compares the paintings of early-phase schizophrenics to the art-work of pre-operational children and concludes that both groups are entrenched, to begin with, in primary thought processes, what is known in Freudian terms as the id. The art at that stage is highly

**Figure 12. Right-Damaged Style in a Skilled Artist: The Scream (1893) by Edvard Munch**

**Figure 13. Left-Damaged Style in a Skilled Artist: Example of Psychotic Art Brut by Adolf Wölfli (1917) (Di Leo, 1983)**

subjective, he says, "dominated by feelings, imbued with fantasy, and largely free from cultural and logical constraints" (189), all of which is very suggestive of the right-hemisphere graphic style discussed earlier, not to mention that of the suicidal painters Van Gogh and Munch.

As a schizophrenic stabilizes, however, Di Leo says secondary process—the left hemisphere, which is heretofore underactive in certain areas—then intervenes and produces a peculiar form of art known as Art Brut, exemplified in a piece created by Adolf Wölfli (Figure 13). Here we see much individualism and non-conformity, repeating geometric figures, crowding, and an almost fanatical preoccupation with symmetry and order. The elaborate patterns in it are reminiscent of a Persian rug.

Compulsive repetition of ideas, called *perseveration*, is common in people with impaired frontal lobes, which the schizophrenic has, and the symmetry, as we have seen, happens when there is underactivity on the left side, and from which the schizophrenic is attempting to recover. The positive facial affect in the example by Adolf Wölfli—the opposite of the serious and frowning faces seen in right-damaged drawings—may be indicative of functioning in the right parietal areas governing such qualities. The main difference between this style and that of Munch, however, is the order, the logical linear precision, and the extreme attention to detail. The general busyness and complexity of it all makes it a visual rendition of Faulkner's prose or Bach's counterpoint, and is very clearly the work of a leftward-moving thinker.

So, it would seem art reflects the side and to some extent even the areas of special activity or underactivity, which can be a very helpful tool in guesstimating the laterality of a given creator. Carrying our hypothesis that style mirrors laterality a step further, it would seem that the child and the psychotic have in common the fact that they are both at first "rooted" in the right hemisphere. The difference is that the maturing child then apparently shifts leftward very quickly (Rourke et al., 1983) while the psychotic essentially stays put for some time, with only incomplete left-hemisphere contributions—the detail, the logical order—producing the outcome that is Art Brut.

Developmentally speaking, laterality can be demonstrated even at the fetal stage and in the very young baby. Speech laterality (and therefore handedness) is demonstrable anatomically preterm, and musical laterality at 22–140 days (Kolb & Whishaw, 1985), which suggest an innate component to the basic sidedness of functions that is later acted upon by hormonal and other environmental influences. For instance, deaf children who learn how to sign have the same asymmetric speech pattern as hearing children, but illiterate people and deaf children who don't know how to sign do not have this organization, which demonstrates the effects on laterality of exposure to language. Aberrant cognitive behavior may therefore be related to atypical lateralization or a failure to shift during critical periods of human development (Rourke et al., 1983; Thatcher et al., 1983).

Laterality is very loose and flexible at the beginning of life, as we can see in the shifting of preferences at various stages in normal child development. At birth and for some time afterwards, the hemispheres functionally overlap each other and are in a state of bilateral organization while each side processes the same low-level behaviors, such as yawning and head turning. Handedness and a same-sided eyedness begin to become perceptible in the first three months of life, left-handedness (right hemisphere) becomes apparent at four to five months, but obvious preference for one hand over the other, usually the right (left hemisphere), doesn't begin to become clear until six to nine months. After that, until age eight or nine, the child usually becomes increasingly right-handed and increasingly specialized for language in the left hemisphere and for nonverbal forms of communication in the right, even if he is not right-handed. Two-year-olds make one-word holistic expressions (right hemisphere), four-year-olds show sensitivity to word order (left hemisphere), and six-year-olds integrate the two, suggesting to Bever (1983) that *language development proceeds from right to left hemispheres and finally to bilaterality by the age of reading readiness, between ages five and six.*

The development of drawing laterality, in contrast, complements that of speech. *Drawing, like language, appears to be bilateral in the preschool years but right lateralized by the age of reading readiness.* The child starts scribbling by the time he is a year and a half, uses simple symbols such as the circle before age three (left hemisphere), and adds greater graphic detail (left hemisphere) by age four. Also about this time, the child, especially the left-hander, tends to draw numbers, letters, profiles and the direction of circles (clockwise) in reverse, suggestive of a rightward shift. By age seven, they are drawn in the accepted direction—letters and numbers facing right, profiles left, and circles counterclockwise—implying that the right hemisphere has become lateralized for drawing by the time speech lateralization is complete (Blau, 1977; Di Leo, 1983; Edwards, 1979; Milner, 1973). Drawings at this age are symmetrical and balanced, and possessing a freedom, simplicity and abstractness that rapidly disappears with maturity.

By the beginning of puberty, between age nine and ten, each hemisphere has developed its own unique functions and handedness is fixed, which suggests that hormonal influences and other factors contribute to the various critical stages in laterality and child development (Kolb & Whishaw, 1985):

The maturational hypothesis argues that both hemispheres are initially involved in language but gradually the left hemisphere becomes more specialized for language control. Lenneberg refined the maturational hypothesis by proposing that lateralization of function develops rapidly between the ages of two or three to five, and then proceeds slowly until puberty, by which time it is complete . . . Lenneberg defined the time span from about age two to fourteen as the critical period for the development of language, and more broadly, of cerebral lateralization (618).

At puberty, then, children's art undergoes a radical transformation toward detailed complexity, laborious realism and thematic repetitiveness (non-fluency), all of which suggests a leftward shift. Frustration with drawing skills grows, and artistic interest and productivity decline. For most people, drawing development doesn't evolve much after that. They may experience another upsurge in interest, or perfect the details of symbols learned earlier (e.g., Snoopy, Garfield), but in general, most adults are left with what we might term a "dysartistica"—effectively a drawing disability—which makes them draw like ten-year-olds.

Again we sense verbal-nonverbal competition and the winning out of one talent at the expense of the other. The child starts out interested, creatively motivated and productive, making sparse, right-sided drawings of symmetrical shapes and composition. But as propositional-conceptual knowledge increasingly takes hold, there is a leftward migration, a preoccupation with realistic detail, and a parallel decrease in artistic quality and output. The corollary, of course, is that only those individuals who are not so dependent on language, whether as a result of nature or nurture, can avoid this outcome.

The drawing study mentioned earlier (Juschka, 1990) uncovered a very interesting apparent pattern in laterality development that has considerable bearing on later discussions of type, talent and disease. The development of laterality for drawing, as suggested by mean handedness scores in 120 test subjects, and their placement of drawings on a page, was found to be the mirror-image of the development of lateralities for language, as proposed by Bever (1983). Furthermore, the laterality for drawing in female subjects, measured in the same way, was the mirror image of that for male subjects, and the sex-by-handedness relationship in drawing placement was found to be statistically significant at the .05 level.

Specifically, *Bever proposed that language development moves from a state of bilaterality in early childhood, through left laterality in adolescence, and again to bilaterality in adulthood. This trend, when graphed, produces a U-shaped curve (Figure 14). The drawing study found that the reverse pattern apparently occurs for graphic skills*—bilaterality in early childhood (as suggested by group tendencies toward ambi-handedness and symmetrical drawings), right laterality in adolescence (right handedness and asymmetric drawings), and bilaterality again in adulthood. This pattern, when graphed, forms an inverted U-curve. Overall drawing skill, as measured by drawing tests, also exhibited a curvilinear relationship with handedness, with highest scores occurring in strong right-handers and left-handers, and lowest scores in ambi-handers.

Primary school boys, as a group, had a mean tested handedness score indicating ambi-

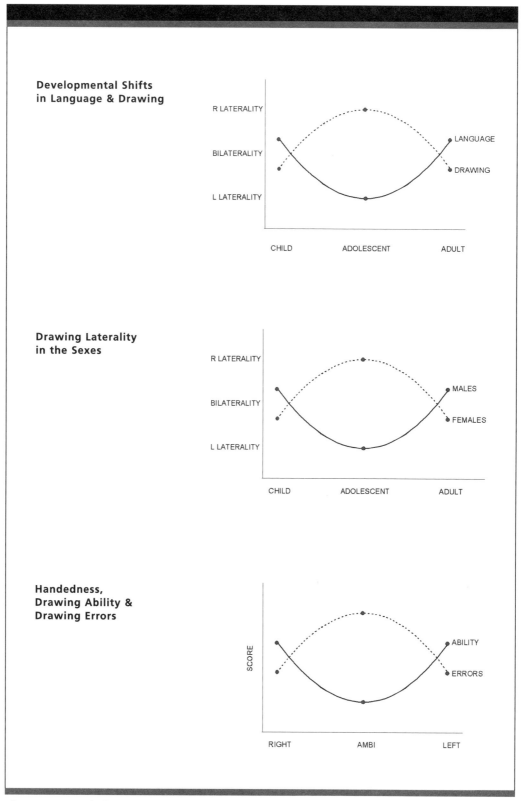

**Figure 14. Trends from the Drawing Study (Juschka, 1990)**

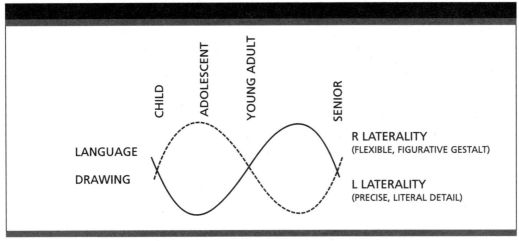

**Figure 15. Hypothetical Development of Lateralities for Drawing and Language (Juschka, 1990)**

handedness, and made symmetrically placed drawings (bilaterality). Adolescent boys tended toward right-handedness and made asymmetric drawings (laterality). Adult males again tended toward ambi-handedness and made symmetric drawings when they were artistically untrained (bilaterality), and asymmetric drawings when they were trained (laterality). Female subjects exhibited the opposite pattern, by comparison, meaning that the sexes produce yet another pair of inverted U-curves (Figure 14, page 73).

The gender pattern is of interest in light of the opposing sex difference in Thinking (left laterality) and Feeling (right laterality) in psychological type, and makes sense because it jibes with other well-known trends in cognitive development. For example, the boys group found to be approaching bilaterality in this study belong to a demographic group that is known for its high incidence of learning disability, which we would anticipate where there is bilateral interference. The women found to be approaching left laterality in young adulthood, and the men approaching right laterality, are "in sync" with gender differences in career preferences at that stage—verbal in women, spatial in men.

Clearly, maturation does not end with entry into adulthood. The next major life transition after reading readiness and puberty happens in middle age when the individual tries on new kinds of cognition peculiar to the third and fourth type functions. To the extent that the less preferred functions are geographically opposite the dominant and auxiliary preferences in the brain, another reverse shift would appear to occur at this stage, making the U-curves just referred to into an undulating S-curve through to old age (Figure 15). The S-line, if it exists, would appear to have all the regular periodicity of a unit sine curve or light wave, the "bumps" in it reflecting the transitional shifts in thinking that occur at puberty and midlife (Figure 16). Following it along, it suggests that type preferences are built into the personality in accordance with the laterality shifts in the line. The dominant function is represented by the segment approaching the first major curve in life (puberty), the auxiliary function begins to be added in at that juncture, the tertiary function is incorporated as the person approaches the second major curve in his development (midlife), and the inferior function is added in later life at a

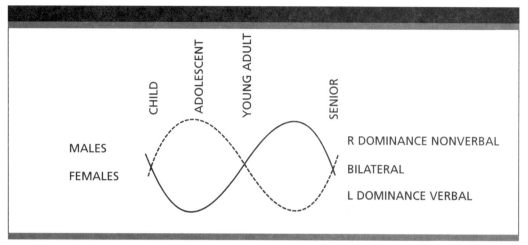

**Figure 16. Hypothetical Development of Verbal and Nonverbal Tendencies in the Sexes (Juschka, 1990)**

time when male-female cognition is less differentiated (bilateral).

In this way, the involvement of the hemispheres in the verbal and nonverbal thinking of the sixteen types is not a static, rigid division between left and right, but a variable, fluid and flexible dynamic that corresponds to, and perhaps gives rise to, the stages of cognitive and typological development. *Special talent in some fields, as with the one-sidedness of personality, might appear to result when there is disequilibrium, a failure to regress to the mean.*

❋ ❋ ❋

**Chapter 3 shows some effects** of deficit, disorder and disease on three example talents—writing, music and visual art. Because damage to *both* sides of the brain impairs writing talent, we conclude that writing is a *bilateral* talent. Because damage to the *right* side of the brain has more serious consequences for musical and artistic abilities, we say that these talents are *lateral* talents, which tend to "lean" in a rightward direction. Other talents, though we cannot illustrate for all kinds of ability, will likewise be lateralized right or left, or will be bilateral like writing; a person may excel in one domain at the expense of another. It is implied in this chapter that healthy, more attenuated cognitive imbalances are analogous to these pathological states, and that this connection, as we shall see, allows us to learn from pathology for applications to health.

What is especially interesting about brain and cognition for the purposes of this book, is that sidedness of function can change to some extent with various internal and external influences such as learning. This is known as a *cognitive shift*. There are individual differences in laterality; sidedness of function can vary with gender, handedness, age, intelligence and psychopathology, and will have an impact on a person's cognitive style. Special talent seems to be related to the extremes of laterality.

# CHAPTER FOUR
## A TALENT-DEFICIT THEORY OF GIFTEDNESS

✱ ✱ ✱

In this chapter, we consider *why* giftedness and talent arise in an individual, from a laterality perspective. Surely there are as many reasons for exceptional ability as there are abilities, but this chapter explores some nature and nurture arguments that are in line with a compensatory laterality hypothesis and Jung's notions of the one-sided personality. In doing so, it becomes clear that there appear to be undeniable associations between talent, deficit and disease, and the personalities that may be associated with them.

Chapter 4 covers the following topics:

* ✱ Talent-deficit theory; a theory of talent development *in utero*, in which a desirable quality is tied to an undesirable quality in the same individual
* ✱ The verbal-nonverbal spectrum of talent which hypothesizes the placement of a variety of talents along a continuum ranging from bilaterality to laterality
* ✱ Deficits and disorders known to be related to various talents
* ✱ Other biological etiologies of talent: heredity, illness and injury
* ✱ Gender and handedness in talent and as a reflection of the verbal-nonverbal spectrum
* ✱ The interaction of the precocious child with the environment
* ✱ Focused and non-focused states in talent, and their extreme expression as problem behaviors, learning disabilities and mental illness
* ✱ Disease correlates added to the verbal-nonverbal talent continuum
* ✱ A *circular talent-deficit continuum* linking laterality, talent and its associated deficits.

The circle is a theoretical model of these relationships in the brain and is consistent with the Jungian conception of individuation, which is also circular. Connections between the talent-deficit continuum and psychological type are proposed, the exploratory investigation of which begins in chapter 5.

✱ ✱ ✱

Having studied some effects of brain injury so as to understand the relative placement of abilities in the brain, we see that abilities vary around the geography of the brain, depending on the kind of talent, and that, far from being fixed—as early notions of hemisphericity seemed to claim—the localization of ability is often very inconstant and of varying degrees of strength because of internal and external influences like heredity (e.g., handedness, gender) and education. In fact, Sternberg and Powell (1982) have suggested that abilities in the brain actually "shade off" into each other, from one into another around the circumference of the brain, which helps to explain the differences in potency as we move around the circle:

> Circumplicially related abilities are not hierarchically ordered but rather are arranged *circularly*, with adjacent abilities essentially shading off into each other. Thus, adjacent abilities may be seen as overlapping each other so that, for example, numerical ability shades off into reasoning ability (989, emphasis added).

## A Biological Theory of Talent Development

The organizational rainbow of abilities that results, as seen earlier in Figure 1 (page 29) (Restak, 1984), is not a modern-day version of phrenology, which places human qualities and skills in a patchwork quilt-like arrangement around the skull, but is rather a loose guideline of lateralities for several different everyday varieties of talent that all of us possess. Reducing these kinds of ability still further, we notice that *there appear to be four general talent "genera" (plural of "genus"), as we might call them, around the circumference of the brain* (Figure 17, page 80). One of these encompasses spoken verbal abilities and is localized in the left-anterior quadrant of the brain. A second genus comprises certain introspective intellectual abilities like written language, linear "scientific" logic and mathematical reasoning, and is found in the left-posterior quadrant. A third genus consists of three-dimensional spatial activity and body awareness, and is located in the right-posterior quadrant. The fourth genus, involving certain social and artistic abilities, is in the right-anterior quadrant.

To the extent that language, especially the creative or expressive use of language, is particularly related to the Intuitive function, mathematical reasoning to the Thinking function, visuospatial-physical activity—whether sculpting, playing hockey, or constructing a house—to the Sensing function, and social-artistic activity to the Feeling function (particularly

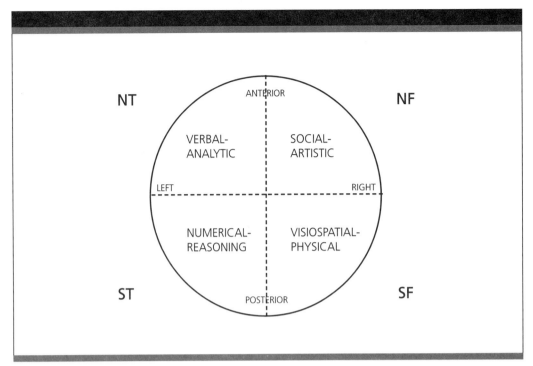

**Figure 17. Approximations of Type and Talent Lateralities in the Brain**

Intuitive Feeling as we saw in our artists), there appear to be clear geographical parallels here between the laterality of talent, and the localization of type and temperament (Figure 17). N, as we have said, would seem to be at the planful, articulate, forward-looking, artistic, front end and right side of the normal brain, S toward the sensory parietal-occipital areas at the back end and detail-oriented left side, T on the analytical left side, and F on the nonlinear, affective right side. Logically then, the dominant-auxiliary category of NT should emphasize the left-front quarter of the brain, ST the left-rear, SF the right-rear, and NF the right-front. In this way, *the four talent genera have the same approximate brain geography as the four type "genera" (NT, ST, SF, NF), within which we should find the many individual species of type and talent that variously comprise the human population.*

James Newman (1989) was one of the first to theorize about the neuropsychological foundations of type, and he conceived of Thinking–Feeling and Sensing–Intuition as left-right distinctions, Judging–Perceiving as a front-back distinction, and Introversion–Extraversion as an up-down distinction driven by the reticular activating system of the brainstem. Though he puts different type functions at slightly different sites, Newman, too, sees quadrants of logical, analytical reasoning in the left-anterior corner; ideational, abstract, symbolic thought in the left-posterior corner; visuospatial, experiential reception in the right-posterior corner; and visuospatial, emotional expression in the right-anterior corner. As he so correctly points out, the brain is an enormous frontier within type research that has yet to be adequately explored using the wonderful technologies available for this purpose. In the meantime, there is little choice but to continue working with small, informed hunches to make somewhat larger educated guesses.

As before, to say that T is probably lateralized toward the left side of the brain, and F toward the right, is not to suggest that T and F are restricted to these locations or that they are unlikely to be found on the other side. On the contrary, just as we are cautioned to remember always that Thinking types feel and Feeling types think, we must likewise recognize that laterality for type functions, like laterality for individual cognitive abilities, moves and tilts at least two ways; that aspects of the Thinking function will most certainly exist on the right side, as aspects of Feeling will most assuredly exist on the left. Facets of Sensing will also be found at the front end and right side of the brain, just as features of Intuition will be found at the back end and left side. Clearly, laterality, like type, is a relative term, rather than an absolute one, which says only that a function leans in a particular direction, and that the direction will be variable, because of natural factors like handedness and maturation, and man-made influences such as experience and education.

Thus, the laterality of talent suggests a loose four-way arrangement of "brain centers" very similar to Jung's original conception of dominant and auxiliary functions. And together they imply a four-way mapping of the major symbolic constructs in cognition—words (NT), numbers (ST), physical shapes (SF) and emotional expression (NF). The "shading off" in the brain that Sternberg and Powell envisioned is probably not simply about unit abilities, therefore, but of types, talents, and perhaps even the four critical elements in literary experience that they might seem to represent—mind (T), body (S), heart (F) and soul (N).

This sort of geography offers nothing radically new. Attempts to localize various cognitive abilities in the brain have been made for centuries. Just as involved, obviously, has been the study of disease. Less common, at least in the twentieth century, is the combination of the two—the localization in the brain of the cognitive relationships to disease. *What kinds of cognitive activity, if any, are related to certain kinds of disease expression?* We know instinctively as well as rationally that thinking affects, or is related to, our physical well-being—from the link between worry and headaches, to the hostility of "Type A" behavior and heart disease—but as yet have no way of *systematizing* the kinds of thinking we do and their physical effects and associations so as to determine what could and shouldn't be done to minimize the effects. We begin our attempts at creating such a system by exploring the links between *talent and deficit, a principle advanced by American scientists Norman Geschwind and Albert Galaburda (1985), in which a desirable quality is tied to an undesirable one, in the same individual.*

The once popular notion of "genius and insanity" is a well-known example of the talent-deficit relationship, and although the genius-insanity pairing is no longer considered accurate, there are others where the relationship is painfully real. For instance, within non-normal groups, such as those defined by autism or bipolar disorder, the expression of a talent and an accompanying deficit of some kind can be extreme, and is often explained in terms of regional enlargement in the brain, compensations for injury, or even epilepsy.

The talents of the prodigious calculator Henry Mondeau, for example, began to emerge at the same time as his seizures, following a bout of scarlet fever at the age of four. Later he could do incredible computations—which we suspect occur in the Introverted Thinking area of the left-posterior quadrant—but, at the same time, "He [was] tormented by nerves. He [was] subject to violent and frequent nervous attacks, which in an instant would cause him to lose his strength and his reason" (Smith, 1988: 29).

Mondeau's gift unfortunately developed at great personal cost, which was also the case for the Russian composer Dmitri Shostakovich:

> The 'secret' of [his talent for composition], it was suggested—by a Chinese neurologist, Dr. Dajue Wang—was the presence of a metallic splinter, a mobile shell fragment, in his brain, in the temporal horn of the left ventricle. Shostakovich was very reluctant, apparently, to have this removed: Since the fragment had been there, he said, each time he leaned his head to one side he could hear music. His head was filled with melodies—different each time—which he then made use of when composing. X-rays allegedly showed the fragment moving around when Shostakovich moved his head, pressing against his 'musical' temporal lobe, when he tilted, producing an infinity of melodies which his genius could use (Sacks, 1985: 135).

In autistic children, the repeated coexistence of deficits and special talents like this has prompted some investigators to consider that:

> . . . the exceptional abilities are, in a sense, the 'flip' side of the characteristic autistic impairments. This possibility carries with it the intriguing corollary that 'average,' non-exceptional abilities are the price that most of us pay for overall 'normal' cognitive and emotional function-ing, that normal functioning places limits on the development and/or exercise of isolated exceptional abilities (Bogyo & Ellis, 1988: 272).

On closer inspection, however, it appears that the talents of even healthy people may be subject to the limitations and advantages of subtle deficiencies.

The late neurologist Norman Geschwind (1985a, 1985b, 1985c) proposed a neuro-anatomical theory of talent around this notion, and his coauthor Albert Galaburda conducted tissue studies to provide limited proof for it, that there are indeed structural differences (cells and cell clusters) in the brains of otherwise normal people who have cognitive disabilities as well as unusual abilities. Exceptional visuospatial skills in some with dyslexia would be an example. *Like Jung's view of the mind, the Geschwind model of the brain is a compensatory one that says essentially that greater abilities in one area of the brain result in weaker areas in another, or that weakness in one area is compensated for elsewhere in the brain by a particular strength or talent.* Accordingly, Geschwind saw giftedness as "the pathology of superiority," an idea which, quite surprisingly, puts a number of physical and psychological traits in the same individual, includ-ing non-right-handedness (left-handedness or ambi-handedness), autoimmune disorders such as allergies, learning disabilities, and various kinds of talent. Indeed, special abilities and characteristics clearly related to laterality, such as handedness and dyslexia, seem to cluster, for genetic reasons, in entire families.

The theory postulates that this unlikely coexistence of physical and psychological traits begins in the third or fourth month of pregnancy for some fetuses, when the right hemisphere is developing faster than the left. Exposure to high levels of testosterone at this point, perhaps due to stress factors operating on the mother, or high fetal sensitivity to testosterone, acts to further slow the development of the left hemisphere, simultaneously affecting immune development; French immunologist Gerard Renoux had shown, in mice at least, that immune functions are stimulated by the left hemisphere and suppressed by the right hemisphere (Somerville et al., 1993). The hormone factor at this stage of human development acts to delay cell migration in certain areas of the left hemisphere, effectively causing "lesions" of sorts and cortical diminution on the left side, enlargement of areas adjacent to the impaired site(s), and enlargement of the same general region on the right side. As a result, exposure to prenatal testosterone atypically enhances right-hemisphere functioning in advance of the left, such that the individual, and other family members to whom this has happened, are found to exhibit combinations of talent and disability reflecting the skew. Talents relying heavily on right-hemisphere processing—the spatial aspects of mathematics, engineering, music, architecture, athletics, art—are consequently found to be associated in the individual or the family with deficits, disabilities and disorders comprising what will hereafter be referred to as *Geschwind "cluster disorders" or "cluster traits"*:

* Non-right-handedness
* Blonde hair, premature graying
* Birthmarks
* Twinning
* Immune disorders, e.g., allergies, urticaria
* Endocrine disorders
* Epilepsy
* Psychopathology, e.g., clinical depression, bipolar disorder
* Homosexuality
* Upper-body somatotypes
* Dyslexia, stuttering and other language deficits and learning disabilities
* Hair lip, cleft palate
* Asymmetries of face and ears
* Asymmetries of disease, e.g., breast cancer predominantly on the left side
* Skeletal abnormalities, e.g., scoliosis, extra digits on the hands or feet

In the last instance, it is a bizarre reality that the same fetal hormones purported to produce unusual hemisphere organization for mathematical abilities also seem to interact with other developing organs to produce skeletal oddities such as extra fingers and toes. In a study by Steven Smith (1988) of nine calculating prodigies, for example, in whom counting is the basic preoccupation, two had six fingers on each hand and one of them also had six toes on each foot. Among calculators, there is also a high incidence of hyperactivity, homosexuality and a difficulty in recognizing faces, while for prodigious mathematicians—whom the type literature suggests are predominantly NT—the cluster factors appear to be left-handedness, immune disorders and myopia (Benbow, 1988).

The adult male C. J., a gifted second-language learner described by Novoa et al. (1988), is an illustration of what is presumed to be "adjacent site" enlargement. C. J. had slowed development, poor spatial skills, and mild reading difficulties, yet exceptional abilities in second-language acquisition on the same side of the brain as the impaired reading. A graduate student in education, this man learned French, German, Spanish and Latin in high school, and is reported to have acquired native-like Arabic and Italian "in a matter of weeks." His cluster traits, in addition to the cognitive disabilities, include premature, firstborn, identical twinning, allergies, hives, prepubertal homosexuality, ambi-handedness and schizophrenia in a maternal grandfather. C. J.'s visuospatial skills are significantly inferior to his verbal skills, which the research team studying him interpreted as exceptional verbal ability having "crowded out" spatial skills in a language organization that is more bilateral than that of right-handed males: "As with females who may show such a pattern, verbal skills appear to benefit from bilateral organization, whereas for the same individuals visuospatial abilities seem to suffer" (301).

As this comment suggests, the Geschwind model may help to account for gender differences in certain talents. Specifically, the presence of intrauterine testosterone excreted by the male fetus, in addition to that contributed by the mother, slows development of the fetus' own left hemisphere and leads to compensatory enhancements in the development of the right hemisphere. In the female fetus, on the other hand, where there is less exposure to testosterone, left-hemisphere development is not so slowed and there is no need for the compensatory overdevelopment of the right side. The result is a male brain with a right-hemisphere advantage for certain tasks, a female brain of comparatively balanced bilaterality, and sex differences in the incidence and performance of right-sided abilities, particularly spatial skills.

For males or females, exposure to high testosterone should make a naturally right-sided ability, such as drawing, even more right-sided, as it were, while exposure to testosterone of a left-sided ability, such as language, should slow its development in some way, allowing its right-sided counterparts to catch up and making the left-sided ability more bilateral. And although Geschwind never alluded to it, it seems possible that exposure to excessive testosterone in females—perhaps because of maternal stress, as we have said—could produce so-called masculine women with right-lateralized talents, just as it might also produce feminine men with bilateral talents, as we see in the exceptional language learning of C. J.

To complicate matters, intrauterine hormonal effects on talent are affected by gender as well as birth order of the fetus. A study by Eleanor Maccoby et al. (1979) found more testosterone in the umbilical cords of males than females, and more estrogen, and particularly progesterone, in the umbilical cords of firstborns than latterborns. The authors thought these findings could be related to hormone depletion and raised this as a factor contributing to the generally higher intellectual aptitudes of firstborns (Zajonc, 1976). In Smith's study of calculating prodigies, for example, 45 percent were firstborns, and in Benbow's study of more than 9,000 intellectually precocious students, 60 percent were firstborns, with the rest well spaced with respect to their siblings. Elevations in hormone levels may therefore play a role in verbal forms of talent, it seems, such as mathematical talent and writing, where lower levels, we interpolate, might help to produce other talents such as drawing and athletic ability.

Most amazing, hormonal effects on talent may even be subject to the *time* of birth—or more accurately, time of conception—as hormone levels in the mother respond to cyclical, seasonal changes in light. Geschwind and Galaburda (1985c) note that eminent people, as well as schizophrenics and people with various mental deficiencies, tend to be born more often in the early months of the year, meaning conception for such people was more often in spring and summer when intrauterine concentrations are high:

> Children conceived in March or April will spend most of their months in utero at a time when hormones are high. The child conceived six months later, in September or October, will tend to spend their early period in utero under much lower hormonal influences . . . It has been confirmed repeatedly that schizophrenics are born predominantly in the first half of the year and particularly in the first quarter. They are thus conceived between approximately the first of April and the first of October, i.e., predominantly during the period in which the days are longer than 12 hours. It is possible that schizophrenia is more common in those people who have spent the first six months of pregnancy under maximal hormonal influences. Mental defectives are also more likely to be born at the beginning of the year. On the other hand many extensive studies of the months of birth of eminent people have shown that they too tend to be born predominantly early in the year and even more consistently to be born at low-rate in the mid-summer months of July and August . . . It appears at first glance that *people born early in the year are likely to be more variable, and thus to contain an excess of both eminent and highly disadvantaged individuals*. It is of interest that mental defectives contain an excess of left-handers. It is, therefore, speculatively conceivable that one is dealing with an influence on the brain that will, when properly controlled [by the body], lead to superiority, but that in excess may lead to deleterious influences. It is obvious that hormonal influences deserve consideration, but they are far from being the only possible candidates (646, emphasis added).

Thus, if high hormone exposure helps to produce the gifted person of high verbal-intellectual ability, as Maccoby contends, and if this type of person is more often born early in the year, as Geschwind notes, it follows that the more nonverbally talented individual might be conceived in the low-hormone seasons of fall and winter, and be born in the last half of the year. *The observations suggest a continuum; therefore, that strangely encompasses time of year, exposure to light, hormone concentrations, talent and certain kinds of disability. To the extent that Jungian traits are associated with various kinds of talent, we may also be witnessing a continuum that indirectly links light and these other factors to psychological type.* Is it possible, for example, that verbal Intuitives are more often born in the first part of the year, while nonverbal Sensing types are more often born in the last half?

Hormonal effects on ability continue long after birth, but it is not known how these specifically affect talent. Some inferences can be drawn from work with normal populations. For example, investigations of sex differences by Doreen Kimura (1989), at the University of Western Ontario, show that merely having an XY or XX chromosome does not in itself ensure male or female development. In rats, she notes, sex hormones can alter brain organization during the perinatal period when the genitals have already been formed. Similarly, XX girls can be mildly androgenized by early exposure to natural or synthetic androgens to the point where, even if raised as girls, they will engage in rough-and-tumble play and show masculine preferences in toys, which in turn influences how they are socialized. In another hormonal anomaly, males with early testosterone deficiency, as a result of disease, will perform worse on some spatial tasks, but not on verbal intelligence tests, all of which might seem to suggest that early exposure to sex hormones has lifelong differential effects on the behavior of men and women.

To examine the effects of hormones on specific cognitive abilities, Kimura tested isolated verbal functions such as articulation, manual skills, and spatial abilities at different times in the menstrual cycle of a sample of women. She observed a definite change in the abilities at different levels of sex hormones. The women did significantly better on the verbal and manual tasks during the high estrogen-progesterone phase in the week leading up to menstruation, and significantly better on the spatial tests during the low phase about five days after onset. To check this, Kimura then tested the effects of estrogen replacement therapy on the abilities of postmenopausal women. Synthetic estrogen, like naturally occurring estrogen, was found to have a strong, positive effect on motor and articulation skills but no effect on spatial skills, demonstrating once again that female hormones can have a positive effect on some "female" skills.

More specifically, and unlike testosterone, estrogen positively impacts the left hemisphere:

> In our human studies, estrogen seems to have a strongly positive effect on functions which we know depend critically on the left hemisphere. Performance on the Manual Sequence Box and on speech articulation tasks requires an intact left hemisphere. What's more, these functions are carried out differently in the left hemisphere of males and females: The left anterior part of the brain is more critical in females, suggesting that estrogen somehow facilitates activity of the frontal regions, of the left hemisphere, or of both (Kimura, 1989: 66).

Additional evidence favoring a left hemisphere-estrogen model, Kimura notes, is the demonstration of a right-ear superiority in dichotic listening during the estrogen surge just prior to ovulation in normally cycling women.

Reducing the work of Kimura, Geschwind and Galaburda to its simplest common denominators, we are left with the impression that *high estrogen-progesterone levels (or perhaps high sensitivity to normal levels) contributes to some kinds of left-sided verbal talent (e.g., articulation, perhaps vocabulary, grammar), especially in women, but that high testosterone levels (or high sensitivity to normal levels) may induce the development of right-sided talents such as music, and bilateral-verbal talents such as creative writing or math, in both men and women.* Putting this thought within the context of a deficit theory of giftedness, we might speculate that any natural or artificial disruption of the endocrine system (pituitary, hypothalamic, thyroid, adrenal, gonadotrophic) may lead, sequentially throughout that system, to some form of talent and its associated cluster weaknesses, particularly if it happens in the very early stages of human life.

Thus, biological factors would seem to play at least a partial role in the creation of abilities comprising talent, without it being a completely deterministic process. Environmental factors, though not the focus of this chapter, are crucial links in the symbiotic nature-nurture dynamic that fosters talent and the disabilities that often go with it. As Fein and Obler (1988) put it:

> What we suspect is that a certain biological predisposition for a talent or a cluster of talents develops in some cases for hormonal reasons and in other cases for familial non-hormonal reasons. Along with it, a biological predisposition for concentrating permits development of special abilities in the case where the subject is (1) exposed to the necessary knowledge-based materials, (2) encouraged to learn—or at least not discouraged from learning—the materials, and (3) encouraged to practice—or at least not discouraged from practicing—the ability (9).

## The Verbal-Nonverbal Spectrum of Talent

Soon after Geschwind's original publications of 1985, a number of researchers began working in the area of talent-deficit theory, studying a variety of talents and their correlated problems. Across some of the findings, at the level of the "bigger picture," we discover an unusual pattern—what appears to be a continuum of talent that ranges from the verbal to the nonverbal, from apparently bilateral to lateral brain states, in many of the common, as well as the not-so-common, talents (Figure 18, page 88). The remainder of this chapter will attempt to show how this spectrum complies with the Geschwind model, using a survey of talent studies compiled by Loraine Obler and Deborah Fein (1988). In doing so, it will become apparent that not only might the talents be part of a spectrum, but also their associated deficits.

We know from lesion studies in chapter 3 that talent extends from the verbal to the nonverbal in proportion to the degree of emphasis on the hemispheres. Verbal talents, such as

| Verbal-Bilateral Talents | Hemisphere Emphasis | Examples* |
|---|---|---|
| • Talents That May Require High IQ, e.g., Mathematics, Writing | Both Hemispheres, With Emphasis on the Left | Verbal Reasoning Talent |
| • Birth in First Half of Year | | Hyperlexia |
| • Conception in High Light Season | | |
| • Firstborn or Well Spaced | | Second-Language Acquisition |
| • High Testosterone | | |
| • High Estrogen-Progesterone | | Verbal Memory (Mnemonists) |
| • Higher Incidence of Schizophrenia, and Mental Deficiencies | | Creative Writing |
| | | Calculation |
| Nonverbal-Lateral Talents | | Mathematical Talent |
| | | Chess Talent |
| • Talents Not Necessarily Requiring High IQ, e.g., Drawing, Athletic Ability | | Musical Talent |
| • Birth in Last Half of Year | | |
| • Conception During Low Light Season | | Eidetic Imagery |
| • Laterborn or Closely Spaced | | Visual Art (Drawing) |
| • High Testosterone | | |
| • Low Estrogen-Progesterone | | |
| • Lower Incidence of Schizophrenia and Mental Deficiencies | Right Hemisphere | Autistic Savants Generally |

* Source: Studies on each of the talents compiled by Obler and Fein (1988)

Figure 18. A Verbal-Nonverbal Spectrum of Talent

writing, are selectively disrupted by damage to either side of the brain and are therefore what we might term "bilateral" talents. However, nonverbal talents, such as drawing, are disrupted by damage more to one side of the brain and are consequently what we might call "lateral" talents. It is between these endpoints that we find our continuum of special abilities ranging from talent in second languages, for example, which is a bilateral talent with a leftward emphasis, to the more lateral talents of calculation ability (a verbal ability, with left-posterior emphasis) and visual art (a nonverbal ability, with right-posterior emphasis). Within these larger talent categories, we find still further left-right subdivisions along this continuum. Within the talent of second-language learning, for instance, more to the left side of the brain's spectrum, we discover a "verbal" talent for grammar-learning dissociated from accent (e.g., in a Henry Kissinger), and a "nonverbal" talent for accent-learning dissociated from grammar (e.g., in a Peter Sellers). Within creative writing, too, there is the sterile "verbal" style of the practical guide or manual, as well as the metaphorical "nonverbal" manner of the poem or play:

It would not be theorized here that syntax and vocabulary *per se* are the elements of Stevens's poems or Shakespeare's sonnets or plays that so amaze and entrance us. It is in fact the arresting and powerfully *vivid images as well as the 'music' of the language* that makes us call their poems and plays works of genius (Waterhouse, 1988: 502, emphasis added).

We know talent in verbal reasoning is localized in the left-posterior area, though it, too, would appear to have bilateral tendencies:

Verbal reasoning ability may be more directly affected by right-hemisphere processes than language production or syntactical aspects of verbal ability, because verbal reasoning ability involves comprehension and the understanding of difficult words and their relationships (Benbow, 1988: 60).

The bilateral condition also seems to be the case for mathematical talent. Studies of people with a severe math disability called "dyscalculia," and studies of EEG during problem solving, implicate the left hemisphere, particularly left-posterior areas (parietal, occipital areas) in computation functions, mathematical sign literacy, logic and pattern recognition, but the right hemisphere in the understanding of numerical and spatial relations and concepts (60). Within calculation ability, we find compelling verbal-nonverbal distinctions between so-called auditory and visual calculators (Smith, 1988). Where the auditory calculator "hears" numbers in his head, verbalizes and fidgets as he speedily calculates a multiplication problem from left to right (a linear, speech-like strategy), the visual calculator "sees" numbers in his head, and quietly and placidly writes the problem down from right to left (a spatial, nonverbal strategy).

Certainly these illustrations and the lesion data which support them help to debunk the myth of right-hemisphere genius, if only for verbal forms of giftedness at one end of the talent spectrum. In more nonverbal talents though, such as athletics, music or visual art, laterality in the direction of the right hemisphere would still appear to be the advantageous, though not mutually exclusive, state. Thus an individual might very possibly exhibit, concurrently, a bilateral verbal talent for writing and a right-lateral nonverbal talent for visual art, perhaps as a result of some earlier mild dysfunction on the left side, which might have produced calculation deficits, for instance, and a rightward shift. As we have said, however, the coexistence of "opposing" talents in a person is presumably contingent upon a dissociation of verbal and nonverbal functions—from side to side, or from front to back—allowing a combination of anterior language and posterior art, as it were, but less frequently a combination of anterior language and anterior music. Consequently, there might appear to be many more artists who would write than writers who would sing.

In the last instance, Judd (1988) has estimated that 5 percent or more of the general population is highly intelligent—and normally, but not necessarily, verbal—yet tone deaf and lacking musical skills, essentially learning disabled in music. Poor-pitch singing is actually quite common among well-educated people, even instrumental musicians, and its incidence

**Table 14. Frequency of Talents in a Sample of Savants (n = 119)**

| Spectrum | Talent | Incidence* |
|---|---|---|
| Verbal | Calendar Calculation | 11% |
| ↓ | Math | 14% |
| | Pseudoverbal Abilities | 16% |
| | Art | 19% |
| | Memory | 40% |
| Nonverbal | Music | 53% |

\* Source: Rimland & Fein (1988)

among males outnumbers that in females by 7:1, a ratio closely aligned with that for developmental dyslexia. For this reason, Judd has proposed that monotonic singing is a kind of musical dyslexia related to linguistic dyslexia. Yet there is little interest in explaining this failure to develop skills, though it can be just as severe as the parallel language deficits, because music has much less social significance than does language. What Judd does not mention is that the condition is perhaps to be anticipated if bilateral verbal functions in verbally talented people do in fact crowd out right-hemisphere musical functions. The greater the shift in a rightward direction, more so in males than in females, the greater the bilaterality for language which, for music if not language, is apparently the non-talented state.

"Musical dyslexia" in intelligent, well-educated people is the mirror image talent-deficit condition to savants who are musically talented yet nonverbal with mental retardation. In savants, who are comparatively unimpeded by words, it is often abilities in music that come to the fore. In fact, among autistic savants generally, there would appear to be yet another mini-continuum of verbal and nonverbal gifts that heavily favors nonverbal, right-hemisphere forms of expression, which is not surprising given the language deficits and social withdrawal characteristic of autism. In a study of 119 savants by Rimland and Fein (1988), the talents in Table 14 were observed, though the authors didn't comment on the apparent gradations.

Bearing in mind there is mental retardation here, it is remarkable what some verbally talented savants can do. One subject in the study recited the alphabet backwards for the first time—without hesitation, and without practice. Another had a working knowledge of French, Spanish, Japanese, Russian, Arabic and Hebrew. Another could mentally compute square roots, and worked out all the prime numbers to 1100—at the age of nine. Another could awaken and tell the precise time, to the minute, without looking at a clock. Still another could give instant answers to impossible calendar problems like, "During what years between 1780 and 1795 did the seventh of August fall on a Wednesday?"

Equally astounding are the reports of nonverbal achievement. One subject in the study could balance himself and walk around the rail of a crib. One had "photographic" memory at the age of two. At the same age, another could draw an outline of the United States and place all the capital cities. Another subject could write in Japanese and Old English-style scripts. Another was able to type, without error, a page of complicated sentences which he had seen only once, a year and a half earlier. Another could name every turn, every landmark along a route traveled once, years earlier. One subject could guess the size of various objects, with accuracy to the quarter-inch. And especially strange, one savant was able to predict his parents' arrival, though the parents had only just decided to come, and the child had not been informed of the decision. Similarly, another subject in the study could "hear" conversations out of the range of hearing, and could pick up thoughts unspoken. The authors described these very unusual abilities as "ESP" talent.

Specifically within the artistic realm, there are the cases of Nadia, the six-year-old creative genius mentioned earlier; Richard Wawro, a very talented visual artist who is legally blind; Alonzo Clemens, an African American with mental retardation who makes beautiful sculptures, initially from tar he dug from a parking lot with his fingernails; and Leslie Lemke, blind, palsied and unable to speak a sentence till his mid-twenties, yet able to awaken his parents one night with the playing of Tchaikovsky's *Piano Concerto No. 1* (Rimland & Fein, 1988). The very sad "flip side" of these talents, of course, is that most savants cannot be counted on to recognize or to write their own name.

## Deficits and Disorders in the Talented

Clearly, savant talent is associated with, and is probably caused by, serious brain impairments. For savants of all types, the related deficits and disorders include a long list of problems like mental retardation, deficient orienting behavior, excessive focusing, a lack of drive for novelty, cerebellar impairment and familial bipolar disorder. On top of this, specific talent types may have additional deficits and disorders. The musical savant, for example, often displays prominent emotional disturbances, epilepsy, cognitive rigidity, a lack of abstract reasoning skills, and blindness (Judd, 1988). J. L., a savant with severe mental retardation studied by researchers at the University of Waterloo, is epileptic, hemiplegic on the right side, blind, and institutionalized because, among other things, he does not know when a bowl or plate is empty and will continue to go through the motions of feeding himself when no food is there. Yet the same man is capable of one-handed (left-handed) jazz improvisation on the piano, and recitations of the *William Tell* overture (Charness et al., 1988). He could also play Beethoven's well-known *Moonlight Sonata*, a brooding, complicated piece written in four sharps.

Among other abnormal groups, there are, for calculating prodigies, problems with exaggerated motor function such as "twitches," hyperactivity, extra fingers and toes, abnormal EEG, epilepsy, spatial inabilities, an inability to recognize faces, poor memory for names and places, drawing disabilities, and design memory and orientation deficits (Smith, 1988). Yet the autistic calculator Elly, at age thirteen, loved the formal symmetry of numbers like 10,001, and enjoyed encrypting integers of the kind in the following problem (Bogyo & Ellis, 1988: 270):

13,691,369 X 53 = 725,642,557 (53 is encrypted)
725,642,557 / 37 = 19,611,961 (A formal duplication)
19,611,961 / 37  = 530,053 (53 appears in duplicate)

For hyperlexic children who possess advanced reading abilities in one or more languages, but a marked inability to understand any of what they read, the associated disorders include childhood psychosis, mental retardation, autism, inconsistent patterns of cerebral dysfunction, hyperactivity, repetitive motor sequences like head-banging, and difficulty in learning patterned motor sequences such as those required in toileting (Aram & Healy, 1988). Yet Isabelle, an epileptic and microcephalic hyperlexic with an IQ of 55, could read French, Dutch and English, all before the age of five (Lebrun et al., 1988).

Stories like this of amazing abilities amidst overwhelming disabilities are in reality very rare, with savants comprising perhaps only 10 percent of the autistic population. Nevertheless, case studies like these are often cited as evidence that talent and deficit do coexist in abnormal states. Researching that connection in normal groups, however, is socially and politically more difficult, regardless of its biological probabilities, as it begins to look like support for stereotypes of the gifted as frail, bespectacled bookworms. There is a certain humanistic reluctance among us to attach any notion of a flaw to giftedness lest it perpetuate outdated perceptions. Psychology in this decade, however, may play a mitigating role in this regard, finally discarding old pejorative labels and newer rose-colored lenses in favor of specific physiological correlates for specific kinds of talent.

For example, contrary to once popular mythology, there are apparently only two kinds of talent associated with the wearing of glasses. As Camilla Benbow (1988) discovered in her sample of over 9,000 gifted young people, mathematical talent and talent in verbal reasoning correlate with the incidence of immune disorders and the early onset of myopia, to the extent that vision problems for both talents are four times the population norm, greater in girls than in boys, and greater in the verbally talented than in the mathematically talented.

Vastly superior memory of the kind displayed by a mnemonist has been suspected of having roots in some, as yet unknown, form of brain damage (Brown & Deffenbacher, 1988), but the deficits of other "normal" gifted groups are more subtle. In gifted second-language learners, often active in immersion programs of one kind or another, visuospatial disabilities may emerge in some students as bilateral verbal strategies presumably crowd out right-sided nonverbal skills (Schneiderman & Desmarais, 1988). In chess talent, there is a preponderance of stress disorders and decreased longevity (Cranberg & Albert, 1988). In young children with eidetic imagery in whom a visual image of a picture or photograph is "seen" in space and can be moved from surface to surface around a room, or erased with the blink of an eye, there is a suspicion that this is a stage in the hierarchy of the visual system not normally accessible to introspection (Haber & Haber, 1988). Among visual artists, there may be weaknesses in verbal-academic domains. And in both visual artists and creative writers, there is a considerably higher risk of affective disorder, more unipolar (depression only) in artists, and more bipolar (mania and depression) in writers, and leading to higher rates of alcoholism and suicide, particularly in writers (Andreasen, 1987; DeLong & Aldershof, 1988; Jamison 1986, 1995).

Certainly it is possible to attribute these problems, at least to some degree, to the doing of the talent, to say that the verbal child has eye strain and needs glasses as a result of reading or computing too much, that the talented immersion student has poor drawing skills because the school concentrates on language, that the chess master has anxiety disorders because he performs under a great deal of pressure, and that artists and writers drink to excess because of the mercurial nature of the work they do. But this is only part of the answer because, as has been noted more than once in our descriptions of compensatory brain activity, having the weakness may produce the strength just as readily as performing the strength produces the weakness, meaning that neither of them may ever really let up so long as the other exists. The Geschwind model suggests there may be definite neuro-immuno-endocrinological reasons for the emerging principle that we apparently do not get one without the other.

All this has interesting implications, and may even present odd ethical dilemmas, for educators, psychologists and other professionals. On the positive side, a talent-deficit view of giftedness may be of help in the identification of students. If a talent is not immediately obvious (e.g., mathematical ability), perhaps a deficit will be (e.g., allergies, myopia) and over time, we might watch for evidence of both. Likewise, in students identified solely for their disabilities (e.g., tone deafness), we could take the optimistic approach that the disability may be tied to a special ability (e.g., exceptional intelligence). But on the negative side, there are two disquieting possibilities. One is that rehabilitation of the disability may ultimately harm or neutralize the talent, as appears to happen in the drug treatment of bipolar writers who may actually need a mild, reflective, introspective mood in order to hone the creative edge for some kinds of work (Jamison, 1995). The other more foreboding possibility is that encouraging the talent may also encourage and worsen the deficit, as might happen, we speculate, in encouraging more chess playing in an already anxious player, or in prescribing art therapy for a depressed artist.

Perhaps this is something of an overstatement for the normal talented population. While it may be possible, for example, to demonstrate that remedial work in visuospatial areas impedes second-language learning, we would likely be hard pressed to show that corrected vision is linked causally or otherwise to a decreased ability to do math. Yet in abnormal groups, the disappearance of a talent as an outcome of treatment is described on more than one occasion. Shostakovich was reluctant to have the splinter removed from his temporal lobe for fear of the musical, rather than medical, consequences. Nadia lost much of her drawing ability, and Elly her calculation ability, following training in language and sociability. And in the case of the hyperlexic Isabelle, therapists tried the reverse tactic of getting at the disability (reading comprehension) by repressing the talent (reading in a foreign language), but were met with only limited success as the mother began teaching her to read in yet a fourth language, at the age of eight. The point which begs study in this is that there may be a direct, positive relationship between ability and disability in which remediation may very possibly induce a regression to the mean of both talent and deficit, and greater activity in the given talent area, a wider deviation from the norm on both counts.

## The Etiology of Talent: Heredity, Illness, Injury

Essentially, the Geschwind theory begins where genetics leaves off, claiming that some hereditary components trigger the hormonal activity that influences the unusual asymmetric development of talents and disabilities. According to Geschwind, exceptional verbal and nonverbal abilities and their associated weaknesses would seem to occur almost randomly, depending on the extent to which their respective cortical territories are accidentally exposed to testosterone. Naturally it becomes impossible to predict which of the cluster disorders might be co-morbid with any one talent.

Another possibility, extending from the same model, is that talent and specific deficits are genetically paired at the outset, with hormones only facilitating a later intermediate step in the execution of the program. In this perspective, inherited disorders might be tied to cognitive abilities as they are sometimes also tied to personality (e.g., heart disease and hostility), the three of them waiting recessively opposite some other important trait, such as a preference for Thinking perhaps, for the rare opportunity for phenotypic expression. Consequently, in addition to the known paired associations of allergies and math, myopia and verbal abilities, tone deafness and verbal intelligence, or dyslexia and athletics, there could also conceivably be relationships between things like sickle cell anemia and music, Tay Sachs disease and high IQ, endocrine hyperfunction and verbal-mathematical skills, hypofunction (hence depression and alcoholism) and visual art, the latter of course suggesting possible group tendencies in disease and cognition. A disorder may one day turn out to be a genetic marker for talent, and vice versa, in much the same way that color blindness has been thought to be a marker for alcoholism, or the whorls of thumbprints markers for schizophrenia (Blau, 1977; Gibson, 1985).

This view would seem to be the logical extension of a conception of inherited talent and disease in the individual. If, for example, it is agreed that a boy's athletic ability, and certainly his dyslexia, runs in the family, it must also be possible that such traits exist, singly or together, in larger interbreeding gene pools, especially one that encourages athletics. The idea would appear to be clean from a biological perspective in which all human traits, good or bad, are equally "valued," but runs into serious ethical difficulties in other spheres which insist on ranking talent, if not deficits, in pecking order of their social and economic importance. So because one kind of talent, such as physical speed and agility, tends to accrue greater socioeconomic advantage than another kind of talent, such as calculation ability, it is unpopular, even discriminatory, to suggest that one group has such ability when another does not, even though it is quite acceptable, even progressive, to point out the same distinctions between individuals—hence the term "individual differences." Considering now the possible relationship between talent and disease, we may be wise to re-evaluate this double standard to ensure our open-mindedness in one respect does not make us close-minded in another. We very much need to be open to the possibility that some groups (e.g., left-handers) may genetically carry some cognitive abilities more than other groups, and that this may therefore expose them to different disease risks than groups with different sets of attributes. Even Geschwind notes,

> If the above interpretation is correct it opens up another way of looking
> at acquired immunodeficiency syndrome (AIDS) . . . [An alternative

explanation is that] the virus is capable of attacking individuals with a specific immunologic constitution. Some individuals have this immunologic pattern as the result of a particular pattern of intrauterine hormonal experience. Other vulnerable populations, e.g., Haitian males and Central African females, may have the same immunologic pattern for quite different reasons . . . in either case it might be useful to study the handedness patterns . . . of those with AIDS (Geschwind & Galaburda, 1985b: 546).

There are firm suggestions of heritability in most of the talents surveyed. Only in calculation prodigies and in chess talent has heredity been patently ruled out, in light of the fact that no family members of talented individuals usually possess the same abilities, either in degree or in kind (Cranberg & Albert, 1988; Smith, 1988). But for math, music, and visual memory in drawing, the spatial ability inherent in all three seems to be what is passed on. Inheritance of exceptional verbal memory is also likely, as is the heritability of a certain cognitive flexibility in second-language acquisition. In hyperlexia, there is sex-linked (male) expression of the talent on the paternal side, which is a plain indication, for some, of an association with dyslexia (Aram & Healy, 1988). And in creative writing, one study of accomplished writers (Andreasen, 1987) implicates polygenic, recessive, X-linked (female) transmission of the talent because of a higher incidence of creativity of all kinds among siblings (41%) as compared to parents (20%)—which is to say, while writing talent does not completely skip a generation, as do most recessive traits, it is recessive-like in that it occurs less frequently in alternate generations.

The talents of autistic savants may also have a hereditary component given that similar abilities often run in a savant's family, especially in the case of the "spatial" talents of music, art and mathematics. Autism in general has familial links, so it is not unreasonable to expect that the talents will have links, too. But in the main, savant talent appears to originate with illness or injury in childhood. In the musical savant, for example, there are reports of encephalitis, premature birth, epilepsy, movement disorders, anoxia, Down syndrome, meningitis, cerebral palsy, schizophrenia and microcephaly (Charness et al., 1988; Rimland & Fein, 1988). In calculators, the list includes asthma, scarlet fever, epilepsy, childhood diseases, typhus, bipolar illness, and physical trauma (Smith, 1988). It is difficult to escape parallels here between these events and themes of the sickly child in other domains such as art (e.g., Tom Thomson, Whistler, Toulouse-Lautrec, Escher), granting however that the effect in the latter is likely more psychological than neurological.

## Gender and Handedness in Talent

Geschwind gives gender and handedness major theoretical importance in the development of many kinds of talent. Indeed, as the product of both genetic and endocrine input, they are among the strongest indications we have of the role of biology in the creation of talent. We say this because, in addition to the familial and hormonal arguments put forth so far, handedness has many physiological correlates (e.g., eyedness, footedness, speech laterality), including gender; because the size of the gender gap in some talents does not seem adequately explained by social determinism alone; and because gender and handedness, singly or in combination, are found again and again to correlate with various kinds of talent. Even the placement of drawings on a page, as we saw in chapter 3, involved the interplay of these two factors.

This chapter's survey of exceptional abilities adds support to the theory's prediction that, among gifted people, there will be more males than females, and a higher-than-average incidence of non-right-handedness (i.e., greater than 10 percent), apparently because of hormone exposure and a rightward shift. In both normal and abnormal states, male-female ratios are heavily weighted in favor of males, particularly at the more posterior and nonverbal-lateral end of our proposed talent spectrum (Table 15).

Only toward the anterior or verbal-bilateral end of the continuum would the incidence of females seem to equal or exceed that of males—that is, in creative writing, verbal reasoning, and second-language acquisition. In fact, in second-language learning, women as well as children, both of whom are believed to be more bilaterally organized than men, have generally been considered to be the more talented groups (Schneiderman & Desmarais, 1988).

In the talent studies for which handedness data are available, we find scantier allusions to a graded pattern from verbal to nonverbal, in which the connection to non-right-handedness is present for all talent groups, save eidetic imagery, but is possibly stronger or more frequent at the verbal end of the scale (Table 16). Consequently, the incidence of non-right-handedness in "nonverbal" eidetic imagers is at normal levels, is about twice the population norm in visual art, chess talent, mathematical talent and calculation talent, but is as much as six to eight times the norm in "verbal" hyperlexics at the other end of the spectrum (Aram & Healy, 1988; Rosenblatt & Winner, 1988). This is of course an extremely speculative generalization which cannot be taken seriously without further study in healthy individuals. But it is helped by Benbow's (1988) observation that there are more left-handers among verbal reasoners than mathematical reasoners, and by the drawing study (Juschka, 1990: 214) which revealed possible relationships between left-handedness, higher levels of drawing talent and nonverbalization, and between ambi-handedness, lower levels of drawing talent and verbalization. The incidence of non-right-handedness in non-talented "verbal" students was more than double the frequency in "nonverbal" art students.

This means that, should there really be more non-right-handedness in verbal forms of talent than in nonverbal forms, we might predict it to be composed of more ambi-handedness than left-handedness, in keeping with the bilateral nature of verbal abilities; this is in fact what happens in hyperlexia. If there is more non-right-handedness generally, among the verbally talented, a retrospective deduction might be that these people have undergone greater exposure to testosterone than other groups, and may therefore be subject to higher associated risks of developing cluster disorders—immune disorders, endocrine disorders, skeletal abnormalities, depression, dyslexia, etc. If Intuitives as a group can be said to be more verbal, perhaps, than Sensing types—related to a preference that emphasizes anterior functions in the brain—Intuitive types may be at greater risk than Sensing types of developing these problems.

So, while right-handedness would appear to be the majority condition for most talent, the frequency of non-right-handedness in any one group may foretell something of the group's collective past as well as perhaps some aspects of its probable future. As such, frequency of non-right-handedness may be a kind of talent-deficit index around which different groups might be systematically compared.

## Precocity, Puberty and the Environment

The investigators of two kinds of talent—hyperlexia and mathematical talent—claim that environment has rather little to do with the emergence of these abilities; hyperlexia arises spontaneously and seems to be in no way related to parental input, and for prodigious

**Table 15. Incidence of Males to Females in a Survey of Exceptional Talents**

| Spectrum | Talent | Male:Female Ratio* | |
|---|---|---|---|
| **Verbal-Bilateral** | **Second-Language Acquisition** | < | **1.0** |
| | **Creative Writing** | | **1.0 ?** |
| | **Verbal Reasoning Talent** | > | **1.0** |
| | **Hyperlexia** | | **7.0** |
| | **Calculation** | | **12.0** |
| | **Mathematical Talent** | | **13.0** |
| | **Chess Talent** | | **4.0** |
| | **Musical Talent** | > | **1.0** |
| | **Musical Savants** | | **1.5** |
| **Nonverbal-Lateral** | **Autistic Savants Generally** | | **5.0** |

\* Source: Obler & Fein (1988)

**Table 16. Incidence of Non-Right-Handedness in a Survey of Exceptional Talents**

| Spectrum | Talent | Incidence of Non-Right-Handedness* |
|---|---|---|
| **Verbal-Bilateral** | **Second-Language Acquisition** | >10%, Left |
| | **Verbal Reasoning** | >10%, Left (Males) |
| | **Hyperlexia** | 67-83%, Non-Right (Especially Ambi), Familial |
| | **Calculation** | 22%, Left |
| | **Mathematical Talent** | 25%, Left, Familial |
| | **Chess Talent** | 19%, Left (Males) |
| | **Visual Art** | 24%, Left |
| **Nonverbal-Lateral** | **Eidetic Imagery** | 10%, Non-Right |

\* Source: Obler & Fein (1988)

mathematical talent, spatial toys and amount of mathematical instruction received are apparently not terribly relevant (Aram & Healy, 1988; Benbow, 1986a, 1988). For the other exceptional abilities examined here, however, experts in the various domains describe varying degrees of environmental instigation.

From a philosophical point of view, we could probably argue that opportunity, access and exposure are necessary for the development of all talent, though from a neuropsychological perspective, it would appear to be more the case for some abilities than for others. In some fields, such as music and second-language learning, to say that exposure is crucial is an understatement. In chess, for example, there is a strong cultural press in Jewish and former Soviet societies, in which chess talent is most prevalent, to play the game, particularly in boys for whom it is a kind of war game, not unlike a manual video game (Cranberg & Albert, 1988). A supportive family environment also appears to be important for savant talent, and the development of normal forms of talent in music and visual art (Judd, 1988; Rosenblatt & Winner, 1988).

For talented art students, social reinforcement by teachers and peers is additionally motivating but evidently not sufficiently so, given they often drop out of art in adolescence if they happen to also excel in a subject area that is more socially condoned. In the verbal domains of mathematical talent and exceptional verbal reasoning, "bilateral" specializations are observed in the parents—fathers tutoring in quantitative areas, mothers in verbal areas. For creative writing, a creative family environment, particularly among siblings and not necessarily of the literary variety, is believed to be a contributing factor (Andreasen, 1987; Benbow, 1986a, 1988). Finally, a disturbingly common feature of the gifted environment is physical, social or psychological isolation, perhaps most pitifully illustrated in calculators who regard numbers as companions because they have few others:

> Numbers are friends for me, more or less. It doesn't mean the same for you, does it, 3,844? . . . But I say 'Hi, 62 squared' (Wim Klein, quoted in Smith, 1988: 45).

> I do admit to a very personal affection for the ingenious, adventurous 26, the magic, versatile 7, the helpful 37, the fatherly, reliable (if somewhat stodgy) 76 . . . Life in this irrational world is chaotic, confusing, unfair. The response to love is contempt; backbreaking efforts go unrewarded; results seem to bear little relation to input. In the world of numbers all comes out right in the end. Figures never fail you (Hans Eberstark, in Smith, 1988: 45–46).

Recurring themes in the data on precocity converge on these kinds of environmental factors and together suggest that some or all of them have most impact on the young talented mind before the onset of puberty. As a result, the concept of critical periods in the development of abilities, developed by Lenneberg (1967), can be extended to talent so as to suggest that much of it is actually "fixed" prior to, or during, puberty. And again, there may be

**Table 17. Average Age at Onset of Various Talents**

| Spectrum | Talent | Age (Yrs)* |
|---|---|---|
| **Verbal** | **Hyperlexia** | **2.5-3.5** |
| | **Second-Language Learning** | **< Puberty** |
| | **Auditory Calculation** | **< Written Numbers** |
| | **Visual Calculation** | **20s** |
| | **Mathematical Talent** | **< Puberty** |
| | **Chess Talent** | **< Puberty** |
| | **Musical Talent** | **< Puberty** |
| | **Visual Art** | **Preschool** |
| | **Eidetic Imagery** | **Preschool, 90s** |
| **Nonverbal** | **Autistic Savants** | **5.5** |

* Source: Obler & Fein (1988)

verbal-nonverbal differences across talents, this time in the average age of emergence of an ability (Table 17).

If there is a trend at all, it is toward "early" development of verbal talents and "later" development of nonverbal talents, which might have been anticipated considering the known maturational lag of some spatial abilities at puberty, particularly in boys, and in the second half of the menstrual cycle in women, both of which have been shown to be related to hormonal activity (Kimura, 1989; Waber, 1976). Thus the hyperlexic child often learns to read before she can fully speak sentences (as early as two and a half), the auditory calculator begins calculating before he can write numbers, and the talented immersion student is most prodigious as a child, losing her capacity for native-like language acquisition and becoming "fossilized," as they say, for language, about the age of twelve (Aram & Healy, 1988; Schneiderman & Desmarais, 1988; Smith, 1988).

Nonverbal talents also tend to emerge before puberty—profound insights can occur during childhood in mathematics, music and chess—but there is limited evidence that some more visually oriented abilities arise much later. Visual calculators are often recognized in their twenties, chess masters reach peak strength in their forties, and eidetic imagery has been reported in elderly people in their nineties (Cranberg & Albert, 1988; Haber & Haber, 1988; Smith, 1988).

Where verbal development is advanced, there might also be, according to a talent-deficit theory of giftedness, nonverbal development that is delayed. In point of fact, the hyperlexic child who reads at three cannot draw spontaneously like other three-year-olds, the auditory calculator has many spatial disabilities including drawing problems and a difficulty in recognizing faces, and the gifted language-learner may also exhibit visuospatial slowness, albeit much less severe. Consequently, adults marveling at early speech and reading abilities in a child may also be unwittingly announcing concordant nonverbal lags. And it is at least theoretically possible that they may have only until the child reaches puberty to correct them. As Fein and Obler (1988) note:

Puberty appears to be a crucial point with respect to the development of talent . . . The hormonal influences, presumably on the brain, can facilitate development of the talent for a few, but inhibit it for all others (7).

The drawing study revealed that for most subjects, with the exception of artists, development of simple drawing skills levels off about the age of twelve, showing no apparent age-related improvements thereafter. Similarly, for second-language learning, only 5 percent of the population is apparently capable of native-like language acquisition beyond puberty, the vast majority losing their neurocognitive flexibility for language to hormonal fixation between the ages of twelve and fourteen (Schneiderman & Desmarais, 1988). Lest these trends be interpreted in terms of changing social pressures at the junior-high level, it should be mentioned that the artistic or musical savant with prominent asocial tendencies, who is not interested in following the crowd, also appears to exhibit the same basic pattern (Rimland & Fein, 1988; Selfe, 1977). Of course, this is not to suggest that these people are incapable of learning from adolescence onward. It does suggest, however, that precursors of talent, and its associated deficits, may be essentially preserved for life at a very young age.

## Strategy, Obsession and Mental Illness in Talent

Talented people in many diverse fields often have in common a strong ability to see patterns in a sea of detail, to see wholes, to see the essential rather than the extraneous. What allows them to do this, in many cases, is an ability to concentrate and to focus. Cognitive psychologists refer to this strategy as cognitive rigidity. Personality theorists might call it unyielding inflexibility, stubbornness, persistence, or determination. Counseling psychologists might call it obsessive, compulsive and ruminating, and neuropsychologists might refer to it as nonfluency and perseveration. Whatever the terminology, it would all appear to be the same construct—namely, a repetitive, voluntary and involuntary tendency to remain "stuck" and focused on one or more ideas or behaviors.

In other fields, though, it is flexibility rather than inflexibility that is the more desirable trait in determining a talent, especially a creative talent. This leads us to say that, within the context of all giftedness, both are of value, which is again suggestive of a continuum, this time ranging from a state of complete flexibility (Extraverted Perceiving?) to that of comparative rigidity (Introverted Judging?). For example, an ability to leap across many thoughts in a short period of time is probably of great advantage to a hockey player at the nonverbal end of the spectrum, but may be of questionable help to an engineer, toward the verbal end of the spectrum, whose success depends on long-term, focused concentration on only a few ideas at a time.

In the survey of various kinds of talents for this chapter, three talents—mathematical ability, music and second-language learning—emerge as requiring some measure of neurocognitive flexibility. Benbow (1988) notes that gifted math students, as compared to non-gifted students, have a certain plasticity of cognitive processing that allows them to reverse their reasoning and shift easily from one problem-solving strategy to another. Judd

(1988) believes the talented musician is also a flexible thinker as a result of having developed many alternate neural pathways to accomplish musical tasks:

> That person may show little loss of musical ability in the face of aphasia, alexia, deafness, blindness, some forms of amnesia, or even a major right-hemisphere stroke, because alternate strategies may be available for most musical activities (151).

In second-language learning, too, it is thought that alternate neural pathways may lead to a propensity for language-learning and divergent thinking by providing resistance to transfer from the first language and "older" ways of thinking, but it is not known whether the pathways are innate or actually created by the learning of a new language:

> The process of acquisition is one of a reduction of possibilities, both in terms of parameter settings and processing routes as strategies. In the initial stages of acquisition, the child can be viewed as maximally flexible. As the first language develops, flexibility gives way in favor of the fixing of a grammar and the establishment of corresponding processing strategies . . . Child second-language acquirers seem to have more [flexibility] than most adults, probably because pre-pubescent children are still undergoing cognitive changes that will lead to further fixing of the neural pathways that represent the most efficient [short-cut] processing of the first language (Schneiderman & Desmarais, 1988: 1089).

Generally, flexibility—in cognitive abilities, neuromuscular skills, and personality—seems to be necessary for, or perhaps produced by, second-language learning. Neuromuscular flexibility, for example, is thought to be a factor in talented accent acquisition, while an adaptable, divergent personality willing to absorb other sociocultural identities is believed to be a prerequisite for, or product of, exceptional second-language ability overall (Novoa et al., 1988; Schneiderman & Desmarais, 1988).

But for numerous other exceptional abilities, some degree of rigidity, fixation and sameness would appear to be the more prevalent state. In cognitive psychology, there is something known as the "ten-thousand-hour or ten-year rule," referring to the time it takes to master chess, music and many other skills. Before we begin to think that it is this kind of training alone that is the basis of special talent, we are reminded of the persistent presence of the Mozarts, Clara Schumanns and Picassos whose talent arises before massive training effects can be expected to have an impact (Waterhouse, 1988). The belief is further challenged by the sudden appearance of great skill in the savant, who is otherwise a poor learner. Yet even these prodigies, whose abilities are clearly not initiated by practice, then go on to hone their abilities through ceaseless repetition.

The talent survey for this chapter reveals that such practice is important for, but only rarely an actual predictor of, talent in visual art and creative writing, as well as music and second-language learning, despite these talents' additional need for a certain mental pliability. Practice is apparently not crucial to gifted mathematical ability, and it is described as important but secondary to neurological determinants of the skills of the mnemonist and the chess master. But for many talented individuals, repetition of ideas or skills moves beyond the realm of mere practice and into that of obsession, at which point it no longer seems to be a matter of choice, nor under the talented person's voluntary control.

Musicians, for example, often talk of an obsessive inability to get a piece "out of one's mind," to forget musical patterns they may or may not have intentionally committed to memory. The same repetitive phenomenon in the visual modality occurs frequently enough in art to warrant terminology—"incidental visual memory" (Rosenblatt & Winner, 1988). In addition, artistically talented children are known to develop one property of a drawing, such as linearity, over several drawings. Adult artists may do the same thing, as illustrated by the remarks of an art student in the drawing study: "The trouble with art students is that they get real hung up on just one drawing" (male student, quoted in Juschka, 1990).

The hyperlexic preschooler has a compulsive preoccupation with reading so extreme it replaces normal play activities, and even her speech is repetitive in a condition known as "echolalia" (Aram & Healy, 1988). The prodigious calculator, too, is aware of compulsive practicing and ritualistic counting at an early age. Smith (1988) writes of the nineteenth-century calculator Henri Mondeux as a young boy:

> If he went into the fields, he walked with his eyes closed and counted until an accident or fear of an accident forced him to open his eyes. Then he would take a step with his eyes open for the first five steps taken with his eyes closed, two for the second five, three for the third five, and so on . . . he tried to take the largest number of steps possible with his eyes closed so as to be able to take a greater number with his eyes open (25).

Mathematician Karl Friedrich Gauss described himself in a similar way:

> From time to time as I am walking I begin to count my steps mentally (incidentally always when I am walking rhythmically). So I count up to 100 and then I begin from one again. I do all this, once it has started, unconsciously. I think of other things, observe whatever happens to catch my eye; the only thing I am not able to do is speak during that time (Smith, 1988: 25).

In the autistic savant, of course, repetition is at its zenith—the insistence on sameness, the intense, "undistractable" preoccupation with the talent (e.g., practicing piano nine hours a day in J. L.). These occur in addition to the typical autistic symptoms of asocial behavior, echolalia, perseveration, obsessive interests and rituals, and repetitive motor behaviors such as head banging and hand-flapping (Rimland & Fein, 1988). Some of the obsessive interests and rituals, at least, seem not a long way off from the focused, absent-minded eccentricities of an

Einstein, the bizarre habits and mannerisms of a Bobby Fisher, or the compulsions of a Howard Hughes. Inventor Hughes used to measure his daily chocolate cake to make certain it was twelve inches on each side. Canadian novelist Malcolm Lawry, while institutionalized for alcoholism, ritualistically washed his hands in milk before drinking it. Such tales have prompted Smith (1988) to wonder about the trait these people may have in common:

> There is a property, shared by those at either end of the mental spectrum, which would account for such an unequal distribution [of talent]—a tolerance for what ordinary folk find intolerably dull . . . People on either end of the intelligence scale seem to be less limited in what they may find interesting. Perhaps that is because they are already regarded as so peculiar that peer support for their interests is not required, or perhaps it is because the brilliant and retarded are not required to shoulder the responsibility of nurturing and transmitting popular culture (37).

Repetition in the talented can be a kind of habituation, like a mantra, that may or may not lead to divergent thinking. Neither can it be said that the gifted person necessarily tolerates it. Calculator A. C. Aitken once remarked that he sometimes squares numbers he happens to see: "This isn't deliberate—I just can't help it" (Smith, 1988: 39).

What is it that keeps the individual in contact with a domain for the time it takes to perfect a skill? What is behind the drive, determination and emotion that moves him simply to practice, on a normal and voluntary level, or to think obsessively and behave compulsively on a more disturbed and involuntary level? Psychological explanations abound, such as that the talented person has a need to control some aspect of an impoverished environment. One theory has it that physical or psychological isolation produces sensory deprivation, loneliness and anxiety, which in turn lead to concentration, focused attention and extensive practice because "focused mental activity appears to suppress the normal stress reaction to sensory deprivation" (Anders Ericsson & Faivre, 1988: 456).

In this light, it seems highly relevant that a very large proportion of children with exceptional abilities are found to have grown up in sterile environments, that many famous calculators were shepherd-boys, for example, or that Beethoven, Fauré, Franz, Vaughan Williams and Smetana all continued to compose in their later years despite the auditory and social isolation of deafness. Such seclusion may actually have helped their productivity by lessening distractions, perhaps in particular verbal distractions. As Smetana wrote, "I have completed in these three years of deafness more than I had otherwise done in ten" (Judd, 1988: 135).

For a great many other talented individuals, however, the isolation that may or may not induce repetitive behavior, is more internal than external. The emotionally disturbed and asocial savant, the socially backward chess player, the disturbed and withdrawn hyperlexic, the nonconformist second-language learner, the introverted and achievement-oriented writer (I), the withdrawn and creative artist (IN, NF)—all have traits very likely to come into conflict with a dominant social world that is principally outgoing (E) and practical (S), and which ethnocentrically views itself as mentally healthy simply because its condition—which has its own problems under this theory—is the majority condition. In many instances, therefore, a perceived lack of social skills would appear to be one of the more acknowledged forms of deficit accompanying giftedness—simple reservedness at normal levels of talent (I), progressing to reclusive unsociability at intermediate levels, and ultimately to pathological obliviousness to the human face in the autistic in whom talent may be statistically more frequent (10%) though not qualitatively superior. Just as deficit is apparently the flip side of talent, or obsession the flip side of persistence and practice, so would isolation seem to be the unavoidable other side of originality:

> Consider the personality of a typical auditory calculator: nervous; verbal; likes to be the center of attention; has nervous 'twitches' (sometimes even epilepsy) which may put people off; may be inclined toward violence directed at himself or herself or others. What do we do with such children? Give them something to do that isn't likely to be dangerous or annoying to the neighbors. Tell them to go count how much wood is in the woodpile and get back to you (Smith, 1988: 45).

This circular argument, that alienation breeds unusual behavior, which is itself further alienating, is common in the literature on giftedness and creativity, but may be flawed in three ways: (1) the cycle is usually described as beginning with an environmental determinant rather than with the odd behavior itself; (2) it seldom goes beneath the behavior to determine what other factors may be contributing to its expression; and (3) in the case of obsession, at least, it almost never says the behavior is important, or even essential to giftedness, preferring instead to merely note when the talented possess it, and the non-talented do not.

A talent-deficit theory of giftedness, on the other hand, would argue that asocial and obsessive tendencies are as much tied in a correlational sense to calculating and numerous other exceptional abilities as are allergies and math, anxiety disorders and chess, depression and art, alcoholism and writing. Such a theory would also argue that the underlying causative factors are more genetic, hormonal, metabolic and neurological than social, leading to personality traits such as introversion, anxiety level and temperament that may ultimately interact with environment in the production of "drive." Haier et al. (1987), for example, have compiled PET-scan data to suggest that Eysenckian introversion, like Jungian introversion, calculation and some functions in writing and math, is left-lateralized, while extroversion (spelled this way in the Eysenck system), like many abilities in music and drawing, would appear to be right-lateralized, generating speculation that our inward or outward focus in life may be bowed in one direction or the other, alongside our cognitive predispositions, at a very early age, perhaps even at the fetal stage.

This suggests more of a biological foundation, as do blood-type A and dopaminergic relationships in obsessive-compulsive disorder, a syndrome often coexisting with depression and known to respond to treatment with antidepressants like clomipramine and imipramine (Gazzaniga, 1988; Mellman & Uhde, 1987). From this perspective, we can envision a situation in which some serotonin deficiency, perhaps as part of a larger endocrine imbalance characteristic of cluster disorders, contributes to social withdrawal, perseverative firing and obsessional thinking in the talent domain as well as in unrelated areas, and which is only relieved, as with other obsessions, by replenishment of transmitter reserves or by the acting out of repetitive impulses. In doing so, ". . . special abilities in fact may lead to special efforts of great intensity. It may be that the exercise of such special abilities is accompanied by internal brain reward, such that the practice of the activity engenders its own particular pleasures" (Waterhouse, 1988: 508).

While admittedly microscopic, this view serves to remind us of two possibilities: (1) that because of the apparent intertwining of talent and deficit, treatment of an obsessive disability may in some way also alter the ability; and (2) that the talented individual himself may unintentionally contribute, at least in part, to his own asocial and repetitive eccentricities, the resulting alienation, and the cumulative and compounding effects thereafter of both factors together. Thus, repetition in the form of lonely, intensive practicing or execution of the talent over many years can be seen not as a cause but as a consequence of talent, a by-product of whatever processes create talent, rather than a primary or intermediate step in its early evolution. The logical extension of this position is that, if the person engages excessively in the talent, he can expect the associated problems to respond proportionately—in this case, to cause serotonin levels to fall, depression to worsen, and repetitive or obsessive tendencies to become more frequent. Doing the talent thus increases the likelihood that he will *want* to do the talent, in order to attain the brain reward. It is not "practice makes perfect," in that sense, but a state of perfection that makes him practice.

The end result, of course, is that those inflexible individuals who would ruminate on the "good" (i.e., that which is positive, productive, desirable) will also ruminate on the "bad" (i.e., something negative, unproductive, undesirable), whatever the targets of these values may be. This has ominous implications for talents coexisting with affective disorder, or requiring plasticity. Conversely, those flexible individuals who would not dwell on the "bad" may also not persist long with the "good," another double-edged sword in domains demanding high levels of concentration. This would seem to say that there are states of focus and non-focus in talent, each with its own particular advantages and disadvantages to the person in his chosen field.

Moreover, since the focused condition selectively screens out extraneous input while the unfocused condition openly accepts it, theoretical parallels are easily drawn between focusing and the strategy of thinking and grouping in wholes, as described earlier, and between not focusing and the strategy of attending to detail. For example, we might speculate that the focused gifted person in calculation or chess, perhaps for reasons of fewer, more direct neural pathways or compromised electrochemical activity, has repetitive or obsessive tendencies that are best managed by chunking, categorizing, structuring, and generalizing similar stimuli so as not to have to respond to each incoming byte of information. In contrast, the more flexible, unfocused gifted person in languages, math or sports, perhaps with redundant or alternate networks, may have fewer such repetitive inclinations and is therefore freer to process each piece of scattered, unrelated information in as disordered a fashion as it may present itself.

In this way, a state of unfocused attention to detail might be seen as an adaptive response to neurocognitive flexibility, or an inability to categorize, while a state of focused watchfulness for patterns and wholes could be seen as a response to neurocognitive rigidity, or an inability to itemize. Considering the role of frontal and parietal lobes in sorting, categorizing and recognizing patterns, this may be a reflection of some anterior-posterior difference in talent, or differences in the frontal and parietal areas themselves.

Since few people could be said to be all of one or the other condition, this is very possibly pointing again toward our continuum, between the endpoints of focusing and non-focusing, which conforms to the verbal-nonverbal spectrum already discussed. At one extreme is the highly perseverative predicament of the autistic savant; at the other, the very unfocused world of the wholly non-academic child with attention deficit hyperactivity disorder (ADHD), each with his own particular array of talents and deficits. Remediation in both cases involves modification toward the center of the individual's natural inclination to fixate and repeat—to reduce it in the savant, to increase it in the hyperactive child—so as to ultimately make him concentrate less, or concentrate more, and render him generally less exceptional. Somewhere in between, theoretically, are the rest of us, with moderate repetitive tendencies, mild or nonexistent levels of disability, and perhaps lesser amounts of talent.

The repetitive end of the spectrum may be the more important one for many kinds of talent:

> It is a matter of considerable interest, and possibly of considerable importance, that a number of people at the genius or near-genius level in the 'normal' population have also exhibited some signs of autism . . . Insistence on the preservation of sameness is regarded as one of the cardinal signs of autism. It is at least possible that some autistic individuals are incipient geniuses whose eccentricities are so severe and incapacitating that all but minimal participation in the normal world is precluded (Rimland & Fein, 1988: 477).

An investigation of talent in 121 disturbed children and youth, by DeLong and Aldershof (1988), suggests that bipolar disorder may be only one level removed from the repetitive extremes of autism. The arrangement of exceptional abilities in Table 18 was found in four deficit sub-groups within their sample. While the authors failed to discuss the larger continuum we see here between autism and ADHD, they did discern a smaller segment of it between autism and bipolar disorder:

> We find it hard to escape the impression that we are observing a spectrum showing all gradations in the expression of special abilities and obsessions between the manic-depressive and the autistic children (394).

**Table 18. Distribution of Talents in a Sample of Disturbed Young People (n = 121)**

| Spectrum | Talent* | Deficit* |
|---|---|---|
| **Verbal-Bilateral** | **Superior Memory (4)** <br> **Hyperlexia (4)** | **Developmental Disorders** <br> **e.g., Autism (n = 8)** |
| | **Hyperlexia (6)** <br> **Precocious Categorization** <br> **& Writing (3)** <br> **Calendar Calculation (3)** <br> **Art (2)** <br> **Music (1)** <br> **Poetry (1)** <br> **Superior Memory (1)** | **Bipolar Disorder** <br> **(n = 17)** |
| | | **Unipolar Depression** <br> **(n = 61)** |
| **Nonverbal-Lateral** | | **Attention Deficit Disorder** <br> **(n = 35)** |

*Source: DeLong & Aldershof (1988)

Of the children with special talents, they found fully 40 percent were bipolar and 35 percent autistic, which of course supports a talent-deficit view of giftedness. More convincing, however, is that the special talents group was more severely abnormal than non-talented subjects with the same disorders, in terms of obsessive characteristics and interests concerning violent, sexual, antisocial and death themes:

> The group with special abilities showed a considerably higher frequency of autistic characteristics, such as stereotypes, rigidity, and self-abuse; these features are virtually absent in the bipolar patients without special abilities (392).

The incidence of obsessive characteristics was 100 percent in the autistic children and 82 percent in the bipolar children, with the qualitative difference between them that talents and obsessions in the autistics were narrower and more stereotyped, and in the bipolar patients broader, more creative and imaginative. Furthermore, the occurrence of special abilities in the bipolar patients was found to be positively related to the severity of the illness and a heavy genetic loading for affective disease. *All* the bipolar patients with special talents had a family history of affective disorder—mostly bipolar, and usually involving the mother—and the loading was heavier than for unipolar children who, we speculate, are lower on the focus-nonfocus spectrum. Indeed, the lesser the severity and the lower the family incidence of bipolar disorder in this sample, the lower was the incidence of special talents altogether, which suggests the operation of a genotypic or phenotypic spectrum behind them. In support of the latter, Gazzaniga (1988) has proposed the existence of a spectrum of blood types from A to O, from obsessive-compulsive disorder to unipolar depression. In addition, anecdotal evidence suggests that autism and bipolar disorder run in the same family.

Thus rigidity and obsession, and not flexibility in this instance, would appear to be the more prevalent circumstance in the kind of "insanity" frequently associated with genius—an intense, highly focused perseverative intellectual style which DeLong and Alderschof characterize as "attention excess disorder." Though apparently beneficial to some forms of talent, it is a style which is very possibly unhealthy to the individual, physically as well as emotionally. Goldberger et al. (1990) have studied electrophysiological patterns in illness and have discerned periodicity in some kinds of disease and chaotic behavior in health:

> In 1988 [we] did a retrospective study of the ambulatory electrocardio-grams of people who had severe heart disease. We discovered that the pattern of heartbeats of those patients often became less variable than normal anywhere from minutes to months before sudden cardiac death. In some cases the overall beat-to-beat variability was reduced; in others highly periodic heart-rate oscillations appeared and then stopped abruptly. Somewhat similarly, the nervous system may show the loss of variability and the appearance of pathological periodicities in disorders such as epilepsy, Parkinson's disease and manic depression (49).

A suspected contributing factor in the motor rigidity of Parkinson's disease is abnormally low levels of dopamine. In the behavioral rigidity of autism, there is a deficiency of serotonin, and for depression, too, there can be a functional deficiency of serotonin or norepinephrine or both, which may or may not cause agitation and obsessive behavior, and which is often treated with antidepressants designed to increase the activity level of the sufferer and calm him at the same time. At the other end of the scale is the hyperactive child, hyperattending to every detail but not focusing, who has often been treated with the stimulant Ritalin which has the paradoxical effect of slowing him down. Again we see two basic yet transient processes in the system (Figure 19).

While a "too little, too much" neurotransmitter hypothesis may be an oversimplified interpretation of the differences between affective disorder and schizophrenia (Kolb & Whishaw, 1985), a theory of subtle electrochemical gradations may not be out of line for conditions more closely resembling each other, as for example in unipolar depression and bipolar disorder. If so, Smith's (1988) account of the two varieties of calculator is illuminating. He notes that the typical auditory calculator displays exaggerated motor activity, especially while calculating, which includes St. Vitus' dance-like contortions, hand-biting, eye-rolling, nervous "twitches," head-banging, extreme anxiousness, and very active movements that produce a feeling of inhibition if suppressed. The visual calculator, by comparison, is placid, relaxed and still:

> Wim Klein [an auditory calculator nicknamed the 'human computer'] was an anthill of agitation. His friend, Hans Eberstark, a visual calculator, exudes monolithic placidity. As Wim described Hans . . . 'He's big and fat. He's so quiet. He never gets nervous. Just the opposite of me' (28).

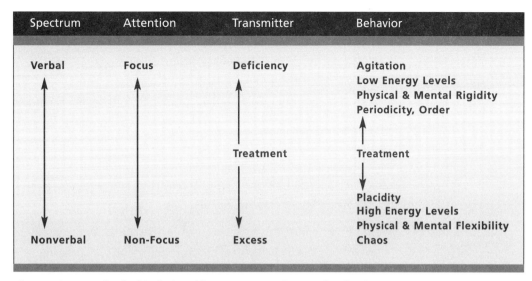

| Spectrum | Attention | Transmitter | Behavior |
|----------|-----------|-------------|----------|
| Verbal | Focus | Deficiency | Agitation<br>Low Energy Levels<br>Physical & Mental Rigidity<br>Periodicity, Order |
| | | Treatment | Treatment |
| Nonverbal | Non-Focus | Excess | Placidity<br>High Energy Levels<br>Physical & Mental Flexibility<br>Chaos |

**Figure 19. Hypothetical Relationships Between Talent and Behavior**

In this we see an apparent connection between agitation, repetitive movement and *verbal* facility, and between placidity, flexibility and *nonverbal* ability, perhaps even relating to ectomorphic and endomorphic body types. The idea is further advanced by closer inspection of the talent distribution within the bipolar subgroup, in the study by DeLong and Alderschof (Table 18, page 107). The list shows that fully 82 percent of the bipolar patients were talented in a verbal domain which, quite strikingly, is the same proportion of them plagued with obsessive thoughts and rituals. Only three bipolar subjects had exceptional nonverbal abilities and as one moves further down the spectrum toward the non-focused condition of attention deficit disorder, we encounter no reported talents whatsoever. However, Jamison's (1986, 1995) link between visual art and depression can be added to the continuum, as can proposed relationships between athletic ability and attention deficit disorder, to form the scheme shown in Figure 20, page 110.

DeLong and Alderschof maintain that autism, now recognized as a neurological disorder in its own right, is also an extreme form of bipolar disorder which, if true, would seem to place autism higher on the spectrum in this model. But because autism is to a very large extent non-verbal, in spite of its verbal-like repetitious characteristics, it would really seem to be at a place *between* the verbally focused condition of bipolar disorder and the nonverbally unfocused condition of ADHD. And because there are surely other examples of nonverbally-focused talent and its associated deficits—such as ballet dancing, perhaps, and immune deficiency, that may or may not be found to accompany it—this suggests that our linear spectrum is not really linear at all, but is in fact circular, and bent into a continuous, nonlinear talent-deficit continuum loosely approximated in Figure 21, page 111. Such a depiction seems to make especially good sense when it is remembered that all of this is brain-based to start with; that this drawing therefore also approximates the "placement" of talent-deficit pairings in the brain, which returns us once again to our circular conceptions of type and talent lateralities at the beginning of this chapter. To those notions, however, we have now added the dimension of disorder and disease.

*It is not perfect.* Because of the circumplicial "shadings," as Sternberg and Powell (1982) put it, of one ability into another around the circumference, and because the placements are also deduced theoretically in many ways, there are some confusing cross-functional overlaps in the pairings that cause us to wonder whether chess talent, for example, as a nonverbally focused talent, is more left-sided or right-sided. Yet it also manages to account for the fact that allergies, as another example, are a correlate for both mathematical and verbal talents which are geographically close together. The mapping also helps to make sense of other apparently random relationships in the literature—such as the high incidence of affective disorder, and especially obsessive-compulsive disorder, in women, who as a group, we know, happen to be inclined towards verbal-bilateral talent domains (Fuller & Thompson, 1978).

A tremendously important implication of this view, as far as the remainder of the book is concerned, is that limited movement is theoretically possible around the circle, depending on the extent to which the talent, the deficit, and implicitly the transmitter, are engaged. Hypothetically, for instance, the active, flexible athlete might use up excess transmitter through excessive practice of the talent, eventually moving himself into the areas of greater rigidity; perhaps for this reason, or some other combination of injury and genetics, boxer Mike Tyson developed bipolar disorder, and Mohammed Ali Parkinson's disease, both of which of course decrease physical activity. Drugs are used as a means of indirectly increasing rigidity in hyperactivity, and reducing it in autism and affective disorder, but the model implies it may also be possible to modify these problems behaviorally to some extent, by attacking not only the deficit, but also the talent opposite to a problem. That is, like the hyperlexic child who is not allowed to read and is encouraged to play, perhaps the suicidal writer should not write and should instead unfocus himself, temporarily or concurrently, on the more relaxed, flexible, active and nonverbal domain of sport. In this manner, for the writer, natural physical activity replaces the artificial chemical stimulation of caffeine, nicotine and alcohol in raising low endorphin levels that may ultimately contribute to his or her talent and deficit in the first place. The drawback, however, which is inconsequential compared to the alternative, is that

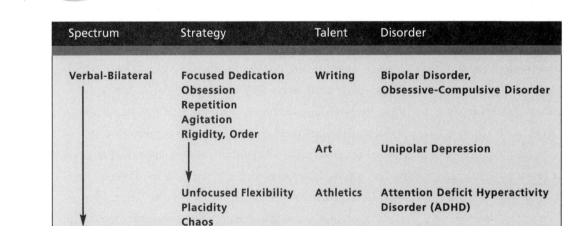

| Spectrum | Strategy | Talent | Disorder |
|---|---|---|---|
| **Verbal-Bilateral** | **Focused Dedication**<br>**Obsession**<br>**Repetition**<br>**Agitation**<br>**Rigidity, Order** | **Writing** | **Bipolar Disorder,**<br>**Obsessive-Compulsive Disorder** |
| | | **Art** | **Unipolar Depression** |
| | **Unfocused Flexibility**<br>**Placidity**<br>**Chaos** | **Athletics** | **Attention Deficit Hyperactivity**<br>**Disorder (ADHD)** |
| **Nonverbal-Lateral** | **Attention to Detail** | | |

**Figure 20. Proposed Relationships Between Laterality, Talent and Deficit**

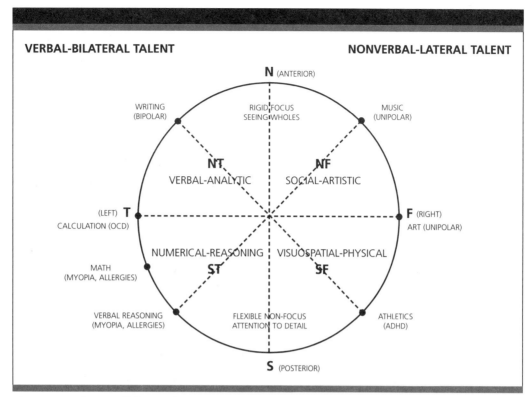

**VERBAL-BILATERAL TALENT**

**NONVERBAL-LATERAL TALENT**

N (ANTERIOR)

WRITING
(BIPOLAR)

RIGID FOCUS
SEEING WHOLES

MUSIC
(UNIPOLAR)

NT
VERBAL-ANALYTIC

NF
SOCIAL-ARTISTIC

(LEFT) T
CALCULATION (OCD)

F (RIGHT)
ART (UNIPOLAR)

NUMERICAL-REASONING

VISUOSPATIAL-PHYSICAL

MATH
(MYOPIA, ALLERGIES)

ST

SE

VERBAL REASONING
(MYOPIA, ALLERGIES)

FLEXIBLE NON-FOCUS
ATTENTION TO DETAIL

ATHLETICS
(ADHD)

S (POSTERIOR)

**Figure 21. Talent-Deficit Continuum in the Brain**

he or she may experience less of an urge to write.

That low endorphins should contribute to negative mood states and be elevated by physical exercise is probably common sense and common knowledge. It is not so common that low endorphins should contribute to a person's writing talent, perhaps as the "cutting edge" of creativity, the anxiety motif that is indeed common in the literature on creativity. However, the purpose in mentioning this phenomenon of the effect of exercise on endorphins is not to point this out, but to illustrate movement around the talent-deficit circle using a familiar theme. If it is probable that sport can modify the writer's deficit (affective disorder), or sociability exercises the autistic's deficit, it also seems possible, if superficially absurd, that calculation exercises might benefit the hyperactive child, or language exercises the anxious chess master, in each case by emphasizing the talent domain contralateral to a deficit. Odd as it may seem, Rossi (1986) notes that talking to warts speeds up their disappearance, and Jon Kaiser at the Wellness Center in San Francisco teaches his HIV-positive patients to write letters to their virus (Colt, 1996)—a verbal response to what may have started out as a mostly nonverbal problem. Writing about one's problems has been shown to enhance the immune-cell activity of traumatized individuals. Indeed, even the writing of music may have this effect. The leukemia of Hungarian composer Bela Bartok went into remission as he wrote his final concerto, causing Bartok to claim that writing it was "the wonder drug I needed" (Somerville et al., 1993).

However, the fact that writing is also associated with affective disorder does not say that severe depression is a prerequisite for writing or, for that matter, for creativity in other "affective" fields such as music or art. By graphing number of musical works against reported emotional highs and lows, Kay Jamison has shown that Robert Schumann, for example, achieved very little in the severely depressed periods of his life. Similarly, Nancy Andreasen's (1987) study of thirty creative writers over a fifteen-year period at the University of Iowa Writers' Workshop (previously attended by Kurt Vonnegut, Philip Roth and others) finds that the most prolific writing occurred during the writers' normal periods, rather than during their highs and lows.

Yet clearly there is some relationship between writing and the more biochemical aspects of the disease, likely at more moderate phases of the cycle, because both are tied to each other on a hereditary level, and both often present with an alcoholic, or alcoholic-like, mask. In comparison with matched controls, Andreasen found rates of alcoholism in the sample of writers to be more than four times higher, and the incidence of first-degree familial affective disorder, particularly among siblings, nearly seven times higher than that of the non-talented group. In fact, she discovered, "The families of the writers were riddled with both creativity and mental illness, while in the families of the control subjects much of the illness and creativity seemed to be randomly scattered" (1290).

Social learning arguments for these observations are dispelled by doubled rates of creativity in siblings as compared to parents suggesting, as we have said, recessive transmission; by the fact that the writers' families contained various kinds of creativity (art, music, dance, math), not simply literary creativity as social learning would predict (this implies some general factor for creativity is what is inherited); and by the sheer magnitude of the differences between the writers and the controls. The incidence of an episode of any affective illness in a subject's life was two-and-a-half times higher in the writers; for bipolar disorder, it was twice that of the controls. None was schizophrenic, challenging earlier hypotheses connecting creativity and schizophrenia which, as a manifestation of frontal- and temporal-lobe dysfunction and dopaminergic irregularities, is very likely to impede the processes involved in writing.

Beyond this are the more serious indications that to be unfocused and physically talented, like the boxer, is in its most extreme sense to be outwardly destructive, while to be focused and verbally talented is to be in some way self-destructive. In the twentieth century, Ernest Hemingway, Sylvia Plath, John Berryman, Anne Sexton and Virginia Woolf are only some of the writers who died by their own hand. And in the Andreasen study, two of the thirty writers (7%) committed suicide during the fifteen years of the project. As Andreasen herself notes, issues of statistical significance pale before the clinical implications—not to mention the social, spiritual and educational implications—of this fact.

## For Further Study: A Periodic Table of Personality, Talent and Disease

Having distinguished numerous relationships between talent and various kinds of dysfunction, it seems conceivable that these represent only the tip of a talent-deficit iceberg. How many other talents—social, practical, mechanical, dramatic, paranormal, etc.—and how many other kinds of disorder, have been excluded from this interpretation? And what of the personality that in many cases guides not only the development of an ability (e.g., the desire to practice) but also the course of a disability? Certain deficits are related to talent, and certain other deficits are related to personality. In light of these relationships, it seems possible that at least some deficits are related to both talent and personality at the same time. For this reason, this section, and indeed the rest of the book, advances the hypothesis that personality, talent, deficit and disease are closely interrelated, and that it may be conceptually feasible to organize these relationships in periodic, predictable fashion around the verbal-nonverbal talent continuum and Isabel Myers' table of psychological types.

The Myers personality table is already periodic, tying together indicators of personality and talent interests in systematic fashion, but as yet it has only limited evidence directly connecting it to brain function, to a verbal-nonverbal continuum, and to deficit, instead describing only positive recurring aspects, including talents, of its sixteen personality types. In actuality, there would appear to be contained in the table a strong verbal-nonverbal gradient, highly suggestive of a spectrum of laterality, which needs only to be correlated with some measure of laterality in order to make the claim. The simplest indicator is, of course, handedness, concordance with which would put personality indicators as defined by Jung and Myers in league with the talent continuum, its apparent gradations in laterality, and the associated deficits known to date.

It would be interesting enough simply to demonstrate in this manner theoretical connections between laterality, personality, talent, and known deficits such as dyslexia and allergies. But we could go a step beyond this stage to its more important conclusion, which would be to seek out similar relationships with *unknown* disorders through a survey of the medical histories of people in the sixteen personality-talent categories. The result might be statistical statements to the effect that this or that psychological type is most likely to exhibit left-handedness and artistic interests, for example, and is at risk of developing depression or some other physical or mental dysfunction, indicating appropriate strategies of prevention and intervention in addition to the more common educational and vocational advice. Filled in, in this way, for each of the various types, *the Myers chart could conceivably become a kind of neuropsychological periodic table of elements, perhaps doing for psychology, education and medicine what its prototype does for chemistry, geology and physics.*

Thus, just as a hostile personality correlates with cardiovascular problems, it might also be found to correlate with a specific ability; for example, calculation or chess skills or some other agitating, stressful talent (e.g., political strategizing) may contribute to the disability. Likewise, myopia and immune disorders might be found to belong to some particular class of personalities, such as Intuitives, and is perhaps of interest in the prediction of math or verbal talent. Certainly a three-factor covariance—Personality X Talent X Deficit—would be a potentially useful addition to identification techniques. But it is at the same time an ominous addition in that hypothetically it might also forecast deficit, disorder and disease on the basis of personality and one's area of expertise; heart disease or stroke, for example, might be predicted from calculation skills in one particular area of the personality chart. Some type purists will not want to know this information, preferring instead to keep psychological type the positive and validating construct it is. But for those of us accepting that we must explore the negatives along with the positives, hopefully so as to help prevent the negatives, we will attempt to outline how a model of type, talent and disease could be formulated and tested.

In chapter 1 (Table 1 page 8), we noted that Myers' four dominant-auxiliary categories—which we have since renamed type "genera"—have learning styles, academic interests and occupational preferences unique to their respective groups. The Intuitive Thinking (NT) type is attracted to science and art in school, and occupations in research science and law. The Intuitive Feeling (NF) types prefers English, art and music, and often chooses work in counseling, creative writing and theology. The Sensing Feeling (SF) type enjoys practical subjects, the details of music, history and math, and often finds a career in the people-oriented fields of sales, nursing and teaching. The Sensing Thinking (ST) type, too, prefers math and practical skills, and is attracted to business careers in accounting, finance and commerce; SF and ST are also particularly likely to be involved in athletics.

In this is a readily observable progression from verbal to nonverbal that is plainly in agreement with the continuum—the highly verbal and analytic NT, the verbal and artistic NF, the artistic, athletic or practical SF, the athletic or practical ST. What's more, the apparent circularity of the spectrum just discussed seems to overlap with the proposed laterality of type functions, so that each of the four major type genera can be seen as being diagonally oriented across two hemispheres and encompassing one-quarter of a rotation from one genus to another. As a result, and contrary to appearances on the type table, ST is only one step removed from NT (Figure 22).

Consequently, from this it would be proposed that the highly verbal NT is functioning on a bilateral level, but is using disproportionately more of the left-anterior quadrant (i.e., left frontal and temporal areas) than other types. Similarly, the NF would be seen as having a bilateral organization but emphasizing the right-anterior quadrant consisting of right frontal and temporal areas. In contrast, the more nonverbal SF or ST would be hypothesized as having more posterior laterality on either side, rendering the individual in all four cases less adept at functions occurring opposite the "preferred" area of specialization. Jung referred to the resulting weaknesses as "the shadow," Myers termed them the "blind spots" of tertiary and least-preferred functions, and the neuropsychological interpretation in this chapter would call them deficits contralateral to a talent.

These vulnerabilities might be depicted diagrammatically (Figure 23) in four example types, in which the preferred dominant and auxiliary functions (no shading) sit opposite the tertiary function (light shading) and least-preferred function (dark shading).

If it could be established that these dark quadrants of the cortex are responsible for the relative deficiencies in both personality and cognitive ability described by Myers for these types, it would not be unreasonable to expect they are also responsible for deficits in sensory, perceptual, motor, emotional or other realms of functioning governed by these regions. We wonder, for example, to what extent, if any, the myopia of the mathematical and verbal NT

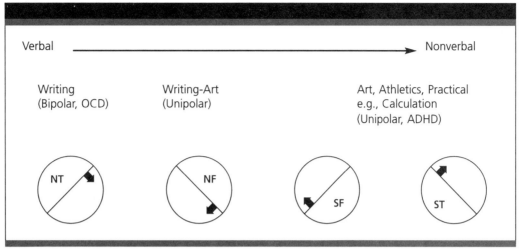

**Figure 22. Hemispheric Emphases in Dominant-Auxiliary Functions**

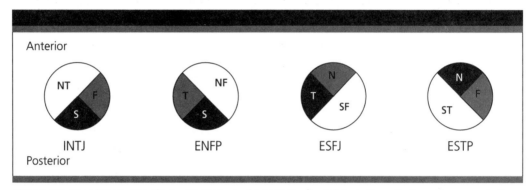

**Figure 23. Dominant, Auxiliary, Tertiary and Least-Preferred Functions in Four Representative Types**

personality may be related to the theoretical lack of emphasis on occipital areas known to play a significant role in the visual modality. Similarly, is the SF personality prone to allergies and other immune disorders, such as diabetes, because the left hemisphere, believed to be involved in immune development, is hypothetically less emphasized than the right? Are SF and ST personalities, in whom it is proposed frontal and temporal areas are de-emphasized, prone to the lateralized frontal and temporal inactivity of schizophrenia, as verbal personalities would appear to be predisposed to develop affective disorder, in many ways the polar opposite of schizophrenia?

Equally unsettling, might the probability of stroke be greater, or the existence of epileptogenic foci or other physiological weaknesses more frequent in accentuated areas or in less-utilized areas in each of the different types? Most strokes, for example, are known to occur in the middle cerebral artery, and epilepsy often affects the temporal lobes (Berg et al, 1987), both of which might seem to suggest some personalities are at greater risk than others. Though they drew no connections to personality, Geschwind and Galaburda (1985c) discuss the findings of Taylor and Ounsted (1971) who suggested that epilepsy is more prevalent in underutilized areas. Studying the predominance of left-sided lesions in boys who had their first febrile convulsions before their first birthdays, they noticed that ". . . epilepsy was more likely to invade a less active region and that it was immaturity of the left temporal lobe in male infants that endowed it with special susceptibility" (641).

Additional support for the possibility that disease occurs in less-utilized areas might come from patterns in degenerative neurological diseases. In Alzheimer's dementia and Parkinson's disease, there are transmitter deficiencies similar to those in depression which cause mimicry of depressive symptoms, and which would seem to stand these disorders alongside verbal talents rather than nonverbal talents, possibly putting NT and NF personalities at greater risk of contracting these diseases. Verbally talented NT and NF, it is proposed, "neglect" posterior areas of the brain, and in Alzheimer's disease, which afflicts women (also verbal-bilateral) twice as often as men (Berg et al, 1987), and which puts male left-handers at greater pre-senile risk than right-handers (Seltzer & Sherwin, 1983), it is the posterior temporal and posterior parietal areas that become most underactive with the development of neural plaques (Rosenfeld, 1988). Likewise, in Parkinson's disease, it is the degeneration of the substantia nigra, a dopamine-producing nucleus in the mid-brain, that figures prominently in the progression of the disease (Kolb & Whishaw, 1985). In both these instances, it is postulated that "posterior" disease may develop in people with "anterior" verbal personalities and talents, the underlying principle being that vulnerabilities to disease, like the weaknesses of personality and cognitive ability, may lie contralateral to our strengths—a kind of internal contralateral neglect.

The mirror image of this imaginary scenario—"anterior" disease in the "posterior" nonverbal personalities of SF and ST—might involve a disorder like Huntington's chorea. Here, hyperactivity of the dopamine system in the basal ganglia leads to symptoms roughly in opposition to those of depression—excess transmitter, abnormal restlessness, involuntary movement, and psychiatric features such as mania and schizophrenia-like psychoses (Kolb & Whishaw, 1985). Loose parallels to the high motor activity and lack of affective periodicity in the non-focused, nonverbally oriented hyperactive child suggest there might also be nonverbal correlates in chorea. Nonverbally talented SF and ST, it is proposed, have posterior preferences which cause them to "neglect" anterior areas; and in choreics, there is a progressive degeneration of the basal ganglia, the corpus callosum, and the frontal cortex. While Huntington's chorea is genetically transmitted, there is no known way, at present, of determining whether a family member will develop the disease before symptoms actually appear. We can envision the possibility that concordance with type and talent (SF, ST?) could help in this regard.

What is being put forward, then, is essentially a "weak-link-in-the-chain" argument in which all people possess a different weak link, but in which groups of people with similar personality indicators and talents may have similar weak links, all as a result of their functional laterality. In other words, *we are proposing a connection between dominance and disease, as there might also appear to be for dominance and certain personality traits, or dominance and talent domain.*

Ideally, scanning devices and other sophisticated techniques would be required to confirm whether or not any of this is more than fiction. In lieu of them, we might begin by examining handedness frequencies in each of the four personality-talent groups. Because of control by the contralateral hemisphere, a high incidence of right-handedness would be anticipated in NT and ST populations, and a comparatively high incidence of non-right-handedness would be expected in NF and SF groups, with ambi-handedness being the most prevalent form of non-right-handedness in the more verbal-bilateral categories of NF and NT. But until such studies, we must content ourselves with qualitative suggestions of links between the various personality indicators, their talents and deficits, and particular regions of the brain.

To illustrate, within the NT genus on the right side of the type table, highly verbal INTJ personalities in fields such as science, politics and philosophy, are described as having ". . . original minds and great drive which they use only for their own purposes . . . often stubborn" (Myers & McCaulley, 1985: 21). Myers (1980b), too, writes of the extent of the focusing in this type: "Some problems may arise from the INTJ's single-minded concentration on goals. They may see the end so clearly that they fail to look for other things which might conflict with the goal" (24).

This is to say, they fail to see concrete details (S) and subjective realities (F) subserved by the more posterior and right-sided areas of the brain. INTJs, it is proposed, are emphasizing left-anterior areas, known in part for contributions to verbal fluency, verbal learning, associative learning, temporal ordering, categorization, comprehension, verbal memory, behavioral initiative, and some kind of creativity, especially verbal creativity (Kolb & Whishaw, 1985). Lewis Baxter at UCLA has used PET scanning to show that this region is also critically involved, along with the basal ganglia, in the expression of obsessive-compulsive disorder; even after drug therapy, the orbital gyri of both frontal lobes, but particularly the left frontal lobe, are metabolically overactive (Rosenfeld, 1988). In line with earlier observed connections between focused rigidity, verbal facility, and affective disorder, the INTJ's ensuing shadow, blind spot or deficit is said to be a certain weakness in the more subjective domain of social behavior and feeling (EF). As Keirsey and Bates (1984) note, INTJs are vulnerable in the emotional area and may make serious mistakes here (183).

Indeed, one of the rare instances in the literature of an association between type and a negative attribute is a relationship between types on the right side, the verbal side of the Myers table (NT, NF), and emotionality. Within the NF group, for example, imaginatively verbal ENFPs, often attracted to careers in counseling, art and journalism, are said to be ". . . hypersensitive and hyperalert; they may suffer from muscle tension" (173).

The very verbally talented and artistic INFP, also attracted to counseling and frequently gifted in writing, as was Myers herself, would appear to be predisposed toward some form of affective disorder, as the talent-deficit continuum would predict:

> The problem with some INFPs is that they may feel such a contrast between their ideals and their actual accomplishments that they burden themselves with a sense of inadequacy . . . If they find no channel for expressing their ideals, INFPs may become overly sensitive and vulnerable, with dwindling confidence in life and in themselves (Myers, 1980b: 17).

It is this group—the verbal, artistic, musical, and social NFs—that is hypothesized to have a kind of right-anterior "dominance" recognized as contributing to design copying, block construction, metaphor comprehension, melody production, pitch detection, movement programming, temporal ordering, categorization, spatial orientation, associative learning, face recognition, design memory, rhythm memory, behavioral spontaneity and social behavior (Kolb & Whishaw, 1985). Scanning of blood flow and metabolism (PET) by Eric Reiman and colleagues at Washington University has demonstrated that this area, indeed the whole right side, is also involved in panic disorder (Rosenfeld, 1988). Furthermore, Tucker (1981) has used EEG to show that right frontal areas are actually activated during depression, rather than deactivated like the left-frontal area, and this, too, would seem to lend physiological support to the premise that right-anterior talents of the kind seen in NFs (literary, artistic, musical, social) can exist on the same side as affective deficits. NFs are also said to have an apparent deficiency in employing impersonal logic (T)—which is surely in other ways a positive attribute—which might imply a certain de-emphasis of left-posterior areas and account for the fact that NFs do not, as a rule, have a preference for math.

At this point, it is worth digressing to illustrate these and earlier claims with neuropsychological features of the life of Dutch graphic artist Maurits C. Escher (1898–1972). The collection of events to be described here will show that Escher might have belonged to the right side of the proposed table of type, talent and deficit.

Escher was born to older parents, the third child of his mother, the fifth child of his father, who was a fifty-five-year-old civil engineer at the time of his birth. Described as a sickly child, Escher was placed in a special home for children at age seven, and was the subject of taunts by village children. He failed, and had to repeat, his second grade. Escher himself acknowledged:

> '. . . at school in Arnheim I was an extremely poor pupil in arithmetic and
> algebra, and I still have great difficulty with the abstractions of figures and
> letters. I was slightly better at solid geometry, because it appealed to my
> imagination, but even in that subject I never excelled at school' (Bool et
> al., 1981: 15).

He didn't complete his first graphic piece until the age of eighteen, but once he did begin drawing, music was ". . . a great source of inspiration for his work, as we see repeatedly in his letters and essays" (15). He played piano and flute, and formed a string quartet in which he played cello. He and two close friends were attracted to psychological literature, read poetry aloud, and are said to have talked together "endlessly" (16). With this group, Escher began writing poetry and prose which later developed into letters, speeches and essays on his graphic work.

Escher enrolled in a technical school to become an architect—he was left-handed—but failed in history, constitutional organization, political economy and bookkeeping. He missed many classes because of "an intractable skin infection" (17), and his "eternal complaint—

constipation and weakness caused by being too thin" (29). In 1930, at age thirty-two, he suffered one of many periods of depression:

> His health was failing and as a result of his own and his family's many illnesses, he could not make ends meet, especially since he was not selling any of his work. He doubted his own skills. These depressions occurred repeatedly throughout his life. However, as soon as he could gather fresh impressions or start on a new project, the mood would pass (35).

He was "plagued," as he said, throughout his life with various recurring ideas and repeating patterns. In 1951, he wrote of these:

> '. . . the fact that a symbol [in my work] is sometimes discovered or remarked upon [by other people] is valuable for me because it makes it easier to accept the inexplicable nature of my hobbies, which constantly preoccupy me. The regular division of the plane into congruent figures evoking an association in the observer with familiar natural objects is one of these hobbies or problems . . . I have embarked on this geometric problem again and again over the years, trying to throw light on different aspects each time. I cannot imagine what my life would be like if this problem had never occurred to me; one might say that I am head over heels in love with it, and I still don't know why . . . An understanding of the relationships between plane and space is a source of emotion for me; and emotion is a strong incentive, or at least a stimulus for making a picture' (Bool et al., 1981: 67).

A letter to his son near Montreal, and other letters of the late 1950s, reveal the emotional turmoil and self-deprecation he experienced in spite of his artistic success:

> 'God, I wish I could learn to draw a bit better! It takes so much effort and perseverance to do it well. Sometimes I am close to delirium with pure nerves. It is really only a question of battling on relentlessly with constant and, if possible, merciless self-criticism. I think that making prints the way I do is almost only a matter of very much wanting to do it well. For the most part, things like talent are mere poppycock. Any schoolboy with a bit of aptitude might draw better than I; but what is usually lacking is the unwavering desire for expression, obstinacy gnashing its teeth and saying "Even though I know I cannot do it, I still want to do it". . .' (81).

> 'I'm plagued from time to time by an immense feeling of inferiority, a desperate sense of general failure; where do these crazy feelings come from?' (93).

Escher died at seventy-three of stomach problems, following surgical removal of cystulas.

Clearly, this artist could be an example of the NF personality which, it is proposed, emphasizes right-anterior areas of the brain to the relative "disregard" of left-posterior areas. The verbal, musical and artistic talent, the mathematical impairment, the left-handedness, the episodic unipolar depression with repetitive obsessions, anxiety and focused perseveration, all would seem to point to the NF area of the talent-deficit chart. The "intractable skin infection" and possibly even the stomach problems may also reflect immunological weaknesses which, after Geschwind, suggest relative underdevelopment of the left hemisphere. That Escher might belong to the Feeling category within type theory, which is very likely a right-lateralized function, is evidenced by his own distinctions between "feeling people" and "thinking people":

> 'There is a noticeable difference between two groups of people which can be distinguished and compared because they have ideas and opinions with an apparently different orientation . . . For want of anything better I have called them "feeling people" and "thinking people". . . By "feeling people" I mean those who, amid everything surrounding them, are most interested in the relationship between themselves and others, and in relationships between people in general . . . Most artists belong to this group. This is clear from the preference they have had since time immemorial for depicting the human countenance and the human form; they are fascinated by specifically human qualities, both physical and spiritual. And even if they do not depict man himself, even when a poet is describing a landscape or a painter is doing a still life, they almost always approach their subjects from their interest in man . . . I do indeed believe that there is a certain contrast between, say, people in scientific professions and people working in the arts . . . *Fortunately there is no one who actually has only feeling or only thinking properties. They intermingle like the colors of the rainbow and cannot be sharply divided. Perhaps there is even a transitional group, like the green between the yellow and the blue of the rainbow*' (Bool et al., 1981: 72–73, emphasis added).

At the other end of the personality "rainbow," opposite NF and NT on the left side of the type table, are the more nonverbal categories of SF and ST. Here, ESFP personalities are described as:

> Outgoing, easygoing, accepting, friendly, fond of a good time. Like sports and making things. Know what's going on and join in eagerly. Find remembering facts easier than mastering theories. Are best in situations that need sound common sense and practical ability with people as well as things (Myers & McCaulley, 1985: 21).

Similarly, ESTPs are said to be:

> Matter-of-fact, do not worry, enjoy whatever comes along. Tend to like

mechanical things and sports, with friends on the side. May be a bit blunt
or insensitive. Can do math or science when they see the need (21).

The more relaxed, flexible posture, the attention to factual detail and the athletic interests all conform to the talent continuum. The deficits, too, on this side of the table, would appear to be foretold by it. Keirsey and Bates describe ISTPs:

> Like ISFPs, ISTPs communicate through action, and show little interest in developing verbal skills. Indeed, this lack of interest in communication may be mistaken for what well meaning but misguided medics and educators call 'learning disability' or 'dyslexia', both preposterous notions when meant as explanations. Let ISTPs get near a tool of any complexity and power and see how fast they pass everybody in learning to use it and how precise their lexicon in talking of its features (201).

Surely in some instances it might be argued that individuals with attention or learning difficulties should no more be given medications to quell their physical propensities and make them more verbal than should the language abilities of the verbally talented be artificially suppressed to make them more physical. As in the case for a musical dyslexia, learning disability may be to a large extent in the eye of the beholder, the beholder invariably possessing a verbal talent the "disabled" person lacks. But from a nonverbal perspective, the tables are turned, pointing to the need for tolerance of personalities, talents and deficits outside our own domains.

In terms of brain function, the abilities of SF personalities (artistic, athletic, practical) seem to suggest greater involvement of the lower right quadrant of the circular continuum and the right-posterior areas (temporal, parietal, occipital) of the brain—the awareness of sensory and perceptual stimuli (visual, auditory, tactile), verbal and nonverbal memory for detail, gregarious social behavior, movement, constructional abilities and spatial abilities (Kolb & Whishaw, 1985). The talents of ST personalities (athletic, numerical, practical) would seem to have similar origins but are also suggestive of a left-posterior bias—the naming, recognizing and using of objects, movement, constructional abilities, visual and tactile preferences, spatial abilities, organization and categorization, and above all, calculation skills in a personality category populated by accountants, bankers and business people.

Apparent weaknesses in these groups may include more anterior verbal deficits and focusing problems, essentially opposite those of the NT and NF, with additional blind spots involving logical analysis in the SF, and interpersonal skills in the ST, suggestive of left and right under-emphasis, respectively. In the last regard, it is significant that poor social adjustment is often a feature of the dyslexia that would appear to sometimes accompany the ST, particularly the SP, personality. Kolb and Whishaw describe their sample of dyslexics:

> [They] suffered through a miserable and usually short school career and then suffered a miserable social life full of disappointments and failures.

They also had a relatively poor chance for advanced training and skilled employment. They did not, however, have a higher incidence of juvenile delinquency or psychiatric problems (718).

Dominant-auxiliary functions are, for the most part, relatively unchanging from about the age of fourteen (Lawrence, 1982). The parallel to the fixation of talent at puberty suggests that a corresponding deficit may also be well entrenched at this age. Combined, they imply that mindsets, preferences and ways of thinking, whether advantageous or disadvantageous, are rather set by a very young age. So, too, may be the macroscopic outcomes of these factors. The general direction of career paths, for example—verbal-analytic, verbal-artistic, practical, physical, etc.—may be essentially predetermined by personality, talent and deficit, and the laterality that may or may not underlie them. Perhaps even personal sociopolitical inclinations are a function of the internal verbal-nonverbal system. Considering some 70 percent of the general adult population in North America is believed to be Sensing (Lawrence, 1982: 39), we could speculate that a majority of voters in this society is more posterior-functioning, and is therefore more interested in the practical, tangible aspects of present reality than in the verbal imaginations of left-wing theory. As a consequence, the political pendulum must always return to find its own conservative level.

Finally, a convincing suggestion of a relationship between laterality, personality, talent and its implicit deficits is a correlation of 0.47 in some 3500 high school students between intelligence and academic achievement in the sixteen different types (Myers & McCaulley, 1985). High levels of ability and achievement were found to be associated with Introverted Intuition (IN), while lower levels were found to be associated with Extraverted Sensing (ES), although as Myers and McCaulley warn:

> It is important not to conclude that ES types are less intelligent than IN types. Scholastic aptitude tests measure the I and N aspects of intelligence [left-anterior areas?] particularly valuable in academic work; they are not designed to measure the practical applied intelligence of E and S [right-posterior areas?] (109–110, brackets added).

In other words, scholastic aptitude tests are not equipped to measure the more nonverbal talents in which ES groups excel, and instead screen for global thinking and pattern recognition in the structured, focused world of verbal abilities. Thus NTs and NFs, especially Introverts, are found at the high end of verbal achievement—presumably along with bilaterality, focused thinking, and problems related to rigidity, obsession and affective disorder—while STs and SFs, especially Extraverts, are found at the low end, presumably along with laterality, nonverbal skills, flexible personalities, and problems having to do with focusing and concentrating.

There are, in the literature, frequent assertions, and data to support them, that intelligence is not a sufficient condition for giftedness or creativity. Yet not very far beneath the surface of this pronouncement is, in all of us, an instinctive belief that a Mozart or any other gifted person must be highly intelligent. In actuality, intelligence as measured by IQ may not even be a necessary condition for most kinds of talent, as a survey of minimum IQ requirements shows (Figure 24, page 124).

For example, in calculating prodigies, genius tends to fall into three categories—brilliant mathematicians, performers, and those with mental retardation—with sizeable over-representation in the brilliant and individuals with mental retardation (Smith, 1988). The talented C. J., described earlier in an illustration of cluster disorders, could speak seven languages, yet possessed poor visuospatial skills and only average IQ (Novoa et al., 1988). And J. L., the musical savant of the one-handed piano playing, can transpose entire pieces by key, yet is virtually untestable at an IQ level of perhaps 50–60, and at the developmental level of a two-year-old (Charness et al., 1988).

Numerous other cases testify to the lack of importance of IQ in talent. Only in the more verbal talents of creative writing and mathematics—that is, toward the verbal-bilateral end of the talent spectrum, where a higher incidence of ambi-handedness and cluster disorders have been postulated—does IQ appear to matter, and even then it does not predict for creativity in those fields (Andreasen, 1987). But because words and numbers have infinitely greater importance in today's schools than notes, line or movement, high IQ and the power it symbolizes continue to have conspicuous social value. Academic preoccupation with IQ is probably also governed by the fact that teachers, researchers and school psychologists are, by and large, verbal, meaning in effect that they and the tests they design are essentially screening for talents like their own.

So, while intelligence- and achievement-testing is an exceedingly useful tool in the assessment of deficit, it would appear to be only moderately helpful in the assessment and prediction of giftedness, in that it separates out a relatively small number of verbal talents from a much larger array of nonverbal talents. The scope of testing may one day also encompass nonverbal skills, such as acting, comedy, social skills, leadership, mimicry, altruism, hypnosis, mind reading, healing, prophesying, telekinesis, and extrasensory perception. A great many nonverbal talents, even more than Howard Gardner's intelligences would include, are likely falling through the wide cracks of tested IQ and the academic grade.

Given the verbal biases of such selection processes, an appropriate addition to identification techniques might be one that assesses manifestations and degrees of laterality and bilaterality. Ultimately this might involve a more biological approach to assessment—perhaps handedness questionnaires, talent-specific and site-specific tests, family histories of talent, and medical histories probing information on birth order and cluster factors. Some or all of these data could conceivably be combined with information on personality, learning styles and cognitive preferences to form a comprehensive picture of the individual, and his or her strengths and weaknesses, without resorting to the prejudices of verbal measures. The subject's place on the proposed type table would then provide some approximation of what might be expected in terms of personality, talent and accompanying deficits, disorders and diseases.

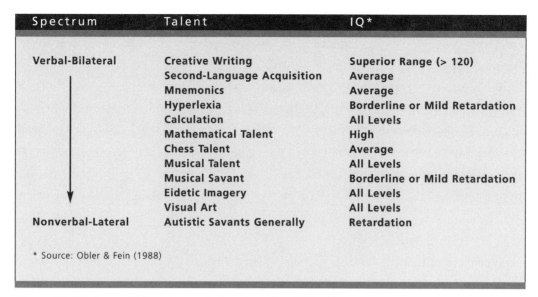

| Spectrum | Talent | IQ* |
|---|---|---|
| Verbal-Bilateral | Creative Writing | Superior Range (> 120) |
| | Second-Language Acquisition | Average |
| | Mnemonics | Average |
| | Hyperlexia | Borderline or Mild Retardation |
| | Calculation | All Levels |
| | Mathematical Talent | High |
| | Chess Talent | Average |
| | Musical Talent | All Levels |
| | Musical Savant | Borderline or Mild Retardation |
| | Eidetic Imagery | All Levels |
| | Visual Art | All Levels |
| Nonverbal-Lateral | Autistic Savants Generally | Retardation |

\* Source: Obler & Fein (1988)

**Figure 24. Minimum IQ Requirements in a Sample of Talents**

A periodic table of personality, talent and disease—which we will begin to develop in the next chapter—may accomplish precisely that, with the equitable caveat that neuro-psychological gains and losses so organized do live, and probably must live, in symbiotic union in all types. It is a theme that is at once pessimistic and optimistic for special abilities, disabilities, and the people who have them.

*** * ***

**Chapter 4 proceeds along the** following lines of reasoning: (1) that talent and the psychological types drawn to various talent domains can be localized in four quadrants of the brain; (2) that some kinds of talent are linked with various kinds of deficit and disease; (3) that psychological type and the ability quadrants of the brain they represent are also therefore related to deficit and disease; (4) that emphasis on any area of the brain depends on *cognition*, on what a person is thinking in order for the brain to be activated in that region; and (5) that *change* in disease risk may therefore require a change in thinking, a cognitive shift, away from a problematic mode. Individuation would suggest that a person might want to shift toward his typological blind spots to achieve this end.

Chapter 4 explores some etiologies of talent and notes that the essential sidedness of talent is probably determined very early on through an interplay of genetic, hormonal and environmental influences. This leads to concomitant risks for deficit and disorder that may not express themselves for many years. In the case of hormonal influences, for example, time of conception during the calendar year (maternal exposure to light) may play a role in deciding the level of exposure to fetal androgens, which in turn influence cognitive shifting in the developing brain and later indicators of these preferences such as handedness, talent predispositions and immune system functioning. The range of possibilities produces the verbal-nonverbal spectrum of talent and its associated deficits. The talent-deficit continuum that at first appears to be linear eventually becomes a circular model in keeping with the brain organization on which it is based and the Jungian concepts which define the dynamics of psychological type.

# CHAPTER FIVE
## TOWARD A MODEL OF THE RELATIONSHIPS BETWEEN TYPE, TALENT AND DISEASE

—————————— ✳ ✳ ✳ ——————————

In this chapter, a preliminary investigation is described that explores *possible* connections between psychological type, talent and disease. The study is included for the purposes of hypothesis building only, and does not represent definitive conclusions on the subject.

The study looks at the diseases that famous gifted people have contracted or died from, in order to assess the question of whether some talent domains are associated with some diseases more than others. Given that certain types are associated with some talent domains more than others, we postulate that the *talent*-disease relationships discovered in this small study may also suggest *type*-disease relationships. At the least, the study appears to suggest a relationship between *laterality* and disease, in which a person's dominant cognitive style is associated with tendencies for cardiovascular or immune dysfunction.

—————————— ✳ ✳ ✳ ——————————

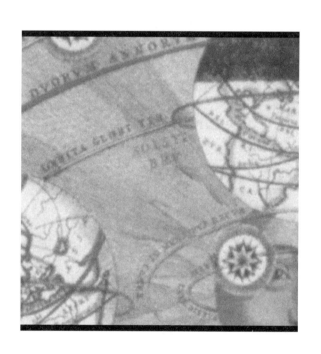

**For all the considerable literature** on type and its various applications, there is surprisingly little information on the possible relationships to disease. Yet the same instinct and laws of probability that tell us there might be other life in the universe, even though we cannot prove it at this stage, tell us that the personality and temperament that are so connected to the mind, which is so connected to the body, must also relate to, and perhaps even predict to some extent, disease. It is a leap of faith, to be sure, a belief without evidence that constitutes so much of human endeavor. But despite the intangibility, many of us "know," sense or believe that the relationship between type and disease is, like love, trust or God, simply there.

## Hypotheses

Three key studies give us important clues as to the disease patterns that might actually be hidden within the type table. Julia Fife, Thomas Carskadon and Michael Thorne of Mississippi State University (1986) were among the first to publish evidence that cardiovascular disease is more prevalent on the left side of the type table. Ernst Roberts and Dayton Young Roberts of Texas Tech University (1988) studied age-matched patients with coronary heart disease and provided additional support for the idea that heart disease may indeed be a problem specific to "Type A" personalities on the left side of the chart—particularly ISTJ and ESTJ in men, and SFs in women (Tables 19–20, page 130). Intuitive types in both these studies were noticeably under-represented. On the other hand, a study of allergies by Herman Staudenmayer and Murray Camazine (1989), at the Allergy Respiratory Institute of Colorado, inadvertently discovered more asthma, IgE documented allergy, gastrointestinal problems, dermatology problems, tension or migraine headaches (which have been suspected of being associated with stroke in later life), hypertension, and menstrual pain in their control group which was composed mainly of Intuitive types.

To this we can add indirect, more suspect associations such as that gifted chess players have been found to be predominantly Intuitive, especially INT (Kelly, 1984) and have often died early of stroke (Cranberg & Albert, 1988). We know that INFP is more likely than other types to have suicidal tendencies (Komosin, 1992), and that EP is apparently more prone to substance abuse (Luzader, 1984; Anchors & Dana, 1989) which might seem to put these groups at greater risk for diseases related to affective disorder and chemical dependency, e.g., certain kinds of cancer. Certainly Geschwind believed that talent and immune dysfunction go hand in hand, which would again suggest a propensity of immune problems on the right

**Table 19. Male Heart Patients (n = 71; Roberts & Roberts, 1988)**

| ISTJ | ISFJ | INFJ | INTJ |
|---|---|---|---|
| n = 21<br>29.58% | n = 11<br>15.49% | n = 0<br>0.00% | n = 1<br>1.41% |
| **ISTP**<br>n = 3<br>4.23% | **ISFP**<br>n = 3<br>4.23% | **INFP**<br>n = 0<br>0.00% | **INTP**<br>n = 2<br>2.82% |
| **ESTP**<br>n = 2<br>2.82% | **ESFP**<br>n = 1<br>1.41% | **ENFP**<br>n = 0<br>0.00% | **ENTP**<br>n = 3<br>4.23% |
| **ESTJ**<br>n = 14<br>19.72% | **ESFJ**<br>n = 6<br>8.45% | **ENFJ**<br>n = 0<br>0.00% | **ENTJ**<br>n = 4<br>5.63% |

**Table 20. Female Heart Patients (n = 50; Roberts & Roberts, 1988)**

| ISTJ | ISFJ | INFJ | INTJ |
|---|---|---|---|
| n = 5<br>10.00% | n = 9<br>18.00% | n = 0<br>0.00% | n = 0<br>0.00% |
| **ISTP**<br>n = 3<br>6.00% | **ISFP**<br>n = 8<br>16.00% | **INFP**<br>n = 1<br>2.00% | **INTP**<br>n = 0<br>0.00% |
| **ESTP**<br>n = 3<br>6.00% | **ESFP**<br>n = 4<br>8.00% | **ENFP**<br>n = 0<br>0.00% | **ENTP**<br>n = 0<br>0.00% |
| **ESTJ**<br>n = 3<br>6.00% | **ESFJ**<br>n = 12<br>24.00% | **ENFJ**<br>n = 1<br>2.00% | **ENTJ**<br>n = 1<br>2.00% |

side of the chart where many abstract artistic, mathematical and reasoning talents may tend to proliferate.

Looking at this extremely sketchy evidence alone then, a very general overall pattern might be that heart problems tend to be associated with SJ on the left of the type table, and stroke and immune or autoimmune disorders with N on the right. Continuing with the notion that the type table mirrors the brain in a sense—with the left side of the table approximating left-sided and posterior functions, and the right side of the table various right-sided and anterior functions—*we are very tentatively proposing that left-hemisphere and posterior cognition on the left side of the chart may be related to heart disease, and right-hemisphere and anterior cognition on the right side of the chart to immune dysfunction, particularly cancer, but also to stroke which has been linked to migraine, a peculiar form of immune problem.*

The research compendium *Portraits of Type*, compiled by Avril Thorne and Harrison Gough (1991) shows that Sensing is related to Introversion, Thinking and Judging, while Intuition is related to Extraversion, Feeling and Perceiving. The correlation between SN and JP scales, for example, is about 40 percent. Peter Harasym et al. (1996) at the University of Calgary, using factor analysis, actually collapsed N/P and S/J into one scale instead of two, which would further suggest that these apparently disparate traits might be related and perhaps even one and the same thing. So we would fine-tune our guess and further posit that *types tending toward I, S, T and J will be predisposed toward heart disease and stroke, as types tending toward E, N, F and P will be predisposed toward immune problems and stroke.* Stroke is listed for both sets since stroke can happen on both sides of the brain.

But how to prove such ideas in the absence of solid typological data? Clearly, there is a great need for extensive research into psychological type and disease—through the typing of patients with certain disorders, and the longitudinal investigation of health problems in random collections of types, particularly those distinguished by handedness, and so forth—but what do we do in the meantime? In the meantime, type researchers have an equally strong need for theory, hints of evidence, and reasonably well-documented hunches so as to convince authorities to allow and fund the work. These may be some of the functions of this book.

There are basically two ways of approaching the type-talent-disease problem—inductively, by doing studies, gathering bits of data and building a theory to explain them (the "bottom up" approach), and deductively, by first formulating a theory and then conducting studies to support or refute it (the "top down" approach). In actuality, all theory building is some of both, but what follows is mainly a step toward the latter.

Ideas here are based on the assumptions that (a) various kinds of cognition, as we have seen, tend to highlight certain localized areas of the brain when in operation; (b) certain types have specific cognitive gifts, highlight some areas of the brain more than others, and gravitate to occupations that allow their use (Myers & McCaulley, 1985); and (c) if a talent area or occupation can be shown to have a higher relative incidence of a particular disease, it follows that the predominant types, cognition and areas of the brain underlying that talent area *may* also be associated with greater risk for the disease. There are, of course, a myriad of other factors from heredity to diet that will also contribute, and which would have to be ruled out in controlled studies to convince ourselves of even a partial role of a typological factor. But for the sake of systematic hypothesis building, it is enough to draw out *possible* relationships so as to have a point of departure for future study. We are imagining, in other words.

One potential outcome of this kind of exercise is probably obvious—perhaps the use, one day, of the *Myers-Briggs Type Indicator®* (*MBTI®*) instrument as a 30-minute lifestyle screening tool, a laterality "balance indicator" as it were, to help in the identification of risk and perhaps even the prevention of disease. We can imagine the possibilities—a simple, reliable and nonjudgmental self-report instrument with half a century of research behind it, to complement various clinical assessments, to help pinpoint potential health problems in some areas and perhaps even reduce concern in others.

*If* it could be shown that Disease X, for example, is more common in Type Y or Temperament Z, the *Atlas of Type Tables* (Macdaid et al., 1986), so familiar to professional type users, could turn out to be a ready-made compendium of disease risks in occupations in North America from which health care practitioners, patients and well individuals could take their cue. Occupations and individual types at risk for heart disease, for example, would have demonstrable warning for taking the necessary preventative steps in diet and exercise, and practitioners would have type-specific and development-specific learning style tips on how best to coach them to do so.

Types at risk for cancer might take special precautions to avoid known causal agents such as cigarette smoke or ultraviolet radiation. People with genetically transmitted disorders in their lineage (e.g., Huntington's chorea, diabetes, schizophrenia) could perhaps assess their own particular risk relative to other personalities in the family. All other factors being equal, perhaps it is type and the cognition, attitudes, and orientation that go with it—past (SJ), present (SP) or future (N)—that actually tip the scales in favor of health or disease in some cases. What a comfort it might be to these people, well before the anticipated age at onset, to discover that Disease X is statistically rare within their own type category. This is all the largest of fantasies today, of course, but perhaps a very real possibility for the future, given enough research into such questions.

Why research another lifestyle inventory when so many already exist? Because few such measures have the psychometric checks and balances and the wealth of correlated information that the *MBTI* instrument has, at all age levels, in so many diverse realms of human endeavor. Few are so widely used, positive, holistic and predictable in a periodic table of people. But mostly, it simply makes sense that an instrument that has successfully helped people of diverse cultures and languages with so many aspects of daily living—from learning in schools to relationships to career choice—might also help patients and health care practitioners with matters of health and disease. This, by itself, would appear to be the essential reason for pursuing this line of questioning.

In a preliminary step toward that goal, a small descriptive study was undertaken to answer the question, *"Are there patterns in the diseases that famous gifted people have contracted or died from? Is there a higher incidence of a given disease in particular talent areas known to attract specific types?"* With each edition of the nightly news, we hear of a famous actor or Nobel prizewinner who has succumbed to this or that illness, and it seems wise to attempt to find order in this, if there is any order to be found, in the event it can provide clues to health maintenance in the rest of us. Perhaps it is time to begin to look for an organized system of *whole personalities and disease*—beyond the linking of disease with isolated traits like optimism or hostility—that could well have the predictability of a periodic table of elements.

Nine talent areas were chosen according to their prevalence in biographical literature and their relatedness to type and temperament categories. Famous and exceptionally talented people in business, sports, music, writing, science and mathematics, acting, political leadership, art, and chess were recorded by the diseases they contracted.

Rightly or wrongly, several assumptions were made as to the laterality of the chosen talents. We have demonstrated that music and art are right-lateralized activities (Chapter 3) and know that these talents tend to attract NF, particularly IN in the case of art (Myers & McCaulley, 1985). We have indicated that writing is likely a bilateralized activity (Chapter 3) and know that it has special appeal for NF and NT types. But because it is beyond our present scope and intentions to offer such extensive proofs for the remaining six talents, it will hopefully suffice to say that we believe business (T), science and mathematics (NT), politics (T) and chess (INT) to be predominantly left-lateralized activities because they require comparatively quiet, logical, linear, reflective, and impersonal analytic thinking involving words and numbers. We get sketchy hints of the type distribution in these talents from existing literature on these and related groups, e.g., that politicians, who are often trained lawyers, should show a preponderance of T (Appendix A, page 301). On the other hand, sports (SP/EP) and acting (EP) should be predominantly right-lateralized activities because of the greater emphasis on physical or social functioning in comparatively noisy, active, personal, emotional, flexible or spontaneous working environments. Further, those talents that involve strategizing, forward thinking or imagination (N) might be more anterior in the brain, while those involving calculation or physical activity might be more posterior (S). Talents that require some of both, such as science and math, may be bilateral talents much like writing.

Within the nine talent groupings, fifteen very general disease categories were defined according to the kinds of illnesses biographers record—heart, stroke, lung, kidney/urinary, psychiatric disorders (e.g., bipolar disorder), suicide, sensory disorders (e.g., blindness, deafness), AIDS, infectious disease other than AIDS, cancer, degenerative neurological disorders (e.g., MS, ALS), substance abuse, gut disorders, autoimmune disorders (e.g., arthritis, diabetes, allergies), and "other." Of these, cardio/cerebrovascular disease and cancer were given most attention because they are currently the biggest killers in North America. In Alberta, for example, coronary heart disease, lung cancer and stroke are the main diseases afflicting men; while for women they are coronary heart disease, breast cancer, and lung cancer. It is intriguing, therefore, that preliminary work by Eduardo Casas of the University of Ottawa suggests that Anglophone Canadian men tend toward NT, and women toward NF.

A total of 680 very well known talented people comprised the initial database in this small study. Great figures such as Howard Hughes, Babe Ruth, Beethoven, Henrik Ibsen, Albert Einstein, Audrey Hepburn, Lyndon Johnson, Paul Gauguin, and the great chess player Johannes Zukertort were compiled alongside the major diseases that killed them or seriously interfered with their lives. Accidental injury and death were not recorded, and the names were controlled only for talent category, and not for age at onset, gender, period of history and the like, which would have been extremely informative but beyond the scope of this initial hypothesis-building exploration. Names were selected from encyclopedias in print, and other specialized sources specific to a given talent area—such as Anne Sunnucks' (1970) *The*

*Encyclopedia of Chess*—according to whether or not the primary talent, disease process and other particulars were listed.

The size of the sample is exceedingly small by epidemiological standards, but perhaps of more acceptable size for hypothesis building in gifted populations that are often estimated at 3–5 percent of the general population. To achieve a more acceptable sample size, we would need to collect many Einsteins and Van Goghs, who are, of course, much harder to come by than large numbers of more "ordinary" scientists and artists, or cardiac patients. So for now, we accept a less-than-exceptional sample size of highly exceptional individuals and all the normal constraints and limitations that go along with that.

To compare these exceptional talent groups so collected in a statistically fair manner, a total of 360 names was then randomly drawn from the larger database—forty from each of the nine talent areas (Table 21)—and analyzed descriptively and inferentially using the statistical software SPSS (Statistical Package for the Social Sciences). Means and chi-square analyses were used to test the statistical significance, albeit limited, of the talent-disease distributions.

The results, described graphically, make the point quite clearly. Plotting the frequency of heart disease and stroke by talent group (Figure 25, page 136), we find that those talents that tend to require physically inactive, analytic thinking (politics, chess, NT)—in other words, those talents presumed to employ left-lateralized cognition or attract left-lateralized types—exhibit the highest incidence of disease, while those talents requiring the more active social or spatial activity of right laterality (acting, sports, EP/SP) have the lowest incidence. Heart disease and stroke affected 70 percent of the political leaders in the sample—such as Woodrow Wilson, Nelson Rockefeller, John Diefenbaker, Leonid Brezhnev, Lyndon Johnson, René Lévesque, and Charles De Gaulle—but only a scant 10 percent of the athletes.

Now this comes as no great surprise, since exercise is a well-known factor in the prevention of cardiovascular and cerebrovascular disease. But what is surprising is that cancer frequencies are precisely the opposite in these gifted people, with the left-lateralized talents of chess and business (T) having the lowest incidence of the disease, and the right-lateralized talents of acting (EP) and sports (SP), the highest, as in the case of Mario Lemieux, Ty Cobb and Casey Stengel (Figure 26, page 136). Indeed, no cancer deaths were to be found in the group of randomized chess players, in contrast to an incidence of more than 50 percent among randomized actors. The list of cancer deaths in actors is astonishingly long—Bette Davis, Audrey Hepburn, John Wayne, Rex Harrison, Humphrey Bogart, Yul Brynner, Spencer Tracy, Ingrid Bergman, to name just a few.

Similar apparently linear relationships between frequency of disease and talent laterality were found for other disease categories examined in this way. Stroke, lung disease, and infectious diseases other than AIDS all exhibited the same general pattern as for cardiovascular disease—namely, that the incidence was highest in talent groups presumed to be high in analytic processing, physical inactivity or introversion, and lowest in talent groups requiring social or spatial functioning, physical activity or extraversion (Appendix B, page 307). Political leaders, musicians, chess players and business people had the highest incidence of heart

**Table 21. Frequency of Disease by Talent Category (n = 360)**

### TALENT CATEGORY

| | L Laterality? Analytic, Inactive I-S-T-J Tendencies | | | Bilaterality? Spatial, Inactive | | | | R Laterality? Spatial, Social Active E-N-F-P Tendencies | |
|---|---|---|---|---|---|---|---|---|---|
| | Bus | Pol | Mus | Chess | Sci | Art | Writ | Act | Sport |
| Heart | 21 | 17 | 13 | 8 | 8 | 7 | 5 | 6 | 3 |
| Stroke | 3 | 11 | 8 | 6 | 5 | 5 | 6 | 1 | 1 |
| Senses | - | - | 1 | 3 | 2 | 1 | - | - | - |
| Infectious (Excl. AIDS) | 1 | - | 1 | 3 | 5 | 7 | 2 | - | - |
| Alcohol/ Drugs | - | - | 3 | 2 | - | 1 | - | - | 3 |
| Suicide | - | - | 1 | 1 | - | 3 | 3 | - | - |
| Lung | 3 | 1 | 2 | 7 | 3 | 3 | 10 | 2 | 1 |
| Kidney | 1 | 1 | - | 2 | 2 | 1 | 1 | 2 | - |
| Psych. | - | - | - | 3 | 1 | 2 | 3 | - | 1 |
| Degen. Neuro. | - | 1 | - | - | 2 | 1 | 1 | 2 | - |
| Gut | - | - | - | 1 | - | 1 | 1 | 2 | 1 |
| Cancer | 8 | 7 | 10 | - | 9 | 3 | 7 | 21 | 12 |
| Immun. (Arth., Diab., Allergy) | 1 | 1 | 1 | 2 | - | 3 | - | - | 13 |
| AIDS | - | - | - | - | - | 1 | - | 3 | 4 |
| Other | 2 | 1 | - | 2 | 3 | 1 | 1 | 1 | 1 |
| Total n | 40 | 40 | 40 | 40 | 40 | 40 | 40 | 40 | 40 |

disease. Stroke was highest in politicians, musicians and chess players (N) and affected people like Menachem Begin, Joseph Stalin, Lenin, Richard Nixon, Franklin Roosevelt, Woodrow Wilson, Bach, Verdi, Sibelius, Mendelssohn, Prokofiev, and great chess players like Jose Capablanca, Paul Morphy, Harry Pillsbury, and Johannes Zukertort. Writers such as Franz Kafka, John Keats, Marcel Proust, Henry David Thoreau and Leo Tolstoy had the highest incidence of lung disease—have writers smoked more, perhaps, than other groups?—and artists, scientists and mathematicians the highest incidence of infection like meningitis, typhoid fever or cholera (Frank Tenney Johnson, Camille Pissarro, Georges Seurat, Georges Cuvier, Wilbur Wright, Benjamin Rush).

Having the same general profile as for cancer are the patterns for diseases of the digestive system, AIDS, autoimmune disease and degenerative neurological disease (Appendix B, page 307). The numbers here, with the exception of cancer and autoimmune disease, are almost

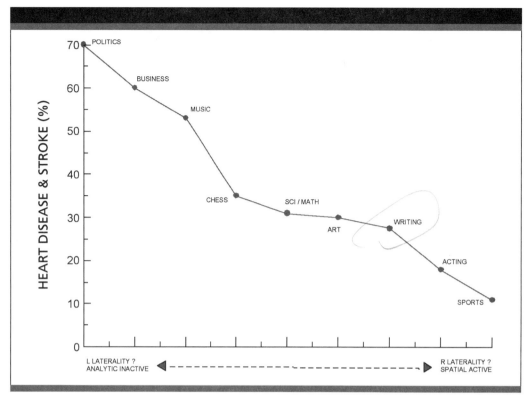

**Figure 25. Incidence of Heart Disease and Stroke in Nine Talent Areas**

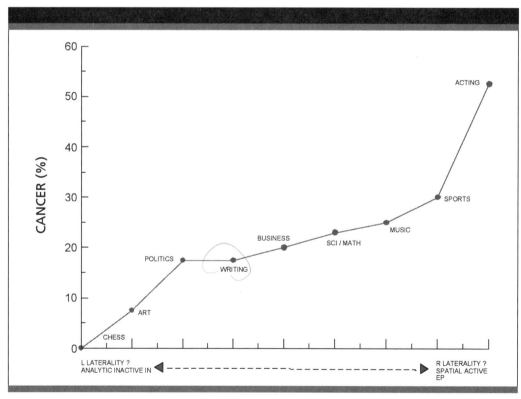

**Figure 26. Incidence of Cancer in Nine Talent Areas**

meaninglessly small yet the same principle appears to apply—that the incidence of these disorders is more prevalent in talent groups presumed to employ social or spatial functioning, physical activity, extraversion or intuition.

Gut disease, including ulcers—which we now know to be associated with the overactivity of bacteria (immune processes) rather than stomach acid—was highest in actors like Rudolph Valentino. HIV/AIDS was highest in actors like Rock Hudson and athletes like Magic Johnson, and autoimmune diseases such as arthritis, diabetes, asthma and other allergies were most prevalent in athletes like Sandy Koufax and Joe Namath. Degenerative neurological diseases such as MS, ALS and Alzheimer's disease were most common in actors such as David Niven and Ronald Reagan, and also scientists and mathematicians like Stephen Hawking. Nephrological disorders are unusual in that chess players, actors, mathematicians and scientists like Benjamin Franklin, Jacques Brandenberger and Jean Harlow—talent groups which may have physically inactive *spatial* functioning in common—have the highest incidence of such disease.

There are very significant problems here pertaining to the definition of disease, which is purely under the control of biographers who may or may not be qualified to comment on such things. There are problems concerning disease etiology and history—is it reasonable to consider AIDS alongside other communicable diseases through history when AIDS has only been recognized in recent decades? There are problems of treatment variability—would the person have been so vulnerable to a particular disease by today's standards if antibiotics, for instance, had been available in his lifetime? There are problems of talent definition—should an Elvis Presley be placed in the same talent category as a Bach?

There are also problems of changing type patterns over time, in various fields. There are problems with occupational hazards that are present for some talents and not others, e.g., radiation exposure in scientists like Marie Curie. There are problems associated with making across-the-board cross-cultural comparisons that ignore age, gender and so on. Be that as it may, we can maintain that it would be unethical *not* to consider the possibility that there could be an emerging trend here—that disease *may* be related in some way to the predominant cognition and laterality of various talents.

A statistical analysis of disease frequency in this sample by presumed talent laterality (Table 22, Figure 27, page 138) also suggests such a relationship. Talents presumed to be predominantly left-lateralized, such as business, politics, chess, science and math, have a comparatively high incidence of heart disease, while the bilateral talent category of writing has a relatively high incidence of lung disease, and the right-lateralized talents of acting, music and sports, cancer. The distribution in the chi-square analysis is sufficiently different and dependent to warrant further study ($\chi^2$ = 71.37, df 30, p<.001). An additional analysis attending to the need for cell size to be greater than five—an analysis of presumed talent laterality by disease rating—again suggests a significant relationship between talent area and disease expression ($\chi^2$ = 23.43, df 8, p<.01).

Striking as these suggestions may be, it is observations of our musicians (Table 21, page 135) that are most intriguing, and perhaps most hopeful for the future of disease prevention.

**Table 22. Incidence of Disease by Talent Laterality\* (n = 360)**

| | TALENT LATERALITY (%) | | |
| --- | --- | --- | --- |
| DISEASE | Left | Bilateral | Right |
| Heart | 38 | 15 | 18 |
| Stroke | 16 | 15 | 11 |
| Infectious (excl. AIDS) | 5 | 5 | 6 |
| Kidney | 3 | 3 | 3 |
| Senses | 2 | - | 3 |
| | | | |
| Lung | 7 | 23 | 8 |
| Psychiatric | 1 | 8 | 3 |
| Suicide | 1 | 5 | 3 |
| Degenerative Neurological | 3 | 3 | 2 |
| Gut | - | 3 | 3 |
| | | | |
| Cancer | 19 | 20 | 23 |
| Immune (Arthritis, Diabetes, Allergies) | 1 | - | 10 |
| AIDS | - | - | 4 |
| Alcohol/Drugs | - | - | 5 |

\* Presumed Talent Laterality: Left (Politics, Business, Chess, Science, Math), Bilateral (Writing), Right (Acting, Music, Art, Sports). Total n: Left = 121, Bilateral = 40, Right = 199, e.g., 38% of 121 individuals with left-lateralized talents had heart disease, 23% of 40 individuals with bilateral talent had lung disease, 23% of 199 individuals with right-lateralized talent had cancer.

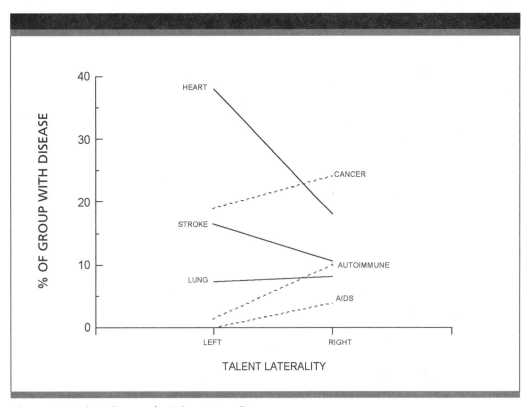

**Figure 27. Major Diseases by Talent Laterality**

Here, heart disease is the number one killer, affecting over 30 percent of the sample, and ranking the musicians third to the politician and business groups, ahead of all the other possibilities, including the left-lateralized talents of chess, science and math. Here we have John Mellencamp (who survived), Roy Orbison, Bobby Darin, Karen Carpenter, Elvis Presley, Charles Mingus, Hank Williams, Jim Morrison, Harry Chapin, and many others.

Critics might challenge that many of the heart attacks in these musicians were drug-induced, or were in some other way lifestyle-related, and are therefore not necessarily related to the occupation or the thinking per se. But perhaps we can answer them by noting that (a) heart disease and stroke were also prevalent among great composers who presumably didn't use street drugs—Richard Wagner, John Philip Sousa, Leopold Stravinsky, Giuseppe Verdi, Jean Sibelius, J. S. Bach, George Friedrich Handel, Felix Mendelssohn, and so forth—and that (b) substance abuse and addiction are more common in our athlete group, yet heart disease (less than 10%), is not as much of a factor for them, unlike cancer (30%). So perhaps the doing of the talent, or the types or lifestyle attracted to the talent, are indeed related.

Singer-songwriter Billy Joel, commenting on the essence of music, once said, "It's the heart, it's the ears, it's the groin. And a little bit of the stomach, sometimes" (*Calgary Herald*, March 11, 1994). He names the chest, head, and lower abdomen here. So it is perhaps of interest that the diseases afflicting our musician group are first heart and stroke (over 50 percent), then cancer of the lower abdomen (25 percent). The reference to ears may also be important in that so many great figures in music, art, science and chess had sensory impairments of one kind or another—deafness in Beethoven, Robert Schumann and Homer Watson, blindness and other vision problems in Camille Pissarro, James Thurber, Bach, Handel, Stevie Wonder, Ray Charles. Among chess players, there are many examples of this—Eileen Tranmer losing her hearing, Richard Teichmann and Theodore Tylor their sight, and so on. And earlier (chapter 4) we noted how myopia has also been associated with exceptional mathematical ability (Benbow, 1988).

To the extent that we do not find sensory deficits in our athletes or actors—not at all, in fact—we can suggest that sensory impairment is more likely a problem associated with left-lateralized talents which may be reflected in impaired eyes and ears on one side more often than the other, the severity perhaps dependent on the *degree* of left-sidedness in a person's life. Sunnucks (1970) notes that "Chess is the *introvert's* football" (emphasis added) and that many chess players, whom we know to be predominantly INT, are also mathematicians or musicians, which hints that all these sensory-impaired people might have Introversion in common. It seems clear that they do neglect some aspects of Sensing—perhaps the visual sense in musicians, the auditory in artists—which, as we have discussed (chapter 4), may have been responsible in some cases for the development of their Intuitive talents in the first place.

Nevertheless, according to our original hypothesis, music, as a right-lateralized group, should not have such a high incidence of heart disease. So why does it?

As we will recall, musical cognition is one very clear case—we have PET scan pictures to support it (Mazziotta and Phelps, 1985)—where the processing involved in the doing of the talent shifts from the right side to the left as a result of training (chapter 3). The person starts out appreciating musical wholes, unable to read or dissect music (right hemisphere), and progresses to ever-deeper levels of naming, reading, counting and analysis (left hemisphere) with guidance. As a result, what starts out as a right-sided talent becomes ever more left-sided, and with that, for the serious musician, may come increased risk for diseases perhaps associated with left-sided functioning. We also saw that art becomes more right-sided with experience—left-hemisphere brain damage has very little effect on an artist's work (Gardner & Winner, 1981)—which might explain why our artists do not exhibit the high incidence of heart disease that the musicians do but instead have a comparatively high rate of infection (Table 21, page 135).

Thus the musicians are key to an eminently flexible and therefore exciting concept of the relationship between type, talent and disease which holds that, yes, *certain types and talents may indeed run inherently greater risks of contracting certain diseases, but that it may be possible to alter those risks by gradually encouraging a shift toward a contralateral cognitive activity or less preferred type function.* Implicit in this is, as we have said, that too much of a good thing can be a bad thing: "If the string is too tight, it will snap. If it's too slack/loose, it will not play" (Siddhartha, the Buddha).

Carrying this a step further, we can wonder if it is even remotely possible that focused, analytic and introverted activity, such as that found in the playing of chess, could have the preventative or healing benefits for cancer or other immune disorders that the less focused, physical and extraverted activity of playing sports has for heart disease? Our success at questioning, researching and/or accomplishing these feats may ultimately determine the degree of balance we attain in our lives and perhaps even our overall health.

For want of better names, the two predominant systems proposed above will be referred to as the *"Cardiovascular" and "Immune" patterns*, respectively. The Cardiovascular pattern (heart, stroke, lung disease, infection) is hypothesized to represent left-lateralized or posterior-lateralized cognition and/or types tending toward I, S, T or J (hereafter written as "I-S-T-J" tendencies). The Immune pattern (cancer, stroke, gastrointestinal disease, AIDS, autoimmune disease, degenerative neurological disease) is hypothesized to represent right-lateralized or anterior-lateralized cognition and/or types tending toward E, N, F or P ("E-N-F-P" tendencies). *We note that both patterns include stroke since stroke can happen on both sides of the brain.* Now this is not to suggest that the above disorders are restricted to ISTJ or ENFP *types*, or that they cannot be associated with reverse lateralities, only to say that they are likely more common with preferences for I,S,T or J, or with preferences for E,N,F or P, in these directions, as was the case for cognitive skills (chapter 3).

As Jung conceived originally, and as Harasym et al. (1995) have demonstrated statistically, E–I, S–N and T–F may be the most important scales to consider in assessing an individual's true type. If, as we have indicated, IT has predominantly left-sided positioning in the brain, EF right-sided, N right and anterior, and S left and posterior, any two of these scales might predict an individual's relative predisposition for Cardiovascular or Immune patterns. For example, we might suggest that IST (three scales left-sided) and EST (two scales left-sided) will be at greater risk for the Cardiovascular pattern, ENT (two scales right-sided) and INF (two scales right-sided) *for the Immune pattern. Adding the fourth scale (J–P), we could propose that types like ESFJ and INTP* (two scales left, two scales right) will have interests in bilateral talents like writing, and that their risk for either of the two patterns will also be roughly equally distributed. Jung himself was an INTP writer/scientist (two preferences left, two preferences right) who died following two strokes. Isabel Myers was an INFP writer/scientist (three preferences right) who died of cancer.

In effect, then, we are proposing that *the incidence or probability of disease, like giftedness, is proportionate to the degree of native talent laterality*, which can be indexed by handedness scales, subtests of standard intelligence tests, sophisticated electronic technologies like EEG, and perhaps even the sub-scales of a popular instrument like the *MBTI* instrument. *Natural laterality and its associated disease risks are then compounded or modified by various kinds of cognition that are performed over long periods of time.*

Under this system, the naturally left-lateralized person is ultimately threatened by excessive left-sided cognition, which tips the scales, but is helped by right-sided cognition, which restores the balance. Similarly, the naturally right-lateralized person is threatened by excessive right-sided cognition but is helped by left-sided cognition. The naturally anterior-lateralized person is threatened by excessive anterior cognition, but is helped by posterior cognition. Thus, if this notion is correct, extremes of laterality should exhibit extremes of disease expression—either very high or very low frequencies—and "bilateral" groups, such as writers and ambi-handers, should exhibit moderate rates. Bilateral groups should effectively split the risk for Cardiovascular and Immune patterns, and may even be the most stable of groups—in a physical sense, if not a psychological one. The Old Testament put it another way:

> Get wisdom, get understanding: forget it not . . . My son, attend to my words; incline thine ear unto my sayings . . . For they are life unto those that find them, and health to all their flesh. Keep thy heart with all diligence, for out of it are the issues of life . . . *Turn not to the right hand, nor to the left* (Proverbs 4, emphasis added).

We are well acquainted with cardiologists Friedman and Rosenman's (1974) term, the "Type A" personality, for characters most at risk for coronary heart disease. Such people are said to be impatient, aggressive, often highly competitive, and prone to outbursts of hostility—in a word, perhaps T, specifically TJ, as one type study discovered (Spencer et al., 1986). We may also recall from the same work the Type B personality who is said to be, in contrast, patient, non-competitive, and having a comparatively placid exterior and lower risks of heart disease.

We might be collectively less aware, however, of psychiatrist Steven Greer's profile of the cancerous Type C personality—compliant, unassertive, nice to a fault, cooperative, well-behaved, prone to depressive moods and, above all, to suppression of feelings, most especially anger. In such a person, there is often a significant loss and a profound sense of hopelessness, alienation and despair preceding tumor development. Even before that, there is a long history of pleasing others to the neglect of the individual's own desires and of holding in needs, frustrations and anger to avoid troubling people (Dreher, 1988)—in a word, perhaps F, possibly introverted F. A study using the Minnesota Multiphasic Personality Inventory (MMPI) found that cancer deaths were associated with high scores on the MMPI Depression scale (Dreher, 1988), which we know correlates moderately (0.39) with the Introversion scale of the *MBTI* instrument (Myers & McCaulley, 1985).

As a consequence, the Type C cancer personality is "the polar opposite of the Type A behavior pattern which has been demonstrated to be predictive of coronary heart disease," (Dreher, 1988: 256) and which has been characterized as the receiver of repression (C) and the emitter of repression (A), respectively. The Type B personality, which is calm but not unduly depressed, angry or competitive beneath the surface, has less of both problems and would seem to be somewhere in between. So, Types A and C could represent laterality extremes of T and F, among other things, while Type B could be the bilateral compromise that is the healthier state. To the extent that hostile cardiac patients can learn to channel their aggression in healthful pursuits, and cancer patients with a fighting spirit who gripe, complain and "misbehave" can recover more often and more swiftly than "good" patients (Dreher, 1988; LeShan, 1977), there would seem to be much hope for the use of contralateral shifting in healing and prevention.

## Anecdotal Evidence

Let us consider a few anecdotes in illustrating the trends implicit in these data. There is Ron, an ISTJ, who sits at his desk reading, writing and contemplating for long periods, and over time develops a circulatory problem in his leg, which requires surgery. Brad, an ISFJ in a similar work setting, acquires a similar condition and also has surgery to correct it. John, another ISTJ, has elevated blood pressure and exercises regularly to reduce it.

Tom, an ISTJ, writes continually for three months and develops a duodenal ulcer. David, an INTJ epitomizing the critical thinker, has a sluggish lower bowel. Donna, an INFJ doctoral student of religious studies, has the same problem. Warren, an INTP, analyzes and writes for long periods and develops a persistent kidney infection. Jane, an INTJ, works hard in her math class, and develops unbearable menstrual cramps, which are helped by eating and heat. Elise, another INTJ, notices burning urination when she writes and thinks for long periods. Roy, an INTJ, works too hard in his business and develops lower back problems. Robert, an ISTJ, has had a growth removed from the prostate gland, and Bill, an INTJ, is recovering from prostate cancer.

The Old Testament notes that "A wise man's heart is at his right hand" (Ecclesiastes 10: 2). In these few examples of people who happen to be right-handed, circulatory problems and health difficulties in the lower parts of the body have emerged in types well known for their focusing abilities, and especially during or following intense periods of excessive left-sided activity, such as that involved in the physically inert activities of reading, writing, concentrating and analyzing.

On the other side of our abstracted fence, there is Natalie, an ENFP, who has experienced a thyroid episode, temporary sore throats with work anxiety, and an immune deficiency. Douglas, an ENTJ, worries about support payments and develops a "cold" that hangs on so long his physician thinks it is mononucleosis. Teresa, an Extravert, has had a growth removed from her thyroid. Glenda, another Extravert, has had a malignant growth removed.

Rose, another ENFP, worries in her noisy, active work environment and gets recurrent one-sided headaches which disappear when she goes home. Natalie, Rose, Ellen and Janet, all ENFPs, have recurrent neck problems and appreciate the benefits of chiropractic treatments. Sandra, an ENTP, suffers migraine headaches after exercise classes. Bob, an ESTP, suffers recurrent joint problems, herpes simplex and tension headaches after driving long distances. Carol, an Extraverted athlete, is completely deaf in one ear. Mitchell, an elderly Extraverted writer, has a cancer that has gone into remission.

In these contrasting examples then, in which two of the individuals are left-handed, immune problems and problems in the upper parts of the body have emerged in types generally less known for their focusing abilities, or during and after periods of excessive right-sided activity, such as might happen with the spatial, social, physical or emotional activities of driving, working in a group, playing sports, or worrying. None of these people has had to deal with these problems as they sit at a desk.

Lest it begin to look as if we're trying to paint a frozen still-life of particular diseases in specific types, we should also describe some individual cases that illustrate an apparent motility and shiftability of some disease states, which might one day be shown to be very much like the shifting that takes place with music training.

*A compensation model of the disease process may go something like this. The patient starts out healthy enough, and then overexerts himself using his dominant preferences in one area of the brain, to the relative exclusion of functions on the contralateral side.* (The whole brain is at work at all times, to be sure, but we will accept the possibility that some areas are emphasized more than others in the expression of certain traits.) *He becomes stressed, the brain then "tilts" in the direction of the inferior functions to compensate for the indulgences, and the patient develops an apposing set of problems. He gets sick. He may recover (i.e., reach physical homeostasis) when he purposely or accidentally achieves psychological and physical balance. He may also not recover if he does not make the shift,* if he stays rooted in one kind of thought process, which is often but not always a negativistic one. Clearly, there is less need for kickback to the inferior function, less need for the drastic rebalancing measures of compensation, if the person is cognitively balanced to begin with. Again, we must point out there is absolutely no proof for this notion, only hypothesized principles which, if they could be shown to exist, might very well offer tremendous hope for the future of disease prevention and health maintenance.

Ruth, as one example of the shifting that may take place, was a well-mannered and analytically minded teacher, likely Introverted, who suffered a left-sided stroke which caused her to lose her speech and control of her urinary and bowel functions, the corollary there being that her left hemisphere mediated her language, self-control, and elimination processes to some extent. With the left side of the brain effectively disabled through brain damage, the balance scales tipped toward the right, and she exhibited less social anxiety, less awareness for social conventions generally, decreased immune function, and she eventually died of pneumonia. So, what started out as normal left-sided type preferences and normal left-sided inhibition of primal functions like elimination, shifted right as a result of a stroke, altered her personality, and caused her to become suddenly vulnerable to the immune problems that may or may not be associated with the right hemisphere and loss of the left. Moreover, the infection she succumbed to was an upper body problem of the kind described in our earlier examples.

A grieving person may go through a similar process. The loss of an object of great affection and personal value—whether a person, marriage, pet or job—produces depression, anxiety and a rightward shift that increases vulnerability to immune disease, like infection. As a result, the grieving person often becomes ill himself, possibly to recover only when he has adapted to the loss, looks at things more rationally and regains a leftward balance.

A contrasting example illustrating a shift in the other direction is Jerome who was an active, social Extraverted businessman who lived with diabetes for much of his life. He developed gangrene in his left foot, which was about to be removed when he suffered a heart attack from great pre-operative anxiety; an ensuing diabetic coma eventually killed him. In this instance, then, a man started out with normal right-sided preferences which increased his risk for autoimmune disease that weakened physiology on the left side of the body, including the foot and the heart. In the end, a stressful leftward shift toward his Introverted inferior functions produced decreased cardiac function, and he died of a heart problem that may or may not be associated with left-sided cognitive functioning.

How often has it happened to us that we work and work, studying perhaps (heightened left-sided activity), while fighting off the common cold (immune dysfunction)? And then as soon as the exam is over, we relax and socialize with friends (shift to right-sided activity) and come down with the cold! For some disease states, resting—as in retirement, for example—may not be the best thing a person can do. In cardiac patients, for example, once the condition has stabilized, the first advice physicians often give them is to get active and exercise—that is, to nonverbalize and shift right—and if they'd only done that to begin with, we can wonder whether they would have ever contracted the problem in the first place.

But in most other disease states, rest is absolutely essential. Brett Hull, a gifted hockey player with one of the best goal-scoring records in the National Hockey League (right-sided activity) developed what has been called a "yuppie" disease, Epstein-Barr syndrome (immune dysfunction), and left the game temporarily to recover. Mario Lemieux, another gifted hockey player, developed Hodgkin's disease after a particularly active and successful goal-scoring period in his career. He, too, decreased his level of physical activity to undergo treatment for the disease, is said to have done a lot of reflection in that time (left-sided activity), and didn't return to the game until it was felt the disease was largely under control.

Terry Fox, on the other hand, was a long-distance runner with tremendous spirit and persistence, as well as ineffable courage. He didn't slow down following removal of a leg from cancer and set out on a charity run across the country. He never made it. Tragically, the cancer returned and effectively forced him to stop and rest after only a third of the distance, and he died of a metastasized cancer as a very young man. Canada was heartbroken. Certainly this is not at all to discount existing theories of disease remission, only to suggest that, *additionally*, type in combination with the activity levels that are associated with a type's cognition may be a factor—the energy that the Introvert gets, for example, from quiet, physically inactive internal stimulation, and the energy the Extravert gets from social and physical interactions with the external environment.

It is well known that physical activity (right-sided) is a critical factor in the prevention of certain cardiac problems (left-sided), and physical inactivity and rest (left-sided) in the treatment of immune problems (right-sided). Many heart attack victims take up carefully monitored aerobic programs, while flu and headache patients are usually told to "rest and drink plenty of fluids." In the latter case, perhaps it is not only the absence of physical activity that helps, but also the replacement kinds of cognition we do while we lie around resting— we may read, reflect, contemplate, analyze and think as we sit there doing "nothing," all of which is the concentrated left-sided activity we saw in our earlier examples. Purposeful shifting, in other words, might actually help make us well.

In retirement, then, exercise, rest and relaxation may have very different effects on different types. Golf, ballroom dancing and other physical activity may be very beneficial to the person with heart trouble, for example, because it forces him to shift right and correct for the imbalance of the inactive left. But precisely the same activities might be detrimental to the right-sided thinker who may already be unbalanced, as it were, in the direction of the active right, and it may put him at risk for an immune disorder of one kind or another, when the intent all along was to help him relax so as to keep him well.

A reductionist and likely much oversimplified version of the underlying lateralization of health and disease might be that *left-hemisphere activity offers some immune protection but cardiac vulnerability, while right-hemisphere activity offers some cardiac protection but immune vulnerability. Since neither endpoint of this continuum is desirable—illness and death are at both ends of it—the object for each of us must be to attempt to strike a balance between these extremes by stressing our less preferred modes of cognition in an effort to move toward the "middle."* As type theory instructs us, complete transfers are probably not possible, perhaps because of the basic sidedness we're born with. But the Introvert can try to socialize more, the Sensing type to imagine more, the Thinking type to feel more, the Perceiving type to get better organized, and so forth, not only to integrate oneself with the rest of a typologically diverse community, but also to integrate oneself with the rest of one's Self in the creation of a healthy whole. Cognition of all kinds, not just of the positive variety—inner, outer, sensory, imaginative, rational, emotional, linear and structured, or non-linear and unstructured—may have enormous prophylactic and healing benefits we have hitherto ignored.

Naomi Quenk (1993) believes that the inferior function of a type surfaces when the person is fatigued, stressed or ill. That is, largely external "trigger events" cause the person to shift in the direction of the inferior function, which is then acted out in grossly exaggerated fashion because he or she is not accustomed to functioning in that way. Here again is the suggestion that fatigue, stress and disease are related to underuse, or at least to an uncommon occurrence, which forces the person to activate less familiar quarters of the brain. This raises the possibility that *practice* may make the shift less traumatic. Like the Introvert who practices public-speaking (E) so as to lessen the shock when called upon to speak, or the Intuitive type who learns to exercise (S) so as to avoid fatigue climbing stairs, perhaps all types need purposeful practice in their less preferred modes so as to increase the balance of functions and buffer any unexpected shifts and transitions in those directions.

Perhaps even marrying a typological opposite, much as it might occasionally be psychologically difficult, may have the effect of encouraging practice in less preferred modes, thereby pulling each partner toward the middle, magnetizing and depolarizing the system to keep both partners healthy. Should one of them leave, the system destabilizes and one or both of them may develop a physical malady. But what might this mean for couples of identical or similar type? Could it be that these people are psychologically comfortable but physically at greater risk because both of them tend to neglect the same kinds of processes?

Perhaps even a job that requires a person to use her less preferred functions—such as an ENFP in accounting, or an INTP in teaching—may also have a balancing effect with practice, even though career counseling with type tacitly recommends that the individual seek out like-minded work environments. Loved ones may then take over where the job leaves off. The Introvert who sits quietly all day at work may do more of it at night and risk heart disease were it not for Extraverted partners and friends who demand that he play or socialize with them. The Sensing type may likewise get stuck in a dangerous workaholic rut were it not for the Intuitive type who sees other possibilities and room for change. Much as we may not like it, cognitive stretching in the direction of our inferior functions, or in any direction contralateral to the functions we're performing excessively, may actually be good for us.

Type theory maintains that stress usually occurs when we are forced to stretch beyond our typological comfort zones, implying that we risk disease when we do this. However, we would expand this notion by suggesting that it is the continued absence of such stretching that puts us at risk by causing our minds to rigidly ignore certain modes of thinking and feeling that in turn underemphasize certain parts of our bodies. As a result, when stress does force us in an unusual direction, we are comparatively inexperienced, both cognitively and physically, in coping with the change and the body rebels. The athlete who never reads or the party animal who never reflects may therefore be just as much the time bomb as the workaholic who never exercises or the thinker who can't relate to people, simply because they continue to emphasize some states of mind, even good ones, to the neglect of other states of mind that are very likely positively connected in some way to physiology.

We can consider, for example, a condition like headache—exertion headache, tension headache and perhaps even migraine—which may very well be related to excessive right-sided activity, such as running too hard, driving, emoting or contending with too much social activity at work or at play. We can suggest, therefore, that the treatment should perhaps not involve visual relaxation techniques by themselves, since that entails even more right-sided activity, but may instead require quiet, complicated, analytical thinking because that will promote a shift to the left. "Rest and take two aspirin" could well become something like "Rest and read two essays," or "Rest and do your algebra," as initially ridiculous as that must sound!

A syllogism makes us take this more seriously (the symbol * means "is associated with"):

If N * Artistic Talent
Artistic Talent * R Laterality (Left-Handedness), Immune Disorders
Immune Disorders * Migraine
A Suspicion that Migraine * Stroke (Mostly Left Hemisphere)
Then, N * Immune Disorders, Migraine, Stroke
(Coren, 1993; Geschwind & Behan, 1982; Myers & McCaulley, 1985)

The *Canadian Journal of Neurological Sciences* says that 16 percent of Canadians suffer from migraines in a given year (29 percent from tension headaches), 50,000 from stroke. Similarly, 15 percent of our randomized artist group (N) suffered strokes, as compared to less than 5 percent of the athlete group (S), and earlier we noted (chapter 3) how comparatively easy it is to find descriptions in the literature of musicians who have had left-sided strokes, but not right-sided ones. In point of fact, most strokes happen in the middle cerebral artery of the left hemisphere (Kolb & Whishaw, 1985), which might suggest that strokes in people with right-lateralized talents may be more often precipitated by neglect of the left hemisphere as a result of preferred or excessive activity on the right, e.g., N. If this were true—and we repeat that this is all mere conjecture—then perhaps it is possible to help prevent stroke in such people by working to increase left-sided capacities, e.g., S. Of course, in doing so, they may trade one risk for another—perhaps heart disease, or stroke on the other side—but it is also possible that balance will be attained through such an effort so that both risks are actually reduced.

The same could hold true for some allergies. Exercise-induced asthma, for instance, like headache, would also appear to be a nonverbally induced (right hemisphere) disease state that flares up with physical exertion, heavy breathing and anxiety in cold or dry environments believed to contain allergens. An episode happens more rarely with quiet inactivity (left hemisphere)—it is not called "contemplation-induced asthma"—and that is precisely what an attack forces a patient to do to bring it under control. He gets away from the crowd, sits down and visibly concentrates on slowing his breathing. So, intense right-sided activity and neglect of left-sided functions such as Introversion may contribute to some autoimmune problems as well, which may also be managed to some extent by purposeful shifting in a leftward direction.

In this regard, we can observe Heather, an INTP whose allergies act up at Spruce Meadows equestrian events. Horse dander is unquestionably a troublesome allergen, but perhaps we should also consider the crowds and the anxiety (Extraversion, right hemisphere) such affairs may present to INTPs who might rather be elsewhere; Heather's problem improves when she goes home (Introversion, left). Another Introvert, Tom, an ISTJ, skis and socializes for four days (Extraversion, right) and has a bad asthmatic reaction that is corrected by resting at home for a week (Introversion, left). Brad, an ISFJ, has asthma attacks when there is office conflict (Extraversion, right), which he deals with by shutting the door and getting away from it all (Introversion, left). Jane, an INTJ, whose episodes are triggered while playing sports and getting silently angry with a coach (right), is helped by sitting down and verbalizing her grievances (left), rather than suppressing them. Sherry, an ESFJ, gets hay fever and hives when she spends summer vacations with relatives who make her feel anxious (Extraversion, right); once again, the symptoms improve when she goes home (Introversion, left), away from the allergens, certainly, *and* the social activity.

As we can see with the Extravert in the last example, it may not be simply a case of allowing Introverts to be Introverts so as to avoid stress and allergic reactions, but of allowing a cognitive shift to take place in a direction that carries the patient, whether Introvert or Extravert, away from an allergenic mode. In the above examples, hypoallergenic cognition might appear to be leftward moving, which makes sense if there is an association between right-sided functioning, left-sided neglect, and autoimmune difficulties of the order we saw in our athletes. Collectively, autoimmune diseases affected nearly 35 percent of that group.

We reaffirm our hypotheses, then, with the proposition that *disease occurs where an area of the brain is underutilized, the corollary being that we must "use it or lose it," emphasize it and use it, and "live in the Shadow," at least to some extent, in order to achieve a healthful balance.* Or, as actress Helen Hayes once put it, "If you rest, you rust," characteristically doing neither herself and passing away in her sleep at the age of ninety-two. The New Testament makes the same point:

> We cannot do without the parts of the body that seem to be weaker; and those parts that we think aren't worth very much are the ones which we treat with greater care . . . God himself put the body together in such a way as to give greater honor to those parts that need it. And so there is no division in the body, but all its different parts have the same concern for one another. If one part of the body suffers, all the other parts suffer with it; if one part is praised, all the other parts share its happiness (I Corinthians 12: 22-26).

Even in epilepsy, there would appear to be evidence that trouble happens when an area of the brain isn't active:

> Although one is struck by the wide range of factors that may precipitate seizures, one consistent feature is that the brain is most epileptogenic when it is relatively inactive and the patient is sitting still (Kolb & Whishaw, 1985: 125).

Could it be that epilepsy is more prevalent in Introverts who are likely more often the types sitting still? Could epilepsy possibly be helped by action-oriented shifts to the right, as

Oliver Sacks' Parkinson's patients in the movie *Awakenings* were chemically helped to do? Or what of mitral valve prolapse patients—mainly women with an anatomical anomaly on the left side of the heart, toward the left side of the body, who are "well-educated," "hypervigilant" and who "never have energy" (Frederickson, 1988)? Physical conditioning has been shown to help them lead more active lives. Could this, too, be an example of an underactive right hemisphere that is helped by a purposeful shift to the right? We cannot begin to know the answers to these and other questions without a great deal of research into the whole field of the sidedness of cognition and its relationship to disease.

In the meantime, we can think of the biases there may be in existing studies of disease, which do not take the spectrum of psychological types into account. Heart studies overwhelmingly investigate men, which means there is an automatic T bias inherent in the data and results that may not apply to the same extent to women. Likewise, cancer researchers might be wise to consider the F bias in female populations that won't be present in male samples. And what of studies that examine only one occupation, such as asbestos poisoning in miners, chemical toxicity in firefighters, or mercury poisoning in fishermen, groups which are probably overwhelmingly ST? What of studies of smokers and alcohol abusers who may tend to represent one portion of the type table more than another? What of any study, in fact, where an experimental or control group is not a representative cross-section of types? The inability to generalize to the rest of the population may be staggering. And then we imagine the investigations that could be.

---

✳ ✳ ✳

---

**Chapter 5 describes a small,** exploratory study designed to probe the notion of whether some talents, and perhaps the types mainly associated with these talents, are at greater risk for certain diseases. The diseases contracted by a total of 680 well-known talented people were compiled in a database from which 360 names were randomly selected for study—forty from each of nine talent areas including business, politics, music, chess, science and mathematics, art, writing, acting and sports.

Statistical analyses of the data suggest that talents presumed to be predominantly left-lateralized, such as business, politics, chess, science and math, have a comparatively high incidence of heart disease, while the bilateral talent category of writing has a relatively high incidence of lung disease, and right-lateralized talents such as acting, music and sports have a comparatively high incidence of cancer. For the remainder of the book, the two predominant systems here are referred to as the "Cardiovascular" and "Immune" patterns, respectively. The Cardiovascular pattern (heart, stroke, lung disease, infection) is hypothesized to represent left-lateralized or posterior-lateralized cognition and/or types tending toward I, S, T and J. The Immune pattern (cancer, stroke, gastrointestinal disease, AIDS, autoimmune disease, degenerative neurological disease) is hypothesized to represent right-lateralized or anterior-lateralized cognition and/or types tending toward E, N, F and P. Both patterns include stroke since stroke can happen on both sides of the brain.

Musicians, as a right-lateralized talent group with a high incidence of heart disease, are an exciting anomaly in these data in that they may represent the effects of contralateral shifting on disease risk. The position is advanced that it is to our collective benefit to stretch toward our typological and neuropsychological opposites so as to achieve and maintain a healthful balance.

# PART TWO

The Spiritual Perspective

# CHAPTER SIX
## REINVENTING THE WHEEL OF COGNITION AND DISEASE: TYPE AND CHAKRA THEORY

*** 

In this chapter, the ancient Hindu tradition of chakra philosophy is used to add further insights to the building of a theory of psychological type, talent and disease. Having spent the first half of the book on more scientific interpretations of these things, we now move to the second half, which weaves spirituality into the same phenomena. Like Jung, we do so in the conviction that the wisdom of the ancients may very possibly enhance our rudimentary understanding of relationships binding cognition and health.

Chapters 6 through 10 look at Hindu chakra theory, Chinese medicine, native medicine wheels and Christianity's Book of Revelation, all of which have something to say about circles, energy, circling or spiraling motion, and the importance of balance, which, in each case, has something to do with being centered or at the center. This movement, of course, is reminiscent of individuation. Chapters 9 and 10 look at these subjects in mathematical terms in an attempt to show that there have been many symbolic ways over the centuries of describing the same basic processes. Type may be one of the newest of such symbol systems.

In the case of chakra theory, *color* and swirling vortices of invisible energy centers in the body are used to convey some of the principles we have seen to this point. Ancient references to color, light and disease are of interest in view of Geschwind's modern-day thinking that coloring and exposure to light are associated with talent, deficit and disease.

Because following chapters incorporate ancient teachings in our circular talent-deficit continuum in the brain, we say we are *reinventing* the wheel of cognition and disease.

***

**With chapter 5, we leave** the more mechanistic, scientific aspects of Western psychology, for the relative subjectivity and acausality of ancient, Eastern and indigenous spirituality. We do this in the hopes of one day effectively bridging them both. Why? Because the new discipline of the millennium—bioenergetic, or spiritual, psychology— is neither a pure science nor a pure art, but a combination of the two. As in any transition or change process, it is often difficult for us to stretch beyond comfortable norms and known quantities into strange new worlds of knowledge that sometimes test our sensibilities, belief systems and patience. But we must give it an honest try because, like brain hemisphericity, handedness, type dimensions, and life itself, the Whole comprises both versions of any directional duality, including these two very different, apparently opposed, ways of knowing— science and spirituality.

So to continue with the building of a theory of type, talent and disease by adding a spiritual perspective, we will now attempt the construction of an imaginary balance wheel of personality and health based on the very little we know. Recall from chapter 5 the circular concept of dominant-auxiliary functions that is actually the brain, and following Jung's (1969a) study of the mandala (*"circle"*) which finds circular archetypes all over the world, we stand to learn much from the balance wheels that have been so described in different cultures throughout history.

In all the examples to follow, it will become apparent that very diverse cultures separated by vast expanses of geography and time may have been describing the same basic constructs in different ways for centuries. Using different symbols—colors, heat, animals, words, numbers—they all describe an energy system, whether of thermal, chemical, electrical or magnetic energy, that goes round and round on a microscopic level (the person) and on a macroscopic level (the globe, universe). Central to all of them is the belief that a balanced mixture of personality traits (energies) is needed for optimum health of the individual and his environment, and that neglect or blockage of specific traits leads to disease. Putting type to these ancient ideas adds some very interesting perspectives to our main question concerning the relationships linking cognition and disease.

To start with, we can consider a very unusual and magical variable in matters of health and disease, one that doesn't have typological or epidemiological statistics to go with it, but does leave many lasting impressions—color. Without a lot of probing, it is not difficult to see that the spectrum of light energy that is color may have vague symbolic links to the type spectrum that moves, like a rainbow in a sense, in graduated steps across the type table. At one end of this continuum, we find bankers and business people (SJ) who for some cultural reason covet the quintessential blue or grey business suit, intellectuals (IN) who may have chosen earth tones as their unofficial symbol, and athletes and entertainers (EP) who have been known to buy bright cars and brighter clothes. Why would business people choose navy as a social convention, and not red? Why would rock bands historically choose brighter colors, and not navy?

It is not simply cultural custom, we could propose, but rather a tendency on the part of the various types attracted to these professions to function in, and respond to, particular wave lengths of the energy spectrum, whether high energy (purple), moderate energy (green-brown), or low energy (red). Like dogs who have species-specific ranges of audition that are much higher than ours, or plants that need high-energy ultraviolet light to photosynthesize, it is probably no accident that ENFPs gravitate to the faster waves of purple and other bright colors in their personal effects, and ISTJs to the slower waves of conservative blues and browns. Radeloff's work (1991) supports the observation that certain types tend to be drawn to certain colors, leading us to consider East Indian chakra theory which, very oddly from a Western point of view, relates color to disease.

Chakra theory comes from ancient Hindu yogic literature and, like five-thousand-year-old Chinese medicine, is gaining more and more credibility with Western scientists as its precepts are validated by Western technologies capable of measuring subtle, ephemeral and ethereal energies. Acupuncture meridians, as just one example, have been tested with Western equipment and now show a release of morphine-like endorphins at acupuncture sites, which helps to verify ancient claims of pain reduction in patients treated by this method (Pomeranz, 1978; Gerber, 1988). Among non-scientists, however, the fact that these systems have been practiced by intelligent people in successful cultures for so many thousands of years—surely they wouldn't have done this if it didn't have some benefit—is itself validating.

"Chakra" is Sanskrit for *"wheel"* and there are said to be at least seven of these mysterious wheels of energy in the human body, all resembling whirling vortices of subtle energies, which somehow manage to take in energies from outside the body, pull them toward the center of each vortex, and transform them into forms utilizable inside the body. Anatomically, each chakra is said to be associated with a major nerve plexus and an endocrine gland, and they are arranged in a vertical line from the base of the spine to the head (Figures 28–29). At least three independent modern-day studies (Motoyama & Brown, 1978; Bentov, 1977; Hunt, 1977) have recorded changes in electrostatic emissions at the proposed sites.

The lowest wheel of energy, called the root chakra, is believed to be located near the coccyx and is associated with the adrenal glands. The second chakra is in the lower abdomen and is associated with the ovaries, prostate, testicles and urinary tract. The third chakra is said to be in the solar plexus region and is related to the pancreas and the adrenals. The fourth is situated in the heart area and is associated with the thymus. The fifth is thought to be in the throat area and is associated with the hypothalamus and the thyroid. The sixth chakra, also known as "the third eye," is located in the forehead region and is said to be related to the pineal gland. The seventh wheel of energy, or "crown" chakra, is located at the top of the head and is associated with the pituitary gland.

Each chakra is also said to be connected to specific organs, a particular type of cognitive or perceptual functioning, and a specific color which represents the energy frequency at which each chakra operates, whether of high, medium or low wave frequency (Table 23, page 158). The root chakra, for instance, is represented by the low-frequency color red, and is said to be involved in "grounded" thinking and the functioning of the elimination and reproductive systems. The crown chakra, at the opposite end of the scale, is signified by the high-frequency color violet, and is thought to be involved in spiritual thinking and the functioning of the central nervous system. For years many Westerners, of course, wondered with great skepticism what color had to do with these associations, and where the proof was for any of it.

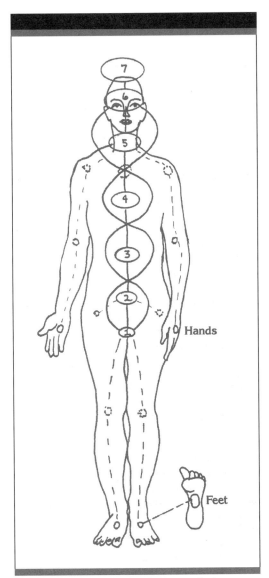

**Figure 28. The Major and Minor Chakras and Their Chief Pathways (Judith, 1987)**

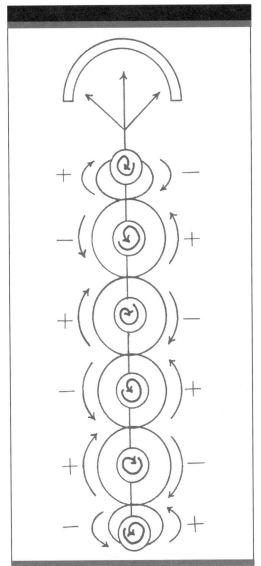

**Figure 29. The Spinning of the Chakras as a Result of Polaric Currents, Ida and Pingala (Judith, 1987)**

In 1975, a study by Valerie Hunt, then head of the Kinesiology Department at UCLA, used spectrum analysis, Fourier frequency analysis, and Sonogram frequencies to show the different energy emissions in color and sound that radiate from major chakra and acupuncture sites on the body with different thoughts and feelings (Bruyere, 1989). EMG electrodes, attached to four subjects during ten sessions of deep muscle manipulation therapy, enabled electronic readings to be taken in another room at the same time that the subjects' comments were recorded. Also at the same time, an aura reader independently perceived the predominant colors emanating from the body.

Aura readers, perhaps in some ways similar to those with eidetic imagery, have

**Table 23. Properties Said to Be Associated with Chakras (Gerber, 1988)**

## NEUROPHYSIOLOGICAL & ENDOCRINE ASSOCIATIONS OF THE CHAKRAS

| CHAKRA | NERVE PLEXUS | PHYSIOLOGICAL SYSTEM | ENDOCRINE SYSTEM |
|---|---|---|---|
| 1. Coccygeal | Sacral-Coccygeal | Reproductive | Gonads |
| 2. Sacral | Sacral | Genitourinary | Leydig |
| 3. Solar Plexus | Solar | Digestive | Adrenals |
| 4. Heart | Heart Plexus | Circulatory | Thymus |
| 5. Throat | Cervical Ganglia Medulla | Respiratory | Thyroid |
| 6. Third Eye | Hypothalamus Pituitary | Autonomic Nervous System | Pituitary |
| 7. Head | Cerebral Cortex Pineal | CNS Central Control | Pineal |

## ENERGETIC DYNAMICS OF THE CHAKRAS

| CHAKRA | POSITION | INNER ASPECTS | FORCES | NATURE |
|---|---|---|---|---|
| 1. Root | Base of Spine | Grounding | Kundalini | Physical |
| 2. Sacral | Below Umbilicus | Emotion Sexuality | Prana | Physical |
| 3. Solar Plexus | Upper Abdomen | Personal Power | Lower Astral | Personal |
| 4. Heart | Mid-chest | Love | Higher Astral | Personal |
| 5. Throat | Neck | Communication Will | Lower Mental | Personal |
| 6. Brow | Forehead | Intuition Inner Vision | Higher Spiritual Forces | Spiritual |
| 7. Crown | Top of Head | Spiritual Seeking | Higher Spiritual Forces | Spiritual |

a rare intuitive ability to see and feel a rainbow of subtle electromagnetic energies surrounding the body. These layers are largely invisible to most of us but are detectable with Kirlian photography which, like X-ray or CT scanning, can image energy frequencies the naked eye cannot (Figure 30). Many authors believe it is auras, in fact, that have been depicted as halos in frescos and cave paintings since the beginning of recorded time. There are said to be at least three of these layers circling the body at different frequencies; these create an egg-shaped envelope of energy from head to foot, that are perceived as colors by the talented few who have learned how to see them. The colors vary with organ systems and the thoughts, feelings and activities

**Figure 30. Artist's Rendering of an Aura Around the Head**

of a person, showing up as unusually patchy, brown or black shadings when disease is present, and often enabling an aura reader to locate a health problem in a person without even touching him. As a result, the oval aura, which stands vertically with the body, is not unlike a natural, life-size PET scan of a person whose shifting colors represent changing thought patterns and disease processes mediated, we presume, by the brain.

The subjects in the Hunt study—a dancer, an actress, an artist and a psychologist who was experienced in meditation—showed greatest waveform activity over different parts of the body: the dancer in the feet and legs, the actress in the heart area, the psychologist in the throat and third-eye area, and the artist in the crown chakra. More importantly, the wave patterns for sound and color correlated directly with each other, and with the aura reader's reports of the colors she saw. In fact, the equipment was able to measure seven varying frequency bands of sound and color at each chakra, which moved from slow frequencies during physical experiences, to higher frequencies with mental experiences. Frequencies of the *auric* spectrum, measured in cycles per second (cps, or Hertz), were found to correspond approximately with the *visible* electromagnetic spectrum, which is measured in the same units (Figures 31–32, pages 160 and 161).

For instance, when the reader saw a red aura around a subject, the waveform coming from the subject experiencing the muscle therapy registered on a frequency band of 640–800 cps, and the subject expressed *physical* pain, in both sounds and muscular agitation (Figure 31, page 160). When the reader saw an orange aura, the frequency band was at 600–740 cps and the subject expressed pain as well as emotional reactions, such as weeping and clenching of fists. With yellow, the frequency band was at 400–600 cps as the subject exhibited a strong

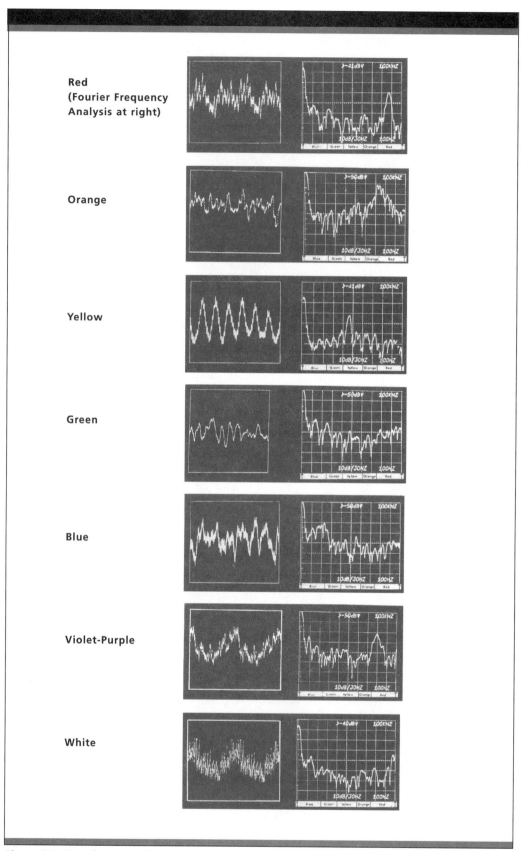

**Figure 31. Waveforms and Frequencies Associated With Auric Colors (Bruyere, 1989)**

will to overcome the pain and an *intellectual* coping with frustration. Green frequencies, at 240–400 cps, which have been attributed to transition from yellow to blue, were rarely seen in this experiment, but blue, the most prevalent auric color for these subjects, was observed at 100–240 cps and at 800 cps. A violet-purple aura, which has been associated with *creative or spiritual* thinking, was seen at about 900 cps, and a white aura, which is the visual equivalent of white noise and comprises all colors, was seen at 100–1000 cps. White auras were seen with altered states during meditation to cope with pain, and have been associated with *spirituality*, out-of-body experiences, and the highest level of consciousness or mind (Hunt, 1977; Bruyere, 1989).

This study, then, was among the first of its kind to offer Western-style physical proofs for this ancient Eastern metaphysical system. It showed the relatedness of light and color to body, mind, emotion and "higher" states of consciousness, and it outlined a spectrum of electromagnetic activity that moves from slower waveforms with physical thinking and feeling, to faster waveforms with more cerebral tasks.

Believers in chakra theory think the seven chakras translate energy of a higher frequency into glandular-hormonal output, which subsequently affects the entire body. In this instance, chakras sound no less real than chlorophyll in plants, which traps photons of light and converts light energy into the chemical energy that is eaten by animals as food. Also like plants, energy trapped by the chakras is said to flow upward through the body as something called "Kundalini" through winding channels called "the nadis," from the red root chakra to the violet crown (Gerber, 1988). A blockage of this flow at any chakra in between, like a blockage in a stem or leaf, is thought to result in the disease of the associated organs, nervous system or glands at that site.

Alterations in food, exercise and thought patterns (e.g., meditation) are recommended under this theory so as to unblock stuck energy and return the body to a healthy state. In the Hunt study, the frequency of the auric energy of the subjects became increasingly higher as they improved physically as a result of the muscle therapy. It even occasionally showed what the investigators called a "DC shift"—which, incidentally, may be the equivalent of a laterality shift—when they experienced an altered state through meditation (white aura) to cope with

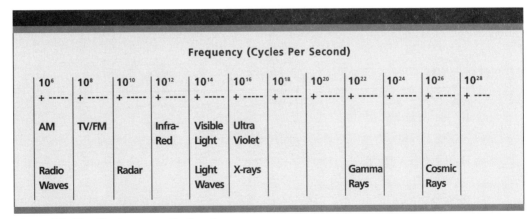

**Figure 32. The Electromagnetic Spectrum**

the pain. Like placing chicks under red light (low energy) to warm and calm them, plants under purple light (high energy) to help them grow, or people with Seasonal Affective Disorder under violet light to lift their spirits, even *wearing* the color of the affected chakra is said to help return the chakra to its preferred frequency (Judith, 1987). Of course, equal emphasis of all the chakras is advised so as to prevent disease from ever gaining a foothold in the first place.

Thus, according to ancient Hindu philosophy, a blockage of the flow of energy at the root chakra level (red) over issues of stability and security may produce elimination problems, such as constipation, and problems in the reproductive organs. Sexuality issues, or desire and frustration issues, may result in problems in the genitourinary organs of chakra two (orange). Concerns over personal will and power may manifest themselves as a blockage in chakra three (yellow) and cause problems in the digestive system, such as ulcers. Issues of love, compassion and particularly balance may affect the heart, lower lungs and general circulatory system of chakra four (green). Themes related to expression, communication and creativity may cause upper respiratory or other throat-chakra problems (blue). Issues pertaining to intuition, visualization, imagination and dreaming may cause headaches, visual problems and difficulties in the autonomic nervous system of the "third eye" (indigo). Finally, issues of spirituality, understanding and knowing may cause a blockage of energy in the crown chakra (violet) and tangible problems in the central nervous system.

Now it is not difficult to imagine the dilemmas at each of the various chakras as themes central to the make-up of various temperaments and types—much like the conflicts to be resolved at each stage of Freudian, Eriksonian or Maslowian development. Stability and security (red) would clearly seem to be an SJ theme; sexuality and physicality (orange) perhaps more an SP value; power (yellow) a TJ value, love (green) perhaps primarily an F matter; expression, creativity and visualization (blue, indigo) all N values; knowing (violet) perhaps an NT issue. This might hypothetically mean health for those types who are comfortable in their lives with these subjects, and potential disease for those types who are not. Thus, to have unresolved conflicts in these areas may be to risk disease at the site of the respective chakras in temperaments and types known to have problems with these issues.

For example, NP, the opposite of the security-minded SJ, might be expected to experience "red" health problems (reproductive, excretory) by virtue of the insecurity inherent in risk-taking. NJ, the opposite of the fun-loving SP, may have "orange" problems (genitourinary) because of an under-emphasis of sexuality, or frustration over other wants. FP, the gentle opposite of TJ, may have "yellow" health problems (digestive) as a result of living in non-power positions and not having control, or dealing with the TJs who do. Thinking types may have "green" health problems (circulatory) because of an under-emphasis of Feeling. Sensing types may have "blue" problems (respiratory) for placing too little importance on creative expression, and "indigo" problems (visual) for seldom trusting intuition and visualization. Finally, Feeling types may have "purple" health problems (CNS) because of a consistent under-emphasis of the Thinking function.

We remind ourselves that this is all purely whimsical speculation, but can continue for the sake of argument to see where it leads. For instance, believers in chakra theory claim that wearing, eating, visualizing or otherwise immersing oneself in the color of a problem chakra can help in the restoration of functions at that level. Is it even possible, then, that the temperaments and types on our cognitive spectrum gravitate to specific ranges of the color spectrum in unconscious reflection of physiological weaknesses peculiar to their preferences? Do businessmen and other Thinking types, for example, announce to the world their respiratory and cardiac weaknesses through their unfailing attraction to blue? Do INFPs similarly reveal their depressive tendencies through an uncommon attraction to black? Are academics on university campuses (IN), who may seem to stereotypically gravitate to earth tones, foretelling of potential difficulties in the middle abdomen? Are extraverted athletes and entertainers expressing potential problems in the central nervous system with their unique attraction to purple and bright primary colors? And what of our once unquestioning attachment to the color blue for boys (T, respiratory, cardiac), and pink for girls (F, reproductive)?

Why, in fact, are there certain colors for certain social groups? Most would argue that it is simply learned tradition and custom that governs the color statements of groups. But we could question that assumption on two grounds: (a) what made the group choose the color to begin with, before it became tradition? and (b) can convention alone explain enhanced appearance and increased comfort that is afforded by some colors and not others? It seems at least possible that, in some cases, there is a biological component to color selection that is in the same phenomenological company as using warming red light for chicks, and energizing purple light for plants and SAD patients. Indeed, work by Hathaway et al. (1992) shows the numerous positive and negative effects of light on the body and mind, including effects on academic achievement and health (Table 24, page 164). Ott (1973) suggests that an absence of any segment of the light spectrum—as in fluorescent lighting that tends toward the pink end of the spectrum, rather than the blue end—may be related to abnormal growth, whether of tissue or bacteria. Together, these studies suggest that exposure to the "slower," pink end of the color spectrum may be related to lower levels of achievement and higher rates of infection.

A color coordination system based on the seasons of the year was popular in the early 1980s, and might very well have reflected this idea. Proponents of the system actually "tested" clients to identify the ranges of the color spectrum to which the biology of a person—hair color and complexion—was best suited. Apparently backed by consumer surveys, supporters claimed that very dark-haired people, belonging to the so-called "Winter" group at one end of the spectrum, are perceived as livelier and more attractive when framed by bright-colored clothing such as red. Brown, red and auburn-haired individuals, belonging to the "Autumn" group, were said to look their best in fall colors of orange and brown. Opposite "Winter" and "Autumn" were fair-haired, fair-skinned people—"Spring," who look best wearing pink and yellow, and the fairest, "Summer," who were advised to build pastel wardrobes of blue and mauve.

In this system, highly pigmented dark-haired people were advised to wear colors toward the red end of the color spectrum, just as less pigmented light-haired people (blonde or grey) were told to wear colors toward the blue end. *Not* wearing the opposite energies of contrasting colors was said to make a person appear "washed out," less vibrant-looking, less robust, or simply odd, which may be saying that the natural biologically determined color of our physical

**Table 24. Some Biologic and Medical Effects of Light on Humans (Hathaway et al., 1992)**

|  | Direct | Indirect |
|---|---|---|
| **Physiologic** | Erythema<br>Pigmentation<br>Epidermal thickening<br>Vitamin D synthesis<br>Blood levels of amino acids<br>Immune systems | Vision<br>Entrainment of rhythms<br>Reproductive activation<br>Entrainment and suppression<br>of melatonin synthesis |
| **Pathologic** | Photosensitization porphyrins<br>Drugs; toxins<br>Ocular damage<br>Carcinogenesis | Indirect behavioral and<br>medical effects not well<br>characterized |
| **Therapeutic** | Hyperbilirubinemia<br>Rickets<br>Light-drug interactions<br>(psoriasis, leukemia) | Depression, Seasonal<br>Affective Disorder (SAD)<br>Jet lag |

features is usually opposite the culturally aesthetic balancing act that is our clothes. To the extent that fair-haired, fair-skinned people are in fact at greater risk for certain diseases such as skin cancer and lupus erythematosus that are much less a concern for African Americans, say, whose number one killer is heart disease, the colors we choose to wear may indeed highlight the disorders more endemic to one end of the energy spectrum than the other—perhaps lighter, "slower" colors (e.g., red) for diseases lower in the body, and darker, "faster" colors (e.g., blue) for problems higher up.

Light and color in an analysis of cognition and disease! An initially outrageous idea, from Western scientific perspectives, but we will examine it to see if it can provide any clues to hidden disease patterns in types for which we currently have almost no aggregate data.

We can return to our anecdotal evidence to test its potential for further study. We may recall Ron, Brad and John, all middle-aged ISJs with "green" circulatory problems that had to be acted upon. Tom, David, Donna, Jane, Elise, Roy, Robert and Bill, all IJs, particularly ITJs, had "red," "orange" and "yellow" problems in the excretory, sexual and digestive areas of the lower body. These people also tended toward dark hair, right-handedness, near- and far-sightedness requiring corrective eyewear, and problems at the "green" heart level or lower.

We also had Janice, Natalie, Douglas and Teresa, all Extraverts with "blue" thyroid and throat infections. We had Natalie, Rose, Ellen, Janet and Sandra, all ENPs with "blue," "indigo" and "purple" neck problems, headaches and migraines, Bob, an EP with a "blue" shoulder problem and a "purple" nervous system infection, and two other Perceiving types, Mary and Carol, with "blue" hearing problems. By comparison, this group tended toward blonde hair, left-handedness, hearing problems, and immune problems in upper parts of the body above the heart.

ITJs versus EPs—it is very possible we are noticing a dichotomous trend here that once again distinguishes between the pathological associations of the left and right hemispheres. We acknowledge the fact that typological dichotomies might also go front (N) to back (S), and top (I) to bottom (E), but the left-right distinction seems the most obvious. Exaggerating considerably to make the point, we notice that we have careful, serious, hard-working, orderly ITJs in the left, operating in a perpetually anxious, high energy "purple" state, as it were, who badly need to get away from it all and to lighten up, loosen up and relax. They don't, so they eventually develop hypertension and other circulatory or respiratory problems (green) that could one day lead to heart attack. They neglect their more basic functions in the name of work—controlling and putting off physical needs like eating, sex and exercise for "later"—and may also develop various problems in the digestive (yellow), genitourinary (orange), or reproductive (red) systems. Even when an ITJ takes sick leave, he will attempt to keep busy to get his mind off it, which is probably precisely what he shouldn't do, considering it was just such compulsive orderliness that likely put him there.

ITJs, who spend a lot of time reading, writing, thinking, analyzing and working would seem to need to *nonverbalize* and shift toward the slower, lower, more disordered "red" energy states of the right side that, paradoxically, are achieved through physical and social *activity*. Their reflective verbal chatter goes on in their heads even when they aren't talking, contributing to worry, insomnia and other problems, which they might try to squelch with excessive drinking, eating or sleeping. But more often than not, they simply avoid any situation that promises more stimulation—crowds, parties, risky adventures—because they already have enough neuronal firing going on inside them and don't want any more. Pushed to the limit of their internal stimulation threshold, they may attack others, whether literally or figuratively, which can only increase their risk of heart disease.

On the flip side of this exaggerated coin, we have the gregarious, easy-going and fun-loving EPs who enjoy the solitary, stationary deskwork of the ITJ about as much as they enjoy taxes. Relative to ITJs, EPs live in the comparatively relaxed, unfettered world of the "red" right side, and generally pay more attention to food, sex and exercise, sometimes to the point of neglecting organized verbal-analytic activity (especially ESPs). They can push things to the limit, too, but in their case it is with *excessive* physical or social activity rather than not enough. They will burn the candle at both ends being active—perhaps partying, playing sports, and thrill seeking—and badly need to slow down and reflect. They don't, so they eventually come down with (we speculate) an immune problem (blue), stroke (indigo) or nervous disorder involving the central nervous system (violet). Even when sick, the EP's solution to the problem is to relax and do something fun to get his mind off it, which probably only makes him sicker as he stresses the disordered, chaotic processes that may have contributed to his illness in the first place. ("Chaos" here is used in the nonjudgmental Gleick (1987) sense and is taken to mean not ordered, structured or regimented, and not easily predictable.)

EPs, who spend a lot of time socializing, being physical and seeking external stimulation, would seem to need to *verbalize* and shift toward the faster, higher, more ordered "purple" energy states of the left side, and these are achieved through physical and social *inactivity*. EPs need to increase the level of internal stimulation doing the very activities of which the ITJ must do less—reading, writing, reflecting and thinking, alone. If they don't, when pushed to the limit of nonverbal rather than verbal stimulation, they might attack themselves—whether through depression, substance abuse, suicide, autoimmune disease, stroke, or degenerative nervous disorders.

In the end, the ITJ might have a comparatively strong immune system—indeed overactive, in the case of allergies—but a vulnerable heart (perhaps especially on the left side of the heart) as a by-product of consistent under-emphasis of the chaotic right hemisphere. Following Geschwind's (1985) reasoning, we would expect him to exhibit right-handedness and darker features and, from our own observations, to be drawn toward lower energies as are found in warm colors, low sounds, and types like EP who live in a more relaxed way.

The EP, in contrast, may have a comparatively strong heart—perhaps because he spends much of his life attending to "affairs of the heart"—but a vulnerable immune or central nervous system as a result of consistent under-emphasis of the ordered left hemisphere. We might expect him to exhibit more left-handedness and lighter features, and to be drawn toward higher energies as are found in cool colors, high sounds, and types like ITJ who exude great intensity in operating at a high, intense internal pitch. The unspoken attraction for both parties, of course, is a balancing of the energies associated with opposite lateralities. The EP is thus attracted to situations where he can "fill up" on the energies of the people, places and things that surround him (positive polarity), and the ITJ avoids them because he already has an excess of his own energies (negative polarity), but both may come together in the comfortable give-and-take union of opposite polarities.

The idea of stopping or calming the internal verbal "chatter" of the ITJ to shift right (a form of something called "verbal inhibition") or increasing the same activities in the EP to shift left ("verbal disinhibition") is really quite common, though we usually know it in different terms. Rightward-shifting in the form of meditation, hypnosis and jogging, for example, are well-known verbal-inhibiting techniques, and leftward-shifting is usually synonymous with reading and formal education.

ITJ—as we know from the database at the Center for Applications of Psychological Type in Gainesville, Florida (Macdaid et al., 1986)—is a common managerial type, or engineer, while EP is a rarer artist, musician, actor or athlete. Accordingly, the above description of ITJ risks is more likely the norm, and the EP risks the less common condition. No surprise, then, when we rank the top three diseases in America today and find that heart disease (green) is number one, followed by cancer (blue), then stroke (violet). Indeed, if a solid connection between type and disease could be demonstrated, the frequency of various diseases in the general population might even be found to mirror type frequencies. For example, the ratio of heart disease to cancer in the general population might be something equivalent to the ratio of Thinking types to Feeling types, which is roughly 1.2 to 1 at this time, and stroke and lung disease might be rarer because there are fewer Intuitive types.

In all of this, it is clear that color is at the least a *metaphor* for, and is perhaps even a visible *reflection* of, energy levels and energy states that are somehow related to health and disease. Energy concepts are comparatively easy to see when considering metabolic disorders like diabetes and hypoglycemia, or psychiatric conditions like schizophrenia and depression—one seems to have too much energy to burn, the other not enough—but the relationships are more complex when dealing with problems like kidney infection or arthritis. To explore these issues, we turn briefly to Chinese medicine, which, like chakra theory, also puts energy processes at the root of disease states.

* * *

**Chapter 6 uses ancient associations** between color (frequencies of light energy) and disease to add further insights to our knowledge of possible relationships between type, talent and disease. Chakra theory postulates the existence of seven major energy centers in the body, spiraling from the base of the spine to the head, which correspond to ever increasing levels of energy, enlightenment and holistic well-being when all centers are open and functioning in unison. Each chakra center corresponds to a certain kind of thinking or emotional state which progresses from a "red," physical state of mind in the lowest chakra through to a "purple," spiritual state of mind in the highest chakra. A blockage of the flow of energy due to personal issues at the level of any particular chakra is said to produce disease in the associated organ system. Thus, it becomes the task of the individual to change one's thinking or feeling to work through an issue, thereby releasing "stuck" energy and restoring balance.

As some of the issues at the different chakra sites sound remarkably like issues confronted by certain types, chapter 6 explores the possibility that types and chakra issues are related. It suggests there are two basic energy systems among types which correspond to the essential left and right lateralities they represent—intense, verbal, "purple" types (e.g., ITJ) which typify a neglect of, and heightened disease risk in, the lower chakras; and social, nonverbal, "red" types (e.g., EP) which typify a neglect of, and heightened disease risk in, the higher chakras. It is recommended that these types purposely shift toward their contralateral sides to achieve and maintain an energy balance.

# CHAPTER SEVEN
## REINVENTING THE WHEEL OF COGNITION AND DISEASE: TYPE AND TAOISM

✳ ✳ ✳

The correspondences outlined in chapter 6 are expanded here to include those in Chinese medicine for a fuller understanding of their possible applications to type, talent and disease processes. Here, the "Kundalini" energy of chakra centers becomes the "chi" energy of Chinese medicine, which flows through rivers of meridians throughout the body. Again, disease appears to occur wherever there is a blockage of the energy flow and in the thinking that may attend it.

Central to the Chinese view is a perpetual swinging, back and forth, between yin and yang states, which sound very much like the dichotomies of left and right lateralities. Chinese medicine also incorporates notions of color, spatial direction and especially *time*, whether daily or seasonally, in its interpretations of bodily functioning. Chinese philosophy is embodied symbolically in the circular T'ai Chi and suggests that the energy of a system can be *changed* by adding opposite energies to the system.

✳ ✳ ✳

The logic underlying ancient Chinese medicine is dialectical, like the left and right hemispheres of modern-day neuropsychology, yet holistic like chakra theory in the sense that disease is seen as a part of the whole rather than as an isolated problem to be fixed. Two well-known opposing processes, yin and yang, govern its principles and practice:

> Yin-Yang theory is based on the philosophical construct of two polar complements, called Yin and Yang. These complementary opposites are neither forces nor material entities. Nor are they mythical concepts that transcend rationality. Rather, they are convenient *labels* used to describe how things function in relation to each other and to the universe. They are used to explain the continuous process of natural change. But Yin and Yang are not only a set of correspondences; they also represent *a way of thinking*. In this system of thought, all things are seen as parts of a whole. No entity can ever be isolated from its relationship to other entities; no thing can exist in and of itself. There are no absolutes. Yin and Yang must, necessarily, contain within themselves the possibility of opposition and change (Kaptchuk, 1983; emphasis added).

The familiar symbol for the T'ai Chi, "the One," depicts the dynamic polarity of black yin processes on one side of a circle and white yang processes on the other (Figure 33, page 172). Much has been made of the similarities between yin and negative, "feminine" right-hemisphere functions and between yang and positive, "masculine" left-hemisphere functions, and more and more Western scientists—such as physicist Fritjof Capra (1975), author of *The Tao of Physics*, and physicist Mitchell Waldrop (1992), author of *Complexity: The Emerging Science at the Edge of Order and Chaos*—are subscribing to the Chinese view generally, though using the terms and symbols of their own disciplines.

For instance, Chinese medicine holds that the yin-yang polarity is the source of all that exists in the world, and that, perhaps like electrical charges or the attraction of types, the black correspondences (right, negative, feminine) need the white (left, positive, masculine), the white needs the black, in order for the One to exist at all. In the founding Taoist book, the *Tao Te Ching*, it is written, "From the One came the Two. From the Two came the Three. From the Three came the Ten Thousand Things" (Kaptchuk, 1983).

**Figure 33. Traditional Yin-Yang Symbol**

This notion, against the backdrop of T'ai Chi and the hemispheres, might remind us of Christian references to the Father, the Son (right hand of God), and the Holy Spirit (left hand), the growth of the nuclear family and its descendants, and an immense array of physical processes from mitosis to splitting of the atom. In all of these, it is recognized that the One—whether that be the organism, the family, the ecosystem, the globe or the universe—has essential parts in its makeup that are connected, interdependent and cannot stand alone.

We would probably never think of asking, "What singular factor causes a tornado?" but would look for a pattern of correspondences in the earth's atmosphere most likely associated with it—humidity, pressure disturbances, movement of air masses, heat followed by a sudden drop in temperature, and so forth—recognizing that any one element is not a sufficient condition for the appearance of tornados. Similarly, the Chinese physician asks not, "What X is causing disease Y?" as is often the Western approach, but "How do X and Y relate? What goes together with Y?" and looks for imbalance in the yin and yang of a patient and the essential patterns of disharmony that give clues about how to restore the balance:

> If a person has a symptom, Chinese medicine wants to know how the symptom fits into the patient's entire bodily pattern. A person who is well, or "in harmony," has no distressing symptoms and expresses mental, physical, and spiritual balance. When that person is ill, *the symptom is only one part of a complete bodily imbalance that can be seen in other aspects of his or her life and behavior.* Understanding the overall pattern, with the symptom as part of it, is the challenge of Chinese medicine. The Chinese system is not less logical than the Western, just less analytical (Kaptchuk, 1983: 7, emphasis added).

Energy in the body, or "chi," is said to travel through a complicated web of pathways called "meridians," and the Chinese physician believes he can alter this energy at various access points along the way using acupuncture, moxibustion, cupping, acupressure, and applications of heat and cold. He may also recommend traditional yin and yang herbs whose content seems to effect energy shifts from yin to yang states or vice versa (skeptics who acknowledge that pasta has a different latent energy of heat than, say, celery, may have less trouble accepting this notion of yang herbs and yin herbs). The Chinese physician cares little about whether or not the meridians or herbal effects can actually be proven using Western techniques, only that the theory works in practice. Nevertheless, Western research methods have in fact demonstrated the positive effects of Chinese therapies on peptic ulcers, angina pectoris and a variety of other conditions not requiring surgery. They also show that, in general, such therapies can often complement Western approaches to the treatment of illness (Aung, 1993; Gerber, 1988; Harpur, 1994; Kaptchuk, 1983).

Like inhalation and exhalation, photosynthesis and respiration, night and day, or the ebb and flow of tides, yin and yang create each other, control each other and transform into each other in a constant, cyclical, give-and-take flux that is health. It is only when yin is excessive that yang becomes weak, when yang is excessive that yin becomes weak, that one cannot support the other. It happens not necessarily because of the prior actions of other things, as we tend to believe in Western medicine, but because of "their position in the ever-moving cyclical universe . . . which made that behavior inevitable for them" (Kaptchuk, 1983: 15). Like a pendulum that swings ever wider, there may be no telling what actually causes circumstances to be at any one place at any one moment in time.

The front, inner and lower parts of the body are considered to possess more yin elements in them, the back, outer and upper parts of the body more yang, and the elements are often described as the body's Water and Fire, respectively. Chronic illnesses and illnesses characterized by weakness, slowness, coldness and inactivity are thought to be yin illnesses, and usually relate to a deficiency of some kind in the person's body, especially in older people. Acute illnesses and illnesses manifesting strength, forceful movements, heat, and overactivity are considered yang illnesses, and usually relate to excess, especially in younger people. Fatigue or pain relieved by eating, for example, may be a sign of deficiency, while severe headache, insomnia, urgent diarrhea or fever can be a sign of excess.

Grossly oversimplified, the Eight Principal Patterns of symptoms in Chinese medicine are complex combinations of two fundamental equations:

Yin = Interior + Deficient + Cold
Yang = Exterior + Excess + Heat

Thus, what the Western world knows as stroke can be related to something called "liver yang ascending" and can produce symptoms of deficiency like slurred speech and numbness. Or, it can be related to deficient chi or deficient liver or kidney yin, and produce symptoms of excess like insomnia, anger, red cheeks, headache, a hot body and tremors. A red sore throat can be a sign of excess heat. Coronary heart disease can involve a pattern of deficient heart, liver or kidney yin which is unable to support the yang, and manifests itself in headache, red face, night sweats, palpitations, insomnia and so forth.

Lung disharmonies like pneumonia also commonly involve deficient yin, producing fever, headache, cough, and irritability, while liver disharmonies, such as liver cancer, may relate to deficient spleen and kidney yang and produce emaciation, low spirit, and lack of appetite. Problems in the middle abdomen such as diabetes and pancreatitis involve "fire," and produce excessive eating, urination or pain. The kidneys, which are said to be the root of yin and yang in all organs, may affect and involve other organs, kidney disharmonies often being related to conditions of deficient yang. Chronic urogenital infections, on the other hand, appear to be conditions of deficient yin, and intestinal disharmonies can be associated with stagnant or obstructed chi and excess heat (Kaptchuk, 1983).

As we trace these common disorders the length of the body—openly admitting that this is not even scratching the surface of the subject—it becomes apparent that ancient East Indian and Chinese practitioners might have been using different metaphors to describe something very similar. In fact, the odd-numbered chakras (1, 3, 5, 7) have been thought to roughly approximate left-hemisphere yang processes, the even-numbered chakras (2, 4, 6) right-hemisphere yin processes (Judith, 1987), which we might further extend to our hypotheses for a left-hemisphere or posterior I, S, T, and J Cardiovascular pattern, and a right-hemisphere or anterior E, N, F, and P Immune pattern. (Bear in mind that we are referring to functional lateralities as opposed to individual whole types. Thus, the type INFP would appear to have a greater functional laterality in the direction of N, F, and P.) Numbers, letters, technical jargon— different symbols spanning many centuries, but all, perhaps, striving to capture the same essential observations and relationships of health and disease in the human body.

For instance, we can see that the intestinal and urogenital problems of the security-minded lower chakras are related to deficient yin (perhaps created by left hemisphere excesses), the kidney problems of the sexual chakra two to deficient yang (right hemisphere excesses), the digestive problems of the power-minded chakra three to deficient yin (left hemisphere excesses), the heart and lung problems of the relationship-conscious chakra four to deficient yin (left hemisphere excesses), the sore throat in the expression-minded chakra five to excess heat (left hemisphere excesses) and stroke in the visionary sixth chakra and spiritual crown chakra to problems with either yin or yang because stroke can happen in both hemispheres.

We will recall that we proposed the "physical" lower chakras to wrap themselves in Sensing values primarily, the "dominance" chakra in Thinking, the "social and emotional" chakra in Feeling, and the "creative and spiritual" chakras in Intuition. Thus, following Chinese logic, disease is associated with either too much of the quality or not enough in these types, and may affect the corresponding chakras accordingly. TJ, for example, might have gastrointestinal third chakra problems in association with too much left-sided yang emphasis on dominance or control issues, while FP might have the same problems because of insufficient emphasis. T might have heart problems in chakra four related to excessive emphasis on impersonal left-sided yang logic, and F might have them because it wasn't stressed enough.

Table 25 summarizes these correspondences listing the seven chakras, and the issues, physiological systems and yin-yang disease processes said to be involved for each of them. Added to this are dominant type functions that seem to best fit the description of the chakras, as well as the talent categories from the database that earlier were found to exhibit disease in

**Table 25. Correspondences Linking Chakras, Yin-Yang, Laterality and Type, in the Localization of Disease**

| CHAKRA | SYSTEM | ISSUE | TYPE[1] | PROCESS[2] | LAT.[3] | TALENT[4] |
|---|---|---|---|---|---|---|
| Seven/Crown (Violet) | CNS | Spiritual | N | +Yang | +LH | Politics |
| Six/3rd Eye (Indigo) | ANS | Visual Creativity | N | +Yin | +RH | Science |
| Five/Throat (Blue) | Respiratory Immune | Verbal Creativity | N | +Yang | +LH | Writing |
| Four/Heart (Green) | Circulatory Immune | Social-Emotional | T[5] | -Yin | +LH | Politics |
| Three (Yellow) | Digestive | Dominance-Control | T | +Yang | +LH | Acting |
| Two (Orange) | Genito-Urinary | Sexual | S | -Yang | +RH | Chess |
| One/Root (Red) | Reprod. | Physical Security | S | -Yin | +LH | Sports |

[1] Dominant type functions implicated in the chakra issue
[2] Pattern of deficiency or excess contributing to disease in this system
[3] Postulated pattern of deficiency or excess in laterality (LH = left hemisphere; RH = right hemisphere)
[4] Talent area(s) in the database with highest disease frequency in this physiological system
[5] T, here, refers more to the talent category than the chakra category and interestingly may reflect deficient F

these systems. The result is an interesting arrangement of possibilities that might seem to warrant baseline and controlled study to investigate the links. Until such time, however, we can only wonder whether too much left-sided activity (or anterior activity?) somehow increases the risk of developing lung disease, as was endured by the writers in our sample, whether the actors with gastrointestinal cancers were Thinking types as the table suggests, or whether genitourinary disorders might have been related to excessively high levels of sexual activity in our athletes and excessively low levels in our chess players.

If yin-yang processes can be superimposed in this way on the arrangement of chakras in the body, then it follows that yin-yang might be a rainbow of traits and talents, too—left-hemisphere yang needing the balance of lower body activity, symbolized in chakra theory by the lighter colors (red), and right-hemisphere yin needing the balance of upper body activity, symbolized by the darker colors (purple), as in the light and dark halves of the T'ai Chi. Chakras may in fact be a series of smaller energy wheels on the T'ai Chi, or smaller versions of T'ai Chi, a never-ending circle of processes that blend from one state into another and, in health, can never be stuck in one place. Once again, what appears to be linear, vertical and unmoving—like the spectra of left-right lateralities, talents, and types—are really circular, changing and evolving. At their root, in man, could be a "circular" and changeable brain.

As a consequence, types tending toward I, S, T and J should be yang types, as it were, who may neglect their yin elements to the point of producing deficient yin disorders, such as constipation, urinary tract infection, ulcers, and heart and lung problems. Types tending toward E, N, F and P might be yin types who neglect their yang aspects, causing the pendulum to swing in an unbalanced rightward or forward direction, and producing deficient yang or excess yin disorders such as kidney disease, migraine, and problems associated with the autonomic nervous system.

In fact, the essence of each type may actually have *both* yin and yang versions of it such that INTP is the yin of INT, for example, where INTJ is the yang. Typological opposites might therefore seek to fill in their complements of the One by consorting with yin or yang personalities that their own energy is missing. So, a yin type like INFP may gravitate to yang types like ENTP, while a yang type like ISTP may have a special affinity for yin types like ENFJ. In all of this, we can see that any one type is only yin or yang relative to another type, that it is not absolute. The ENTP (three scales right) may be yang to an INFP perhaps, because of the T, but will be yin relative to an ISTJ (four scales left). INTP and INTJ will be yang *relative* to most other types, but perhaps a balance of yin and yang to each other. In relationships, as in the body, it is only when yang is excessive that yin becomes weak, when yin is excessive that yang becomes weak, that one cannot support the other.

Fundamental to Chinese medicine is the belief that states can be altered to some extent by changing the energy of the system. Of course, Western medicine acknowledges this too, in recommending heat for chills and sore muscles, ice for inflammation, tepid baths for fevers, juice for low blood sugar, and pressure for certain circulatory problems, and so on. But Chinese physicians see these thermal, chemical and mechanical energies—not to mention the energies associated with wind, dampness and dryness—as treatments for health problems as well as their contributors. They believe we can change these states and help to achieve balance, in many cases, simply by adding opposite energies to the system.

For example, leafy green vegetables, which are considered yin, are believed to be healthier food energy for a person when balanced with ginger, which is yang. High blood pressure (yang) can be relieved by physically releasing some of the pressure with a special pinprick to the toe (yin). Pain in a broken right arm that is aggravated by pressure (excess yang) may be helped by needling acupuncture in the left ear (yin). A dislike of hot weather can be a sign of excess heat (yang), which might be relieved by the addition of something cold (yin), just as chills and a dislike of cold weather signifies a yin problem that might require the addition of heat (yang). Traditional Chinese medicine claims, "Winter injures with Cold, in Spring there will be warm illness" (Kaptchuk, 1983: 271), which suggests different vulnerabilities at different times of the year—risk for diseases of Cold (yin) higher in the cold months, and for diseases of Heat (yang) in the warm months. These are again helped by reducing the energy extremes to moderate ranges. Indeed, the seasonality of mortality is a concept that has been accepted in Western medicine since the seventeenth century (Smith, 1979).

If, as has so often been suggested, yin processes are related to right-hemisphere function, yang processes to left-hemisphere function, and now perhaps to certain types, it follows that the simple addition of opposite energy—thermal, chemical, mechanical, even the electromagnetic energy of light—may induce leftward and rightward shifts that have differing healing benefits for the various types.

To illustrate the possibility, we can consider what happens in the menstrual cycle. Premenstrual syndrome (PMS) is often associated with anxiety, irritability, lack of motor coordination, moodiness, muscle tension, compulsive cravings, angry or introverted behavior, constipation (red chakra) and, as we know from Doreen Kimura's (1989) hormone studies, relatively high verbal activity, all of which might seem to suggest left-sided functioning. Chinese medicine calls it deficient yin, and perhaps Jung would have called it an introversion of energy, or the conservation of energy, in preparation for a fallow interval. The condition is helped by a reduction of salt and stimulants, like caffeine and chocolate, in what should otherwise be a balanced diet, and by a rightward shift to extraverted nonverbal activities such as exercise, sex and relaxation—in other words, a *release* of blocked energy.

According to Kimura, with the onset of menstruation, verbal activity dissipates in comparison with pre-menstrual levels, and fatigue, depression, diarrhea or cramping may ensue—the cramping (orange chakra) helped by eating often, and by massage, rest, analgesics, heating pads and warm baths. That is, the physical deficiencies of right-sided functioning (yin) are helped by the *addition* of energy to shift left, just as the excesses of left-sided functioning (yang) were first balanced by a *release* of energy to shift right. In the space of a week, a woman has experienced both states.

The menstrual cycle is really an excellent example of yin-yang, plus-minus, positive-negative cycling in the human body, of how yin creates and becomes yang and vice versa, and how cognition and personality are just a part of that cycle at any moment in time. A woman literally flows back and forth across the laterality "lines" exhibiting both mental and physical changes as she does so—yin, perhaps, before ovulation, yang afterwards from the time of ovulation to menstruation—and through it all, it is quite clear that one state is needed in order to produce the other. It is when imbalances occur along the way that the stages in the cycle can become problematic.

Our tenuous applications of yin-yang theory to type would suggest that because some types seem to stress one form of laterality more than another, they may experience greater difficulty than other types with one or the other of the two main phases. ISTJ women, for example, who naturally lean toward left-sided or posterior functioning, might experience more PMS difficulties than ENFP women who, as right- or anterior-lateralized types, may have more trouble with cramping and other post-onset symptoms. As a consequence, ISTJ women may especially benefit from purposeful rightward or anterior shifting before a period, just as ENFP women may particularly benefit from leftward or posterior shifting once it begins.

Now this begs the question of whether excessive menstrual activity (e.g., endometriosis) is generally associated with excessive right or anterior lateralization (E-N-F-P), and whether amenorrhea or premature menopause—effectively an atypical blockage of the orange chakra—is associated with excessive left or posterior lateralization (I-S-T-J). Could hormone replacement therapy be helped along, or even delayed in some instances, by conscious cognitive shifting toward right-hemisphere functioning? Once again, this is mere conjecture that remains to be explored.

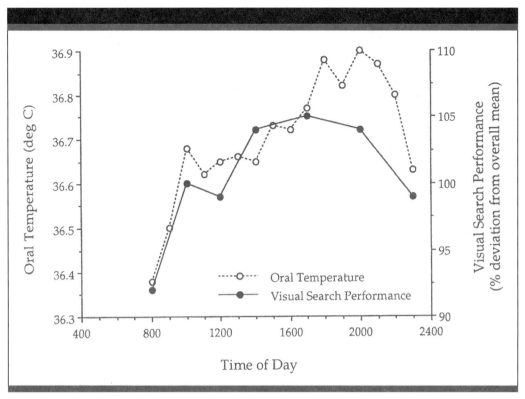

**Figure 34. Performance as a Function of Time of Day for Visual Search Tasks (Adapted from Smith, 1992)**

From: Proctor, Robert & Dutta, Addie. *Skill Acquisition and Human Performance*. pp. 343, copyright © 1995 by SAGE Publications, Inc., Thousand Oaks CA. Reprinted by Permission of SAGE Publications, Inc.

The ebb and flow of yin and yang are not restricted to the month, but can also be seen even in organ sensitivities in the course of a day. Western science is well aware of the daily Circadian rhythms of body temperature and some cognitive tasks (Smith, 1992; Figures 34–35). But Chinese medicine tracks the internal biological clock, which tells the time of peak energy flow of the different organs (Figure 36). Considering that the heart, lungs, spleen, pancreas, liver, and kidneys are yin organs, and the intestines, stomach, gall bladder and bladder are yang organs, we can see in Figure 36 that the body apparently shifts from yin (right) to yang (left) states at four-hour intervals, and that the circulatory and digestive systems, for example, are functioning at optimum levels during the high-light energy periods of daylight hours, while the respiratory system functions best during the low-light energy period that is night. Acupuncturists therefore attempt to treat their patients at these most beneficial times.

Of course, the converse is also true, that these systems should be at their weakest during periods of similar energy—heart yin during the night (low-light energy), liver yang during the day (high-light energy), and so forth—which practitioners and patients alike may do well to bear in mind. Equally important, from our perspective, is that yin and yang systems in yin and yang types may be at greater risk in different seasons of the year when the energy of heat and light most contradicts the energy requirements of a given system. We would anticipate, from the theory, that left-sided yang types will be most susceptible to yin deficiencies such as

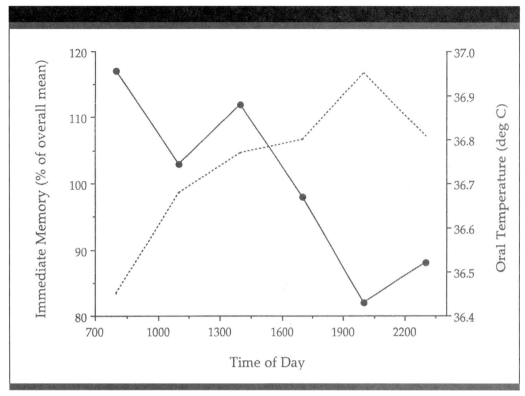

**Figure 35. Immediate Memory Performance as a Function of Time of Day, With Oral Temperature Shown by the Dotted Line (Adapted from Smith, 1992)**

From: Proctor, Robert & Dutta, Addie. *Skill Acquisition and Human Performance*. pp. 343, copyright © 1995 by SAGE Publications, Inc., Thousand Oaks CA. Reprinted by Permission of SAGE Publications, Inc.

cardiovascular disease when heat and light energies are most yang—in hot summer months. Right-sided yin types should be most susceptible to yang deficiencies such as immune disease during the cold yin months of winter.

While yin-yang theory stretches back into China's remote antiquity, Five Phases elemental correspondence theory (Wu Xing), which deals with this issue of seasonal effects on organs, is a little more recent. Today a system of loose one-to-one correspondences meant to augment but not replace yin-yang theory, Five Phases theory is especially interesting in comparison with the health wheels of other cultures, which propose similar kinds of relationships.

In essence, the Five Phases are the four seasons of the year with symbolic names—

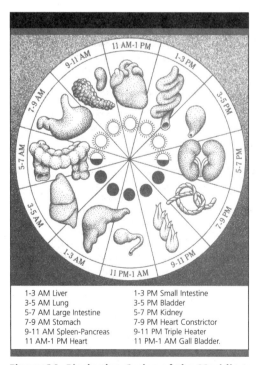

| | |
|---|---|
| 1-3 AM Liver | 1-3 PM Small Intestine |
| 3-5 AM Lung | 3-5 PM Bladder |
| 5-7 AM Large Intestine | 5-7 PM Kidney |
| 7-9 AM Stomach | 7-9 PM Heart Constrictor |
| 9-11 AM Spleen-Pancreas | 9-11 PM Triple Heater |
| 11 AM-1 PM Heart | 11 PM-1 AM Gall Bladder. |

**Figure 36. Biorhythm Cycles of the Meridians**

Gerber, Richard. Vibrational Medicine: New Choices for Healing Ourselves. pp. 183, copyright © 1988 by Richard Gerber. Reprinted by Permission of Bear & Company, Santa Fe NM 87504-2860.

**Table 26. Five Phases Correspondences in Chinese Medicine**

| | SPRING<br>Wood<br><br>YANG | SUMMER<br>Fire<br><br>YANG | INDIAN SUMMER<br>Earth<br><br>BALANCE | FALL<br>Metal<br><br>YIN | WINTER<br>Water<br><br>YIN |
|---|---|---|---|---|---|
| DIRECTION | East | South | Center | West | North |
| COLOR | Blue<br>Green | Red | Yellow | White | Black |
| CLIMATE | Windy | Hot | Damp | Dry | Cold |
| EMOTION | Anger | Joy | Pensiveness | Grief | Fear |
| YIN ORGAN | Liver | Heart | Spleen | Lungs | Kidney |
| YANG ORGAN | Gall<br>Bladder | Small<br>Intestine | Stomach | Large<br>Intestine | Bladder |
| ORIFICE | Eyes | Tongue | Mouth | Nose | Ears |
| TISSUE | Tendons | Blood Vessels | Flesh | Skin | Bones |
| LATERALITY | Left? | Posterior? | Bilateral? | Right? | Anterior? |
| TYPE | T | S | Balance | F | N |

Wood (spring), Fire (summer), Metal (autumn), Water (winter)—plus a "centering" phase, called Earth (Indian summer), which is supposed to represent a balancing of the warm yang seasons and the cold yin seasons. With these phases are associated a number of aspects of physiology, emotion, facial color, climate and compass directions on the earth, which are summarized in Table 26. The seasons, when placed on a T'ai Chi in accordance with their respective compass directionalities, bear marked resemblances to the system of humors posited by the Greeks (Figures 37–38). Both systems suggest a greater propensity for kidney, bladder, large intestine and lung problems in the cold yin months of the year, and for liver, gall bladder, small intestine and heart problems in the warm yang months of the year (Kaptchuk, 1983).

To consider the likelihood of this arrangement in a very limited way within the talent database, season of death was sorted to see what disorders were most characteristic at certain times of the year. The numbers, as we have noted, are minuscule, but even here lung disease, cancer, and gut problems were found to have contributed to more deaths in the cold months of the year, while heart disease, stroke, and infectious diseases were related to more deaths in the warm months (Table 27, page 182).

Overall, more Cardiovascular pattern deaths occurred in the warm "East" and "South" seasons of the Chinese system, and more Immune pattern deaths in the cold "West" and "North" seasons. To the extent that cardiovascular disease is primarily a left-sided or posterior disorder of Heat that is worsened by heat, and immune disease primarily a right-sided or anterior disorder of Cold that is worsened by cold, directionality in yin-yang theory would really seem to be a case of latitude as well as laterality, where left is East, from the Chinese perspective, posterior is South, right is West, and anterior is North. In that sense, the T'ai Chi and its circular correspondences are really a schematic representation of the brain as well as the earth.

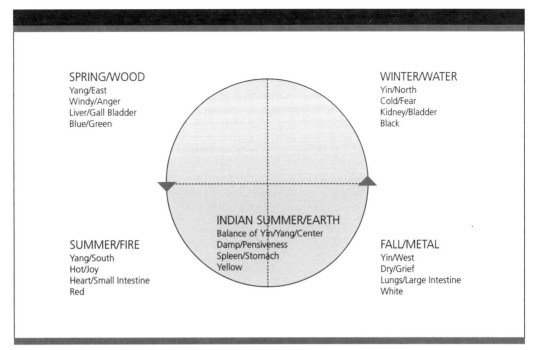

**Figure 37. Order of the Five Phases in Chinese Medicine**

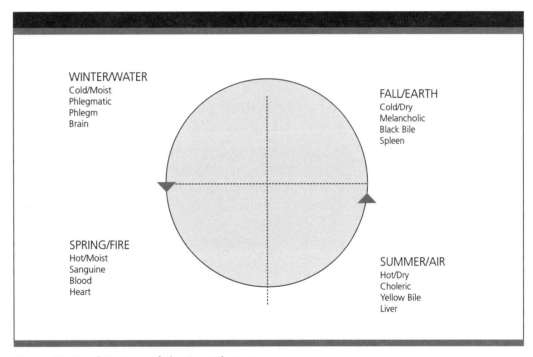

**Figure 38. Greek System of the Four Elements**

**Table 27. Season of Death in Cardiovascular and Immune Pattern Diseases Within the Talent Database**

|  | SEASON OF DEATH (%)* | | | | | |
| --- | --- | --- | --- | --- | --- | --- |
| DISEASE PATTERN | Winter (J/F/M) | Spring (A/M/J) | Summer (J/A/S) | Fall (O/N/D) | TOTAL COLD SEASONS | TOTAL WARM SEASONS |
| **"Cardio."** | | | | | | |
| Heart | 15 | 15 | 17 | 17 | 32 | 32 |
| Stroke | 20 | 24 | 15 | 15 | 35 | 39 |
| Infectious (Excl. AIDS) | 11 | 37 | 5 | 21 | 32 | 42 |
| **"Immune"** | | | | | | |
| Lung | 38 | 13 | 19 | 9 | 47 | 32 |
| Cancer | 10 | 5 | 13 | 13 | 23 | 18 |
| Gut | 0 | 0 | 17 | 50 | 50 | 17 |

* Interpretation: Of all subjects in the talent database who died of diseases belonging to the "Cardiovascular" pattern, a greater percentage died in warmer months of the year in the Northern Hemisphere. A greater percentage of "Immune" pattern deaths occurred in colder months of the year.

✳ ✳ ✳

Chapter 7 applies concepts in Chinese medicine to type, talent and disease questions discussed to this point. Chapter 7 arrives at the following conclusions:

✳ The pendulum-like swinging between yin and yang states seems similar to cognitive shifting between left/posterior and right/anterior polarities. Both states are needed for a balancing of the whole, though extremes of either can cause serious health problems. Yin-yang moves toward equilibrium, implying the very real possibility of *change* with this movement.

✳ Chakra issues might seem to correspond loosely to yin and yang processes, as well as to laterality, type, talent and disease in various physiological systems. Types tending toward I, S, T and J should be yang types who may neglect their yin elements. Types tending toward E, N, F and P should be yin types who may neglect their yang elements. Excessive imbalance in either direction may cause disease.

✳ Chinese medicine claims that patients with diseases of Heat (yang) are more likely to succumb in warm months of the year, while patients with diseases of Cold (yin) are more likely to succumb in cold months of the year. An examination of the talent database shows that subjects with Cardiovascular pattern ailments (left/posterior laterality) did, in fact, die more often in warm months of the year, while subjects with Immune pattern ailments (right/anterior laterality) died more often in cold months of the year, in the Northern Hemisphere.

* The Chinese system draws strong ties between disease processes, *time* (whether time of day or time of year) and *space* in north-south and east-west directionalities of the earth.

# CHAPTER EIGHT
## REINVENTING THE WHEEL OF COGNITION AND DISEASE: TYPE AND THE NATIVE MEDICINE WHEEL

✳ ✳ ✳

We will now look at the third of four ancient kinds of circles and its possible insights for questions of type, talent and disease. The medicine wheel considers colors (races) of man, representatives of which to some extent we are studying in sequence in chapters 6 through 10 in looking at example wheels of various cultural groups.

Space-time leads similar to those in Chinese medicine are also to be found in the native medicine wheel (compass directions, seasons) and, when applied to the circular talent-deficit continuum of the brain, form a unique wheel that is a kind of integration of the wheels we've seen to this point. This modern-day circle of life, the beginnings of the Sundial wheel we are building toward, represents not only the individual brain, but the earth as well, in keeping with the micro and macro aspects of the ancient models.

The medicine wheel speaks of an individual being born into a particular season, which gives him a certain view of life not held by those born into other seasons. It becomes his life task, then, to work his way around the symbolic dimensions of the wheel so as to incorporate these values in his life view and get along with his brothers for health and happiness.

Because Geschwind also had an idea about the effects of time of conception on an individual, we put these and the Chinese views together within the talent database and explore connections of type, talent and disease to time of birth. In doing so, we are exploring whether ancient beliefs bear any relation to our more recent model.

Chapter 8 considers developmental applications of the composite wheel, with special reference to the individuation process throughout life, and looks at this circle's possible ramifications for disease patterns around the world.

✳ ✳ ✳

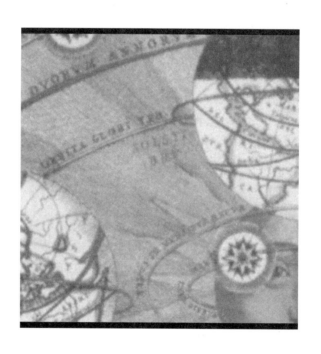

## Circle of Life

From the day we arrive on the planet

And blinking, step into the sun

There's more to see than can ever be seen

More to do than can ever be done

There's far too much to take in here

More to find than can ever be found

But the sun rolling high

Through the sapphire sky

Keeps great and small on the endless round

It's the circle of life

And it moves us all

Through despair and hope

Through faith and love

Till we find our place

On the path unwinding

In the circle

The circle of life

Some of us fall by the wayside

And some of us soar to the stars

And some of us sail through our troubles

And some have to live with the scars

In the circle of life

It's the wheel of fortune

It's the leap of faith

It's the band of hope

Till we find our place

On the path unwinding

In the circle, in the circle of life.

Circle of Life. Elton John and Tim Rice (1994),

Walt Disney Music Company, ASCAP

**The Chinese idea—that cognition,** health and the earth are somehow related—is also described in the ancient medicine wheel by Plains tribes of North America (Figure 39, page 188). These wheels, many of which are visible even today, may take the form of large sacred circles of stone, marking the prairies like flattened Stonehenges across the miles for early travelers who did not have compasses. Or, they can be found as small shields of deerskin and feathers, which at one time adorned native lodges to describe the kind

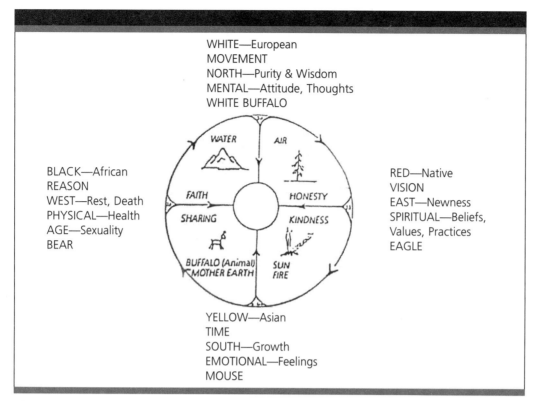

WHITE—European
MOVEMENT
NORTH—Purity & Wisdom
MENTAL—Attitude, Thoughts
WHITE BUFFALO

BLACK—African
REASON
WEST—Rest, Death
PHYSICAL—Health
AGE—Sexuality
BEAR

RED—Native
VISION
EAST—Newness
SPIRITUAL—Beliefs,
Values, Practices
EAGLE

YELLOW—Asian
TIME
SOUTH—Growth
EMOTIONAL—Feelings
MOUSE

**Figure 39. The Medicine Wheel**

of person who lived inside. Like the T'ai Chi, the medicine wheel represents nature from its smallest to its largest—the person, the family, the people, the globe—and is used as a healing tool (e.g., in Twelve-Step programs) to remind seekers of the areas within themselves or their group that are needing work. Some investigators think the medicine wheel was also used for astrological purposes such as determining the equinox (Friesen, 1995).

With the medicine wheel, there may not be the formal literature on the subject that there is for Chinese medicine because of the oral traditions of the native cultures, but the thrust is very similar—that the earth, with its four defined seasons and four directions, is associated with particular human activities and states of mind. These things are symbolized on a cross around a circle by elements, races, colors and now animals, different for each tribe, which are said to protect each stage of the cycle. Some wheels show yet another overlaying X-shaped cross which symbolizes the spirit world. By now, as we go through the meaning of the stages of the wheel, the connections to type and the brain might more readily jump out at us.

For instance, the east or right side of the wheel signifies newness—whether that is spring in the earth's development or early childhood in human development—and this newness is represented by the passionate color red, the lightness of the element Air, and the soaring Eagle, because this place on the circle is about inspiration, illumination, sensitivity, perception, vision and spirituality, qualities which might be found in Intuitive Feeling types (NF). The south or posterior pole of the wheel signifies growth—summer, adolescence—and this is represented by yellow (another warm color), the heat of the Sun and Fire, and the tiny Mouse because this position is about growth, time, small details, innocence, communication with others, understanding, emotional life and feelings, all of which might sound a bit like the qualities of SF. The west or left side of the wheel signifies rest—fall, adulthood—and this is represented by black, the quiet strength of the Buffalo, Mother Earth, and the powerful Bear, to symbolize introspection, reason, individuality, physical health, and sexuality, some of which might sound like Introversion and Sensing Thinking types (ST). The north or anterior pole of the wheel signifies movement—winter, old age—and is represented by the color white, the element of Water, and the Buffalo to symbolize wisdom, mental attitudes, thought, and conflict followed by peace, some of which might remind us of the temperament and goals of Intuitive Thinking types (NT).

The earth "moves" around this wheel in due course—from the birth of a day to the close of the day, from spring to summer, and so on—and each of us is born into one of the seasons, developing from that point onward through each of the stages. The same idea is described in ancient Christian traditions:

> And God said, Let there be lights in the firmament of the heaven to divide the day from the night; and let them be for signs, and for seasons, and for days, and years (Genesis 1: 2–4, 14).

> To every thing there is a season, and a time to every purpose under the heaven (Ecclesiastes 3: 1).

Being born under a seasonal sign is said to have its drawbacks. Marguerite Wood, of New Mexico, has studied the typological relationships of the wheel in Assiniboine culture, and tells of the belief that if we come too much from one direction, we are seen by others as deficient in the other areas. However, she says, "if you have integration of all the medicines, you will have no problem understanding your brothers" (Wood, 1994).

To achieve this state, it is considered the task of the truly holistic person to integrate the mind, body, heart and spirit of all four directions and to not become stuck at any one place around the circle. Native cultures use allegories to make this point. In the Legend of the Singing Stone, for example (Storm, 1973), a young man travels in search of the Singing Stone, believing it to be the embodiment of truth on earth, and is told by grandparents and symbolic animals along the way that the Singing Stone is to be found in a direction other than the one in which he is traveling. At each stop, he is informed that what he has done to get as far as he has is not enough, that the object of his quest is now south, east or west of where he actually is, and he follows their directions, ultimately traveling the whole of the wheel as he does so. Eventually he finds himself in the north, having traveled to all four compass points, where he is given buffalo meat and is greeted ceremoniously as Singing Stone himself. The message, of course, is that the journey of personal growth is lonely in that no one can do it for us, that it requires stretching outside our directional comfort zones to find our way, and that the effort is well worth the wholeness in body, mind, heart and spirit that is achieved as a result.

In mentally superimposing the medicine wheel on the circles that are chakras, Chinese Five Phases theory and even the Greek system of humors (Figures 37–38, page 181), we arrive at some very approximate similarities. The wheels are not identical, to be sure—nor would we expect them to be, given the differences in historical period, culture, and place of origin on the globe—but are related perhaps in a subjective, metaphorical manner that is the way of the ancients. For instance, we notice that the warm seasons and warm colors (red, yellow) tend to be represented on the lower half of each model, with connections to the positive emotions of joy, optimism and anger, and the circulatory (heart) and digestive systems. Cold seasons and cold colors (blue, black, white) tend to be on the upper half of each model, alongside the negative emotions of apathy, fear and melancholy, as well as the central nervous system (brain), immune system (spleen) and urinary system (kidney, bladder).

The warmer the color on this imaginary "combination" wheel, the lower the position on the body, and in the case of the medicine wheel, the more apparently right-sided the cognitive activity. The colder the color, the higher the position on the body, and the more apparently left-sided the activity to some extent. Thus, to become rooted to one side of a wheel is to be excessive on that side, and deficient on the other. To be right-sided, as we have speculated, may be to affect the CNS and the immune system primarily, and be at particular risk in the cold months, whereas to be left-sided may be to affect the circulatory and digestive systems primarily, and be at risk more often in the warm months.

It is entirely possible that drawing such connections between type and ancient beliefs on a series of wheels is complete nonsense and an utter waste of time. On the other hand, it is also possible that these similar efforts by very different cultures underscore the larger and more important question, that *there may actually be a relationship between the sidedness of cognition and disease.* Regardless of the accuracy or inaccuracy of the individual wheels, there seems to be much longstanding wisdom in their collective advice, which is to strive for integration, centering and balance of natural tendencies so as to maintain health.

There is much we can learn from these earlier attempts, to apply to our own modern-day situations. If, for example, being born under a particular sign on the wheel (season, direction) can influence mind, body, heart and spirit as the First Nations peoples believed, and certainly as ancient Egyptian and Chinese astrologers believed, if "coming too much from one direction" can contribute to ill health and interpersonal difficulties, it would be very interesting to test whether season of birth is also related to the type, talent, disease problem. Geschwind (1985) wondered about links between birth month and disease, so a cursory examination of the talent database in this way would not appear to be totally out of line.

Looking at the three main health problems in Canada—heart disease and stroke, representative of what we have called the Cardiovascular pattern, and cancer, representative of the Immune pattern—it becomes apparent that, for the highly talented people in this small sample only, heart disease and stroke are slightly more often associated with birth in the colder seasons of the year in the Northern Hemisphere (fall and winter). Cancer, on the other hand, seems slightly more common in those who were born in warmer seasons of spring and summer (Figure 40). Then, if this is further broken down by talent category, we find that our gifted people in writing, music, art, science, mathematics and politics (Intuitive types?) were more often born in the cold months of the year, while our athletes and business people

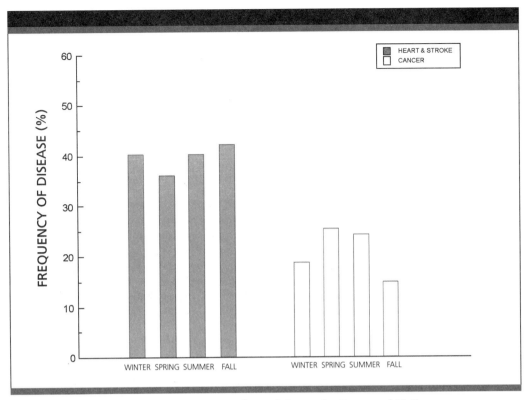

**Figure 40. Incidence of Heart Disease, Stroke and Cancer by Season of Birth**

(Sensing types?) were more often born in the warm months, and the actors and chess players in both (Tables 28–29, pages 192 and 193; Appendix C, page 315).

The tables are not precise and are certainly far from perfect—*clearly, all talents and all types are born in all months of the year*—but it is interesting to note that some talents in our database seem to cluster in some seasons of the year more than others. Our scientists and mathematicians (NT, ST), for example, were more often born in the first part of the year, which would support Geschwind's hypothesis about the birth time of gifted people in verbal spheres. Our more spatially inclined people, however—artists and chess players—were more often born at the other end of the spectrum, in the latter part of the year. When we put such clustered talents together with their presumed temperament and laterality (e.g., math, left-posterior), and the most common disease pattern that was found for them, whether Cardiovascular or Immune or both, we arrive at the system depicted in Figure 41 on page 193—a modern-day version of the medicine wheel which relates the light and heat energy of the different seasons to talent laterality, type and disease.

This wheel certainly isn't precise or perfect either, but is rather a rough metaphorical guide to the patterns that might be going on in each of the four quadrants of the brain, the genus names of NT, ST, SF and NF replacing the element names of Water, Earth, Fire and Air, and the animal names of Buffalo, Bear, Mouse and Eagle.

From the lessons taught us by the ancient wheels, we know that this system, if it even exists, is probably very flexible, and that it may be possible to move from one quadrant to the next, regardless of the one we were actually born into, simply by stressing cognitive activities that promote shifting. The goal, as in times of old, must be to center ourselves, to strive for equality of skill and modes of thought, action and feeling so as to offset the risks that may be coupled with an overemphasis on any one of them.

Following the aboriginal peoples' belief that the seasons are also stages of development in man—spring is childhood, summer is adolescence, fall is adulthood, winter is old age—and Jung's notion of the development of the dominant function in childhood, the auxiliary function in adulthood, the tertiary function at midlife, and the inferior function in old age (Hirsch & Kummerow, 1990), it is also interesting to explore this imaginary system in a developmental sense.

An INTP scientist like Carl Jung, for instance, as a right-handed left-anterior talent who was born in summer, 1875, is said to first develop his dominant Thinking (left) in childhood, his auxiliary Intuition (anterior) in adolescence and adulthood, his tertiary Sensing (posterior) at middle age, and his inferior Feeling (right) in later life. Is it possible that an INTP's disease vulnerabilities also move in this order, from the Cardiovascular pattern in childhood (T), to the Immune pattern in adulthood (N), to the Cardiovascular pattern again in middle age (S), and finally to the Immune pattern again in later life (F)? Without research, of course, we cannot say, but it is interesting to note that Jung experienced fainting attacks as a young boy, following a blow to the head, that like Einstein and Freud, he had a nervous collapse at 38, suffered emboli in his heart and lungs at 68, and finally died following two strokes in spring, 1961, at the age of 86.

**Table 28. Season of Birth and Frequency (%) of Heart Disease, Stroke and Cancer in Nine Talent Categories**

| | DISEASE | | | SEASON OF BIRTH | | | |
|---|---|---|---|---|---|---|---|
| **TALENT** | **Heart** | **Cancer** | **Pattern (CV or Immune)** | **Winter** | **Spring** | **Summer** | **Fall** |
| **Pol.**[1] | 70 | 18 | CV | 23 | 18 | 13 | 28 |
| **Bus.** | 60 | 20 | CV | 5 | 8 | 13 | 8 |
| **Mus.** | 53 | 25 | CV | 25 | 15 | 18 | 20 |
| **Chess** | 35 | - | CV | 8 | 23 | 13 | 23 |
| **Sci/Math** | 33 | 23 | CV/IM | 25 | 23 | 20 | 15 |
| **Art** | 30 | 8 | CV[2] | 23 | 13 | 13 | 25 |
| **Writ.** | 28 | 18 | CV/IM | 25 | 15 | 20 | 30 |
| **Act.** | 18 | 53 | IM | 23 | 20 | 15 | 15 |
| **Sports** | 10 | 30 | IM | 8 | 8 | 15 | 10 |

[1]Interpretation: Of the politicians in the talent database for whom birth dates were available, 70% had heart disease or stroke, 18% had cancer—meaning the Cardiovascular (CV) pattern predominates—and 28% were born in the fall
[2]We might expect to see an Immune pattern for artists or for art, but the data actually suggested a CV pattern. Further data collection may or may not support this finding.

As another example, we can observe the left-handed artist M. C. Escher, who might have been INFJ and who, as a right-anterior talent born in June, should have gone through a dominant Intuition (anterior) stage in early life, an auxiliary Feeling (right) stage in young adulthood, a tertiary Thinking (left) stage at mid-life, and an inferior Sensing (posterior) stage in later life. In actual fact, Escher was a "sickly child" (Bool et al., 1981) all through his

**Table 29. Most Common Season of Birth in Nine Talent Areas, Corresponding to the Quadrants of the Medicine Wheel, Type, Laterality and Most Common Disease Pattern**

| BIRTH SEASON | WINTER | SPRING | SUMMER | FALL |
|---|---|---|---|---|
| TALENT | Music | Science | Sports | Writing |
| | Science | Math | Business | Politics |
| | Math | Chess | | Art |
| | Acting | | | Chess |
| QUADRANT | Vision | Time | Reason | Movement |
| | Stage | Stage | (Common Sense) | Stage |
| | | | Stage | |
| TYPE | NT | ST | SF | NF |
| LATERALITY | Left/Anterior | Left/Posterior | Right/Posterior | Right/Anterior |
| DOMINANT DISEASE PATTERN | CV | CV/Immune | Immune | CV/Immune |

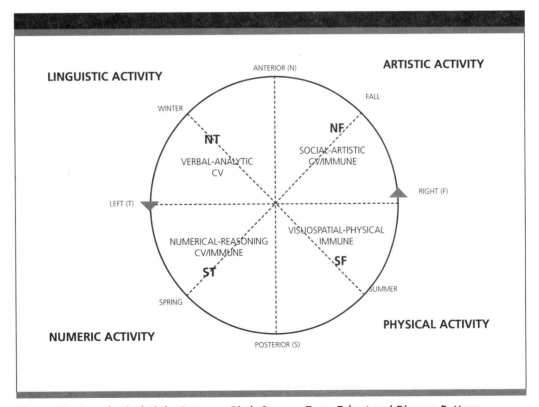

**Figure 41. Hypothetical Links Between Birth Season, Type, Talent and Disease Pattern**

childhood (N development), who developed a persistent skin infection, depression and many illnesses in adulthood (F development), compulsive obsessions at 53 (T development), finally dying of stomach problems (S development) in March 1972, at 73.

Plotting the type development of all sixteen types on the wheel in this way suggests that a person may be born on one side of the wheel and end his life on the contralateral side (Table 30). Thus, a person born into the world as a dominant Thinking type (left) could very well complete the life cycle in his inferior Feeling (right) quadrant, perhaps increasing his risk for the Immune pattern of disease. A dominant Feeling type (right) might ultimately find himself in a Thinking (left) quadrant, perhaps increasing his risk for the Cardiovascular pattern. A dominant Intuitive type (anterior) could complete the life cycle in a Sensing (posterior) quadrant, perhaps increasing his risk for the Cardiovascular pattern. And a dominant Sensing type (posterior) may end up in an Intuitive type (anterior) quadrant, perhaps increasing his risk for the Immune pattern.

With this possibility in mind, it is of interest that the heart and stroke patients in the talent database who were born in cold seasons of the year tended to die slightly more often in the warm months, just as cancer patients who were born in warm seasons of the year tended to die more often in the cold months—in other words, during the opposite light and heat energy into which they were born (Figure 42).

In tracing development of all the types on this wheel, we find that type development appears to move in imperfect clockwise and counterclockwise directions around this circle, which is the brain, depending on the type. Clockwise or rightward movement would seem to be the case for STs with dominant Sensing, SFs with dominant Feeling, NFs with dominant

**Table 30. Stages of Typological Development**

| ISTJ | ISFJ | INFJ | INTJ |
|---|---|---|---|
| 1. Sensing<br>2. Thinking<br>3. Feeling<br>4. Intuition | 1. Sensing<br>2. Feeling<br>3. Thinking<br>4. Intuition | 1. Intuition<br>2. Feeling<br>3. Thinking<br>4. Sensing | 1. Intuition<br>2. Thinking<br>3. Feeling<br>4. Sensing |
| **ISTP** | **ISFP** | **INFP** | **INTP** |
| 1. Thinking<br>2. Sensing<br>3. Intuition<br>4. Feeling | 1. Feeling<br>2. Sensing<br>3. Intuition<br>4. Thinking | 1. Feeling<br>2. Intuition<br>3. Sensing<br>4. Thinking | 1. Thinking<br>2. Intuition<br>3. Sensing<br>4. Feeling |
| **ESTP** | **ESFP** | **ENFP** | **ENTP** |
| 1. Sensing<br>2. Thinking<br>3. Feeling<br>4. Intuition | 1. Sensing<br>2. Feeling<br>3. Thinking<br>4. Intuition | 1. Intuition<br>2. Feeling<br>3. Thinking<br>4. Sensing | 1. Intuition<br>2. Thinking<br>3. Feeling<br>4. Sensing |
| **ESTJ** | **ESFJ** | **ENFJ** | **ENTJ** |
| 1. Thinking<br>2. Sensing<br>3. Intuition<br>4. Feeling | 1. Feeling<br>2. Sensing<br>3. Intuition<br>4. Thinking | 1. Feeling<br>2. Intuition<br>3. Sensing<br>4. Thinking | 1. Thinking<br>2. Intuition<br>3. Sensing<br>4. Feeling |

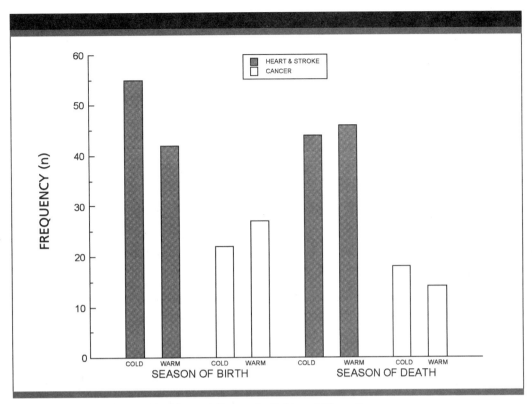

**Figure 42. Heart Disease, Stroke and Cancer in Cold and Warm Seasons**

Intuition, and NTs with dominant Thinking. Counterclockwise or leftward movement would seem to be more often the norm for STs with dominant Thinking, SFs with dominant Sensing, NFs with dominant Feeling, and NTs with dominant Intuition. That is, there would seem to be a veritable "spin" to type development in the brain, both positive and negative like chakra vortices and yang and yin states, and which may be related, in part, to the season of birth, whether of lightness (summer, yang), darkness (winter, yin), or somewhere in between (spring, fall, yin-yang).

The spinning should not surprise us since all of nature does it, from the spinning of atoms in microscopic infinity, which creates net positive and negative charges, to the spinning of orbiting moons, planets and suns in macroscopic infinity, which also create gravitational fields of varying strengths—negative charges on bodies having a counterclockwise spin, and positive charges on those with a clockwise spin. As the First Nations believed many thousands of years ago, personal development may be only a microcosm of this larger activity on the global level, the energy quantities and "spin" of the person creating the "charge," anionic or cationic, which ultimately determines the types of energy and the energic types he or she will be drawn to in the creation of a steady state. The "anion" type (I, S, T, or J?), as we have said, may look to *release* energy because it has a natural tendency to build up excess, the "cation" type (E, N, F or P?) to *absorb* energy because it has a natural tendency to operate at a deficit. Together, following Coulomb's law of electrostatics, they may empty and fill each other in the formation of a quasi-molecular relationship that has prototypes everywhere.

The four directions, the four functions, the four stages of life, and birth and death in opposite quadrants—it is hard not to draw larger metaphysical fantasies from this, such as that existence may be much like a three-dimensional LP on a turntable, with the stylus touching down to determine our starting place on the circle, as well as when and how we get off it. Accordingly, each organism is programmed with its own innate power to create (talent), as well as its own unique power to self-destruct (disease). Thus each of us has qualities of organization, building, creation and *order* within his or her own being, as well as entropy, destruction and *chaos*. Life, then, is a constant and swinging flux between these polarities, with talent or disease occurring when the flux becomes relatively fixed at some place along the continuum. Rigidly insisting on being one kind of person—even a flexible person—very likely allows us to become especially good at something, even gifted, but it is also possible that it can make us unwell in some way if we continue to do it excessively.

Inasmuch as it may be the light and heat energy present in a season—weak energy in winter in the Northern Hemisphere, strong in summer, moderate in spring and fall—that first influences the whole process of talent development in the fetus, which in turn "lights up" some areas of the brain, hormonally and otherwise, while placing other areas in the shadows, a more apt metaphor would seem to be the *sundial.* Over time, whether daily or over the course of a lifetime, parts of the brain are emphasized, highlighted, "lit up," as it were, circumplicially as we move around our developmental wheel. To stop this progression, to focus on only one area or skill set, is to stop the flow of energy, and to do that may be as physically likely or beneficial as stopping the march of time. As the New Testament points out, "If your whole body (brain) is full of light, with no part of it in darkness, it will be bright all over, as when a lamp shines on you with its brightness" (Luke 11: 36, parentheses added).

Movement around the North American medicine wheel, or personal growth as we would call it in humanistic terms, is said to happen in clockwise concentric circles, or orbits, which become ever smaller in moving toward the center. Plains tribes have a "Master Tree" at the center of a Sundance circle, around which are twelve spoke poles representing the Apostles. Buddhists believe God is at the center of such mandalas, and aboriginal tribes of Australia believe something very similar:

> . . . in this world of personalities, there is always a duality . . . It is not black or white; it is always shades of gray. And most importantly all the gray is moving in a progressive pattern back to the Originator (Morgan, 1994: 137).

Jung, too, wrote:

> . . . the goal of psychic development is the self . . . *There is no linear evolution; there is only a circumambulation of the self.* Uniform development exists, at most, only at the beginning; later, everything points toward the center . . . *The center, therefore, is the goal* (Jung, 1969b: 196–199, emphasis added).

Jung believed we are each born with a self, a blueprint of our uniqueness that is all at once the center and the totality of our psyche. In analyzing these thoughts, Corlett and Millner (1993) put it well:

> As an inner, organizing center, the self moves us toward a synthesis of opposites, the different and often conflicting parts of ourselves, through the process of individuation . . . Jung saw individuation not as a self-centered path, but as a search for balance in which both self-understanding and connections with others interact and enhance one another. The path may be linear, or, increasingly at midlife, may be seen as a circular and often spiraling pattern that periodically recycles around the psyche with a different focus to clarify issues and enable us to view our life experiences from a new perspective (Corlett & Millner, 1993: 49–50, emphasis added).

This process of individuation towards integration and wholeness might be seen as a circle, if viewed from above, or a spiral, if viewed from the side, that moves ever inward toward the center of a geometric shape called a whorl, found elsewhere in physical nature as fingerprints, hair crowns, seashells, whirlpools, water spouts, tornados and nebulas, and in ethereal nature as the spinning vortices of chakras (Figure 29, page 157). A physicist's interpretation of the interconnectedness of whorls in nature is illustrated in the following verse:

> Big whorls have little whorls
> Which feed on their velocity,
> And little whorls have lesser whorls
> And so on to viscosity
> (Lewis F. Richardson, in Gleick, 1987:119).

Thus, in very literal terms, individuation is a process of ever-decreasing laterality in the brain, of tighter and tighter circling toward some real or invisible center, of the modification of thought and feeling, of normalizing, to a point where the self is equidistant from the extremes of all four main functions and is, as such, doubly bilateral, or quadrilateral, in space. The directional spin of a particular whorl (left or right) may vary from person to person as a partial function of birth time (conception time) and handedness. So might the "tightness" of the whorl vary with maturational speed, the stresses of life experiences, and a great variety of other factors including conscious choices to shift in different cognitive directions. A person rewarded for his lateral extremes, such as for an exceptional gift perhaps, is surely likely to circle wider than a person somehow punished for his behavior and who seeks to modify his extremes.

Because these are variations on the same basic theme, with the same basic circling structure, the type-disease whorl should be mathematically describable, perhaps ultimately to predict the tightness of the developmental circles and the direction in which the whorl travels so as to actually pinpoint periods of heightened disease risk (times of greatest one-sidedness and imbalance) in a person's life. Our starting place on the "big picture" laterality whorl could be the month of birth, our disease vulnerabilities then changing with type development, such that dominant Intuitive type children, for example, may have more trouble than Sensing types with infectious childhood diseases or allergies, while post-menopausal Sensing types may have more trouble than Intuitive types with heart disease or osteoporosis.

A simple demonstration of how we might use whorl geometry in prediction is the partial whorl that is created by plotting, on a polar axis, number of meditation sessions per week for stress reduction and relaxation against numbers of people who do such things. To illustrate, suppose a sample of 160 fictitious practitioners meditate less than once a week, on average, and are therefore relatively infrequent meditators, yet one person meditates ten times per week and is therefore a frequent meditator. Graphing these cases, and others in between, on a linear two-axis graph would normally produce an L-shaped curve (Figure 43), but on a four-quadrant graph (Figure 44) of the kind we've been using with our health wheels, the logarithm of the same line is suddenly part of a clockwise-spinning whorl which depicts the "disease" state (infrequent meditation, higher stress) on one side, and the healthy state (frequent meditation, lower stress) towards the center.

If we wanted to, we could derive an equation for this line that would allow us to predict the degree of stress or relaxation in a new individual based on how often the person engages in this practice. This is just a simple example, but more complex equations for more complex whorls could be developed in this way for other behaviors and disease states, each line having a different curl in tightness or direction that could shed light on one process relative to another. If we knew what type functions reliably correlated with these states—e.g, what type scales, if any, correlate with the practice of meditation and successful stress reduction—we might have diagrammatic proof of the importance of being at a particular place on the wheel in order for such balance to occur, as well as mathematical sentences to help in the prediction of outcome.

Why should mathematics be relevant in a discussion of ancient health wheels? Because mathematics is the language of physics, and it is physics that will very likely bring new life to these concepts in the emerging discipline of bioenergetic or spiritual psychology. Physics will ultimately prove (or disprove) holistic ideas and will legitimize holistic thought in Western society. For, in the final analysis, Westerners will still require that analysis and logical proofs show that analysis and logical proofs in health are not the whole answer!

For instance, the dynamical yin-yang system underlying Chinese medicine for five thousand years is often criticized by Western skeptics for its non-scientific fuzziness, but is easily described by chaos theory using a strange attractor model (Figure 45, page 201). From that perspective, the laterality pendulum swings back and forth between yin and yang over a lifetime, gradually losing momentum over time as the person meets resistance for his extremes, learns (hopefully) from experience, and modifies his thinking and behavior. The trajectory of this path, when mapped, forms an inward-moving spiral, which is in a static, steady state only in the center, at the moment of death. It is because, in this sense, *type development is actually a three-dimensional spiral*, and not a two-dimensional circle, that the unit "circles of life" for the sixteen types on the chart in Table 30 (page 194) seem imperfect. They are not uniformly

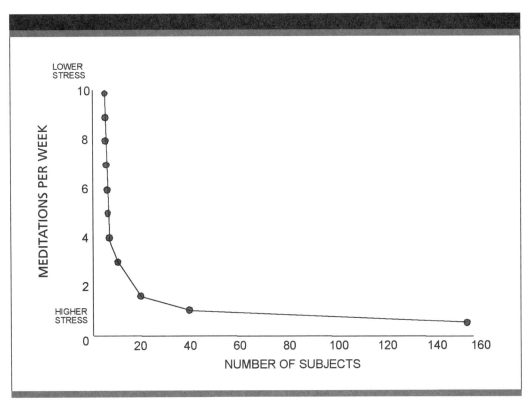

**Figure 43. Frequency of Meditation Expressed as an XY Graph**

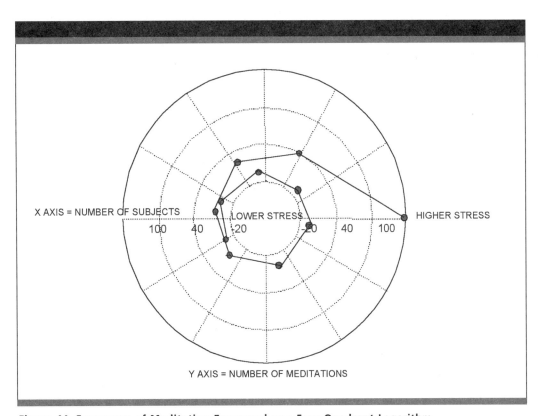

**Figure 44. Frequency of Meditation Expressed as a Four-Quadrant Logarithm**

round, as we might expect from looking at a wheel on paper, but are stretched in vertically spiraling coils because type development happens in a three-dimensional space that is the brain.

In the end, those who would resist the inward flow of the path of their own developmental spiral by practicing a lateralized function to extremes may become ill because they ignore the instinctive balancing process, the resistance, that should keep them well. Physical and psychological symptoms advising of the need for change, for getting on with one's movement around the whorl—like viral infection and chest pain perhaps, or relationship signals like repeated divorce—"speak" to us about potential laterality problems we should probably explore. Veronique Boulangier (1994), an Australian psychotherapist who uses type in her practice, feels mental and physical disease is related to the development, emergence or suppression of a function, which suggests that transitional periods between life stages, and transitional periods generally, could be particularly vulnerable times. The active, physical ST male, for example, who denies the importance of Intuition or Feeling at midlife because he wants to hold onto his accustomed ways, may run greater risks of heart attack than the ST who acknowledges their value, downplays the T, and lets in the F. As Boulangier advises, "heart attack is an attack of the heart" which could be serious for a man who fails to listen to it.

We have said that laterality may be influenced by the light and heat energy of the season at the time of conception. This is not astrology, which makes detailed personal predictions based on the constellations of stars, but is instead about available *light* from the sun and the moon whose patterns are known to influence seasonal growth of living organisms and the rhythmic yin-yang movement of even inorganic nature, like waves and tides. Many organisms, plant and animal, grow and behave differently in the summer than they do in the winter—witness tree rings and hibernation—so it seems not at all implausible to agree with Geschwind that a natural process that affects the development of other life on the planet might also affect our own. It may do this in part through light-mediated exposure to different levels of fetal androgens and other biochemical processes, which contributes to a major developmental shift in the brain before birth. And it may do it again afterwards in conjunction with post-natal environmental effects like parenting, education, and free choice.

This thinking makes us take a second look at language used in the New Testament, which again we do purposely in an attempt to integrate concepts in science and spirituality:

> In the beginning was the Word, and the Word was with God, and the Word was God. The same was in the beginning with God. All things were made by him; and without him was not made any thing that was made. In him was life; and the life was the light of men. And the light shineth in darkness; and the darkness comprehended it not. There was a man sent from God, whose name was John. The same came for a witness, to bear witness of the Light, that all men through him might believe. He was not that Light, but was sent to bear witness of that Light. *That was the true Light, which lighteth every man that cometh into the world* (John 1:1–9, emphasis added).

A. The charts at left depict the left-right swinging of a dynamical system such as a pendulum, as in a pendulum clock. The charts at right map the trajectory of the pendulum on a four-quadrant graph (phase space). One point in phase space contains all the information about the state of the dynamical system at any instant. Two numbers—velocity and position—describe what the pendulum is doing at any point in time. Thus, velocity is zero as the pendulum starts its swing. Position is a negative number, the distance to the left of the center. The two numbers specify a single point in two-dimensional phase space. Velocity reaches its maximum as the pendulum's position passes through zero. Velocity declines again to zero, and then becomes negative to represent leftward motion.

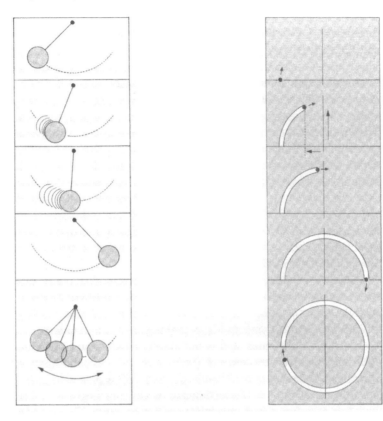

B. Many such points trace a trajectory that provides a way of visualizing the continuous long-term behavior of a dynamical system. A repeating loop represents a system that repeats itself at regular intervals. If the repeating behavior is stable, as in a pendulum clock, then the system returns to this orbit after small disruptions. In phase space, trajectories near the orbit are drawn into it; the orbit is an attractor. An attractor can be a single point. For a pendulum steadily losing energy to friction, all trajectories spiral inward toward a point that represents a steady state—in this case, the steady state of no motion at all.

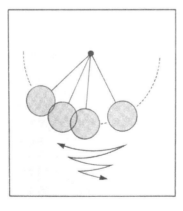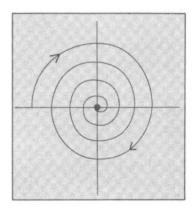

**Figure 45. Strange Attractor Model of a Pendulum**

From: Gleick, James. *Chaos: Making a New Science*. p. 136, copyright © 1987 by James Gleick

Babies born in hot climates near the equator are exposed to greater and stronger amounts of ultraviolet light, before and after birth, than babies born in more temperate climes. Therefore, it might stand to reason that, like the differential effects of light on spring and winter wheat, there may be subtle differences in human development in hotter, brighter parts of the world, especially at certain times of the year when the sun is most direct (Figures 46–47). From a Darwinian perspective, people in these regions are said to have adapted to the light, over many generations, by producing darker skin pigmentation to absorb it. The main ingredient of this pigmentation is a compound called melanin, which acts as a filter for ultraviolet radiation. Black people have more of this substance, while Caucasians, who are said to have evolved as a race in colder climates, have less of it.

Melanin concentrations are controlled by the hormone melatonin. Melatonin is derived from the neurotransmitter serotonin, which we know is more likely to be found in higher concentrations in the left hemisphere (Glick et al., 1977). When serotonin is at low levels, especially in the right hemisphere, it can contribute to depression, and depression we know is related to immune dysfunction. In the end, blacks as a race have also evolved particular problems with hypertension, sickle cell anemia, and cardiovascular disease (left laterality?), while red-haired, fair-skinned people have evolved disproportionately more problems with sun-sensitive immune disorders such as lupus erythematosus and skin cancer (right laterality?).

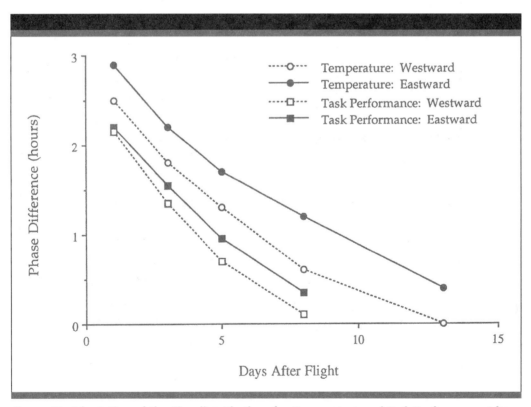

**Figure 46. Adaptation of the Circadian Rhythms for Temperature and Task Performance After Westward or Eastward Flights of 6-Hour Tranzonal Displacement**

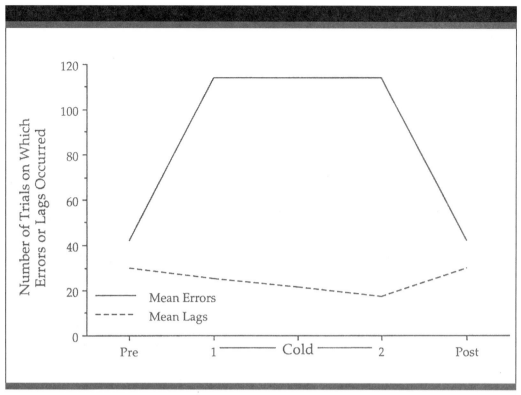

**Figure 47. Mean Errors and Mean Number of Lag Trials for a Serial Choice-Reaction Task Performed Twice Under Cold and Moderate Temperatures**

From: Proctor, Robert & Dutta, Addie. *Skill Acquisition and Human Performance.* p. 347, copyright © 1995 by SAGE Publications, Inc., Thousand Oaks CA. Reprinted by Permission of SAGE Publications, Inc.

Clearly, our bodily adaptations to sunlight, through coloring, are associated at least to some degree with racial variations in disease.

Now to the extent that Geschwind is right, that blonde hair is one of the cluster factors associated with right-sided cognition and immune dysfunction, we can suggest that, like color blindness has been said to be a genetic marker for alcoholic predispositions, or left-handedness a marker for certain learning disabilities, hair color in general might be an external physical marker for broad cognitive tendencies such as verbal or nonverbal talent, as well as the disease vulnerabilities that apparently go with them—darker coloring for verbal-cardiovascular pairings, and fairer complexions for artistic-immune or athletic-immune pairings. If hair color were such a marker, naturally *changing* hair color might foretell of acute changes in health status, not to mention the three major developmental shifts in laterality that we believe take place over the course of a lifetime—the transitional periods of reading-readiness (between the ages of four and seven), puberty, and midlife.

To illustrate, we can imagine a preschooler with very blonde or red hair who might be particularly right-lateralized—outgoing, active, artistic—and perhaps more vulnerable therefore to childhood diseases such as measles and chicken pox. As he learns to read, and later do math, he gradually shifts left, reduces his risk of contracting infectious childhood diseases, and his hair darkens, possibly turning completely dark by adulthood. Covariant with this transformation is a much-bemoaned loss of artistic interest normally blamed on "left-brained" schooling. But what he loses in drawing skills, he gains in verbal abilities, perhaps with even greater control of the immune sensitivities, while at the same time experiencing a concomitant increase in cardiovascular risk throughout midlife. The hair grays, the complexion pales, and with advancing age, he shifts right again, perhaps taking more interest in golf, retirement in the warmth of the sun, or some other right-sided activity, and he is at risk once again for immune problems, such as skin cancer, which may stop the spin of the circle altogether.

We are not for a moment suggesting that coloring, as a genetic adaptation to light energy, predicts for or causes illness. We are only noticing that, as in chakra theory, changes in color seem to parallel, to be *associated with*, other physical and cognitive changes in a person at critical points in human development. Sweeping shifts in laterality and changing modes of thought at these junctures may be collectively responsible for the observations.

Adding the cognitive element to our cultural theme, then, we can look at the Japanese who have a lower incidence of cancer than North Americans, presumably in part because they eat more vegetables than North Americans eat. We can look at the French who have lower rates of heart disease than North Americans do, in part because they consume more red wine than North Americans consume. But perhaps it is not only what they eat and drink—in conjunction with all the various other elements identified as causal factors—but also what they *think*. Is it possible that the dark-haired Japanese, as a culture, are simply more left-lateralized, more verbal-analytic than North Americans are, and are hence less prone to immune dysfunction? Could it be that the French, as a culture, are more right-lateralized, more active-artistic than North Americans are, and are hence less prone to heart disease? And what of fair Scandinavians who for years put the world to shame with their cardiovascular fitness, while at the same time exhibiting great creative and progressive thinking as a region, as well as high rates of depression? (Gibson, 1985). As a culture, have they not been among the most right-lateralized Europeans of all?

In the same way, we can look at the staggering incidence of depression, substance abuse and suicide in aboriginal cultures around the world, and wonder if this tragedy isn't perpetuated in part by political and economic hopelessness (right hemisphere activation) as well as by the very *strengths* of these cultures in the nonverbal arts—painting, sculpture, dance. Perhaps a collective leftward shift with verbal self-education will help to overcome this cycle, but we wonder if that might occur at the possible expense, to some degree, of their wonderful arts.

We noted earlier that the medicine wheel suggests that the four quadrants of the wheel containing personality, cognitive and physical traits in the individual are also the four directions of the compass (Figure 39, page 188). The wheel as brain is a cell of the individual in that sense, the individual is a cell of the earth, the earth is a cell of the solar system, and so on, a multi-layered onion, in effect, of wheel upon wheel, circle upon circle, orbit upon orbit in all of the universe. The medicine wheel describes or implies *space and time* at all these levels—in the individual (the brain, spiraling personal development, the life cycle) as well as the earth (directionality, days, seasons)—and is, consequently, a very Einsteinian model of existence that is centuries old.

Following the space leads of the wheel, we can supply our type genus names from the diagram in Figure 41 (page 193) to the quadrants of the three-dimensional "quadrispheres" that are the globe and arrive at some very interesting possibilities in terms of disease patterns in the four corners of the world. We will recall we hypothesized that NT (left-anterior), and the possible cardiovascular weaknesses associated with this genus, is the typological equivalent of the northwest quadrant of the medicine wheel. Placed on a globe, this part of the wheel would seem to localize the Cardiovascular disease pattern in the northwest corner of the world over North America where heart disease is decidedly the number one killer.

ST and NF, meanwhile, were proposed to exhibit a more equal incidence of Cardiovascular and Immune patterns from observations in the talent database, and to represent traits in the southwest and northeast quadrants of the wheel. Applied to the wheel on a global level, this would seem to place a comparatively equal distribution of cardiovascular and immune diseases in the southwest corner of the world over South America and in the northeast corner over mystical Asia where diseases like diabetes and liver cancer are common health problems (Lappe, 1994) and where SARS and avian flu first originated. Similarly, SF (right-posterior) and its proposed associated immune dysfunction in the southeast corner of the wheel should be localized in the southeast corner of the world, over Australia, parts of Africa and southeast Asia, where skin cancer, malaria and AIDS are extremely significant health problems attracting the serious attention of the rest of the world. Now this is not at all to downplay the role of pathogenic factors like ozone depletion, genetic abnormalities, deficient health care systems, diet and toxins, but only to say that *additionally* we might want to consider the effects of latitude on laterality in these matters. *Cultural cognitive style* may be one factor we have not systematically addressed with respect to illness. Cultural variations in disease, handedness, the direction of reading and writing (right to left in the East, left to right in the West), and East-West differences in philosophical orientation (holistic vs. analytic) may be enough to raise more than an inquisitive eyebrow in this regard.

Following the *time* leads of the medicine wheel, we can go beyond mere seasons and days in the life of the individual, and look at time in the life of the earth, in the global context of millennia and disease patterns throughout the history of civilization. For example, the spiritual "N" period following the Crusades through to the early sixteenth century saw the emergence of the bubonic plague, syphilis and influenza as the most serious health problems facing the world (Smith, 1979). The mechanistic scientific period of Newton's Modern Age, a decidedly "T" period in human history, witnessed the increasing prevalence of cardiovascular disease and a relative decline in the incidence of left-handedness (Harris, 1978). Since the Industrial Revolution, the global preoccupation with technological development for the sake of security, an "S" period, has seen the invention of a wide variety of medical treatments, such as vaccines, and the gradual eradication of a great many infectious diseases. Tuberculosis was a leading cause of death in the nineteenth century, heart disease for much of the twentieth century (Smith, 1979; Cohen, 1989), and in the same time frame there was a rapid decline in the incidence of left-handedness (Coren, 1993).

Now, however, in the early twenty-first century, we have entered another as-yet-unnamed revolution, the New Age or the Information Age, that is watching political and economic decentralization (decreasing order, entropy) on a grand scale, a movement toward holism and wellness, and an expanding human consciousness, a passionate "F" period perhaps, that is heretofore unprecedented. Left-handedness has been tolerated, if not actively supported, since the 1960s. And allergies, tuberculosis, virulent strains of Streptococcus A (flesh-eating disease), AIDS, antibiotic-resistant infection and other immune disorders are inexplicably on the rise.

The history of man itself may thus have moved counterclockwise on the wheel of life, in rough parallels to the typological development of an Intuitive Thinking type (NT) and the counterclockwise orbit of the earth around the sun. This begs the Hindu-like question of how many times we may have been around this circle, not to mention whether we will again move increasingly toward spirituality (N) and the immune problems that may or may not accompany it. It also suggests, perhaps naively, that to heal the world, like the individual, there may need to be a concerted effort to shift and balance these four main thrusts in human endeavor—mind (cognitive needs), body (physical needs), feeling (emotional needs), and spirituality (intangible needs). Taking some poetic license, we might say this idea, too, was expressed by the ancients:

> "Which commandment is the most important of all?" Jesus replied, "The most important one is this: 'Listen Israel! The Lord our God is the only Lord. Love the Lord your God with all your heart (F), with all your soul (N), with all your mind (T), and with all your strength (S)'" (Mark 12: 28–29; parentheses, of course, added).

That there should be a balance of these things is a message common to all the major religions of the world. Nevertheless, nations and governments—who themselves have cognitive biases determined by predominant type functions—normally choose one or two approaches to problems to the disregard of the remaining options. Thus border conflicts and economic problems might be resolved through sheer power (NT) or practical common sense (ST), without exploration of other innovative possibilities (N) or consideration of the human consequences (F). In the Western Hemisphere, disease itself is often approached only from a logical, mechanistic or monetary angle (S, T), with the repudiation of alternative therapies (chiropractic, homeopathy, aromatherapy, acupuncture, etc.) that attempt to augment and complement what we know through intuitive, spiritual and patient-centered means (N, F). Because one-sidedness, as we have seen, may make the organism unwell at the individual level or even the institutional level, modern health care is wise to continue to absorb these perspectives in order to maintain a progressive and moving whole.

Jung (1969) observed long ago, in his study of circles, that the Buddha is drawn in the middle of ancient mandalas that represent the universe. Buddhists, Muslims and aboriginal cultures literally circle their icons on foot, passing each compass direction as they do so, in their walk or dance of the Circle of Life. With God essentially at the center, Jung believed it is the goal of individuation to ride the spiral through life, the path unwinding, ever closer to that center. This is perfection, then—the act of achieving quadrilaterality, as it were, where the person strives to be a jack of all functions, master of none, and is psychologically healthy because there are no extremes. The T'ai Chi, of course, is a circle recommending a similar equilibrium. The medicine wheel and the Christian circle with the cross at the center both advocate the integration of the four directions, to be one rather than four, to be whole. To the extent that we all circumambulate the four functions, we can say that the circle and its center—which is God from some of these perspectives—is in each of us.

* * *

**Chapter 8 is a further integration of** ancient wheels and a modern talent-deficit circle that yields the following key points:

* While all talents and all types are born in all months of the year, some talents in the talent database, and perhaps the types attracted to these domains, seem to cluster in some seasons of the year more than others. This cannot be said to be fact, of course, without further research.

* Given the apparent relationship between talent and disease, it is interesting to note that disease, too, may be related to certain birth seasons. Within the talent database, Cardiovascular pattern illnesses seem to occur more often in talents born in colder months of the year, while Immune pattern illnesses seem more common in talents born in warmer months of the year. Again, this is a *hypothesis* resulting from study of the talent database.

* Jung's process of individuation can be symbolically traced for each of the sixteen types, producing developmental spirals that emphasize certain quadrants of the brain at different life stages. It is proposed that, because of possible type-talent-disease relationships, individual types will exhibit variations in cognitive emphases and disease predispositions throughout the life cycle, not only as a result of aging, but because they are stressing different type functions and the associated talents. An INTP, for example, may have variations in disease risk as he develops his Thinking, Intuition, Sensing and Feeling functions over the course of his lifetime. This notion represents a *time* aspect of our composite wheel.

* Time aspects of the circle on a much larger, historical scale suggest that certain periods in the history of the development of *man* may have been at greater risk for certain diseases. The model may offer insight into the question of why infectious diseases, allergies and other Immune pattern disorders are on the rise, despite medical advances in vaccines and other technologies.

* *Space* aspects of the wheel suggest that certain quadrants of the *globe*, like the individual brain, may be associated with greater risk for certain diseases. For example, the model seems to predict for a high incidence of Cardiovascular pattern illnesses in North America, and Immune pattern illnesses such as skin cancer and AIDS in the southeast corner of the world over Australia, parts of Africa and southeast Asia.

* Chapter 8 begins to consider typological development from a mathematical-physical science perspective and shows that a left-right dynamical system can also be represented as an inward-moving spiral that is consistent with both the laterality hypothesis and Jung's conception of individuation. A steady state of no motion at all occurs at the center of the circle, which is a place of balance and even God from many ancient perspectives.

# CHAPTER NINE
## REINVENTING THE WHEEL OF COGNITION AND DISEASE: ORDER, CHAOS AND THE SUNDIAL WHEEL

* * *

We now complete the construction of a modern Sundial wheel of life that attempts to make theoretical sense of links between psychological type, talent and disease. It is clear it is not a static model but rather a system of dynamical processes that may conform to Einsteinian physics, which governs energy and space-time relationships. The language of physics thus becomes the newest way of describing processes that have been documented for centuries using the simpler symbols of color, elements, animals and seasons.

Two essential states emerge—order and chaos—which may relate to laterality extremes discussed to this point and possible approaches to Cardiovascular and Immune pattern diseases.

In addition, it is demonstrated how a circular or spiraling, dynamical system can be drawn as a repeating wave pattern (and vice versa) as might be found in light waves, EEG waves or the seasonal periodicity of disease. We extend this notion to the spiraling developmental paths of individual types to show that there are four basic helical patterns in type development.

* * *

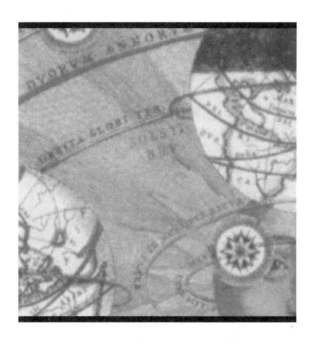

*"In psychological problems, physics and biology come together."*

(Albert Einstein, quoted in Clark 1971: 197)

**The difficulty in working with** these ancient concepts within a scientific community is arriving at tangible proofs verifiable under the scientific method. This is an unfortunate situation in some ways, because some things simply defy such measurement, but it is nevertheless at this place in the history of thought, a period which values measurement, that we find ourselves. Type names help in this pursuit of the rational, because we might more readily identify with laterality scores for something called "NF" than with something less measurable called "Yin," "Air" or "Eagle." But even that is not enough because a name tells only that something is, and not how or why it came to be, or where it is headed in the future. The key, therefore, will be to study the big picture of the wheel using the methods and jargon of the age, in terms no more or less meaningful but perhaps more scientifically acceptable at this point than poetic figurative symbols of nature (colors, elements, animals, seasons)—that is, in the mathematical symbols of the language of physics.

Einstein's famous equation, $E=mc^2$, which says that the energy contained in a tiny particle of matter is equal to its mass multiplied by the speed of light squared, is actually an abbreviation of a longer equation called the Einstein-Lorentz Transformation, depicted in Figure 48. It says, in short, that a particle of matter contains an incredible amount of energy (as in the splitting of the atom), that extremely large amounts of energy are needed to move subatomic particles close to the speed of light, but that matter and energy are interconnected and interconvertable from one to the other (Gerber, 1988). Matter *is* energy, in effect, and energy is matter, and according to the Law of Conservation of Energy, it can never be created or destroyed, only transformed into different states—from light energy into chemical energy (e.g., ATP, neurotransmitters), from chemical energy into electrical energy, from electrical energy into heat energy, and so forth. Perhaps it even converts to another state called psychic energy, or "cognitive" energy.

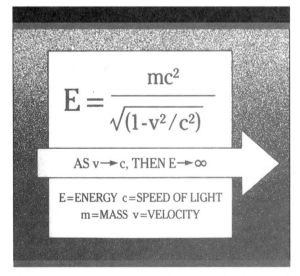

$$E = \frac{mc^2}{\sqrt{(1-v^2/c^2)}}$$

AS $v \rightarrow c$, THEN $E \rightarrow \infty$

E=ENERGY c=SPEED OF LIGHT
m=MASS v=VELOCITY

**Figure 48. Einstein-Lorentz Transformation (Gerber, 1988)**

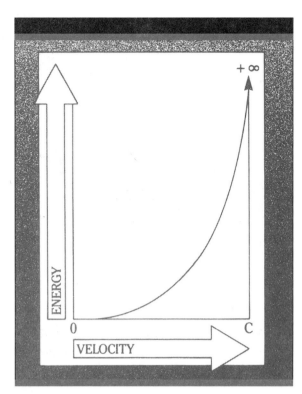

**Figure 49. Relationship of Energy to Velocity
(Gerber, 1988)**

*Vibrational Medicine: New Choices for Healing Ourselves* by Richard Gerber, M.D.,
Bear & Company, a division of Inner Traditions International, Rochester, VT 05767
Copyright © 1988, 1996 by Richard Gerber.

In any event, when velocity components of the Einstein-Lorentz equation that are *less* than the speed of light are plotted against the energy values on a two-axis graph, an exponential curve of the kind in Figure 49 is attained. However, when numbers *greater* than the speed of light are inserted into the equation—in other words, energy values beyond the visible spectrum, as perhaps in chakras or chi—solutions to the equation contain the square root of -1, which is an imaginary number signifying the mind-bending notion that space and time beyond the speed of light are negative. When these solutions are drawn, the graph produced is an inverted, mirror-image curve on the opposite side of the line denoting light velocity—again, a four-quadrant graph of the kind we've been examining

(Figure 50). Figure 50 is an adaptation of the work of William Tiller of the Materials Science Department at Stanford University (Gerber, 1988).

The result of these computations is a mathematical drawing that essentially describes the theoretical existence of two worlds of matter and energy—a *physical* universe that is tangibly demonstrated because the particles have been found, and an *etheric* universe that is intangible because the particles have not yet been found using current technologies. The physical universe, represented on the right side of the line, consists of electrical energy and positive space and time, operating at speeds less than the speed of light. The etheric universe, represented on the left side of the line, consists of magnetic energy and negative space and time, operating at speeds greater than the speed of light. It is of little consequence that we can't see the qualities of the etheric universe—though we can often, but not always, see aspects of the physical universe—because Einstein's work assures us that energy is matter, even if we can't see it, touch it, or use complicated sensory equipment to prove that the matter is actually there. Neither has such intangibility bothered those who have known the effects of Kundalini, chi meridians, animal spirits, love, healing hands, or God.

Space-and-time matter in the context of this graph demonstrates the properties of entropy, which is the tendency toward disorder in a system—positive entropy in the physical quadrant, and negative entropy in the etheric quadrant. Most systems within the physical universe tend toward positive entropy or *chaos*—things tend to fall apart over time—with an accompanying loss of energy. But living systems tend to display negative entropy, or a tendency toward increasing _order_, requiring the continued input of energy to maintain the integrity of the system. Living organisms take the raw material that is food and organize it into complex bodily structures, even thoughts and feelings—unless, of course, disease enters the picture and halts the process that holds everything together.

In addition to describing the energy universe at microscopic and macroscopic levels, the Einstein-Tiller model of positive and negative space and time would seem to be a model of ordered and chaotic disease processes of the kind we have been discussing. The quadrant of negative entropy/positive energy roughly approximates the highly ordered state of the Cardiovascular pattern, which requires much energy to sustain it—a high fat diet, stimulants, and conservation of physical energy—before it finally "snaps." The quadrant of positive entropy/negative energy, on the other hand, parallels the chaotic state of cancer, AIDS and other immune disorders in which the system literally falls apart and out of control with an extreme loss of energy—depression, lack of appetite, fatigue, and weight loss.

In that sense, the Cardiovascular and Immune patterns are polar opposites along a laterality continuum that is really an energy continuum, which sees excessive order, linearity, sameness, focus, control, and energy conservation at one end—perhaps I-S-T-J preferences at their worst—and excessive randomness, nonlinearity, changeability, a lack of focus and control,

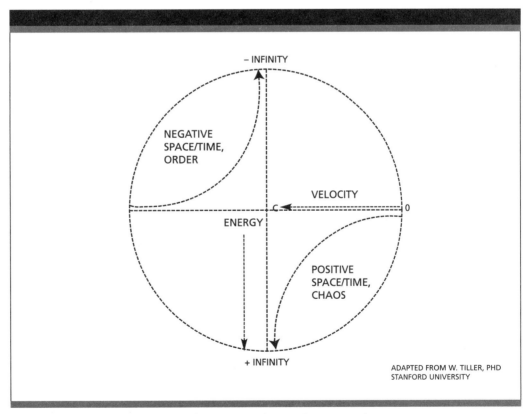

**Figure 50. Einstein-Tiller Model of Positive and Negative Space-Time**

_Vibrational Medicine: New Choices for Healing Ourselves_ by Richard Gerber, M.D., Bear & Company, a division of Inner Traditions International, Rochester, VT 05767 Copyright © 1988, 1996 by Richard Gerber

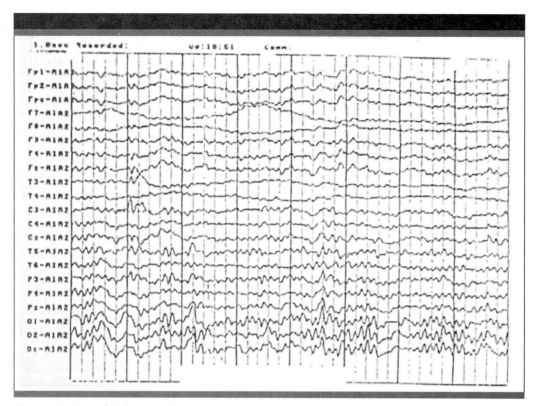

**Figure 51. EEG of Seizure Activity**

and energy expenditure at the other—perhaps E-N-F-P preferences at their worst. Various disease states may happen along this continuum but balance between these two extremes would seem to be related to functioning at moderate energy ranges within the visible and non-visible spectra of thought (T), bodily sensation (S), feeling (F) and spiritual awareness (N).

We may already be able to visibly measure tendencies toward order and chaos, to some extent, using ECG, EEG (Figure 51), oscillators and other equipment capable of monitoring energy wave emissions from the body. ECGs, for instance, show that the waves become tighter, more regular, more orderly just before a heart attack but more irregular and chaotic with ventricular fibrillation (Ruelle, 1980). EEGs show that seizure frequency decreases the looser the waves become, being even less frequent, looser and less repetitive in the lesional state accompanying tumors (Darwish et al., 1994). Indeed, cancerous cells have been found to be low-frequency, low-amplitude embryonic cells which vibrate at a much slower rate than the rest of the body (Becker & Selden, 1985), and lung cancer shows up as red light (slower waves) under laser light which is normally a green glow (faster waves) (Wilson, 1994). In these examples, just the disease states of heart attack and cancer could represent opposing ends of the visible spectrum—higher-energy short waves approaching the violet end of the spectrum, and lower-energy long waves approaching the red end. The notion might sound slightly revolutionary were it not for the fact that Chinese physicians developed sensate ways of relating wave order (yang) and disorder (yin) to illness centuries ago (Figure 52). Chakra theory, too, contains within it the notion of energetic polarities (Figure 53, page 216).

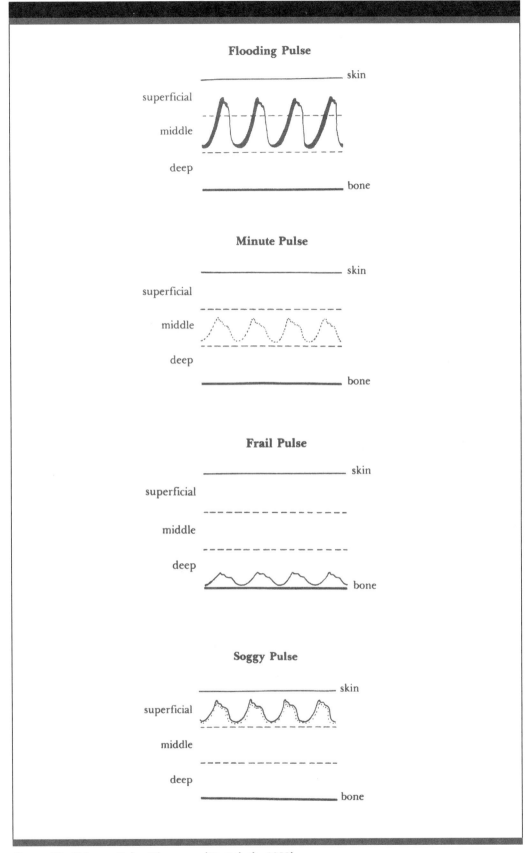

**Figure 52. Chinese Pulse Diagrams (Kaptchuk, 1983)**

If this simple dichotomy between energy order and chaos, between fighting for control and surrendering to it, between left and posterior laterality (I-S-T-J preferences) versus right and anterior laterality (E-N-F-P preferences), is a partial contributor to even some disease processes, it follows that shifting may be possible by altering the energy organization of the system, and that experimentation with this principle could be very worthwhile in relieving, or perhaps even preventing, some kinds of illness. For instance, the *release of energy to shift right* may help to relax, and possibly also inhibit, development of the high-energy (purple) order of diseases that might be associated with left and posterior laterality, e.g., heart and lung disease. This rightward shift might be achieved through low-fat, low-salt diets, cooling, exercise, meditation, sex, laughter, crying, artistic or spatial activity, and the E-N-F-P qualities of social activity, creativity, caring and flexibility.

The *addition of energy to shift left*, meanwhile, may help to slow or inhibit the low-energy (red) chaos of diseases that might be associated with right and anterior laterality, e.g. cancer, AIDS, MS, ALS, ulcers, allergies, diabetes, arthritis. This state might be achieved through high-energy, salt-containing diets, heat, sunlight (with the exception of skin disorders), rest, quiet introspection, reading, writing, or doing math, and the I-S-T-J qualities of reflection, logical thinking, practical, an orderly daily routine, and down-to-earth, common sense. The underlying energy principle in operation seems to conform to the laws of mechanics—such that $F=ma$ at rest, or $Fd=1/2mv^2$, kinetically, as for a pendulum—which means that *resistance does not diminish our energy level, but rather augments it proportionately, just as a lack of force actively depletes it*. So, to avoid physical "explosions" of the kind we see in heart attack and stroke, we may need to do more surrendering, "letting go," and accepting of reality, while to help counteract the "implosions" of cancer and AIDS, we may need to exert more aggressive and structured control, the achievement of which may happen any number of ways.

With diet alone, we know there is considerable variation in the recommendations, which may actually be reflecting shifting—a low-fat, low-salt diet for heart patients, a high-fat

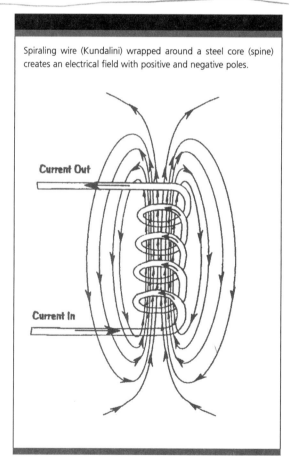

Spiraling wire (Kundalini) wrapped around a steel core (spine) creates an electrical field with positive and negative poles.

Current Out

Current In

**Figure 53. The Structure of an Artificial Magnet and Its Similarity to Chakra-Kundalini Theory in the Body (Bruyere, 1989)**

ketogenic diet for epileptics, a high-energy carbohydrate diet for hypoglycemics—and that many pharmaceutical preparations and other treatments, especially those with paradoxical effects, may also be promoting a change in laterality. Seizures and the aggressive tendencies associated with heart disease and some psychiatric disorders *discharge* energy, which is inhibited with sedating drugs that may promote a rightward shift, while electroconvulsive therapy (ECT) *adds* a jolt of energy (usually to the right hemisphere) where anti-depressants fail and perhaps provides a boost in the other direction. Beta-blockers for heart disease (a rightward shift), Ritalin for attention deficit hyperactivity disorder (leftward), and epinephrine for allergies (leftward) may all contribute to a cognitive shift away from a problematic style.

Some side effects of medications would thus stem from the new trade-off risks associated with a shift once made. Steroids, for example, while very helpful in the treatment of allergies, may also weaken a person's immune defenses (chaos), anti-depressants used to excess can increase episodic mood cycling and cause heart failure (order), and beta-blockers can cause depression (chaos). Greater knowledge of the energy patterns in operation in these systems could possibly help us make more informed choices in this regard.

If, as we are proposing, disease mirrors mode of thought and the degree of entropy to some extent, it should not surprise us that the Cardiovascular pattern of disease predominates in highly structured, cold countries of the developed world, while immune diseases ravage highly chaotic, hot regions of the Third World. Mind and body appear to reflect and absorb the energy of their environment and vice versa, which, if it is extremely ordered or extremely disordered, may help to make the receiver sick.

Aboriginal creationism in Australia is little known in the Western world, but even in this there are parallels:

> . . . In the beginning of time, in what they call Dreamtime, all earth was joined together. Divine Oneness created the light, the first sunrise shattering the total eternal darkness. The void was used to place many discs spinning in the heavens. Our planet was one of them. It was flat and featureless . . . Then Divine Oneness expanded knowingness to each disc, giving different things to each one (Morgan, 1994: 130).

Gifts differing . . . given to the uniquely spinning circle that is the earth as well as the infinitely smaller organic and inorganic circles that have come to inhabit it—the seasons, the cycle of evaporation and condensation in water, the metamorphosis of the butterfly, the life cycle of the salmon, the Krebs cycle within respiration, the replication cycle of DNA, and also very likely the development of man, on levels of time from the colossal to the minute.

We have implied in various places that the brain is a metaphorical mini-earth; because energy is matter, the brain *is* the earth, in a way, with hemispheres, quadrispheres, compass directions, crosses of latitude and longitude, regional disparities, a predetermined "orbit" or rotational spin, and periods of lightness and darkness which inevitably transform into the other, and through which it is possible to move. It is not a new idea that the atom is a

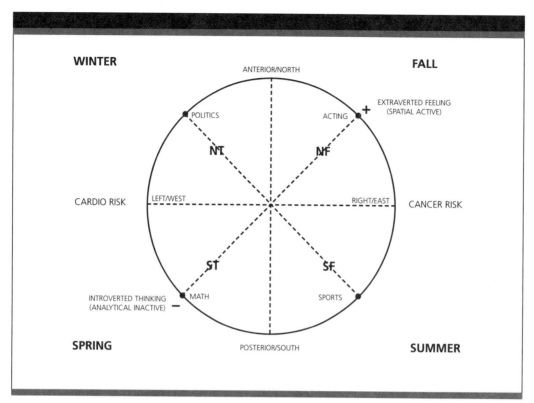

**Figure 54. Talent Laterality and Season of Birth as a Brain Map**

microcosm of the universe, that the individual is a microcosm of humanity, and it can be traced in one form or another to the ancient philosophies of Hindus, Egyptians, Greeks and Romans. But to add to this notion, we would further propose that the brain is a microcosm of the earth, and that the laterality continuum of IT to EF—from the left-posterior area of the brain to the right-anterior—is effectively the polar energy axis of the brain around which all human activity moves. The typological opposites of I-S-T-J and E-N-F-P preferences, and the diseases which may or may not accompany exaggerations of their expression, are thus negative and positive poles on this axis.

We repeat that all types and talents are born in all seasons of the year. But insofar as some types and talents may cluster in some seasons more than others (i.e., the "hump" of the normal curve is in one season), suggesting that dominant birth season may relate to some extent to laterality and type genus—e.g., winter, politics, NT; fall, acting, NF, and so forth—we can draw our own wheel of life of sorts (Figure 54). Here we can see where two laterality lines, one running north and south (S-N) and another running east and west (T-F), intersect to form a cross that separates each of the four functional directions of the circle—T (left), F (right), N (anterior), S (posterior)—as well as the four seasons. Two diagonal laterality lines further delineate the four dominant-auxiliary quadrants that seem to correspond to birth season in our sample—NT (left-anterior), ST (left-posterior), SF (right-posterior), NF (right-anterior). As a result, these diagonals would appear to represent the equinox of spring and fall, and the solstice of winter and summer, which renders time of conception at a point some three seasons prior to any quadrant on the circle.

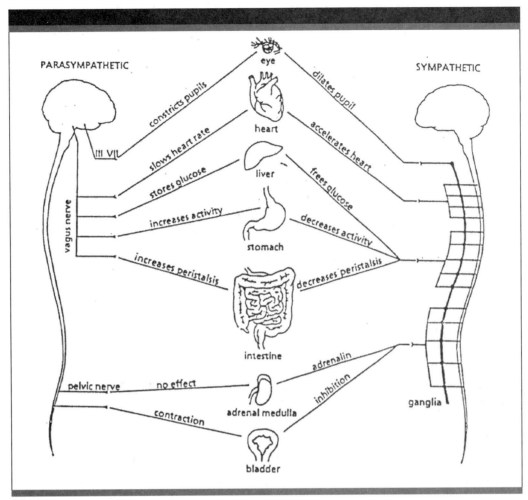

**Figure 55. The Autonomic Nervous System**

One of the diagonals—the equinox line, as it were—is the proposed axial continuum that stretches between energy states of physically inactive, analytic cognition (IT) and physically active, spatial or social cognition (EF), and the disease vulnerabilities that might be paired with them. Tendencies toward negative entropy, high internal speeds of energy transformation, and cardiovascular disease are purported to be where there is left or posterior laterality, and may be related in some way to high metabolic rates, adrenalin production, and the functions of the sympathetic nervous system. On the other hand, positive entropy, low internal speeds of energy transformation, endorphin production, and immune disease (endorphins suppress immune defenses) may be where there is right or anterior laterality, and may be related in some way to the parasympathetic nervous system (Figure 55).

In all, there will be twelve "spokes" to the wheel, like the native Sundance wheel, twelve hypothetical lines of laterality, each corresponding to the monthly changes in light energy experienced hormonally *in utero* that may or may not contribute to the whole system. The result is a pie-like arrangement of mental abilities and physical weaknesses whose pieces "light up" or remain in the shadows, as on a sundial, according to the interaction of the prevalent logical and physical factors of "nature" and the interpersonal and spiritual factors of "nurture."

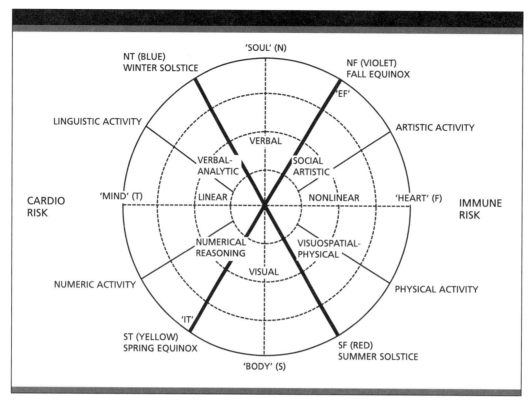

**Figure 56. Sundial Model of Type, Talent and Disease**

From the moment of conception, the wheel might begin to "spin" involuntarily in a leftward or rightward direction, as a figurative needle on a compass drawn by the pull of magnetic north. But after birth, movement around the circle is also subject to the action of voluntary and involuntary influences, and is thus a partially self-determining, hopeful model of health and disease that gives at least as much weight to choices as to chance.

When we generalize exceptional talents to common daily activities—writing and politics as linguistic activity generally, mathematics as numeric activity, sports as physical activity, acting as artistic activity, and so forth—we arrive at the Sundial wheel displayed in Figure 56. The twelve diagonals in this case could signify, like Chinese biorhythms, the *times of day* that a person's energy may be most aligned with these pursuits—physical activity in the "spring" and "summer" of the day, social and verbal activity in the middle of the day, and reflective intellectual pursuits in the twilight "winter" hours.

It may be no accident, for example, that some sensing "morning" people spring into the day with physical gusto when the energy for their preferences is optimum, while some intuitive "night" people may prefer to hibernate through the daylight hours and work quietly into the night when the energy for their preferences awakens. Neither may it be a coincidence that movement around the circle parallels Freudian, Ericksonian, Maslowian, and chakra development through physical, emotional and cerebral stages. Indeed, the corresponding colors for the chakras change from warm reds and oranges in the SF quadrant (physical), through yellow, green and blue in the ST quadrant (emotional), to cool blues and purples in the NT and NF segments (cerebral).

What does the Sundial wheel suggest exactly? Certainly it must be said first that none of it is black and white, as they say, but rather *"shades of gray"* wherein one cognitive ability, type function or associated disease pattern on the circle blends into others, much as the seasons and the colors of the rainbow fade into each other. Consequently, within the larger verbal-nonverbal arc, there should be smaller continua of varying intensities depending on the degree of left-right or front-back laterality at any point around the circle.

Second, the Sundial suggests that there is an *association* only between type, talent, disease and the variable light energy in the year, and in no way implies causal relationships linking these factors. We cannot know whether the playing of music, for instance, contributes to heart disease in some way without controlled study—although we do know from a University of California study by Dimsdale and Nelesen that the playing of high notes on brass instruments can contribute to hypertension, and that operatic singers have a higher incidence of reflux laryngitis and asthma—and can say in the meantime only that a relationship was observed, and even then only on an extremely small scale. Surely we are seeing reflections of common lifestyles and other factors in our talent groups, but cannot tease apart all the various possibilities without an experimental design. Although, on a hypothetical level, the model does suggest that talent and disease may be paired, that we may not get one without the other, and that such expression, if it can be found to actually exist, is highly suggestive of genetic transmission, as in the relationship between male gender and dyslexia or other traits literally tied to each other on the same chromosome.

Third, we emphasize that all of us possess all the various cognitive abilities and type functions in the brain, and therefore presumably a risk of disease in any of the four quadrants. However, just as some of us have greater abilities or type preferences in some areas more than others, some of us will have greater risk for their associated disease patterns, perhaps especially at certain times of the year. The fact that some talent groups seem to be able to minimize disease expression that other groups cannot—e.g., the relative absence of cancer in chess players as opposed to actors—only suggests the possibility that *conscious shifting toward contralateral cognition may moderate certain pathogenic factors and reduce risk or severity.* Just as there is no one best type, there is also no one best place on the circumference to be, as each activity may or may not have its own paired disease risk. The wisest approach, then, would seem to be to integrate the polar functions as much as possible and to strive, ideally, toward reaching the center. Again, however, we cannot know for certain without controlled study.

Finally, we stress that this is a *model* only, a reductionist view of personality, ability and disease which attempts to simplify a great deal of intensely complicated information into a workable scheme that may or may not ultimately add insights into these complexities. It is created on frequencies—e.g., the greatest number of athletes born in a given season—and is therefore subject to all the benefits and pitfalls of any frequency analysis, particularly the problem of where to categorize exceptions to the rule (which fall in the tails of the normal curve). As a result, athletes in our sample (and Sensing Feeling types) are most certainly born in the winter as well as the summer, but apparently to a lesser extent considering the highest frequency for the group was found in the summer. This suggests that perhaps "winter" athletes may have slightly different disease risks than will "summer" athletes. The wheel is therefore a series of normal curves around the circle, with peaks and tails reflecting variable distributions at different places along the way.

In the end, we tentatively conclude that the Sundial is a potential, rudimentary road map for lifestyle changes that takes biology and choices into account. Yes, a person may be born in the summer with certain traits such as left-handedness, athletic abilities, and a weakness for immune disease, but perhaps he can alter the negative realities to some degree by purposely "moving" to another place on the circle, by making a contralateral cognitive shift and occupying himself with less preferred activities. The possibility that reading, working on math, or playing chess may be as therapeutic for some people as exercising is certainly a strange idea but one that may be well worth researching, considering the alternatives. It may also be a very old idea. The notion of using opposite and unlikely strategies to overcome hardship and achieve larger goals has been around, in cryptic form, at least since the New Testament:

> If anyone slaps you on the right cheek, let him slap your left cheek too (Matthew 5: 38–44).

> Whoever wants to be first must place himself last of all . . . (Mark 9: 35).

> Love your enemies, do good to those who hate you (Luke 6: 27).

> The greatest one among you must be like the youngest, and the leader must be like the servant (Luke 22: 26).

> For everyone who makes himself great will be humbled, and everyone who humbles himself will be made great (Luke 14: 11).

> The stone the builders rejected as worthless turned out to be most important of all (Luke 20: 17).

Collectively, these messages would seem to be advising employment of a flexible, human, FP approach to problems—in other words, right-sided cognition—in situations that might normally arouse the colder, competitive, T or TJ strategies of the left side. That is, what some might view as the *least* likely approach to a problem is considered to be the most desirable from this perspective.

To this point, we have looked at time and talent on the wheel only in terms of the season, with some brief mention of daily biorhythms. But observations related to *month* of birth and death are also quite illuminating. Figure 57 (page 224) shows the births and mortality in the nine talent groups by month, and we can see that the pattern in the frequency lines is identical over the course of the year, with the greatest number of births and deaths occurring about the time of the winter solstice (December 21), and fall and spring equinox (September 21, March 21). That is, conception in this sample of highly talented people occurred most often at the spring equinox, and also at the winter and summer solstice, but not in the fall for some reason when, interestingly enough, mortality for this sample also turns out to be highest. Even when the births are broken down by left and right talent laterality (Figures 58–59, pages 224 and 225), the pattern is essentially the same, the peaks in the lines occurring at approximately the same times.

However, when *mortality* is broken down by left and right talent laterality (Figure 60, page 225), an amazing thing occurs: the patterns *mirror* each other, as left-right abilities mirror each other in the brain, with left-lateral deaths occurring most when right-lateral deaths are occurring least, and vice versa. Right-lateral deaths, like births, seem to relate to equinox and solstice dates, while left-lateral deaths seem to happen between these demarcations. This suggests, of course, that *right- and left-lateralized talents might be physically vulnerable at different, energetically apposing, times of the year—right-lateralized talents particularly in the cooler seasons of the Northern Hemisphere, and left-lateralized talents in the high-energy period of summer* (Figure 61, page 226).

That one line seems to be displaced to the left of the other suggests there is variable periodicity in these cyclical patterns. The frequency of undulation in the line for right-siders seems to be somewhat faster than for left-siders, with peaks occurring a month or two ahead of the same peaks for left-siders so that right-lateralized talents appear vulnerable when light and heat energy are in lesser abundance. These observations would seem to make particularly good sense if, as we proposed, left-lateralized talents are often in a state of *excess* internal energy and needing release, and right-lateralized talents are in a state of *deficient* energy and needing absorption of it. Left-siders are perhaps thus weakened by the addition of energy in summer where right-siders comparatively thrive on it, just as right-siders are weakened by the depletion of energy in the colder months and left-siders are apparently less bothered by it.

These patterns distinguish for left- and right-lateralized talents grouped together into these two categories. When we plot disease mortality or specific talent by month of birth, we arrive at still other periodicities. Figure 62 (page 226), for instance, suggests faster periodicity (faster cycling) for heart and stroke, and comparatively slower periodicity (slower cycling) for cancer, which is coincidentally in agreement with our postulations about the wave patterns on ECG and EEG for these diseases—faster, more regular cycling prior to heart attack, slower cycling for seizures related to the lesional state. Periodicity in disease has long been a well-known fact in modern medicine. For instance, we know of annual flu and allergy seasons, the chaotic periodicity of measles, the orderly periodicity of chicken pox (Smith, 1979), sleep-wake cycles and body-temperature cycles in the case of fever. But cycling of disease according to time of birth, and in relation to cognitive abilities, has not been much explored in recent times.

Appendix C (page 315) shows the similarity of graphs for *disease by month of birth*, and *talent by month of birth*. Heart and stroke periodicity (highest frequency in spring and winter births) has roughly the same birth pattern as for left-sided talents in science and math. Cancer periodicity (summer births) has the same birth pattern as for athletes, and lung disease (fall

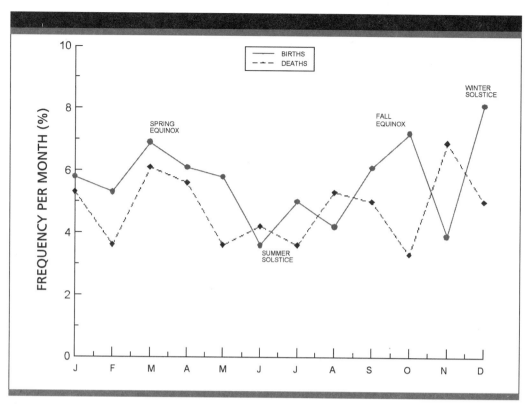

Figure 57. Births and Mortality in Talent Groups by Month of Year

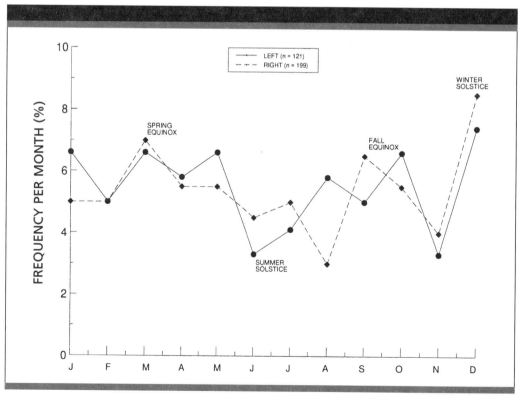

Figure 58. Births per Month of Left- and Right-Lateralized Talents

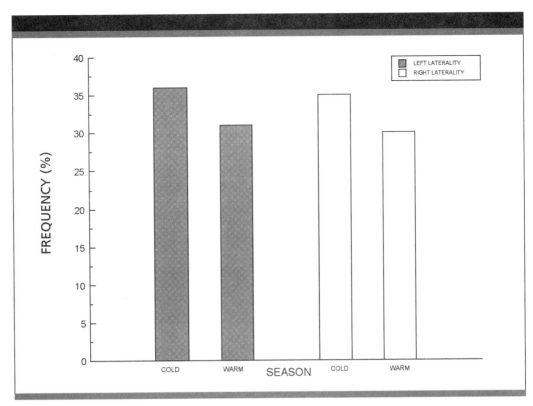

**Figure 59. Season of Birth, by Talent Laterality**

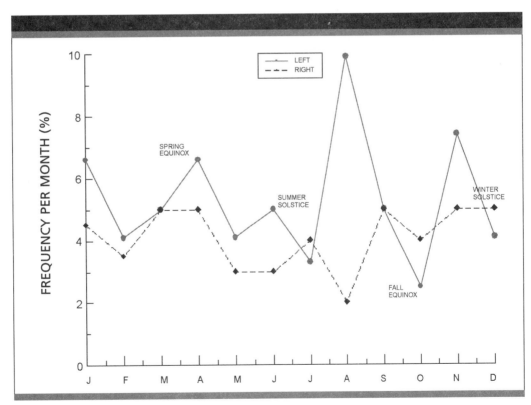

**Figure 60. Mortality per Month of Left- and Right-Lateralized Talents**

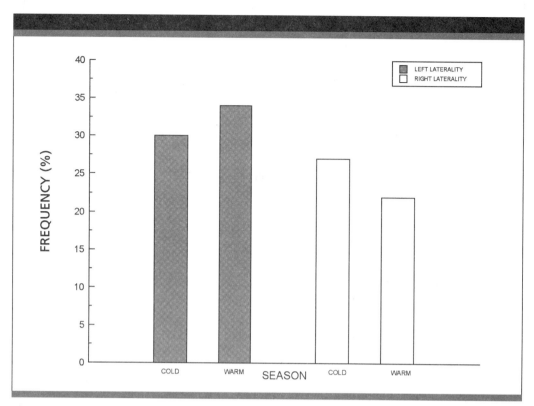

**Figure 61. Season of Death, by Talent Laterality**

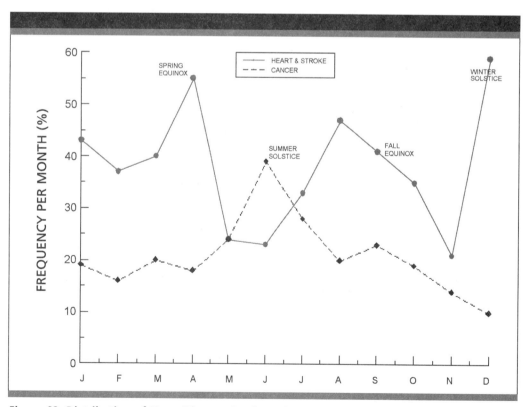

**Figure 62. Distribution of Heart Disease, Stroke and Cancer by Month of Birth**

births) for writers, which would seem to suggest that cognition, and probably the personality that accompanies it, like the biorhythms of disease, might be periodic over the course of the year. *The graphs suggest at what seasonal locations around the Sundial we might place potentially problematic organ systems*, the highest peak in a given line indicating the appropriate season on the wheel, e.g., the respiratory system in the fall quadrant, the central nervous system (stroke) in the winter quadrant, the circulatory system in the spring quadrant, and so forth. The graphs imply relatedness therefore to the periodicity throughout the year of light energy.

Together, the graphs raise some interesting, albeit terribly futuristic, questions:

* Does the shape of the line over a long period of time look anything like the shape of the line over a very short period of time? Is one a sub-system of the other, a fractal that is self-similar in scale? For example, is the shape of the line for disease-by-month-of-birth related in any way to pathological patterns picked up by electronic diagnostic tools, such as the spikes and after-slow waves on EEG?
* Do different types and talents emit particular baseline waves, a change, which might indicate a problem? Are similar types literally "on the same wavelength?"
* Can a wave pattern over the long term be altered by conscious shifting, much as it is now possible to alter it over the short term, e.g., lowering heart rate through meditation?
* Can a certain periodicity in cognition help to explain left-right swings in the history of thought?
* Could there be beneficial times of year to engage in certain kinds of cognition, e.g., sports in summer, writing in autumn? Is insight more common in the "reflective" season of winter when light energy waves are shorter and faster?
* Could there be cognitive periodicity in space as well as time, e.g., in energetically different parts of the world?
* Is it possible to mathematically predict periodicities for use in prevention?

This last point is especially interesting in that the dynamic "pulses" on a line graph are really the longitudinal version of periodicity on a circle, which, after all, is what we've been primarily concerned with. From basic trigonometry, some of us will recall that revolutions on a circle can be spread out, mathematically, onto a periodic XY graph (sine, cosine, tangent curves, etc.), and back again to the circular form (Figure 63, page 228), and it may be helpful to apply this principle to the spirals and circles of type and the longitudinal periodicity of disease. For the sake of discussion, we can walk ourselves through this possibility to see where it leads.

To begin with, and in keeping with Jung's original conception, we have said that type development progresses, for all types over a lifetime, in a clockwise or counterclockwise spiral toward the center of the life cycle. That is, using our jargon, laterality in the brain changes with development, particularly at the critical life stages of puberty and middle age, and becomes decreasingly extreme (i.e., increasingly bilateral) with maturity. The order of the stages of

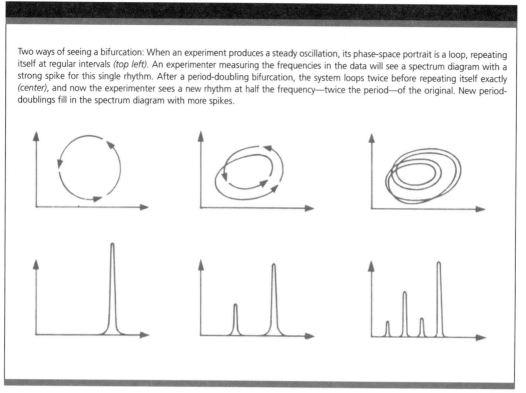

Two ways of seeing a bifurcation: When an experiment produces a steady oscillation, its phase-space portrait is a loop, repeating itself at regular intervals *(top left)*. An experimenter measuring the frequencies in the data will see a spectrum diagram with a strong spike for this single rhythm. After a period-doubling bifurcation, the system loops twice before repeating itself exactly *(center)*, and now the experimenter sees a new rhythm at half the frequency—twice the period—of the original. New period-doublings fill in the spectrum diagram with more spikes.

**Figure 63. An Illustration of How a Repeating Spiraling Cycle Can Be Described Using a Spectrum Frequency Diagram (Gleick, 1987)**

functional development, for all types, was outlined in Table 30 (page 194) (Hirsch and Kummerow, 1990).

In the case of INTP, for example, the person begins life in his dominant Thinking mode (left side), adds his auxiliary Intuitive function in his youth (anterior), begins to appreciate Sensing values at midlife (posterior), and finally adopts a more Feeling approach to being in old age (right side), all the while retaining the essential character of his INTP-ness. His progress around the circle thus begins on the left side (T), moves clockwise through anterior functions (N) in young adulthood, through more posterior functions (S) at midlife, and finally evolves toward more right-sided functioning (F) in his senior years. Certainly, all of the cortex is used at all times, but we recognize, as we have often said, that some areas may be stressed more than others during different periods of a person's development. Overall, then, as we trace the INTP's path through life, we can see that his particular life course is a spiral that progresses clockwise from left to right, as depicted on page 194. He is rightward-moving, in effect.

But, as Table 30 (page 194) suggested, the *direction* of this development is probably not the same for all types. INTJ, for example, would seem to spiral through life from front to back in the brain, developing the N function (anterior) in childhood, the T function (left) in adulthood, the F function (right) at midlife, and finally the S function (posterior) in old age. ESTP, on the other hand, moves in precisely the reverse direction, from back to front, developing the S function first (posterior), the T function second (left), the F function third (right) and the N function fourth (front). INFP moves from right to left, building in F (right), N (anterior), T (left) and then S (posterior). In fact, in looking at all of the sixteen types, it becomes apparent that there are probably four essential developmental patterns, each possessing a clockwise and counterclockwise variation:

    1. Anterior to Posterior Spiral ("Southerly" Development)

        Clockwise:                    INFJ, ENFP

$$N$$
$$T \quad \circlearrowright \quad F$$
$$S$$

        Counterclockwise:        INTJ, ENTP

    2. Posterior to Anterior Spiral ("Northerly" Development)

        Clockwise:                    ISTJ, ESTP

        Counterclockwise:        ISFJ, ESFP

    3. Left to Right Spiral ("Easterly" Development)

        Clockwise:                    INTP, ENTJ

        Counterclockwise:        ISTP, ESTJ

    4. Right to Left Spiral ("Westerly" Development)

        Clockwise:                    INFP, ENFJ

        Counterclockwise:        ISFP, ESFJ

It is clear that these eight patterns can be further reduced to two root directions—"north-south" and "east-west," so to speak. Thus, eight types develop "vertically" between the front and back ends of the brain (north-south), and eight types progress "horizontally" through the right and left sides of the brain (east-west). That is, half the types conceived by Isabel Myers would appear to be on the vertical axis of the cross in the circle of life, while half are apparently on the horizontal axis.

The circumambulatory development that Jung wrote about—with the side-to-side spin of development winding ever closer to the center—suggests he might have been figuratively looking at man from a topographical perspective. From that perspective, the two root paths of type development might look very much like conceptions of chakra revolutions with their net positive (clockwise) and negative (counterclockwise) charges (Figure 29, page 157). However, by plotting the coordinates of type functions from the topographical version of the spiral onto

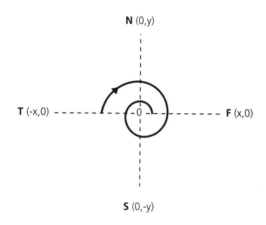

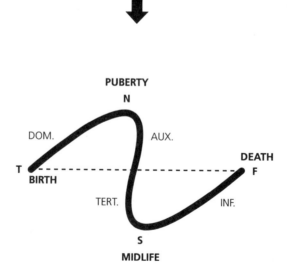

a longitudinal graph—for INTP, as an example—we see that the same plots form an out-stretched spiral viewed from the side, in lateral cross-section. It is this unit cycle, on page 230, that resembles the seasonal periodicities of talent and disease just discussed.

If the single revolution for a type (Table 30, page 194) is extended so that it repeats more than once—as should be the case if indeed there is biorhythmic periodicity daily, monthly, yearly, or over the course of a lifetime and beyond—the unit spiral becomes a long coil of movement traversing dominant and auxiliary functions. To make another leap of futuristic fantasy, this coil is inescapably reminiscent of the shape of the double helix of DNA, the very blueprint and building block of life (Figure 64, page 232).

Perhaps not so strangely DNA, too, has right- and left-handed strands which fit the laws of stereochemistry, is often compared to a spiral staircase, and splits like a zipper in reproductive replication that is itself a cycle lasting a number of hours. DNA, too, is undulating longitudinally until it is X-rayed topographically, at which point it can appear to have an unmistakable cross in it (alpha form) or equinox-like "X" in it (beta form) (Figure 65, page 233). DNA is composed of two root chemical compounds (purines and pyrimidines) that decide the direction of chemical bonding and whose variations are five bases—adenine (A), guanine (G), thymine (T), cytosine (C) and uracil (U). But most striking of all, *paired bonding of opposing bases, in sequences of four,* holds the spiral together and forms a genetic code which can determine everything from handedness to hair color to personality traits to natural talent to disease. A four-by-four matrix exploring possible genetic messages one arrangement of bases can produce coincidentally creates 16 kinds of coding possibilities eerily similar to a type table (Table 31, page 234).

Is it possible that the strands of DNA actually code for the hemispheres (personality, cognition, disease) and determine which side and directional spin are dominant in a person? Is it possible that the sequence of four bases (A,G,T,C/U) are, in effect, the elemental foundations of the four functions (S,N,T,F), with the relative strength and order of development of the functions decided upon by the arrangement of bases? Is it possible that A–T and G–C (or G–U) pairings on the DNA spiral are the S–N and T–F pairings on the typological spiral of life? If so, DNA could provide ample organic foundation for the fact that aspects of personality, talent and disease are so often linked and repetitively cyclical.

> And Jacob dreamed, and behold a ladder set up on earth, and the top of it
> reached to heaven: and behold the angels of God ascending and descend-
> ing on it. And, behold, the Lord stood above it, and said . . . the land
> whereon thou liest, to thee will I give it, and to thy seed; And thy seed
> shall be as the dust of the earth, and thou shalt spread abroad to the west,
> and to the east, and to the north, and to the south: and in thee and in thy
> seed shall all the families of the earth be blessed (Genesis 28: 12–15).

Here, the Jacob's ladder of Christian traditions symbolizes the genetic propagation of the lineage to the four corners of the earth and, if our deductions and fantasies are correct, perhaps also to the four corners of the brain. Even the angelic figures ascending and descending the ladder have broad symbolic parallels to type development, which become apparent in the "staircase" diagrams on pages 234–235.

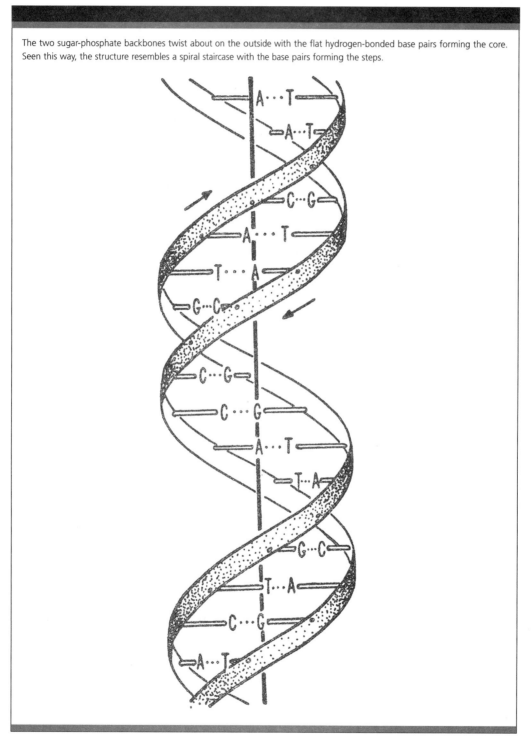

The two sugar-phosphate backbones twist about on the outside with the flat hydrogen-bonded base pairs forming the core. Seen this way, the structure resembles a spiral staircase with the base pairs forming the steps.

**Figure 64. A Schematic Illustration of the Double Helix (Watson, 1968).**

The crossway pattern of reflections, going from 11 o'clock to 5 o'clock and from 1 o'clock to 7 o'clock, and which provided Watson and Crick with the evidence for the helical arrangement of DNA, can be seen very clearly. The elongated regions at the very top and bottom of the pattern provide the evidence for the regular stacking of purine and pyrimidine bases at 3.4Å and perpendicularly to the axis of the DNA molecule. Note the large X in the B Form, a characteristic scattering pattern for helices.

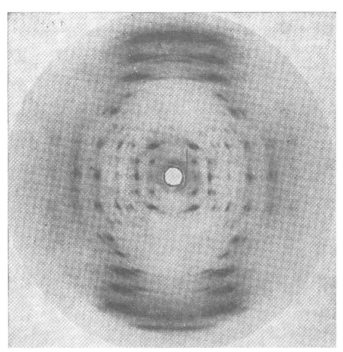

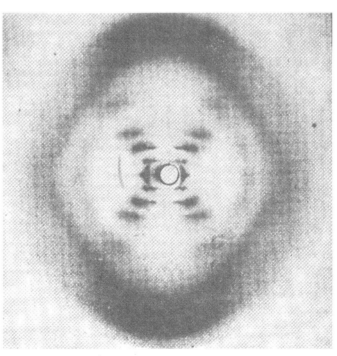

**Figure 65. X-ray Diffraction Patterns of Crystalline DNA Fiber in the A Form (top) and B Form (bottom) (Watson, 1968)**

Courtesy of the James D. Watson Collection, Cold Spring Harbor Laboratory Archives.

**Table 31. Possible Genetic Combinations Resulting from Four Bases in DNA**

|  | MESSENGER CODONS | | | | | | | |
|---|---|---|---|---|---|---|---|---|
|  | SECOND BASE | | | | | | | |
| FIRST BASE | U | U | C | C | A | A | G | G | THIRD BASE |
| U | UUU | Phe | UCU | Ser | UAU | Tyr | UGU | Cys | U |
| U | UUC | Phe | UCC | Ser | UAC | Tyr | UGC | Cys | C |
| U | UUA | Leu | UCA | Ser | UAA | Stop** | UGA | Stop** | A |
| U | UUG | Leu | UCG | Ser | UAG | Stop** | UGG | Trp | G |
| C | CUU | Leu | CCU | Pro | CAU | His | CGU | Arg | U |
| C | CUC | Leu | CCC | Pro | CAC | His | CGC | Arg | C |
| C | CUA | Leu | CCA | Pro | CAA | Gln | CGA | Arg | A |
| C | CUG | Leu | CCG | Pro | CAG | Gln | CGG | Arg | G |
| A | AUU | Ile | ACU | Thr | AAU | Asn | AGU | Ser | U |
| A | AUC | Ile | ACC | Thr | AAC | Asn | AGC | Ser | C |
| A | AUA | Ile | ACA | Thr | AAA | Lys | AGA | Arg | A |
| A | AUG | Met Start* | ACG | Thr | AAG | Lys | AGG | Arg | G |
| G | GUU | Val | GCU | Ala | GAU | Asp | GGU | Gly | U |
| G | GUC | Val | GCC | Ala | GAC | Asp | GGC | Gly | C |
| G | GUA | Val | GCA | Ala | GAA | Glu | GGA | Gly | A |
| G | GUG | Val | GCG | Ala | GAG | Glu | GGG | Gly | G |

\* Initiator codon
\*\*Terminator codon

Legend:

Amino Acids: Alanine (Ala), Arginine (Arg), Asparagine (Asn), Aspartate (Asp), Cysteine (Cys), Glutamate (Glu), Glutamine (Gln), Glycine (Gly), Histidine (His), Isoleucine (Ile), Leucine (Leu), Lysine (Lys), Methionine (Met), Phenylalanine (Phe), Proline (Pro), Serine (Ser), Threonine (Thr), Tryptophan (Trp), Tyrosine (Tyr), Valine (Val)

Nitrogen Bases: (1) Purines: Adenine (A), Guanine (G); (2) Pyrimidine: Cytosine (C), Thymine (T), Uracil (U)

To wit, four types—INTJ, ENTP, INFJ and ENFP—appear to develop on the vertical axis through anterior and posterior functions over the course of a lifetime, a three-dimensional spiraling or helical concept we can try to represent two-dimensionally as follows:

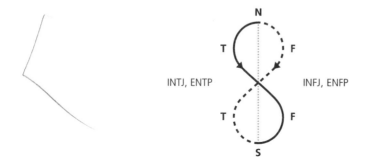

Similarly, four types—ISTJ, ESTP, ISFJ and ESFP—seem to develop through posterior and anterior functions, from back to front, over a lifetime, perhaps experiencing the disease risks associated with these paths:

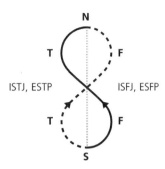

Were they viewed from the top or bottom, these helices would look like the tight, circular spiral Jung hypothesized about, which winds its way inward.

On the horizontal axis, in contrast, four types—INTP, ENTJ, ISTP and ESTJ—appear to develop from left to right over a lifetime:

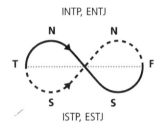

Finally, four types—INFP, ENFJ, ISFP and ESFJ—appear to develop from right to left:

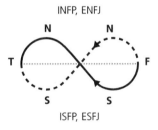

These helices would be seen as a circular, Jungian spiral if they were viewed from either end of the S-shaped line.

When we put these four scenarios together into one construct, superimposing the shapes produced by each of them into one shape, the images created are quite startling (Figure 66, page 236). We see a cross within a circle that is the brain; the four spatial directions of the globe; seasonal "X" axes dividing the four type genera (NT, ST, SF, NF) in time; a rainbow of personality species, abilities, chakra colors and seven physiological systems; chakra-like

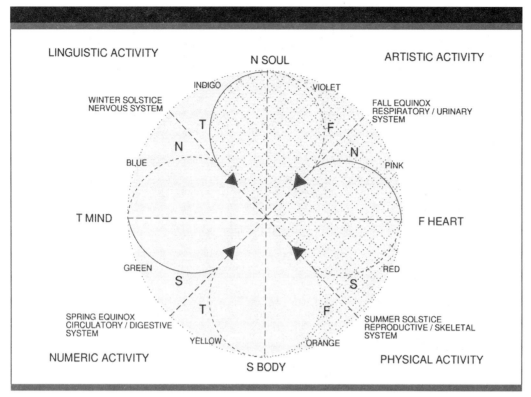

**Figure 66. The Journey: Helical Paths of Type Development Over a Lifetime**

wheels within a wheel (viewed from the top, bottom or sides); and two pairs of three-dimensional helices whose spirals all point to the center. The path unwinding, then, the "journey" as we often call it, moves toward the center, creating the physical and philosophical totality that contains everything from the yin-yang symbol of the macro universe to the cell division of meiosis—"From the One came the Two, from the Two came the Three, and from the Three came the Ten Thousand things." In the mere building of the theory, we would appear to have come full circle.

✳ ✳ ✳

### Key points to arise out of chapter 9 are as follows:

✳ Einsteinian physics—which takes space, time and energy into account— may be one very modern way of describing phenomena which have been described since ancient times. The Einstein-Tiller model of positive and negative space-time posits the existence of two universes—the physical universe we can see, and the etheric universe we cannot see—and shows that order and chaos are necessary elements of the system.

✳ In applying these concepts to type, talent and disease, it is proposed that Cardiovascular and Immune patterns are part of an *energy* continuum, as well as a laterality continuum, which puts excessive order at one end (perhaps I-S-T-J preferences at their worst) and excessive randomness at the other (perhaps E-N-F-P preferences at their worst).

✳ A law of mechanics says that resistance *increases* energy, while a lack of force actively depletes it. Thus, Cardiovascular pattern ailments characterized by high-energy states (e.g., high fat diets) may be best helped by a *release* of energy to shift right, while Immune pattern ailments characterized by low energy states may be best helped by an *addition* of energy to shift left.

✳ The completed Sundial model of type, talent and disease (1) compiles a fluid rainbow of preferences, talents and disease risks which blend one into another around the circle that is the brain; (2) presents associations only; (3) claims all of us possess all type traits, cognitive abilities and risks but that these will vary in strength according to our preferences and the degree of emphasis on particular functions and abilities; (4) proposes that disease risk might be reduced to some extent with a purposeful shifting of one's thinking to a different part of the circle/brain; and (5) is only a theory that needs verification with research.

✳ The Sundial model suggests there will be *time* variations in talent and disease patterns, which are tentatively explored in this chapter using the talent database. In point of fact, many individuals in the database seem to have been born about the time of the spring or fall equinox or the winter solstice. Right- and left-lateralized talents seem to have been physically vulnerable at different, energetically apposing times of the year—right-lateralized talents particularly in the cooler seasons of the Northern Hemisphere, and left-lateralized talents in the high-energy period of summer. Talents as well as diseases seem to exhibit a seasonal periodicity in terms of month of birth. The birth dates of scientists and musicians, for example, cluster around spring and fall equinoxes and the winter solstice, while those of athletes cluster around the time of the summer solstice. Similarly, heart disease and stroke seem to have occurred more often in individuals born at the spring or fall equinox or winter solstice, while cancer seems to have occurred more often in individuals born about the time of the summer solstice. Again, further research is needed to validate these trends.

✳ Chapter 9 shows that a circular or spiraling, dynamical system can also be drawn as a repeating wave pattern (and vice versa) as might be found in light waves, EEG waves or the seasonal periodicity of disease. We extend this notion to the spiraling developmental paths of individual types to demonstrate that there are four basic helical patterns in type development. When the four are superimposed on each other, the resulting picture looks very much like ancient wheels, not to mention photographs of DNA, which can predict, of course, for laterality, handedness, personality traits, talent and disease. All paths in this developmental picture point to the center.

# CHAPTER TEN
## REVELATION AND RELATIVITY:
## HEALING WITH "COGNITIVE" ENERGY

———————————————— ✳ ✳ ✳ ————————————————

And finally, we look at handedness and the lateralities it represents, not as a correlate of disease risk, but as a means of helping to *treat* disease through the practice of Therapeutic Touch. In doing so, we apply the Chinese principle that an *addition* of energy, or the application of apposing energies, may actually act to help soothe or balance energies that may have reached unhealthy extremes. Far from being a kind of faith healing, Therapeutic Touch produces unusual auric emissions in healers' hands, which have been recorded with Kirlian photography. It also produces waveform effects on both healers and patients that have been documented using EEG and other kinds of sensitive, diagnostic equipment. It has even been shown to affect inanimate solutions. Healers, who tend to have a bilaterally balanced EEG when performing Therapeutic Touch, typically report a sense of slowed time, a lack of spatial awareness, and increased energy.

Chapter 10 ponders extensions of the life cycle beyond death and explores near-death experiences which offer clues, including the oft-described perceptions of white light and hovering above one's body. The fourth and final ancient "wheel" to be described in *Sundial*, that of the circle described in Revelation, is considered from the vantage point of previous connections to type, talent and disease. Finally, observations made from the practice of Therapeutic Touch and throughout *Sundial* are explained in terms of Einstein's General and Special Theories of Relativity which show, among other things, that time slows and energy increases as spatial directionality moves toward the center.

———————————————— ✳ ✳ ✳ ————————————————

*"I believe in the brotherhood of man and the uniqueness of
the individual. But if you ask me to prove what I believe,
I can't . . . There comes a point where the mind takes a higher
plane of knowledge, but can never prove how it got there.
All great discoveries have involved such a leap."*

(Albert Einstein, quoted in Daniel, 1987)

Perhaps the circles through history and waveforms throughout science have been there to alert us to the fact that all nature is organized in some way along circular (topographical) or spiraling (horizontal, longitudinal, vertical) patterns in space and time, in both macro and micro directions of infinity, even so far as to include the processes of cognitive development through life. If that were the case, it would suggest that conceptions of afterlife and other invisible, etheric phenomena and entities described since recorded time began might be an extension of the circling, spiraling, laterality energy cycle beyond death, which should recapitulate if for no other reason than that the developmental line appears to be cyclic. Of course, it goes without saying that we cannot determine whether this is even remotely plausible, or how many revolutions and what periodicity, if any, there might really be. But we can nevertheless theorize about it—as in Figure 67—knowing that this is all that's possible.

Viewed topographically in the circular, Jungian form of the spiral, we can suppose that the physical, observable life of a person moves in ever tighter, faster concentric revolutions toward the center. Viewed from the side (Figure 67), the tighter circles suggest increasing frequency of the energy wave in later life ("ultraviolet") and that etheric, unobservable reality is tighter

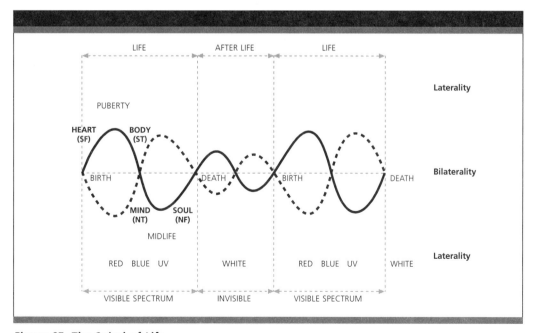

**Figure 67. The Spiral of Life**

**Figure 68. The *Caduceus*, Western Symbol for Healing (Judith, 1987)**

and faster still, beyond the ultraviolet end of the visible spectrum toward white light, or beyond even the speed of light according to the Einstein-Tiller model. Left and right talent lateralities might have opposing developmental peaks above and below the bilateral midpoint—as suggested by the opposing peaks in our talent database—and together they form a double-helix shape when both their lines are drawn on the same graph. Coincidentally, the lines also have the shape of winding chakra pathways (Figure 28, page 157) which some believe helped to form the basis of the caduceus, a well-known Western symbol for healing (Judith, 1987; Figure 68).

Thus, according to the graph in Figure 67 (page 241)—which could just as easily be drawn vertically—body language and the physical-emotional forms of communication of infants happen on the grounded "red" level of slow energy waves (which corresponds roughly to the position of SF on the Sundial wheel), the symbolic adult communication of numbers and words on faster "blue" waves (corresponding to the positions of ST, NT), and the abstract communications of art forms, auras, extrasensory perception and mental telepathy on very fast "ultraviolet" waves (NF). The most evolved of us who have successfully managed to integrate the four functions—perhaps mediums, the elderly, seers like Edgar Cayce, and those at the moment of death—would seem to be, in effect, *between* the visible and invisible spectra of ultraviolet and white light, rendering them able to see (clairvoyance), hear (clairaudience) or feel (clairsentience) communications from the "other side." Christ, as one such individual, is said to have risen on the third day. Could it also have been at the time of the third peak?

If this vacillating pattern of laterality were the norm, then the energy deviations we have discussed, whether deviations of "too much" or "not enough," might serve to contribute to disease processes at any point along the way. Disease has its own energy under this system, which transmits at some frequency on the visible or invisible spectrum, and is picked up by electronic "receivers" designed for this purpose—CT and MRI scans, X-ray, ultrasound, EEG, ECG, and so forth (Figure 69, page 244). That is, abnormal energy frequencies, which might very well be paired with excessively "fast" or excessively "slow" energy frequencies on the cognitive rainbow, emanate from the inside to the outside, regardless of the original causes of the disease.

If "deviant" energy and illness are tied to one set of thought processes, as we ha[?] speculated, it stands to reason that it might be normalized, even healed in some cases, throug[?] a transmission of "corrective" energy and other thought processes—perhaps on an opposing frequency—whether it comes from the environment (machines, drugs, herbs, food, climate, etc.), the individual himself, or literally at the hands of another. In fact, "corrective" energy is the principle behind radiation therapy, pacemakers, electroconvulsive therapy, laser surgery, acupuncture, insulin therapy, *qi gong*, herbal treatments, aromatherapy, special diets and many other sophisticated interventions, but it also seems to occur on a much smaller, less invasive scale in the ancient technique of laying-on-of-hands.

The New Testament describes many instances of this practice:

> Some people brought him a man who was deaf and could hardly speak, and they begged Jesus to place his hands on him. So Jesus took him off alone, away from the crowd, put his fingers in the man's ears, spat, and touched the man's tongue. Then Jesus looked up to heaven, gave a deep groan, and said to the man, "Open up!" At once the man was able to hear, his speech impediment was removed, and he began to talk without any trouble (Mark 7: 32–35).

> All the people tried to touch him, for power was going out from him and healing them all (Luke 6: 19).

Modern experimental explorations of healing hands have demonstrated that there is a magnetic energy field around healers. This has been correlated, in some elaborate double-blind studies, with such effects as reduced rates of goiter development in mice; healing of intestinal infections in rats; faster wound healing; greater seed yield and plant growth; the charging of bottles of water, much like a battery; increased germination rates in seeds treated with such water; elevated enzyme activity (NAD-synthetase) that promotes cell metabolism; repair of a UV-damaged enzyme called trypsin; increased chlorophyll production; increased hemoglobin production in ill individuals; anecdotal reports of improvements in some cardiac conditions, asthma, epilepsy and rheumatoid arthritis; relaxation, pain reduction, and faster recuperation times; and a change in color of copper sulfate crystals from jade green to turquoise-blue (Gerber, 1988; Harpur, 1994; Krieger, 1979, 1993). Benor (1990) was able to find 131 controlled trials in the scientific literature of healing by laying-on-of-hands, fifty-six of which were able to demonstrate statistically significant results at the 0.01 level or better. While it is seldom, if ever, a cure—as most forms of radiation are seldom, by themselves, a cure—healing by laying-on-of-hands often appears to be, at the very least, a help to those who feel unwell.

Equipment capable of detecting infinitesimally weak magnetic fields has found the emissions during laying-on-of-hands to be at about one hundred times higher than normal body activity, but not substantially different from the emissions from non-healer's hands, which suggests that healers may not be much physically different from the rest of us. However, an interesting chemical reaction known as the Beluzov-Zhabotinsky (B-Z) reaction demonstrates the healer's unusual ability to increase order (or negative entropy) by *cognitively* boosting the energy of the system (Figure 70):

> In the B-Z reaction, a chemical solution shifts between two states, which are indicated by unfolding, scroll-like spiral waves in a shallow petri dish solution. If dyes are added to the solution, one observes an oscillation of colors from red to blue to red . . . *Following treatment by [the healer's] hands, the solution produced waves at twice the speed of a control solution.* In another experiment, the red-blue-red oscillation in two beakers of solution became synchronized after [the healer's] treatments. The conclusion of the research team was that *the healer's field was able to create greater levels of order* in a nonorganic system along the lines of negative entropic behavior (Gerber, 1988: 305, emphasis added).

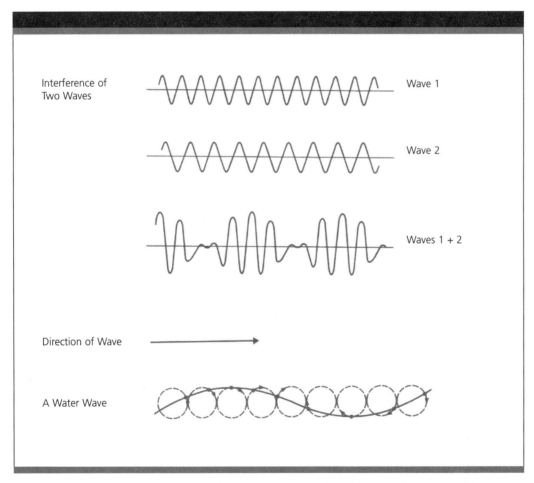

**Figure 69. Some Physical Properties of Waves: Waves Produced by Interference, and by Periodic Circular Motion**

From *The Tao of Physics* by Fritjof Capra. (c) 1975, 1983, 1991, 1999 by Fritjof Capra. Reprinted by arrangement with Shambhala Publications, Inc., Boston, www.shambhala.com.

Chemical chaos: Waves propagating outward in concentric circles and even spiral waves were signs of chaos in a widely studied chemical reaction, the Beluzov-Zhabotinsky reaction. Similar patterns have been observed in dishes of millions of amoeba. Arthur Winfree theorized that such waves are analogous to the waves of electrical activity coursing through heart muscles, regularly or erratically.

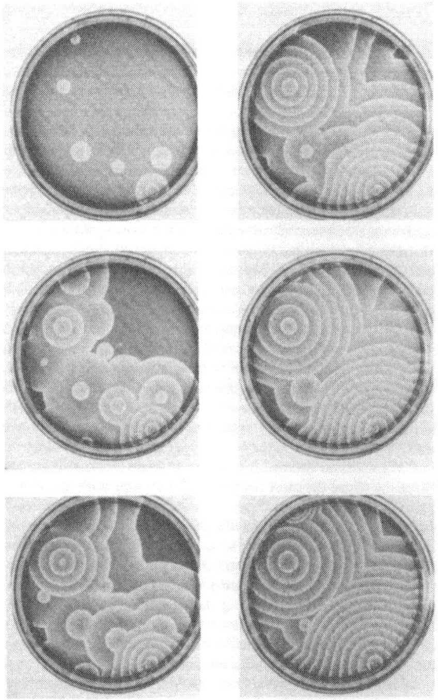

**Figure 70. Waves Produced in the Beluzov-Zhabotinsky Reaction (Gerber, 1988)**

It has been proposed by Dolores Krieger, Ph.D., R.N. (1972, 1976) of New York University, a professor of nursing who has trained thousands of nurses, physiotherapists, chiropractors and other health care professionals in this skill around the world, that psychic healing or spiritual healing, as it is known, which is very distinct from the faith healing seen on television, is not some unique, mystical power only some people possess, but is rather *a universal ability to tap into relevant thought processes*. As Richard Gerber, an American physician, notes:

> To the eyes of the healers, the test tubes [in one experiment] appeared to contain only clear solutions. They were not trying to induce a change in enzyme activity in any particular direction. They were only *thinking* about healing (Gerber, 1988: 301, emphasis added).

Healers apparently do four or five essential things related to meditation when they engage in this kind of activity, which should not be taken lightly in experimentation because it is very probably a method of tinkering with a person's energy. It is said to be possible for susceptible individuals (e.g., children, pregnant women, people with head injuries, traumatized patients) to actually "overdose" on another's energy, feeling agitation and increases in pain (Krieger,

1979) so it is important to be versed in the technique. First, healers ground their own bodies well and strive to quiet and "center" their own thinking (their term) through appropriate visualizations. They create a compassionate meditative state by becoming intensely focused on the person to be healed and by being relaxed, alert and emotionally passive at the same time. Then they intuitively assess the auric energy field of the patient, searching with the hands and the mind's eye for changes or imbalances in the field ("bulges," "holes," hot or cold areas in the space a few inches above the body). They may visualize energy, such as light, coming into their own bodies through the top of the head so as not to give from their own supply, as it were. Finally, they fix the gaze and "deliberately and consciously direct their *excess* body energies," or energy from the auric space around them, to the affected site through simple will and focused concentration (Harpur, 1994, emphasis added).

It is very important to note that there is no forcing of this process. It is instead a kind of "effortless effort" that comes from genuine, selfless caring and which gives both healer and recipient pleasant, relaxed sensations as it occurs. The intense focusing, the undistracted gaze, the instinctive scanning of the body, the "excess" body energies—all this makes healers sound much like left-lateralized talents, according to our earlier hypotheses, possibly Introverted Intuitives (IN), given the internal, imagination components of the activity.

One of the more famous healers, in fact, Godfrey Mowatt (1874–1958) of the U.K., who as a child was described as "blue-eyed with red-gold curls [and] unusually intelligent" (76), was blinded, alienated, despairing and suffering from heart disease when he reportedly had a vision, at age forty-five, to go serve his fellow men. The blindness was said to have helped him in the act of healing by eliminating distractions, and he devoted the rest of his life, to age eighty-four, to this work. He once wrote:

> It means more to me when people write to say they have found new peace and happiness, such as they have never known before, through the Light penetrating their darkness, than when they write that they have received some wonderful healing (Harpur, 1994: 85).

Sometimes healers touch the skin of the person seeking healing, sometimes the person touches the healer, and sometimes healers suspend their hands above the person, or visualize certain colors, e.g., blue to calm a patient, yellow to stimulate him. Some healers claim to have achieved results at considerable geographic distances as much as 1000 miles away (Bro, 1989), apparently only by thinking of the healing they want to accomplish. The healer usually feels heat in his hands as he works; the major meridians are believed to meet in the hands, and Kirlian photography reveals a fireworks display of energetic activity there (Harpur, 1994; Figure 71). The person being healed feels this as a warm, tingling, pulsating or current-like sensation running through his own hands, arms, neck or spine, while the hands are on or near him. In the meantime, the healer becomes unaware of his spatial surroundings, and perceives a marked slowing in the sense of the passage of time. A twenty-minute healing session feels to him as if it is over in no time at all (Krieger, 1979).

Here is a typical account from the journal of one of Krieger's students:

'These successes with Therapeutic Touch have affected me profoundly, and I have found a peacefulness and purposefulness in life through my ability to help those I 'touch.' After I have centered and am working on the ill person, *I feel that I am, in a sense, in a different 'place' than my usual physical surroundings.* It is as if I am alone with the ill person, and I have a deep knowledge of the task to be performed. The quiet is peaceful, and the serenity seems to touch me physiologically as well as emotionally. I am aware of my hands, but only in the sense of them being extensions that work in concert with my other sensitivities toward the end of meeting the needs of the ill person.

'After the assessment, I feel myself getting "stronger" (for want of a better word). I have more confidence and my respirations are quieter, deeper, and slower than usual. I have a sense of inner plenitude that I cannot explain, except to say that I know it to be a feeling within me, not "out there." I do not understand these phenomena . . . *I am aware of an increase in my own energy level*, and a feeling of joyfulness . . . a quiet joy . . .'

'*My sense of time is slowed* during the act of *Therapeutic Touch*. I might spend fifteen or twenty minutes with a person and yet not be aware of the passing of those many minutes at all. This aspect of Therapeutic Touch I find rather extraordinary, because I am usually acutely aware of time. . .

'I feel bonded for the period that I am with the ill person . . . Previous to learning about Therapeutic Touch, I usually felt depleted of energy after a close encounter with a patient. Now I feel no loss of energy; I would even say I feel more energetic!' (Krieger, 1993: 89–90; emphasis added).

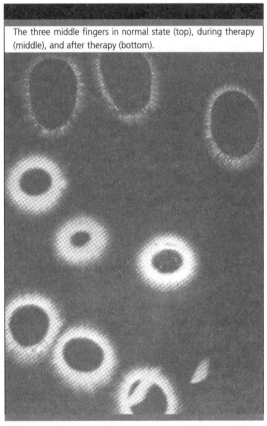

The three middle fingers in normal state (top), during therapy (middle), and after therapy (bottom).

**Figure 71. Kirlian Photography of Effects of Therapeutic Touch on the Healer (Krieger, 1979)**

The objective effect on the person being healed, as on the B-Z solution, appears to be a change in waveform activity that may or may not translate into a change in physical state as the energy is transformed from magnetic to chemical and electrical states. Krieger's research team found that the EEG patterns of both healer and the person receiving the healing change. Those being treated by laying-on-of-hands often enter into a low-amplitude alpha state, indicative of relaxation, which remains for the course of the treatment. *The healer, meanwhile, who has a bilaterally balanced EEG wave pattern at rest (Harpur, 1994), shows a high-amplitude beta state indicative of deep concentration* (Figures 72–73, pages 249–250). Eventually, the waves of both healer and feeling type come to be "in sync," even when the healing takes place at a distance:

> Mrs. Worrall [a healer] sat in a room down the hall from her patient while both were attached to EEG, ECG, GSR, and other physiological monitoring devices. While Mrs. Worrall *visualized* herself working on the patient's throat area, the patient would actually report that he or she could feel a sensation of warmth and tingling in that bodily region. Even more remarkable was the researchers' observation that there was a synchronization of brain wave activity and other bioelectric rhythms between healer and patient during the healing process (Gerber 1988: 320, emphasis added).

Krieger believes the focused work of healers *accelerates* the healing process that is naturally within each of us, and has seen therapeutic touching by health care providers and laypeople alike work with asthma, ailing premature babies, and the pain of terminal cancer. In this respect, it is noteworthy that Jesus is reported to have said, "I am telling you the truth: whoever believes in me will do what I do—yes, he will do even greater things . . ." (John 14: 12).

Just as disease may be tied to cognition, so, too, may be the healing that is its antithesis, which is not a new idea except for the fact that it is probably *specific* kinds of thinking which may serve to bring this about. Perhaps diseases of "slow" waveforms (red) can be changed by cognitive activity characterized by "fast" waveforms (blue) such as beta waves, just as diseases of "fast" wave activity (e.g., anxiety disorders) are often helped by slow-wave cognition (e.g., relaxation exercises) that acts to slow it down. Maybe the hand emissions of people with left-sided talents might be used to *add* energy (negative entropy) needed by those with right-sided disorders, just as those with right-sided talents, in turn, might be able to absorb energy excesses (positive entropy) characterizing left-sided disorders. It is probable that we all do both to some extent—transmitting and receiving—depending on the kind of thinking we do during the act of touching.

Very likely there is even hand differentiation within us, reflecting hemispheric control, where one hand (the dominant) effectively gives energy to the patient (negative polarity), and the other draws it away (positive polarity), as in an electrical circuit (Sherwood, 1985). A simple experiment visibly demonstrates the notion of opposite polarities in the hands.

*Top:* EEG and EOG (eye position) recording of healer D. K. during eyes-open, baseline. Note the preponderance of fast EEG (50μV calibration). *Bottom:* EEG and EMG recording during Therapeutic Touch. Simultaneous recording of the patient (H.P.) and healer (D. K.). Note that the increase in D. K.'s fast beta EEG is not associated with an increase in EMG. Also note the preponderance of alpha in the EEG of H. P. (50μV calibration).

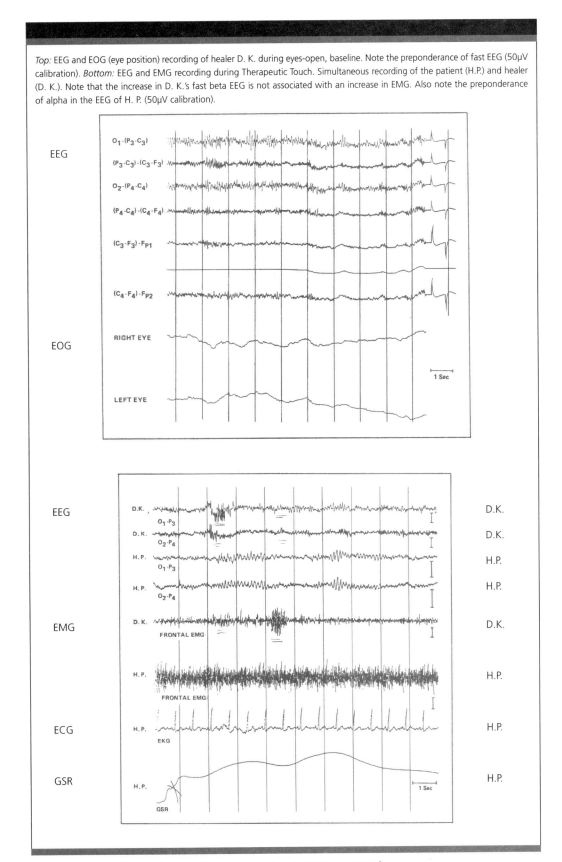

**Figure 72. Wave Recordings of Therapeutic Touch (Krieger, 1979)**

Reprinted with the permission of Simon & Schuster, Inc., from *The Therapeutic Touch* by Delores Krieger. Copyright © 1979 by Prentice-Hall, Inc.

A conductive copper rod spins in opposite directions, and at different speeds, when it is held in the right hand and then in the left hand of the same person. It also spins above the head of the person, in the region of the crown chakra. Incredibly, holding up the left hand near the rod spinning in the right hand will cause the rod to stop spinning and sometimes even to reverse itself, which has the effect of making the person feel weak and nauseated and is therefore suggestive of polarity reversal, from a state of wellness to unwellness, with cognitive manipulation. The same phenomenon, in the opposite direction, can be observed with the right hand near a rod spinning in the left hand, all of which is rather unusual empirical evidence that the hands of normal people do emit an invisible, circular energy of some kind that, directly or indirectly, affects the body.

Most hopeful of all in this area is the fantasy that patients might be able to help themselves in this way by helping others. Through therapeutic touching of the kind Dolores Krieger teaches and Godfrey Mowatt practiced—and which is routinely practiced in neonatal units around the world—perhaps people exercising to recover from heart attack, for example, might give to cancer patients of the blocked energy surpluses they themselves work to dissipate. Considering they might otherwise expend it only on jogging, perhaps they can instead act as "energy donors" for those with little to burn, helping to restore balance for both parties in the process.

If this could be done, energy efficiency through recycling would then extend beyond trees and material waste to the sharing, by touch, of the very life force in each of us—which is

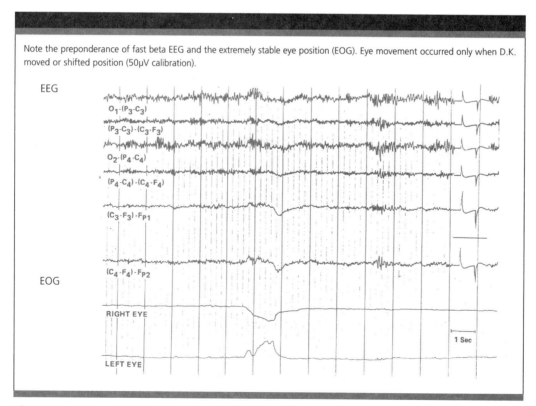

**Figure 73. EEG and EOG Recording of D.K. During Therapeutic Touch**

another interesting dreamscape but one that clearly requires controlled experimentation and verification before it can be taken seriously. Some answers to these questions may lie in testing the physical effects of the rainbow of cognitive abilities around the Sundial, aware of the possibility that even the ability to heal (or feel auras) may have its place on the circle—perhaps in the area of the brain that mediates the "third eye" (frontal lobe?) as is believed in India and Tibet, or in the area associated with abdominal function (left-posterior area?) as is believed in China and Japan. The New Testament also has something to say about this:

> There are different kinds of spiritual gifts, but the same Spirit gives them . . . The Spirit's presence is shown in some way in each person for the good of all. The Spirit gives one person a message full of wisdom, while to another person the same Spirit gives a message full of knowledge. One and the same Spirit gives faith to one person, *while to another person he gives the power to heal . . . as he wishes, he gives a different gift to each person* (I Corinthians 12: 4–11, emphasis added).

The idea of chasing maladaptive "cognitive" energies (read: maladaptive electromagnetic energies) with adaptive ones is only one meaning derived from our original life cycle graph at the beginning of this chapter (Figure 67, page 241). From the vantage point of yet another big picture, we can see that one revolution of the S-shaped line in the graph represents the development of the individual—through an emotional stage (child), physical stage (youth), intellectual stage (adult), and spiritual stage (middle to old age)—and also the cyclical development of man through historical periods that may have tended to particularly emphasize values of the heart and body (early man?), mind (Renaissance?) or soul (Romantic period?). In the twentieth century alone, it could be said that we moved through physical, emotional and intellectual phases. As each stage is necessary to the healthy development of the individual, so, too, is each period and its associated strengths (emotional expression, physical skill, language, the arts) necessary to the evolution of man. This, of course, places the importance of each of the type categories gifted in these forms of expression (SF, ST, NT, NF) on an equal footing. There can be no hierarchies, because all abilities are needed for the orchestrated, forward movement of the whole. Clearly, it takes all spokes of the wheel, we might say, to make it roll!

According to this conception, then, civilization has already passed through an "adolescence" and "adulthood" of logical-material thinking, and is now perhaps at an awkward "midlife" transition between materialism and spiritualism. The blurring or dissolution altogether of former realities in gender roles, east-west political philosophy, economic territoriality, and disease patterns, are all evidence of, and catalysts for, *a transformation toward a new rightward order—or less order—that is increasingly seeking for, and receptive to, bilateral thinking and spiritual explanations. This may not necessarily mean a return to organized religion as we have known it, but rather to a belief in the importance of spirituality for health, and in a conception of bioenergetic medicine which embodies the idea.* To the extent that the transformation is happening in all areas of human endeavor, and not just in health, we may be witnessing a grand paradigm shift (laterality shift) to high-level nonlinear thought. Supposing a God-figure actually had a role in creating evolution, we might even say that evolution has, in turn, brought us full-circle and led us to this renewed interest in spirituality.

What awaits civilization at the end of the cycle? Do we repeat the cycle? Or is it literally the end of the age and the beginning of an afterlife for an entire species? Is the faster cycling beyond a figurative death of the age a rebirth of sorts, in which man enters a "white" phase of development hitherto inexperienced, at least in recorded memory? To answer this question, perhaps we can again generalize to the collectivity from the developmental experiences of the individual. That is, perhaps in the commonalities of reports by individuals who have reached the end of the cycle, as it were, and who have survived near-death experiences (NDE), we can deduce unique glimpses into this portion of the cycle for mankind in general.

Carol Neiman and Emily Goldman (1994), in examining the NDE researches of Kenneth Ring and Melvin Morse, note that NDE travelers, as they are known, are religious and agnostic alike, that they give remarkably similar reports regardless of background or physical attributes, and that they are so changed by the experience, it is difficult to imagine they are telling anything other than the complete truth as they know it. Having first come into the world through a birth canal, these people often tell of leaving it in a similar fashion, through a tunnel that is usually dark but "may be luminous and feature multicolored streaks of light, just like a rainbow" (149). Those who recall any sense of speed through the vortex describe it as "faster than the speed of light" towards a destination far beyond the stars, and at the center of the tunnel is ". . . an extremely brilliant light. It's pure white. It's just so brilliant . . . this most magnificent, just gorgeous, beautiful, bright, white or blue-white light" (150).

The light is viewed as a being of some kind, "a mass of energy" which telepathically exudes an overwhelming strength and compassion that transforms their lives upon returning to their bodies:

> It was all the energy of the universe forever in one immeasurable place . . . There is no doubt in my mind that it was God. God was me and I was God. I was part of the light and I was one with it. I was not separate. I am not saying that I am a supreme being. I was God, as you are, as everyone is (155).

> I saw that bright light and I knew it was all the colors there were, everything was in that light (157).

> And I was talking to this blinding white light that was all colors and no colors at the same time (168).

Usually feeling wonderful during the visit and reluctant to go back, travelers often see "cities of light" and centers of learning in a world that does not value material success or accumulations. They converse with the Being of Light and return with two messages for continued life on earth—*the importance of love, and the importance of knowledge or "knowing"*:

I realized that there are things that every person is sent to earth to realize and to learn. For instance, to share more love, to be more loving to one another. To discover that the most important thing is human relationships and love, and not materialistic things (163).

You realize that you are suddenly in communication with absolute, total knowledge. It's hard to describe . . . You think of a question . . . and immediately know the answer to it (156).

It seemed whole Truths revealed themselves to me . . . Waves of thought— ideas greater and purer than I had ever tried to figure out came to me. Thoughts, clear without effort revealed themselves in total wholeness, although not in logical sequence. I, of course, being in that magnificent Presence, understood it all. I realized that consciousness is life. We will live in and through much, but *this consciousness we know, that is behind our personality, will continue* (157; emphasis added).

From a typological perspective, we may be clear on the message NDE travelers bring to us about love—to play out our lives more and more in the key of F for the sake of those around us—but what exactly is the message about knowledge and "knowing"? Surely it is to learn as we move around the wheel. But it could also be to engage in knowing, in intuiting, by trusting the dominant function that guides the whole developmental process. *The dominant function— N for INTJ, T for INTP, S for ESTP, F for INFP, and so forth—is the compass in each type that instinctively knows the direction that is best for us and advises us in verbal, visual, physical or feeling languages consistent with the preferences we understand. This is the "inner voice" we all recognize, confidence in which may very likely lie the key to staying on course. We fail to hear, see or feel it at the risk of creating a whole spectrum of lateral imbalances.*

One woman asked the Being of Light about sins, the response to which was that "There are no sins. Not in the way you think about them on earth. The only thing that matters is how you think" (158).

This returns us to our original problem, that of consciously shifting our cognition to avoid the "sins" of one-sidedness created by cultural "shoulds" and egotistical "wants," to achieve a nearly centered equilibrium of body, mind, heart and soul characteristics, founded on needs. Full integration may not be possible, by virtue of our more innate aspects of laterality, functional preferences and stage of development. It may not even be advisable insofar as a *total* steady state is, in effect, the death of the organism. But perhaps by striving for *more* of a balance, we might be able to decrease the personal, physical and social risks that may come with not striving for it at all.

Life begins with duality—the meeting of man and woman, sperm and egg, the splitting of DNA, the division of the ovum into two cells, then four cells, right and left laterality, anterior and posterior laterality—and this evolves (or devolves) into conceptions of "I" and "You," mind and body, heart and soul, positive and negative, east-west, north-south, yin-yang,

Sensing–Intuition, Thinking–Feeling, science and spirituality, earth and sky, life and afterlife. Through it all, the fundamental human paradox would appear to be that the tangible material and intangible spiritual natures of man are essentially one, despite our struggle with the apparent opposition of our visible and invisible selves. Finally recognizing that we must accommodate *both* sides, rather than one side, of the coins of life, in contradiction to some of our inclinations, will ultimately determine our physical, intellectual, emotional and spiritual well-being—as individuals *and* as a species.

By way of summarizing many of the principles discussed in this book, we will draw some final parallels now between our modern Sundial and ancient images found in the strange and mysterious book of Revelation, the last book of the Bible, written by the apostle John about sixty years after the death of Christ. Numerous interpretations of Revelation's bizarre symbols and scenes have been put forward since that time—usually relating to a timetable of historical events and the end of the world—yet scholars are still generally uncertain of its meaning. Whatever interpretation might be derived, Revelation is a book of visions that tries to convey a still-crucial message of hope to its readers and, as in the other spiritual systems we have examined, it contains suggestions of a circle and many references to other spatial shapes, colors, and repeating figures of time—the numbers four, seven and twelve.

Taking great poetic license, we can find a number of unexpected similarities to various aspects of the wheel in several of John's reported visions. As before, the accuracy or inaccuracy of the parallels or the visions, or even the genuineness of the visions, is irrelevant; *it matters only that the same general themes crop up again and again in the major doctrines of man,* over vast stretches of geographic space and historical time, this time in Christianity. Wherever the images in Revelation begin to sound excessively mythical, dogmatic, dreamlike or simply hallucinatory, we can reassure ourselves that these tendencies are really no different in that respect from the vision quest of Singing Stone around the medicine wheel, the image of Kundalini rising, or the natural symbols of Chinese Five Phases theory (Earth, Fire, Air, etc.). It was a time in history when expansive allegory was the medium for interactive learning, and given that, we must afford Revelation the same level of open, patient consideration that we give other ancient symbolism.

The first of John's visions is one in which the Spirit takes him into heaven, saying, "Come up here, and I will show you what must happen after this." John follows and sees before him a very odd circle with someone sitting on a throne in the center of the circle, which of course is very much like our Jungian notion of God at the center of the wheel:

> . . . *And all around the throne there was a rainbow the color of an emerald. In a circle around the throne were twenty-four other thrones,* on which were seated twenty-four elders dressed in white and wearing crowns of gold. From the throne came flashes of lightning, rumblings, and peals of thunder. In front of the throne, seven lighted torches were burning, which are *the seven spirits of God* (4: 3-5, emphasis added).

The rainbow might remind us of the Hindu chakra system of cognition and organ systems that may shade off around the wheel, and especially of the heart chakra which is said to be the center of love issues (F) and is represented in that system by the green of the emerald. Green, as the center of the visible electromagnetic spectrum, a blend of primary blues from one end and yellows from the other, is a midway point balancing energy extremes. In the twenty-four lesser thrones in the verses we might see reminders of the Circadian repetitions of the system over the course of a day, and the physical shiftability of this wheel over time and around the circumference, when the self purposely changes its thinking. To the extent that NDE travelers are right, that the love chakra is the all-important chakra, it may indeed be the hybrid "green" energy of love that energizes the system and makes this wheel-that-is-a-world go round. Practitioners of the form of love that is Therapeutic Touch, who seem to have a bilaterally balanced EEG while at rest, can apparently trigger a cognitive shift in themselves, as well as a recipient, when they engage in this kind of thinking. So it seems not at all unreasonable to suggest that a mind state of love in the rest of us may not only lend a certain amount of balance to our own wheels, but may also prevent them from becoming fixed in any one place.

The seven lights in the passage might make us think of the seven colors in the spectrum (red, orange, yellow, green, blue, indigo, violet) and the seven accompanying thought patterns and physiological systems in chakra theory. John himself hinted that the seven torches also symbolize the seven major churches of the world—which ideally would include the four philosophies we have mentioned, aspects of Hinduism, Taoism, native spirituality and Christianity—whose essential message about balance and the altruistic treatment of others is fundamentally the same. Taoism speaks of the importance of the union of masculine (white) and feminine (black) qualities in all of humanity, the medicine wheel teaches of integration of the colors of the four medicines and four races (black, yellow, red, white) and Hinduism and Christianity further advise tolerance for the seven major belief systems within them.

The vision continues:

> Surrounding the throne on each of its sides, were four living creatures covered with eyes in front and behind. The first one looked like a lion; the second looked like a bull; the third had a face like a man's face; and the fourth looked like an eagle in flight . . . Then I saw a Lamb standing in the center of the throne, surrounded by the four living creatures and the elders. The Lamb appears to have been killed. It had seven horns and seven eyes, which are the seven spirits of God that have been sent through the whole earth (4: 6–7, 5: 6, emphasis added).

Here, the sacrificial Lamb, Jesus, stands in the center of the circle, with four symbolic animals surrounding Him—the lion, bull, man and eagle—whose positions are not unlike those of the Buffalo, Bear, Mouse and Eagle on the medicine wheel. Can we venture that John's animals, too, are representative of the four functions on the wheel? We can imagine, for instance, that the lion could represent aggressive Thinking, the bull the physical strength of Sensing, the man's face Feeling, and the eagle the soaring flights of fancy of Intuition. That the creatures are on four sides of the center also reminds us of the four compass directions of the wheel that may be as much the globe, we have speculated, as it is the brain.

Later in Revelation, John sees seven angels, the last of which has an unusual appearance about him similar to an aura: "Then I saw another mighty angel coming down out of heaven. He was wrapped in a cloud and had a *rainbow around his head*" (10: 1, emphasis added).

John is advised to acknowledge the great variety of mankind, the many gifts differing in a sense, in being told to "proclaim God's message about many nations, races, languages and kings" (10: 11). He learns of the seven churches and the seven plagues, which again might have parallels to the seven colors, seven kinds of thought and seven disease processes in the chakra system relating to elimination (red), reproduction (orange), digestion (yellow), circulation (green), respiration (blue), communication (indigo) and visualization (violet). Indeed, it is likely the latter two mental processes—communication (left hemisphere) and visualization (right hemisphere)—that have the most profound impact on the remaining five physiological systems of the body. *As we have said, left-hemisphere verbal activity may somehow mediate Cardiovascular patterns, and right-hemisphere spatial activity Immune patterns, which is to say, the hemispheres could relate to the time components (pulse, periodicity, rhythm, regularity, seasonality, etc.) and space components (size, shape, color, feeling, etc.) of cognition, as well as disease, in the individual. The body follows the directional lead of the mind, in that sense.*

Seven plagues are let loose upon the earth, including plagues of water pollution, weather imbalances, and one in which the people break out in "ugly and painful sores" (16:2). When these trials are ended, John has a vision of the "new heaven and earth," an NDE traveler's City of Light perhaps, in which we see an interesting array of colors represented by twelve kinds of precious stone:

> [The Spirit] showed me Jerusalem, the Holy City, coming down out of heaven from God and shining with the glory of God. The city shone like a precious stone, like a jasper, clear as crystal. It had a great high wall with twelve gates and with twelve angels in charge of the gates. On the gates were written the names of the twelve tribes of the people of Israel. There were three gates on each side: three on the east, three on the south, three on the north, and three on the west. The city's wall was built on twelve foundation stones on which were written the names of the twelve apostles of the Lamb . . . *The first foundation stone was jasper [a precious stone that is usually green, blackish green or clear], the second sapphire [blue, violet blue], the third agate [often red], the fourth emerald, the fifth sardonyx [red and white], the sixth carnelian [orange/red], the seventh yellow quartz, the eighth beryl [green], the ninth topaz [yellow/brown], the tenth chalcedony [blue], the eleventh turquoise, the twelfth amethyst [violet]* . . . The city has no need of the sun or the moon to shine on it, because the glory of God shines on it, and the Lamb is its lamp . . . there will be no night there (21: 10–26, emphasis and brackets added).

When we actually sketch these descriptions in Revelation, plotting the colors of the twelve numbered foundation stones at the hourly positions of a clock, our modern-day sundial of Circadian rhythm, it is possible to arrive at the metamorphosis drawings in Figure 74 (page 259)—in this case, a City of Light which happens to have twelve month-like gates, three on each side of a square.

What might be especially interesting about this vision, for the sake of these very loose comparisons, is that the colors of the numbered stones in this passage are arranged in the same order as colors in the chakra system around the perimeter of the Sundial wheel. Cool colors toward the blue-violet end of the spectrum are to be found on the upper half of the circumference, and warm colors toward the yellow-red end of the spectrum on the lower half, both halves being separated by a diagonal that stretches from the southwest corner of the foundation to the northeast corner. On our wheel, the same color diagonal is both a seasonal diagonal (equinox) and a directional diagonal between south-west (IT) and north-east (EF) which distinguishes between what could turn out to be the neuropsychological foundations of Cardiovascular (blue) and Immune (yellow) patterns of disease. As it happens, there is also a diagonal like this on the globe, a five-degree tilt of the earth's orbit relative to the moon's orbit, called the "line of nodes."

John then sees a flowing river, symbolic of the journey of life, which divides the Whole into halves like the left and right hemispheres of the brain, the Northern and Southern Hemispheres of the earth, or the yin and the yang of the universe:

> The angel also showed me the river of the water of life, sparkling like crystal, and coming down from the throne of God and of the Lamb and flowing down the middle of the city's street. *On each side of the river was the tree of life, which bears fruit twelve times a year, once each month, and its leaves are for the healing of nations* . . . (22: 1–2, emphasis added).

In this we are shown that an important key to life is fortunately to be found on both sides of the border, perhaps at the sites of the various cognitive gates around the circumference, and in the twelve months of the year when these differing gifts are most likely to be born. In this sense, *it is the different types of cognition that would be the leaves of the Tree of Life, and it is these "leaves" that would exist for the healing and making whole of the peoples of the world.*

Finally, the seventh angel says to John, "These words are true and can be trusted. And the Lord God, who gives his Spirit to the prophets, has sent his angel to show his servants what must happen very soon" (22: 6).

And the Lamb apparently says to John, "I, Jesus, have sent my angel to announce these things to you in the churches . . . *I am the bright morning star*" (22: 16, emphasis added).

Figure 74, page 259 shows us that the natural star luminously distorted into radiating spikes and rays by telescopes and the human eye, and the stylized star we so often see in Christian traditions, particularly in connection with celebrations of the birth of Christ, have the same basic two-dimensional geometry as the Sundial.

With the visions of John in Revelation as backdrop, it is interesting to also consider a dream Jung experienced, following his study of mandalas and prior to his publication of *Psychological Types*:

> Finally, there was a dream that had an extraordinary impact on him. He found himself in Liverpool (lit. 'pool of life'), a city whose quarters were arranged radially about a square. In the center was a round pool with a small island in the middle. The island blazed with sunlight while everything round it was obscured by rain, fog, smoke and dimly lit darkness. On the island stood a single tree, a magnolia, in a shower of reddish blossoms. Although the tree stood in the sunlight, Jung felt it was, at the same time, itself the source of light (Stevens, 1994: 21).

Jung drew no connections between the dream and the radial city in Revelation, but again we see the mandala theme, again like the Sundance, with the great tree at the center.

Having sketched some very approximate and unlikely metaphysical parallels to our Sundial model, we can make things a little more tangible and consider some circular analogies in the physical world, from which we might also learn. For instance, central to all our discussions has been the fact that there is movement in the wheel, and that this movement is at least partly described, if not controlled, by the forces and principles comprising the study of physics. Polarity differentials contribute to the linear movement of energy from point A to point B in the hemispheres and elsewhere, but it is other influences, such as gravity, that act on the poles and help drive the system, thereby skewing the lines into nonlinear shapes like circles, ellipses, vortices and spirals.

On a very macroscopic level, we notice that the planets circle the sun, the ones closest to it having the highest gravitational fields. The earth, in its particular orbit as the third planet, rotates eastward, drawing with it easterly trade winds that, in a low-pressure environment, drag hot, moist air in upward spirals into hurricanes and tornadoes. Even in Revelation, "flashes of lightning, rumblings, and peals of thunder" emanate from the circle (4: 5). It rains just outside the center in Jung's dream. On earth, the storms form a spiral that spins in a counterclockwise direction in the Northern Hemisphere, and in a clockwise direction in the Southern Hemisphere. In the Northern Hemisphere, spiraling hurricanes are most common at the equator in the warmest months. Spiraling tornadoes also begin in the south, in spring, and move northward as the summer progresses (read: as the heat moves northward) and they travel on a diagonal from south-west to north-east until they literally run out of steam.

In these large spirals—and even in the little vortex of water that spins in a whirlpool or swirls down a drain, in a clockwise direction in the Northern Hemisphere, and in a counterclockwise direction in the Southern Hemisphere—there are lessons for us about the smaller, invisible spirals of cognitive energy that might occur in and around the brain. For instance, it is apparent from these examples that the velocity of the spinning is proportionate to factors like distance to the center, gravitational pull, the mass, volume or density of the

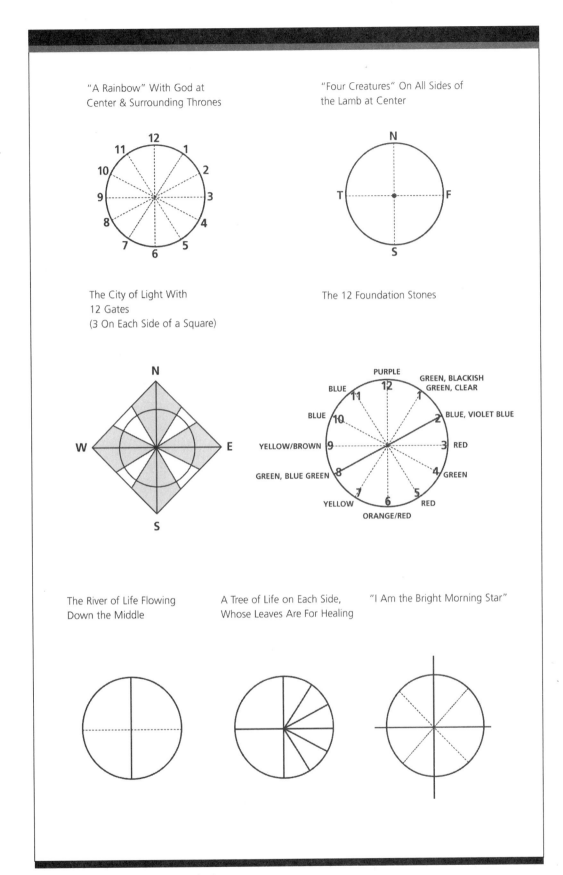

**Figure 74. Revelations in Revelation**

spinning matter, and perhaps especially the distance to the sun. Atmospheric spirals and vortices spin faster and toward the center of the earth—possibly comparable to the bilateral condition because the person is less likely to find himself "rooted" to one side of the brain or the other—when the earth is closer to the sun. In other words, atmospheric spirals spin faster at the equator and during the summer months. They spin slower and wider—the lateral condition, in a sense—when the earth is farther away from the sun, which is to say, farther north or south of the equator, and during the winter months. As we have proposed, bilateral thinking and bilateral births might also be more common in warmer times and space, lateral thinking and lateral births in the colder ones.

Much destruction can occur in the peripheral bands of a spiraling storm, and in the wall of cloud just outside the eye. The constructive side of the storm's presence, however, is that incredible surpluses of moisture and heat energy built up over land and sea are released in the process, and are depotentiated and dissipated over areas that are lacking in a burst of meteorological activity that can last hours or weeks. The spiral storm is thus a compensatory disease of the earth, as it were, an epileptogenic site of sorts, that acts to discharge, stabilize and rebalance the energy asymmetries that build to excess in the atmosphere. In doing so, the storm that can cause so much death also acts in other ways to support life. The spiral of death is also a spiral of life.

The same phenomenon happens elsewhere in the universe, figuratively in the birth and death of spiraling stars, and literally in weather patterns in other parts of our solar system. For example, the fifth planet in our system, Jupiter, is renowned for having at least four moons, twelve satellites, oppositely rotating atmospheric currents—especially in the middle of the planet at its equator—and above all, the Great Red Spot, an anticyclone churning in its Southern Hemisphere. Astronomer William Kaufmann (1985) writes:

> The Great Red Spot spins counterclockwise, completing a full revolution in
> about six days. Meanwhile, winds to the north and south of the spot blow
> in opposite directions. Consequently, circulation associated with the spot
> resembles a wheel spinning between two oppositely moving surfaces (225).

The colored ovals visible in the Jovian atmosphere are gigantic storms—the Red Spot is about the size of the earth—many of which are very stable and persisting for many years. The swirling clouds are multicolored—red, orange, brown, blue, white—and sometimes they behave a bit like the evolution of yin into yang, or the order-disorder oscillation of the Beluzov-Zhabotinsky reaction under Therapeutic Touch:

> The planet's cloudy surface not infrequently displays striking colors. In
> particular the two belts north and south of the equator periodically vary
> from very red to brown, neutral gray or even bluish. When one belt attains
> a maximum of redness the other is colorless or even bluish; between the
> periods of extreme coloration both belts are moderately red. The cycle has
> been found to take place in 12.08 years, which is in close agreement with

the planet's revolution. Minimum redness [maximum blueness, colorlessness] has been found to occur shortly after the autumnal equinox of the hemisphere in which the belt is situated, which would seem to indicate a seasonal effect, despite the fact that Jupiter's axis has an inclination of only 3' 7" to the plane of orbit (*Encyclopaedia Britannica*, 1966, 13:141; brackets added)

Again, in space, we see glimpses of the circle in Revelation and the lateral organization of the Sundial—the colors, the numbers, the circling and spiraling shapes, the cyclical time dimensions, even the diagonal tilt. The onyx-like colors of Jupiter's swirling clouds are poorly understood but, incredibly, even these storms have been related in some ways to biological activity, the spiral of destruction that can often also act as a spiral of creation: " . . . pressures and temperatures are not too different from those on Earth; organic molecules almost certainly exist there" (Kaufmann, 1985: 231).

Spiral storms can be relentlessly violent, as we well know, but the inner eye of a hurricane, on earth at least, is calm. The people who fly into these vertical tunnels often see rainbows there, experience gravity as twice what it is on the ground, and momentarily see unattached equipment, like cameras, surreally suspended in the air (Funk, 1980). Considering the other metaphorical parallels we have drawn, it is not unreasonable to expect that the very center of a Jungian cognitive spiral might also be a place of high gravity that is tranquil, "multicolored" or "white," secure and suspended in time and space, despite the commotion going on in the lateral states, or even in the bilateral states, just outside it.

We have noted that "centering" and "grounding" are important first steps in the meditations of Therapeutic Touch, and that changes in perceptions of time and spatial surroundings are reported by its practitioners. We also know that the practices of meditating and praying benefit the physical and mental well-being of the individuals who do it (Dossey, 1993; Harpur, 1994). We know that the meditations of Therapeutic Touch cause a healer's heart rate to fall, breathing to slow, eye movement to stabilize, and beta wave activity to become synchronized with that of another human being in whom pain reduction, relaxation or some form of healing is often achieved. *It is at the center of the circle, we would suggest, where truly balanced kinds of cognition appear to live, cognition perhaps like Eastern-style meditation and Western-style prayer that is characterized by intuitive knowing (N), focused concentration (T), and compassion (F), in a physically grounded context (S). It is in this place that the healing of the self and others might begin.*

It is also in the center, in the tunnel in the middle of turbulence, that life begins and ends. Revelation puts God and Christ at the center of the circle, and in the same book Jesus asserts, "I am the Alpha and Omega, the First and the Last, the Beginning and the End" (Revelation 22:13).

The God-figure, and the beginning and end of life, are in the center of the wheel, according to Revelation. The idea of centering at these critical moments agrees with our notion of bilaterality in childhood and old age—bilaterality at the beginning, laterality throughout life, and bilaterality, finally, at the end. That is to say, there is relative balance in the wheel to begin with, which is followed by life-long struggles to regain it, and perhaps ultimate achievement of it at the moment of death.

Such metaphysical, metaphorical or literary interpretations of these things are all very well on some level, but they simply will not do for those parts of ourselves, borne of exposure to traditional Western science, which demand proofs and more tangible, testable reason. For the Doubting Thomas in each of us, we can reframe some of these ideas in the language of physics, and say that the space-time relationships we see in the cosmos, and even in the smaller spirals on planet surfaces, might also be found to some degree in, and around, the brain. We say this because the circles of the macrocosm are thematically similar in many ways to the circles of the microcosm—in terms of dynamic, energetic revolutions around an attracting center or tunnel, the presence of cross-sectional axes and magnetic poles, hemispheres, spatial aspects (right hemisphere) and time aspects (left hemisphere) in the revolving entity, magnetic fields surrounding it, cyclical variations in wave production, speed of revolution, and so forth. Because of the correspondences, the brain, like planets and particles, might be appropriately described using Einstein's General and Special Theories of Relativity. Here again is a manifestly monstrous idea, but again we might tolerate it if it can make our talent-disease problem more comprehensible, or our model somehow more empirically defensible. We will consider it, then, to see how it might apply, acknowledging that an understanding of these questions will first require some limited introduction to the theories.

Unlike his predecessors, Copernicus, Kepler and Newton, Albert Einstein believed and managed to prove mathematically that the laws of the universe are the same anywhere in the universe, whether we happen to be sitting on earth or being catapulted through space close to the speed of light. Writing at the same basic time in human history as Carl Jung, in the early part of the twentieth century, Einstein abandoned the ideas of absolute space and absolute time and showed that the reality of these functions varies according to gravity and the speed at which we're traveling relative to another observer. His are mind-twisting notions simplified with the illustration that a clock on the ground floor of a building ticks imperceptibly slower than a clock on the top floor because the clock on the ground floor is more closely bound by earth's gravity. For the same reason, space—which comprises the dimensions of distance (length, width, height, radius, etc.) and mass—is also variable. It is hard to imagine that the space through which planetary probes fly can change in shape, or that the flow of time could be anything other than linear, continually marching onward, and the same for everything in the universe. But variable they are, and this has been confirmed by almost every experiment designed to test the theory (Kaufmann, 1985).

The *general theory of relativity* describes gravity entirely in terms of the geometry of space and time. It says that, when we are far from a source of gravity, which is a mass such as the sun or the earth, space is "flat" and clocks tick at their "normal" rate. As we move closer to a source of gravity, however, clocks slow down and space, even light, becomes increasingly curved. When these space-time phenomena are graphed in a composite drawing, the geometric figure that is created is a vortex, the center of which represents the strong gravitational pull of something like a planet or a black hole. In a weak gravitational field, Einstein's general theory of relativity gives the same results as Newton's classical theory, as we mentioned earlier concerning the force in the swing of a pendulum, for example. But where gravity is stronger, such as near the sun's surface, the two theories give different results. Newtonian mechanics is thus very accurate when applied to weak gravity and low speeds (flat space), but Einsteinian calculations are the better approach when there are powerful gravitational fields and extremely high speeds (curved space).

Imagining the action of an object in a smaller vortex helps in understanding these concepts—a ball rolling into a curved well, water swirling around a drain, or a penny spinning around a plastic funnel before it finally drops into the hole. In each case, the revolving object starts out in the outer, "flat" realms and moves relatively slowly. Gravity draws it downward and inward, and as it does so, the object travels through curved space on a spiral route touching all sides, spinning faster and faster in ever-tighter circles as it approaches the center. Near the center, the object seems to almost hover in place, over the hole, as it picks up speed. Then, when the object reaches a certain maximum speed, the spiraling motion becomes a straight line and the object, which now appears comparatively heavy from the force of its own momentum, disappears into the hole, apparently never to return to the flatter regions from whence it came. The space aspect of this construction is especially malleable, the time aspect less so, which is again easier to understand with an analogy. We as individuals, like the penny, have much freedom to move as we like through the three dimensions of space—left and right, forward and back, up and down—but we do not have the freedom to move at will through the dimension of time. Like it or not, we all move inexorably from youth to old age.

The same action that occurs in little funnels happens in the immensely larger vortices surrounding neutron stars and black holes, and it is the special theory of relativity that describes the effects of this motion on measurements of time, distance and mass. *The special theory says that, as an object approaches the speed of light, mass and time increase and distance decreases,* which is exactly what we observe in our smaller examples—the object becomes relatively "heavier" and the time to disappearance down the hole momentarily seems to lag, as the distance to the center shrinks. At slower speeds, under weaker gravitational pulls, it is the reverse situation—"normal" mass, time and distance which, compared to the strong-gravity scenario, appear "lighter," faster moving in time, and farther away from the center.

The effects of relativity on time, distance and mass become noticeable only at extremely high speeds, but even in the very huge spiraling mass of a dying star, the same process occurs. The overpowering weight of the star's burned-out matter presses inward from all sides, causing the star to contract. The strength of the gravity around the collapsing star then increases dramatically as the matter is compressed to enormous densities inside a rapidly shrinking sphere. Distortions of space and time become increasingly pronounced. Finally, what is known as the "escape velocity" of the circling matter comes to equal the speed of light, and the star actually disappears from the universe, leaving behind only a black hole. At this point, Kaufmann (1985) says, "space has become so severely curved that a hole is punched in the fabric of the universe" (445). Indeed, he calls the black hole an "information sink" because infalling matter takes with it many properties (chemical composition, texture, color, shape, size) that are forever removed from the universe.

A black hole spins very fast and Einstein's theory predicts that this rotation causes space and time to be literally dragged with it around the hole. A spinning black hole is therefore surrounded by space that rotates with the hole. Indeed, around the perimeter of the hole, in an area called the event horizon, it is said:

> . . . the dragging of space and time is so severe that it is impossible to stay fixed in the same place. No matter what you do, you get pulled around the hole along with the rotating geometry of space and time. This region, where it is impossible to be at rest, is called the *ergosphere* (Kaufmann, 1985: 449).

A fictitious satellite in such a place is therefore carried along with the rotating geometry of space and time, while it is conceivable that another satellite, traveling in the opposite direction, would have an extremely hard time of it constantly fighting its way "upstream." Thus the two satellites will have very different orbital periodicities reflecting the apparent ease or difficulty that characterizes their movement with, or against, the natural flow of the revolution.

Although a black hole might have a tiny electric charge, it cannot have any magnetic field whatsoever. Einstein's equations demonstrate that a north-pole/south-pole asymmetry cannot be present in the geometry of space around a black hole. When a star is in the act of collapsing, it may possess an appreciable magnetic field which radiates away from the star in the form of electromagnetic and gravitational waves, carrying energy away from the system as a ripple in the geometry of space and time. Once the star turns into itself, however, and is engulfed in the hole, there are no magnetic reverberations.

It is the Law of Conservation of Energy, as we have noted, that all matter has energy and is convertible from one state into the other. The human body is one such kind of matter, and we have considered the kinds of outpouring of energy from the body, from heat to electrical brain waves to auras. All matter also has gravity and gravitational waves pulsing through the geometry of its own space and time, and general relativity tells us that gravity curves space and time, even for the small mass that is man:

> Thus, the 80-kg man is surrounded by a slight warping of space and time commensurate with his mass. Now suppose that the man begins waving his arms. Although his total mass does not change, the details of how his mass is distributed do change. The geometry of space and time must respond to these changes because the gravitational field of the man with his hands over his head is slightly different than that of the man with his hands by his side. These minor readjustments appear as tiny ripples in the overall geometry of space and time surrounding the man. In the same way,

a bouncing ball, the Moon going around the Earth, or two stars in a binary all produce gravitational waves. From the equations of general relativity, it is possible to prove that gravitational radiation moves outward from its source at the speed of light (Kaufmann, 1985: 448).

Because of the similarities between the circle that is the brain and the circles that exist in space, let us take this small step and go one giant leap further by applying the equations of special relativity—the Lorentz transformations—to man. Suppose, for the sake of argument, that the mathematical relationships of the macro universe adhere for man's micro universe, that on the smaller level *mass equals weight, that time might equal age, and that distance is a laterality measure representing the distance (radius) to the center.* The center is zero laterality, in that sense, or perfect bilaterality, on a laterality scale such as Thinking–Feeling, which moves left and right from zero.

The Lorentz transformation for the effects of motion on distance is as follows:

$$L = L_o \sqrt{1-(v^2/c^2)}$$

where $L_o$ is a measure of starting distance at rest, $v$ is velocity (distance/time), c is the speed of light ($10^{15}$ cycles per second), and $L$ is the new, subsequent measure of distance, relative to the first one, when these variables are factored in. If velocity is

$$v = \frac{distance}{time} = \frac{laterality}{age} = \text{laterality point score/year}$$

Then, at a starting Thinking–Feeling laterality score of 10 ($L_o$), in a 30-year-old person*, the "velocity" of the person's movement around the Sundial spiral is

$$v = \frac{10}{30} = .33 \text{ point/yr}$$

Now if his T–F preference score never changed over time, which is doubtful considering Jung's developmental hypotheses about puberty and midlife, the velocity should naturally slow with age. For example, at a T–F score of 10, the velocity is .33 point/yr at age 30, .25 point/yr by age 40, and .10 point/yr by age 100, suggesting as in any declining speed measurement that less and less distance is covered over time. If, on the other hand, the person's preference becomes more clearly defined by age 40, more lateralized, as we say, to a T–F score of 20, the velocity increases to .50 point/yr, and more distance in the brain is traveled in the identical time frame. Should the person grow instead toward less typological definition and greater bilaterality by age 40, to a T–F score of 1, the velocity slows to .025 point/yr, and even less distance is covered over time than would be the case had either T or F increased or remained unchanged. *Laterality seems to speed up the developmental process, in other words, while bilaterality seems to slow it down.* There is a certain plausibility to this when we consider the precocity that accompanies some lateralized forms of giftedness (e.g., mathematics, music), and the relative developmental lags that can occur in the "non-gifted."

* At this point, the possibility of type scales actually measuring laterality is purely hypothetical. The formulas in this section should be considered as models only.

The Lorentz transformation for distance requires that we express velocity as a fraction of the speed of light, i.e., $v^2/c^2$. To accommodate this, and to test the formula using apples and apples rather than apples and oranges, we can perhaps use brain wave frequency, which can be quantified in the same units as light, in cycles per second (cps). Visible light cycles at $10^{15}$ cps, radio waves at $10^4$–$10^8$ cps, auras at 100–1200 cps (Hunt, 1977), the fast beta activity of Therapeutic Touch at 18–20 cps (Krieger, 1979), and "normal" brain waves at .5–35 cps (Bruyere, 1989).

Consequently, if we use the velocity of a normal, slower brain wave in the Lorentz equation, *at 10 cycles per second and a T–F score of 10 ($L_o$)*, we arrive at the following computation for laterality in motion:

$$L_1 = L_o \sqrt{1-(v^2/c^2)}$$
$$= 10 \sqrt{1-\left(\frac{10}{10^{15}}\right)^2}$$
$$= 10 \sqrt{1-\left(\frac{1}{10^{14}}\right)^2}$$
$$= 10 \sqrt{\text{Almost 1}}$$
$$\sim 10$$

The laterality value, at this comparatively slow speed, is fractionally less than 10. However, at the same original T–F measurement of 10, *at a faster brain wave velocity of 20 cps*, which is the approximate frequency during Therapeutic Touch, we arrive at a second computation for laterality in motion:

$$L_2 = 10 \sqrt{1-\left(\frac{2}{10^{14}}\right)^2}$$

Therefore, $L_2 < L_1$.

*What this means is that laterality "distance" to the center is minutely reduced under the faster meditative cognitions of Therapeutic Touch.* This effect, called the Fitzgerald contraction in other circumstances, is intensified if the person's preference score also approaches bilaterality over time. That is, at a T–F score of 1, at a waveform frequency of 20 cps, a third computation becomes:

$$L_3 = 1 \sqrt{1-\left(\frac{2}{10^{14}}\right)^2}$$
$$= 1 \sqrt{\text{Almost 1}}$$
$$< 1$$

Thus, a relativity equation for the effects of motion on a distance closer and closer to a source of gravity may demonstrate theoretically that laterality shrinks toward bilaterality, admittedly imperceptibly, at faster speeds of brain activity approaching the visible spectrum of light energy. Distance to the center, within the space of the brain, may be distorted and curved as we approach the center at faster speeds. *Laterality may be distorted toward bilaterality with a form of cognition that acts to help another human being.*

We can try the same thing for the effects of motion on mass, using the Lorentz transformation for mass:

$$M = \frac{M_0}{\sqrt{1-(v^2/c^2)}}$$

where $M_0$ is a mass at rest, and M is the new measure of mass when these other variables are factored in. For an 80-kg person, at the faster Therapeutic Touch velocity of 20 cps, the computed mass is greater than the mass computed at a slower brain wave velocity of 10 cps. This suggests of course that *the relative, theoretical mass of a person should increase imperceptibly, or perhaps be redistributed, with the use of Therapeutic Touch.* We might expect this to occur if Therapeutic Touch is a bilateral activity that pulls us, by gravity, through "grounding," to the center of the wheel. If mass increases, so, too, might the available energy in the person for such activities, as we know from Einstein's most famous equation, $E=mc^2$, where $E$ is energy, $m$ is mass, and $c$ is the speed of light. Perhaps because the practitioner gains more energy himself, he doesn't feel the effects of acting as donor or conductor for the person doing the receiving. This relationship might seem to show, then, that *the act of healing recharges the healer as well as the one receiving the healing,* which is exactly what healers tend to report—in other words, the act of healing heals the healer.

Finally, there is the issue of time, or age in this case, using the Lorentz transformation for time:

$$T = \frac{T_0}{\sqrt{1-(v^2/c^2)}}$$

where $T_0$ is time in an object at rest, and $T$ is time in a moving object when these other variables are factored in. The same calculations show that a one-second event at the Therapeutic Touch speed of 20 cps is longer than at the slower brain wave speed of 10 cps. *Time is thus dilated, stretched out, using Therapeutic Touch,* which we would anticipate if such cognition actually brings us to the center of an Einsteinian vortex that is the brain. Again, distortions of time are exactly what healers report.

Thus, relativity may theoretically demonstrate the effects of bilateral cognition on the space, time and energy components of the brain, as well as on the perceptual experience of the individual—suspended space and time, and high energy—during this meditative state. Relativity may show, in effect, that the space aspects of the brain determine its energy and time aspects. To the extent that bilaterality is the healthier state—and we certainly don't know conclusively at this point that it is—relativity may even show that the degree of bilaterality (distance to the center) determines the amount of available life force in the individual, his rate of aging (velocity) and his longevity (time, age). In short, all of this could mean that *maneuverings in cognitive space, which are very much under our control, may actually affect the energy and time components, which are not.*

These formulae may not be able to make detailed, pinpoint predictions about these questions—such as age at death given a certain laterality value—but it could be something like them that eventually does. For example, for the flat, cross-sectional, Newtonian spiral Jung wrote about, perhaps the polar equation for a logarithmic spiral, first discussed by Descartes, is appropriate:

$$r = k_e \, c \, \emptyset$$

where $r$ is the radius of the spiral (laterality), from a fixed point 0, under a constant angle $\emptyset$, and where $c=cot \, \emptyset$. The form of such a spiral is independent of $k$, but dependent on $c$, which could be the variable in this expression that relates to age.

Or, given the apparently infinite scale drawings of spirals that are possible, from neutron stars to tornados to hair crowns to DNA coils, perhaps a mapping from chaos math would be more descriptive. The Mandelbrot set, as one example, writes infinitely smaller spirals inside one spiral:

$$z \; \rightarrow \; z^2 + c$$

where a new mapping, $z$, is created by taking a number (a laterality score?), multiplying it by itself, and adding the original number (Gleick, 1987).

But for a three-dimensional postulation of the general effects of gravity on the brain, and perhaps ultimately on our lives, an Einsteinian relativity model may be best. We accept that gravity, over time, has enormous impact on our physical bodies, but often forget that the brain, too, as part of the body, is not only subject to the same influences, but is perhaps, as a "rotating" entity, a source of the force itself. As we have said, some small, visible evidence of the circular energies in the head region can be seen by holding a conductive copper rod above the head. At this site, the rod spins at different speeds in different directions for different people and moods. As the brain's energies are affected by the gravity and other factors that determine their spin, so, too, are the cognitions and energies that radiate from it and are picked up as rhythmic waves by more conventional tools such as EEG. As in other parts of the universe, space-time may be curved because of the gravitational fields created internally and externally. The curvature may be proportional to local energy content, and space (distance, laterality) and time (duration, age) may be functions of that curvature.

It is definitely possible that, exactly the way they stand, these equations may not apply to the brain or to development. Modifications are very likely needed that take into account anatomical variations, cognitive tilts, the "flatness" of the model at younger ages, the "curves" of it in old age, and other individual differences such as handedness. Or it may be that entirely different equations are required. *Or* it could turn out that it is simply impossible to describe the brain in this fashion and, as attractive an idea as it may be, the pursuit of spiraling mathematical functions for the mapping of health and development may be a complete waste of time, and space! Such is the nature of theorizing. But in their present form, certainly the above expressions begin to raise suspicions that relativity, or some modified version of it, might describe our rudimentary Sundial wheel of type, talent and disease, to some extent. They also suggest that Revelation and relativity might be using different symbols—words, colors, numbers, shapes—to portray the same basic ideas about life and death in the universe. In the spirit of that unity, *we will propose then that the ancient Tree of Life in Revelation, is the modern-day vortex of space and time in relativity* (Figure 75).

Let us consider the possibilities. A life is created at a place on the globe, at a time of the year, such that a baby is born when the earth's gravitational pull is strongest. Using a male example, he enters the world through a tunnel, in a relatively "pure," bilateral state, exhibiting rather little preference for one hand over the other. He is at the center of the circle. Over time, however, his preferences are differentiated and guided, through his own biology and through socialization by home, school, work and life experiences, so that he comes to choose between his natural preferences and to develop some functions at the expense of others. Puberty is a great natural differentiator, after which time young men and women often appear dissimilar, though no less exceptional, in their personality (particularly Thinking and Feeling), cognitive interests (spatial versus verbal), and patterns of abnormality which are often, but certainly not always, cyclically or seasonally related (e.g., schizophrenia predominantly in boys and those born in the first part of the year, versus depression and anxiety disorders predominantly in girls and occurring monthly and in colder months of the year). The person's handedness becomes fixed, the talents emerge, the preferences are reinforced, and there is little apparent facility or advantage to developing the "other side." The lateral mode takes over, and he begins to spin in his life's journey on the perimeter of the circle.

In the lateral state, he may feel comfortable and excel in his chosen talent area but he encounters some bumps along the way—perhaps interpersonal problems from excessive

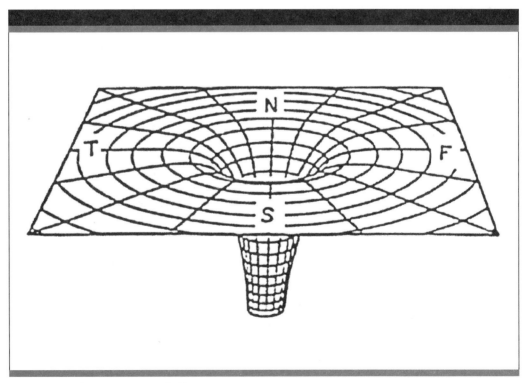

**Figure 75. Relativistic Tree of Life**

Thinking (T), emotional problems from excessive Intuition (N) or Feeling (F), or physical disease from imbalances of Sensing (S)—and he recognizes the need for change. But, knowing nothing other than his own preferred approaches, he seeks to solve these problems using the very strategies that helped to create them. He seeks solutions by becoming an even more concentrated version of what he already is, even more one-sided—by being more critical (T), more sensitive (F), dreaming up more imaginary demons (N), or working harder, faster, better (S), and so forth—and the problems get worse before they get better. His strengths, maximized, rapidly become his liabilities. He ages quickly as he spins out of control on the chaotic periphery, his excesses pushing people away from him at a time when he most needs them. Carried to extremes, his successful cognitive strategies are also his social, mental or physical undoing, in many respects, and he is highly polarized.

The natural compensatory mechanisms of the brain, very likely related in some way to gravity, act to restabilize this situation and bring the wayward scales back into balance and order. As the body or the environment reacts to the imbalances, this is done in small ways (interpersonal conflict, fatigue, the common cold), large, catastrophic ways (relationship failure, mental illness, physical disease) and even developmentally at certain points in the life cycle. It is as if nature always provides a larger back-up mechanism by which the brain can right itself and regress things back to the happier median. If the small messages aren't heard, nature tries bigger, louder ones, and so on until the person eventually dies because of lateral rigidity, or modifies himself and grows out of the stage into the next inward-looping phase of the life spiral. Midlife is a great natural equalizer, after which point men and women begin to spin closer to the center, although their personality, interests (e.g., culturally sanctioned forms of violence in men, pacifism in women) and disease patterns (e.g., heart disease and deafness in men, breast cancer and osteoporosis in women) are still quite dissimilar. In old age, as at birth, there is finally less differentiation as both genders once again approach bilaterality toward the center of the circle.

In the very center of the circle, at a place we have called "perfect bilaterality," when and where on the globe the gravitational pull is again strongest for the individual, where the escape velocity of spinning cognitive energies approaches the speed of light, and where the drag of the cognitive "ergosphere" is so powerful that it can't be resisted, the person begins to die. Perceptions of space and time become distorted; there are imperceptible increases in mass in the brain or elsewhere, the body collapses, and the distance to the center shrinks. Like the penny in the funnel, or the camera in the eye of the hurricane, the person may even find himself temporarily suspended in space and time, overlooking his own body. He then experiences yet another tunnel and eventually disappears through the "hole," the information sink which takes all manner of cognitive or psychic energy with him and leaves behind only the matter which must be converted into other energy. In dying, the person reaches the zenith of energetic homeostasis and possesses no charge or magnetic field whatsoever because, we suspect, the hole allows for no north-pole/south-pole asymmetry. The EEG or heart monitor, which now has nothing to record, exhibits a straight line where there used to be horizontally moving waves.

The child thus starts out balanced and centered in his cognition, and then shifts predominantly right or left, forward or backward through adulthood, to the specialties and imbalances of his lateral extremes, and then shifts back again to the center in old age. At the end, like the star, as increasing gravity causes matter to compress to high densities and to eventually collapse (e.g., blood clots in the circulatory system, mucous in the respiratory system, tumors in the gastrointestinal system, neural plaque in the nervous system), his invisible, conscious or cognitive self abandons the visible self and departs through an energetic escape hatch created by his own circling. The child has started out in the "trunk" of the relativistic Tree of Life, in that sense, has grown outward to its outermost "branches," and back again down the trunk (the brainstem?) to its roots in old age. In many ways, it is much the same path that the lifeblood of a real tree travels in spring and autumn, along a seasonal diagonal of the wheel.

The real tree also has spreading branches visible above ground and spreading roots which are not visible below, and could therefore be said to possess two V-shaped "vortices" meeting apex to apex at the earth—a copper rod also spins above plants—an intersection above which life begins, and below which life "ends" and waits for rebirth in the spring. Is it possible that the relativistic Tree in man is something very similar? Is it possible that a vortex for life energies, made "visible" by EEG, copper rods and other man-made energy receivers, is met by an invisible vortex for anti-life energies beyond the grounded center? If it were, like the tree in the ground, the space-time of the Tree of Life on earth would be shaped something like an hourglass, with one "V" leading rapidly into the other by way of an intersecting gate of sorts where escape velocity equals the speed of light. The hourglass configuration also happens to have the same general shape of a black hole (Figure 76, page 272).

This kind of fanciful musing would be utterly pointless were it not for some of the parallels to other spirals we have drawn. In those analogies, the spiral of death was sometimes also a spiral of life, with oppositely spinning downdrafts and updrafts continually maintaining the geometric shape of the system. *If we accept that development through life is an inward, downward-moving cycle, driven primarily by the action of gravity on oppositely charged poles, perhaps we must at least consider the possibility that afterlife not only exists—in a continuation of the infinite system of visible and invisible opposites in the universe—but that the afterlife moves, as life does, only in an antithetical direction which is both outward and upward like a rising air mass.*

Were that the case, life itself could be yet another ordered hemisphere, like a hemisphere of the brain or of the earth, which needs the opposition of a contradictory hemisphere for the balanced cohesion of the whole and the directional movement of energy from one to the other. A relativistic approach to these things, where the vortex of life spins through a corpus callosum-like tunnel into the vortex of an afterlife, might even predict for the existence of two universes—one universe we can theoretically experience because we're effectively "lateralized" so as to perceive it, if not travel it, and another parallel universe we cannot experience because we're neither in it, nor apparently equipped to perceive it very well.

We reasoned earlier that an important key to life may be found on both sides of the various borders dividing the opposites. In fact, the bridging of the brain's hemispheres in the

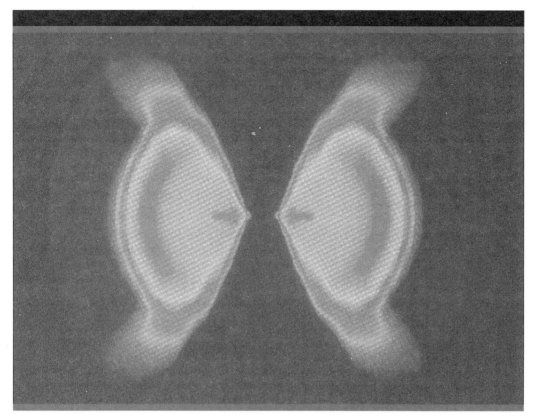

**Figure 76. Accretion Disk Around a Black Hole (Kaufmann, 1985)**

Courtesy of LL Smarr and J.F. Hawley.

bilateral state may be as close as we can ever get to actually tapping both worlds—the one we can see with our senses, and the other one we can only intuit with eyes closed. Attaining complete bilaterality, as we have said, defeats the purpose because total equality of function happens only when the person enters the suction of the ergosphere, cannot reverse the motion, and necessarily slips over to the "other side."

*But a person who tries to live a reasonably balanced variety of the cognitive leaves of the Tree— by emphasizing thought processes that are associated with mind (T), body (S), soul (N) and especially heart (F)—probably helps himself to spin at a more ordered place on the edge of the bodily entropic chaos of the center.* His visual, auditory or kinesthetic "inner voice" likely guides his progress to this end, compliance with which allows him to go *with* the flow of his own developmental river toward the center of the circle, rather than against it, since the latter can only make him socially, mentally or physically unwell in some way. An INTP must grow toward his inferior Feeling function (F), an ESFJ toward Thinking (T), an ISTJ toward Intuition (N), and an ENFP toward Sensing (S), and so forth, in keeping with each type's own developmental game plan. Indeed, realization of the unconscious inferior function may be exactly the knowledge that each type is put on this planet to learn, as it is that function which ultimately gives us the balance peculiar to our own particular set of needs.

Revelation says, "Blessed are those who wash their robes, that they may have the right to the tree of life and may go through the gates into the city" (Revelation 22:14).

From our perspective, the message implicit in this verse may not be so much about being morally virtuous in order to pass through the gate of the vortex, but about cleaning up our lateral act and striving for balance in thought and behavior so as to reach the other side. This is probably the goal not only at the time of death, but also long before it so as to maintain the necessary equilibrium between our Sensing and Intuitive selves, and the material and spiritual worlds they represent.

The other side is a place beyond the speed of light, we speculate, through a posited black hole in the time and space dimensions of the brain. It seems that this place might be at least partially and safely accessed by deliberate acts of cognitive centering such as meditation, prayer and the practice of Therapeutic Touch. Strange, inexplicable occurrences have been recorded during or following these activities, which many of us tend to haughtily dismiss in a catchall "X-file" for phenomena we can't adequately explain with Western science. The prophetic visions had by people praying are legendary, and are described throughout the Bible, and in the oral traditions of native cultures, and other important spiritual works and artifacts of man. Experienced meditators may see visions of something like an umbilical cord connecting them to earth as they fly through cognitive space, and afterwards feel strange bodily sensations of incredible heat, known as the Kundalini syndrome, rising up the back side of the body and down the front (Gerber, 1988). Even novice meditators may start to see colored auras around people, or spots of color near problem sites on the body. Many practitioners of Therapeutic Touch—who are normal, healthy, well-educated caregivers working in our hospitals and clinics—talk quietly of "telepathic" healing over short or long distances, faster recuperation rates, improved intuitive or psychic capacities in themselves, and of strange synchronicities difficult or impossible to explain by chance.

Delores Krieger, for example, reports of catatonics speaking for a few moments, of energizing cotton batten for later use by injured athletes, of patients paralyzed by spinal cord injuries "feeling" hand energies they could not have known about, and of lightning striking close by as she performed an emergency laying-on-of-hands on a febrile patient whose temperature was exceedingly high. Immediately after this particular incident, the temperature was found to have returned to normal. As she describes it:

> There is a discernible point in the Therapeutic Touch process when you know that healing is occurring. Just as I became aware of the culmination of that experience, there was an inexplicable incident: Out of a sky that had seemingly been cloudless, there flashed a huge jagged bolt of lightning, followed by a roar of thunder that shook the house. I had been deeply concentrating on the Therapeutic Touch process when this happened, and my reaction to this is not easily explained . . . still with my hands on Joan, I realized that the skin temperature had changed . . . I really do not know why the synchronicity of circumstances coupled the lightning and thunder with Joan's dramatic recovery (Krieger, 1979: 93–94).

Therapeutic Touch manages to intervene with some apparently powerful energies in a circle from which emanate, in Revelation at least, "flashes of lightning, rumblings, and peals of thunder" (4:5). We speculate that *such thinking might actually build energy and even attract energy, though the hands themselves have a weak magnetic field, because the thinking is geographically close to a gravitational center.* Indeed, the famous differential equation developed by Schrödinger demonstrates that energy is conserved where there is a mathematical symmetry of rotation, and yet it is either gained or lost where there is asymmetry (Truax, 1996). From that perspective, perhaps Krieger's strange stories involving energy should not surprise us in the least. Krieger reminds us that Jung, too, noticed instances of the paranormal during therapy:

> It is of interest to note Jung's findings that transference [which may intensify during therapeutic interactions] can lead to parapsychological phenomena. Obviously, it is not the parapsychological phenomena themselves that one must be cautious of, but rather it is imperative to acknowledge the source of any paranormal happenings (Krieger, 1979: 79).

It is at least not inconceivable that the "source" Krieger mentions in this passage is the other side, the shadow of the present universe we neither know nor understand but perhaps selectively penetrate each time we engage in these selfless kinds of talent, totally free of ego.

The profound experience of bonding with humanity that people commonly report as a result of meditating, praying or performing a laying-on-of-hands is what we might call an experience of Collective Consciousness, in view of the fact that those who do it are very much aware of connecting with others and of what happens to themselves in the process, because they do it purposely. *Centering and bilateral cognition, then, may be a way to access this Collective Conscious where people communicate deeply with each other on a purely energetic level, even in the absence of speech, nonverbal cues, or the physical presence of the other.* Jung himself, who preferred to conceive of a collective *unconscious,* wrote of the strange synchronicities that can occur with such projections.

Toward the center, in a safe zone just outside the event horizon, we suspect there could be high gravity, which has the strange effect of attracting the energies of other people and drawing them in where it is easier to communicate and otherwise connect with them, the charismatic converse to the individual whose lateral excesses serve to polarize and repel. There are probably slight alterations in mass with this higher gravity, some Einsteinian increases in the person's energy as a result, and increases in order that the energy works to hold together in defeat of natural tendencies toward entropy. This occurs not only for the self but also for the others to whom this energy may be directed. The energy can apparently be channeled intentionally through the hands, radiated unintentionally from the head and body in an auric energy field, or conveyed across space—and perhaps even across time judging from our relativity equations—simply by thinking about it.

Also according to relativity, light energy should be curved and bent in the center, such that the visible spectrum in the tunnel of energy there, as light through a prism, approaches the amalgam that is white for the dying person in the ergosphere who is able to perceive it. Practitioners of Therapeutic Touch sometimes see areas of a particular color around ill people, aura readers see a rainbow of about three colors around well people, and the aura of these meditators themselves, for those who can see it, may also approach white, signifying the very balanced union of all the energies of the cognitive rainbow. Thus, the dying person sees the multiplicity that is white but exudes only single colors from his own body, while the healer might see many colors but exude white, predominantly, himself. The rest of us are somewhere in between, most of us seeing no colors whatsoever but nevertheless emitting several colors in our own fields which extend around us in a bubble of silent, energetic communication to those with whom we come in contact. The bubble and the hands "speak" to others according to how we think.

Space shrinks at the center, but time, as we said, is elongated, perhaps even in terms of life expectancy, significant evidence for which might be the reduced longevity of strong left-handers who may happen to be right-lateralized (Coren, 1993), and the greater longevity of women, the "bilateral" gender which still manages to dominate the helping, caring professions of nursing, teaching, counseling and social work. Caring for others, it seems, may not only help these others, but ultimately also ourselves, as we conjectured mathematically in the Lorentz transformations concerning redistributions of mass and energy.

Could these emerging relativistic principles have implications for life expectancy in various parts of the world (space), or at various times of the year (time)? Is it possible that life is extended in temperate mid-latitudes, not only because of economic advantage, but also because of a relative balance in energy extremes? And what of the implications for life expectancy of higher gravity and lower gravity? Weightlessness, for example, suspends the body in space, but not in time, because the body is not necessarily near a strong gravitational center, and the life expectancy of a space traveler should therefore decrease relative to the same person's time on earth. Indeed, current space travelers tell of the intense religiosity of their experience, which would seem to suggest more of a connection to the spirituality of afterlife than to the grounding of life. In contrast, perhaps planets of higher mass, gravity and energy might support life, given the right conditions, better than even our own planet can support it.

Despite this line of mathematical-theoretical reasoning and our best efforts to describe potentialities in an area where there really are no concrete realities, and despite the subjective and objective evidence of the human and practical strengths of these concepts, there will still be those who charge that the benefits of meditating, praying, laying-on-of-hands, and other alternative therapies are simply placebo effects not worth our serious attention, trust or practice. In response, we can challenge that *it is precisely the processes underlying the placebo effect that we should be striving to locate, activate and refine—because it is those functions that are the energetic shift in thinking that is the very foundation of a natural psychology of healing.*

Finally, in view of the binding together of life and death and other opposites in the same relativistic geometry of space and time, it is fitting that we end this initial exploration of type, talent and disease at a beginning, at Genesis. In that instance, the inhabitants of the Garden were prohibited from even going near the Tree of Life at the center of the Garden. Why would that have been the case if sampling of the cognitive leaves of the Tree were important to staying on course? We can guess it is because man and woman were already at the center, in the Garden, and to eat of the Tree, at that point, was to leave an ideal place for the enduring hardships accompanying lateral exorbitance. They did eat from the Tree, however, and we have apparently been spinning outside the inner sphere, on the less-than-perfect lateral periphery, ever since. Ironically, the choice that may first have taken us out of the inner circle may now be the choice that can take us back in. By again trying on, and appreciating, the varieties of thinking around the circumference—the thinking of mind (T), body (S), heart (F) and soul (N)—we keep moving, avoiding the pitfalls associated with lasting rigidity in any one place. Sensing types become more Intuitive, Thinking types more Feeling, and so on, in the unification of opposites for both self and community. It is through cognitive flexibility that we progress inward toward our happier beginnings, while at the same time making an enormous leap into a more positive future.

Certainly it is time to appreciate and develop the many gifts differing *within* ourselves, as much as among ourselves.

*** 

### Key points to be derived from chapter 10 are as follows:

* The vacillating pattern of laterality that is typological development throughout life may extend even beyond death, in keeping with the Einstein-Tiller model of space-time, which predicts for the existence of two universes, physical and etheric. If that is the case, life itself might be a kind of hemisphere that needs a contradictory hemisphere for the balanced cohesion of the whole and the directional movement of energy from one to the other.

* Chapter 10 explores near-death experiences (NDE) to gain insight into what happens after death—in the etheric universe perhaps—and discovers that NDE travelers often have in common perceptions of floating above one's body; speeding through a multicolored tunnel; visions of brilliant, white light, "cities of light" and centers of learning; a sense of God, the importance of love and the importance of knowledge or "knowing."

* We look at the fourth of our ancient wheels, which is found in the Bible's Book of Revelation. The images described there summarize many of the symbols presented throughout *Sundial*, and echo some of the themes reported by NDE travelers, such as a City of Light. Key images in Revelation are the circle, the great Tree of Life, the God-figure, high energy ("flashes of lightning") and the beginning and end of life, all at the center of the wheel.

* In many places throughout *Sundial*, we have seen handedness as a correlate of various abilities as well as deficit and disease. Use of the hands, of course, can also be a way of *treating* health problems. Therapeutic Touch, as an example, is a modern-day version of laying-on-

of-hands, which has documented effects on both healers and patients. While it is seldom, if ever, a cure, it appears to be a help to those who feel unwell, and is accompanied in the healer by a sense of slowed time, a lack of spatial awareness, and increased energy. Healers tend to exhibit bilaterally balanced EEG wave patterns (centered, meditative thinking) while performing Therapeutic Touch. This suggests that, just as disease may be tied to cognition, so, too, may be the healing that is its antithesis. Thus handedness, as an *expression* of the energy of cognitive laterality, may also be a way of helping to *treat* it in another, when it is out of balance. Healing using the hands is a talent that is accessible to us all.

✳ We apply Einstein's General and Special Theories of Relativity to these notions in an attempt to offer mathematical explanation of these phenomena for those who may feel uncomfortable with ancient or metaphysical symbols and interpretations. The General Theory describes gravity in terms of space and time and says that time slows as we move closer to a gravitational center, and space, even light, becomes increasingly curved, forming a tree-like vortex. The Special Theory describes the spiral motion of imaginary objects traveling through this vortex and the effects of this motion on measurements of mass, time and distance. It says that, as an object approaches the speed of light, mass and time increase and distance to the center decreases. We apply the equations of special relativity, which are normally used with space-time phenomena in space (e.g., stars), to the circling and space-time relationships we think might occur in the area of the brain. A macro concept is thereby applied to a micro situation.

✳ If mass can be said to equal weight, if time can be said to equal age, and if distance can be said to equal a laterality measure representing the distance (radius) to the center, relativity equations may add validity to healers' perceptions in demonstrating that time does slow and energy increases with a form of bilateral cognition which acts to help another human being. We conclude that cognitive shifting, which is very much under our control, may actually affect the energy and time aspects of our lives that are not. It is recommended that we strive toward the bilateral state and a balance of typological functions and abilities for the long-term, healthful maintenance of individuals and community.

✳ Thus, earlier biblical references to the Tree of Life, high energy at the center, etc., and the very unusual experiences of NDE travelers and practitioners of Therapeutic Touch, might appear to bear some symbolic relation to relativity and vice versa. We propose that a child is born into the center of the circle (tree); moves to its outer reaches as he develops his laterality preferences and various disease risks over the course of his lifetime; gradually spirals back toward the center with age; and finally dies at the center, which represents both the beginning and end of life, as well as the beginning and end of whatever might lie on the other side.

# EPILOGUE

We have come a long way from uni-dimensional, linear, static views of type, talent and disease, to a three-dimensional, circular and changeable conception of these things, and finally to metaphysical and cosmic fantasies of other dimensions not yet explored. Despite its possible appeal, it must be said that there is, of course, no solid proof whatsoever for the existence of our Sundial wheel, or its pulsating extensions, only suspected theoretical relationships comprising what would normally be called an educated guess. None of the associations or precise locations on the wheel or in the brain may actually exist. Or it may be that *some* of them exist. Or *all* of them may exist. Consequently, for those interested, there is a need to research this theory that is for now a kind of Impressionist painting with broad brushstrokes of trends and hypotheses that blend, obfuscate and approximate detail. Without evidence, it is difficult to do more.

Having many times mentioned our reservations to the contrary, we will repeat our bias that because circles of life linking the energy of human behavior, physical health, and natural forces and cycles have been found in many cultures since antiquity—in the form of Buddhist mandalas, Egyptian and Chinese astrological charts, Hindu chakras, the Chinese T'ai Chi, the web of life of Nordic runes, the Mayan calendar, the native medicine wheel, the dance of the circle of life in Australian aboriginal cultures, the Tibetan cycle of life and death, the Star of David in Judaism, the crossed-circle symbols of Christianity, and so forth—it seems likely that there may be at least some truth to the relationships, and that this warrants renewed investigation in the twenty-first century.

Whether we choose to call it Kundalini, Chi, Spirit, life force, chemical, electrical or magnetic energy, or Light, we would all appear to be describing something very similar using a great variety of different labels which appeal to our cultural and cognitive slants. To the extent that the Sundial, like other balance wheels, offers hope for changing some aspects of the human condition, it will be important for us to explore the "light" of some of our own shadows to discover the vast possibilities that may live beyond them.

> I have come into the world as light, so that everyone who believes in me
> should not remain in the darkness (John 12: 45).

# ✳ BIBLIOGRAPHY ✳

**Abra, J. (1988).** *Assaults on Mount Parnassus: Theoretical Views of the Creative Process.* Lanham, MD: University Press of America.

**Alajouanine, T. (1948).** Aphasia and artistic realization. *Brain, 71,* 229–241.

**Anchors, S. and R. Dana (1989).** Type and substance abuse in college age students. *Journal of Psychological Type, 17,* 26–30.

**Anders Ericsson, K. and I. Faivre (1988).** What's exceptional about exceptional ability? In L. Obler and D. Fein (Eds.), *The Exceptional Brain: Neuropsychology of Talent and Special Abilities.* New York, NY: Guilford Press, 436–473.

**Andreasen, N. (1987).** Creativity and mental illness: Prevalence rates in writers and their first-degree relatives. *American Journal of Psychiatry, 144* (10), 1288–1292.

**Aram, D. and J. Healy (1988).** Hyperlexia: A review of extraordinary word recognition. In L. Obler and D. Fein (Eds.), *The Exceptional Brain: Neuropsychology of Talent and Special Abilities.* New York, NY: Guilford Press, 70–102.

**Aung, S. (1993).** Interrelationships between Western and Traditional Chinese Medicine. Lecture, The University of Calgary Faculty of Medicine, Calgary, AB.

**Bakal, D. (1979).** *Psychology and Medicine: Psychobiological Dimensions of Health and Illness.* New York, NY: Springer Publishing.

**Bakan, P., G. Dibb and P. Reed (1973).** Handedness and birth stress. *Neuropsychologia, 11,* 363–366.

**Becker, R. and G. Selden (1985).** *The Body Electric: Electromagnetism and the Foundation of Life.* New York, NY: William Morrow.

**Beinfield, H. and E. Korngold (1991).** *Between Heaven and Earth: A Guide to Chinese Medicine.* New York, NY: Ballantine Books.

**Benbow, C. (1986a).** Physiological correlates of extreme intellectual precocity. *Neuropsychologia, 24,* 719–725.

**Benbow, C. (1988).** Neuropsychological perspectives on mathematical talent. In L. Obler and D. Fein (Eds.), *The Exceptional Brain: Neuropsychology of Talent and Special Abilities.* New York, NY: Guilford Press, 48–69.

**Benor, D. (1990, September).** Survey of spiritual healing research. *Complementary Medical Research, 4* (3), 9–33.

Benson, F. and E. Zaidel (Eds.) (1985). *The Dual Brain: Hemispheric Specialization in Humans*. New York, NY: Guilford Press.

Benton, A. (1968). Differential behavioral effects in frontal lobe disease. *Neuropsychologia, 6,* 53–60.

Bentov, I. (1977). *Stalking the Wild Pendulum: On the Mechanics of Consciousness*. New York, NY: E.P. Dutton.

Berg, R., M. Franzen and D. Wedding (1987). *Screening for Brain Impairment: A Manual for Mental Health Practice*. New York, NY: Springer Publishing.

Bever, T. (1980). Broca and Lashley were right: Cerebral dominance is an accident of growth. In D. Kaplan and N. Chomsky (Eds.), *Biology and Language*. Cambridge, MA: MIT Press.

Bever, T. (1983). Cerebral lateralization, cognitive asymmetry, and human consciousness. In E. Perecman (Ed.), *Cognitive Processing in the Right Hemisphere*. New York, NY: Academic Press, 19–39.

Bever, T. and R. Chiarello (1974). Cerebral dominance in musicians and non-musicians. *Science, 185,* 137–139.

Bisbee, C., R. Mullaly and H. Osmond (1982). Type and psychiatric illness. *Research in Psychological Type, 5,* 49–68.

Blau, T. (1977). Torque and schizophrenic vulnerability. *American Psychologist,* 977.

Blumstein, S., H. Goodglass and V. Tartter (1975). The reliability of ear advantage in dichotic listening. *Brain and Language, 21* (2), 226–236.

Bogen, J. (1969a). The other side of the brain I: Disgraphia and dyscopia following cerebral commisurotomy. *Bulletin of LA Neurological Societies, 34,* 73–105.

Bogen, J. (1969b). The other side of the brain II: An appositional mind. *Bulletin of LA Neurological Societies, 34,* 135–162.

Bogen, J. (1975). Some educational aspects of hemispheric specialization. *UCLA Educator, 17,* 24–32.

Bogen, J. and G. Bogen (1969c). The other side of the brain III: The corpus callosum and creativity. *Bulletin of LA Neurological Societies, 34* (4), 191–217.

Bogen, J. and H. Gordon (1971). Musical tests for functional lateralization with intracarotid amobarbital. *Nature, 230,* 524.

Bogyo, L. and R. Ellis (1988). A study in contrasts. In L. Obler and D. Fein (Eds.), *The Exceptional Brain: Neuropsychology of Talent and Special Abilities*. New York, NY: Guilford Press, 265–276.

Bokoros, M., M. Goldstein and M. Sweeney (1992). Common factors in five measures of cognitive style. *Current Psychology Research and Reviews, II,* 99–109.

Boller, F. and E. DeRenzie (1967). Relationship between visual memory defects and hemispheric locus of lesions. *Neurology, 17,* 1052–1058.

Bool, F., J. Kist, J. Locher and F. Wierda (1981). *M. C. Escher: His Life and Complete Graphic Work*. New York, NY: Harry N. Abrams, Inc.

Botez, M. and N. Wertheim (1959). Expressive aphasia and amusia following right frontal lesion in a right handed man. *Brain, 82,* 186–201.

Boulangier, V. (1994). Type dynamics and development: A gold mine for professional development in psychotherapy. Paper presented at Navigating Global Transformations and Inner Explorations, Third International Conference on Myers-Briggs Typology, University of Quebec, Montreal, PQ.

Bradshaw, J., N. Nettleton and G. Geffen (1971). Ear differences and delayed auditory feedback: Effects on a speech and a music task. *Journal of Experimental Psychology, 91* (1), 85–92.

Bradshaw, J., N. Nettleton and G. Geffen (1972). Ear asymmetry and delayed auditory feedback: Effects of task requirements and competitive stimulation. *Journal of Experimental Psychology, 94* (3), 269–275.

Bro, H. (1989). *A Seer Out of Season: The Life of Edgar Cayce.* New York, NY: St. Martin's Press.

Brockway, W. and H. Weinstock (1939). *Men of Music: Their Lives, Times and Achievements.* New York, NY: Simon & Schuster.

Brown, E. and K. Deffenbacher (1988). Superior memory performance and mnemonic encoding. In L. Obler and D. Fein (Eds.), *The Exceptional Brain: Neuropsychology of Talent and Special Abilities.* New York, NY: Guilford Press, 191–211.

Brown, J. (1988). Rethinking the right hemisphere. In E. Perecman (Ed.), Cognitive Processing in the Right Hemisphere. New York, NY: Academic Press, 41–52.

Bruyere, R. with J. Farrens (Ed.) (1989). *Wheels of Light: Chakras, Auras and the Healing Energy of the Body.* New York, NY: Simon & Schuster.

Bryden, M. (1965). Tachistoscopic recognition, handedness, and cerebral dominance. *Neuropsychologia, 3,* 108.

Bryden, M. (1973). Perceptual asymmetry in vision: Relation to handedness, eyedness, and speech lateralization. *Cortex, 9,* 418–432.

Buck, J. (1948). The H-T-P technique, a qualitative and quantitative scoring manual. *Journal of Clinical Psychology, 4,* 317–396.

Buxton, H. (1983). Auditory lateralization: An effect of rhythm. *Brain and Language, 18* (2), 249–258.

Campbell, W. (1995). On relapse in recovering alcoholics. Personal communication, Calgary, AB.

Capra, F. (1975). *The Tao of Physics.* Boston, MA: Shambhala Publications.

Carey, S. (1980). A case study: Face recognition. In D. Kaplan and N. Chomsky (Eds.), *Biology and Language.* Cambridge, MA: MIT Press.

Charness, N. (1988). Expertise in chess, music and physics: A cognitive perspective. In L. Obler and D. Fein (Eds.), *The Exceptional Brain: Neuropsychology of Talent and Special Abilities.* New York, NY: Guilford Press, 399–426.

Charness, N., J. Clifton and L. MacDonald (1988). Case study of a musical "mono-savant:" A cognitive-psychological focus. In L. Obler and D. Fein (Eds.), *The Exceptional Brain: Neuropsychology of Talent and Special Abilities.* New York, NY: Guilford Press, 277–293.

Clare, S. and S. Suter (1983). Drawing and the cerebral hemispheres: Bilateral EEG alpha. *Biological Psychology, 16,* 15–27.

Clark, R. (1971). *Einstein: The Life and Times.* New York, NY: Avon Books.

Clynes, M. and N. Nettheim (1982). The living quality of music: Neurobiologic patterns of communicating feeling. In M. Clynes (Ed.), *Music, Mind and Brain: The Neuropsychology of Music.* New York, NY: Plenum Press, 47–82.

Cohen, M. (1989). *Health and the Rise of Civilization.* New Haven, CT: Yale University Press.

Colt, G. (1996, September). Heal me. *Life,* 35–50.

Coren, S. (1993). *The Left-Hander Syndrome: The Causes and Consequences of Left-Handedness.* New York, NY: Vintage Books.

Corlett, E. and N. Millner (1993). *Navigating Midlife: Using Typology as a Guide.* Palo Alto, CA: CPP Books.

Cox, C. (1926). The early mental traits of 300 geniuses. In L. Terman (Ed.), *Genetic Studies of Genius: Volume 2.* Palo Alto, CA: Stanford University Press.

Craig, J. (1979). The effects of musical training and cerebral asymmetries on perception of an auditory illusion. *Cortex, 15* (4), 671–677.

Cranberg, L. and M. Albert (1988). The chess mind. In L. Obler and D. Fein (Eds.), *The Exceptional Brain: Neuropsychology of Talent and Special Abilities.* New York, NY: Guilford Press, 156–190.

Critchley, M. (1953). *The Parietal Lobes.* **London: Arnold.**

Cross, P., R. Cattell and H. Butcher (1967). The personality pattern of creative artists. *British Journal of Educational Psychology, 37,* 292–299.

Crossman, D. and J. Polich (1989). Hemispheric and personality differences between "left-" and "right-brain" individuals for tachistoscopic verbal and spatial tasks. *Personality and Individual Differences, 10* (7), 747–755.

Curtiss, S. (1988). The special talent of grammar acquisition. In L. Obler and D. Fein (Eds.), *The Exceptional Brain: Neuropsychology of Talent and Special Abilities.* New York, NY: Guilford Press, 364–386.

Daniel, C. (Ed.) (1987). *Chronicle of the 20th Century.* Mount Kisco, NY: Jacques Legrand.

Darwin, B. (1979). *The Oxford Dictionary of Quotations* (3rd ed.). New York, NY: Oxford University Press.

Darwish, H., P. Diadori and B. Juschka (1994). Relationship between spike parameters and seizure severity. Unpublished manuscript, Alberta Children's Hospital, Calgary, AB.

Dawson, J. (1977). An anthropological perspective on the evolution and lateralization of the brain. *Annals of NY Academy of Sciences, 299.*

DeLong, R. and A. Aldershof (1988). An association of special abilities with juvenile manic-depressive illness. In L. Obler and D. Fein (Eds.), *The Exceptional Brain: Neuropsychology of Talent and Special Abilities.* New York, NY: Guilford Press, 387–395.

Delbridge-Parker, L. and D. Robinson (1989). Type and academically gifted adolescents. *Journal of Psychological Type, 17,* 66–72.

DeRenzie, E. (1978). Hemispheric asymmetry as evidenced by spatial disorders. In M. Kinsbourne (Ed.), *Asymmetrical Function of the Brain.* Cambridge: Cambridge University Press.

DeRenzie, E. and H. Spinnler (1967). Impaired performance on color tasks in patients with hemispheric damage. *Cortex, 3,* 194–217.

Deutsch, D. (1977). Memory and attention in music. In M. Critchley and R. Henson (Eds.), *Music and the Brain.* London: W. Heinemann Medical Books.

Deutsch, D. (1979). In R. Nickerson and R. Pew (Eds.), *Attention and Performance VIII.* Hillsdale, NJ: Lawrence Erlbaum.

Diamond, M. and A. Scheibel (1985, July 28). Research on the structure of Einstein's brain. In W. Reich: The stuff of genius. *The New York Times Magazine,* 24–25.

Di Leo, J. (1983). *Interpreting Children's Drawings*. New York, NY: Brunner-Mazel.

Dorner, G., B. Schenk, B. Schmiedel et al. (1983). Stressful events in prenatal life of bi- and homo-sexual men. *Experimental Clinical Endocrinology*, 83–87.

Dossey, L. (1993). *Healing Words*. New York, NY: Harpersanfrancisco.

Dreher, H. (1988). *Your Defense Against Cancer: The Complete Guide to Cancer Prevention*. New York, NY: Harper & Row.

Dreifuss, F. (1961). Observations on aphasia in a polyglot poet. *Acta Psychologia et Neurologia Scandinavia, 36* (1), 91–97.

Edwards, B. (1979). *Drawing on the Right Side of the Brain: A Course in Enhancing Creativity and Artistic Confidence*. Los Angeles, CA: J.P. Tarcher.

Eiduson, B. (1958). Artist and non-artist: A comparative study. *Journal of Personality, 26*, 13–28. *Encyclopedia Britannica* (1966), *13* (141).

Escher, M. (1986). *Escher on Escher: Exploring the Infinite*. New York, NY: Harry N. Abrams, Inc.

Fein, D. and L. Obler (1988). Neuropsychological study of talent: A developing field. In L. Obler and Fein (Eds.), *The Exceptional Brain: Neuropsychology of Talent and Special Abilities*. New York, NY: Guilford Press, 3–15.

Feinberg, I., M. Lane and N. Lassen (1960). Senile dementia and cerebral oxygen uptake measured on the right and left sides. *Nature, 188*, 962–964.

Fife, J., T. Carskadon and M. Thorne (1986). Psychological type and heart disease. *Journal of Psychological Type, 12*, 58–64.

Flor-Henry, P. (1976). Lateralized temporal-limbic dysfunction and psychopathology. *Annals of NY Academy of Sciences, 280*, 770–797.

Ford, L. (1988). Cognitive preferences and personality type: Further evidence of a relationship. *International Brain Dominance Review, 5* (2), 15–22.

Franco, L. and R. Sperry (1977). Hemisphere lateralization for cognitive processing of geometry. *Neuropsychologia, 15*, 107–114.

Frederickson, L. (1988). *Confronting Mitral Valve Prolapse Syndrome*. San Marcos, CA: Avant Books.

Friedman, M. and R. Rosenman (1974). *Type A Behavior and Your Heart*. New York, NY: Knopf.

Friesen, J. (1995). *You Can't Get There From Here: The Mystique of North American Plains Indians Culture and Philosophy*. Dubuque, ID: Kendall/Hunt Publishing.

Fuller, J. and W. Thompson (1978). *Foundations of Behavior Genetics*. C.V. Mosby.

Funk, B. (1980, September). Hurricane! *National Geographic, 158* (3), 346–379.

Gaffron, M. (1950). Left and right in pictures. *Art Quarterly, 13*, 312–321.

Galin, D. (1974). Implications for psychiatry of right and left cerebral specialization. *Archives of General Psychiatry, 31*, 572–583.

Galin, D. and R. Ornstein (1972). Lateral specialization of cognitive mode: An EEG study. *Psychophysiology, 9*, 412–418.

Galton, F. (1869). *Hereditary Genius: An Inquiry into Its Laws and Consequences.* London: MacMillan and Co.

Gardner, H. (1975a). Artistry following aphasia. Paper presented at the Academy of Aphasia. Victoria, BC. Cited by Gardner and Winner (1981).

Gardner, H. (1982). *Art, Mind, and Brain: A Cognitive Approach to Creativity.* New York, NY: Basic Books.

Gardner, H. (1983). *Frames of Mind: The Theory of Multiple Intelligences.* New York, NY: Basic Books.

Gardner, H. (1985). *The Mind's New Science: A History of the Cognitive Revolution.* New York, NY: Basic Books.

Gardner, H. (1988). Foreword. In L. Obler and D. Fein (Eds.), *The Exceptional Brain: Neuropsychology of Talent and Special Abilities.* New York, NY: Guilford Press.

Gardner, H., J. Silverman, G. Denes, C. Semenza, and Rosenstiel (1977). Sensitivity to musical denotation and connotation in organic patients. *Cortex, 13,* 243–256.

Gardner, H. and E. Winner (1981). Artistry and aphasia. In *Acquired Aphasia.* New York, NY: Academic Press, 361–384.

Gates, A. and J. Bradshaw (1977). Music perception and cerebral asymmetries. *Cortex, 13,* 390–401.

Gazzaniga, M. (1988). *Mind Matters: How the Mind and Brain Interact to Create Our Conscious Lives.* Boston, MA: Houghton Mifflin.

Gazzaniga, M. and J. LeDoux (1978). *The Integrated Mind.* New York, NY: Plenum Press.

Gerber, R. (1988). *Vibrational Medicine: New Choices for Healing Ourselves.* Santa Fe, NM: Bear & Co.

Geschwind, N. and P. Behan (1982). Left-handedness: Association with immune disease, migraine, and developmental learning disorder. *Proceedings of the National Academy of Sciences, USA, 79,* 5097–5100.

Geschwind, N. and A. Galaburda (1985a, 1985b, 1985c). Cerebral lateralization: Biological mechanisms associations and pathology: 1, 2 and 3. A hypothesis and a program for research. *Archives of Neurology, 42,* 428–459, 521–55, 634–654.

Geschwind, N. and W. Levitsky (1968). Human brain: Left-right asymmetries in temporal speech region. *Science, 161,* 186–187.

Getzels, J. and P. Jackson (1962). *Creativity and Intelligence: Explorations with Gifted Students.* New York, NY: John Wiley and Sons, Inc.

Getzels, J. and P. Jackson (1970). The highly intelligent and the highly creative adolescent. In P. Vernon (Ed.), *Creativity: Selected Readings.* Harmondsworth: Penguin Books, 189–202.

Gianotti, G. and C. Tiacci (1970). Patterns of drawing disability in right and left hemispheric patients. *Neuropsychologia, 8,* 379–384.

Gibson, D. (1985). *Human Behaviour Genetics.* Calgary, AB: Lecture series at The University of Calgary.

Ginn, C. and D. Sexton (1988). Psychological types of *Inc. 500* founders and their spouses. *Journal of Psychological Type, 16,* 3–12.

Gleick, J. (1987). *Chaos: Making a New Science.* New York, NY: Penguin Books.

Glick, S., T. Jerussi and B. Zimmerberg (1977). Behavioral and neuropharmacological correlates of nigrostriatal asymmetry in rats. In S. Harnad et al. (Eds.), *Lateralization in the Nervous System.* New York, NY: Academic Press, 213–249.

Goldberger, A., D. Rigney and B. West (1990, February). Chaos and fractals in human physiology. *Scientific American, 262,* 42–49.

Goldstein, K. (1948). *Language and Language Disturbances.* New York, NY: Grune and Stratton.

Goldstein, K. (1962). The effect of brain damage on the personality. *Psychiatry, 15,* 245–260.

Goodall, H. and G. Brobby (1982). Stuttering, sickling, and cerebral malaria: A possible organic basis for stuttering. *Lancet, 1,* 1279–1281.

Gordon, H. (1970). Hemispheric asymmetries in the perception of musical chords. *Cortex, 6,* 387–398.

Gordon, H. (1975). Hemispheric asymmetry and musical performance. *Science, 189,* 68–69.

Gordon, H. and J. Bogen (1974). Hemispheric lateralization of singing after intracarotid sodium amylo-barbitone. *Journal of Neurology, Neurosurgery and Psychiatry, 37,* 727–738.

Greenacre, P. (1971). *Emotional Growth, Psychoanalytic Studies of the Gifted and a Great Variety of Other Individuals, Volume 2.* New York, NY: International Universities Press.

Griff, M. (1970). The recruitment and socialization of artists. In M. Albrecht et al. (Eds.) *The Sociology of Art and Literature.* London: G. Duckworth, 145–158.

Grossman, M. (1980, February). Figurative referential skills after brain damage. Paper presented at the International Neuropsychological Society, San Diego, CA. Cited by Gardner and Winner (1981).

Guilford, J. (1950). Creativity. *American Psychologist, 5,* 444–454.

Guilford, J. (1970). Traits of creativity. In P. Vernon (Ed.), *Creativity: Selected Readings.* New York, NY: Penguin Books, 167–188.

Haber, R. and L. Haber (1988). The characteristics of eidetic imagery. In L. Obler and D. Fein (Eds.), *The Exceptional Brain: Neuropsychology of Talent and Special Abilities.* New York, NY: Guilford Press, 218–241.

Haier, R., K. Sokolski, M. Katz and M. Buchsbaum (1987). The study of personality with positron emission tomography. In J. Strelau and H. Eysenck (Eds.), *Personality Dimensions and Arousal.* New York, NY: Plenum Publishing, 251–267.

Hall, M., G. Hall and P. Lavoie (1968). Ideation in patients with unilateral or bilateral midline brain lesions. *Journal of Abnormal Psychology, 73* (6), 52–531.

Harasym, P., E. Leong and B. Juschka (1996). Relationship between Myers-Briggs Type Indicator and Gregorc Style Delineator. *Perceptual and Motor Skills, 82,* 1203–1210.

Harasym, P., E. Leong, B. Juschka, G. Lucier and F. Lorscheider (1995). Myers-Briggs psychological type and achievement in anatomy and physiology. *Advances in Physiology Education, 13* (1), S61–S65.

Hardyck, C. and L. Petrinovich (1977). Left-handedness. *Psychological Bulletin, 84,* 385–404.

Harpur, T. (1994). *The Uncommon Touch: An Investigation of Spiritual Healing.* Toronto, ON: McClelland & Stewart.

Harris, J. (1986). *Clinical Neuroscience: From Neuroanatomy to Psychodynamics.* New York, NY: Human Sciences Press.

Harris, L. (1978). Sex differences in spatial ability: Possible environmental, genetic and neurological factors. In M. Kinsbourne (Ed.), *Asymmetrical Function of the Brain.* Cambridge, MA: Cambridge University Press, 405–522.

Harshman, R., E. Hampson and S. Berenbaum (1983). Individual differences in cognitive abilities and brain organization Part 1: Sex and handedness differences in ability. *Canadian Journal of Psychology, 37*, 144–192.

Hathaway, W., J. Hargreaves, G. Thompson and D. Novitsky (1992, February). *A Study into the Effects of Light on Children of Elementary School Age—A Case of Daylight Robbery.* Policy and Planning Branch, Planning and Information Services Division. Edmonton, AB: Alberta Education.

Hebb, D. and W. Penfield (1940). Human behavior after extensive bilateral removal from the frontal lobes. *Archives of Neurology and Psychiatry, 44,* 421–438.

Hemingway, E. (1940). *For Whom the Bell Tolls.* New York: Charles Scribner's Sons.

Hier, D., J. Mondlock and L. Caplan (1983a). Behavioral abnormalities after right hemisphere stroke. *Neurology, 33,* 337–344.

Hier, D., J. Mondlock and L. Caplan (1983b). Recovery of behavioral abnormalities after right hemisphere stroke. *Neurology, 33,* 345–350.

Hines, M. and R. Gorski (1985). Hormonal influences on the development of neural asymmetries. In F. Benson and E. Zaidel (Eds.), *The Dual Brain.* New York, NY: Guilford Press, 75–96.

Hirsch, S. and J. Kummerow (1990). *Introduction to Type in Organizations: Individual Interpretive Guide* (2nd ed.). Palo Alto, CA: Consulting Psychologists Press.

Housser, F. (1926). *A Canadian Art Movement: The Story of the Group of Seven.* Toronto: Macmillan.

Hubel, D. and T. Wiesel (1963). Receptive fields of cells in striate cortex of very young, visually inexperienced kittens. *Journal of Neurophysiology, 26,* 994–1002.

Hudson, L. (1970). The question of creativity. In P. Vernon (Ed.), *Creativity: Selected Readings.* Harmondsworth: Penguin Books.

Humphrey, M. and O. Zangwill (1951). Cessation of dreaming after brain injury. *Journal of Neurosurgery and Psychiatry, 14,* 322–325.

Hunt, V. (1977). *Project Report: A Study of Structural Integration from Neuromuscular, Energy Field, and Emotional Approaches.* Boulder, CO: Rolf Institute of Structural Integration.

Huot, B., Makarec, K. & Persinger, M. A. (1989). Temporal lobes signs and Jungian dimensions of personality. *Perceptual and Motor Skills, 69*(3, Pt 1), 841–842.

Jackson, P. and S. Messick (1967). The person, the product, and the response: Conceptual problems in the assessment of creativity. In J. Kagan (Ed.), *Creativity and Learning.* Boston, MA: Beacon Press.

James, U. (1986). The Herrmann, Myers-Briggs connection. *International Brain Dominance Review, 3* (2), 32–34.

Jamison, K. (1986). Manic-depressive illness and accomplishment: Creativity, leadership and social class. In F. Goodwin and K. Jamison (Eds.), *Manic-Depressive Illness.* Oxford: Oxford University Press.

Jamison, K. (1995). *An Unquiet Mind: A Memoir of Moods and Madness.* New York, NY: Vintage Books.

Jamison, K., C. Gernar, C. Hammen and C. Padesky (1980). Clouds and silver linings: Positive experiences associated with primary affective disorders. *American Journal of Psychiatry, 137* (2), 198–202.

Johnson, P. (1977). Dichotically-stimulated ear differences in musicians and non-musicians. *Cortex, 13* (4), 385–389.

Jones-Gotman, M. and B. Milner (1977). Design fluency: The invention of nonsense drawings after focal cortical lesions. *Neuropsychologia, 15,* 653–674.

Judd, T. (1988). The varieties of musical talent. In L. Obler and D. Fein (Eds.), *The Exceptional Brain: Neuropsychology of Talent and Special Abilities.* New York, NY: Guilford Press, 127–155.

Judith, A. (1987). *Wheels of Life: A User's Guide to the Chakra System.* St. Paul, MN: Llewellyn Publications.

Jung, C. (1969a). *Mandala Symbolism.* Princeton, NJ: Princeton University Press.

Jung, C. (1969b). *Memories, Dreams and Reflections.* Princeton, NJ: Princeton University Press.

Jung, C. (1971). *Psychological Types.* Princeton, NJ: Princeton University Press. First published 1921.

Juschka, B. (1990). *Neuropsychology of Giftedness: Development of Visuographic Skills by Age, Sex, Handedness and Training.* Unpublished doctoral dissertation, The University of Calgary, Calgary, AB.

Kaplan, E. (1980, February). Process and Achievement Revisited. Presidential address, International Neuropsychological Society, San Diego, CA. Cited by Clare and Suter (1983).

Kaptchuk, T. (1983). *The Web That Has No Weaver: Understanding Chinese Medicine.* Chicago, IL: Congdon & Weed.

Kaufmann, W. (1985). *Universe.* New York, NY: W. H. Freeman & Co.

Keirsey, D. and M. Bates (1984). *Please Understand Me: Character and Temperament Types.* Del Mar, CA: Promethean Books.

Kelly, E. (1984). Type preferences of average chessplayers. *Journal of Psychological Type, 8,* 52–58.

Kelly, E. (1986). The MBTI patterns of women chessplayers: Comparisons with other chessplayers and non-players. *Journal of Psychological Type, 11,* 51–58.

Khatena, J. (1978). *The Creatively Gifted Child: Suggestions for Parents and Teachers.* New York, NY: Vantage Press.

Kimura, D. (1960). Spatial localization in left and right visual fields. *Canadian Journal of Psychology, 23,* 445–458.

Kimura, D. (1963). Speech lateralization in young children as determined by an auditory test. *Journal of Comparative Physiological Psychology, 56* (5), 899–902.

Kimura, D. (1964). Left-right differences in the perception of melodies. *Quarterly Journal of Experimental Psychology, 16,* 355–358.

Kimura, D. (1966). Dual functional asymmetry in the brain in visual perception. *Neuropsychologia, 4,* 272–285.

Kimura, D. (1973). The asymmetry of the human brain. *Scientific American, 228,* 70–78.

Kimura, D. (1989, November). How sex hormones boost—or cut—intellectual ability. *Psychology Today,* 62–66.

Kinsbourne, M. (1972). Eye and head turning indicates cerebral lateralization. *Science, 176,* 539–541.

Kinsbourne, M. (1978). Biological determinants of functional bisymmetry and asymmetry. In M. Kinsbourne (Ed.), *Asymmetrical Function of the Brain.* Cambridge, MA: Cambridge University Press, 1–3.

Knox, C. and D. Kimura (1970). Cerebral processing of nonverbal sounds in boys and girls. *Neuropsychologia, 8,* 227–237.

Kolb, B. and I. Whishaw (1980). *Fundamentals of Human Neuropsychology*. New York, NY: W. H. Freeman and Co.

Kolb, B. and I. Whishaw (1985). *Fundamentals of Human Neuropsychology* (2nd ed.). New York, NY: W .H. Freeman and Co.

Komosin, L. (1992). Personality type and suicidal behaviors in college students. *Journal of Psychological Type, 24*, 24–32.

Krieger, D. (1972). The relationship of touch, with intent to help or heal, to subjects' in-vivo hemoglobin values: A study in personalized interaction. Proceedings, American Nurses Association, 9th Nursing Research Conference, San Antonio TX, 39-78.

Krieger, D. (1976). Healing by the laying-on of hands as a facilitator of bioenergetic exchange:The response of in-vivo human hemoglobin. *International Journal for Psychoenergetic Systems, 2*.

Krieger, D. (1979). *The Therapeutic Touch: How to Use Your Hands to Help or to Heal*. New York, NY: Simon & Schuster (Fireside).

Krieger, D. (1993). *Accepting Your Power to Heal: The Personal Practice of Therapeutic Touch*. Santa Fe, NM: Bear & Co.

Kroeger, O. and J. Thuesen (1988). *Type Talk: The 16 Personality Types That Determine How We Live, Love and Work*. New York, NY: Dell Publishing.

Lansdell, H. (1961). The effect of neurosurgery on a test of proverbs. *American Psychologist, 16*, 448.

Lansdell, H. (1962, June). A sex difference in effect of temporal-lobe neurosurgery on design preference. *Nature, 194*, 852–854.

Laposky, A., M. Wilson and M. Languis (1991). A topographic brain mapping study of electrophysiological differences between sensing and intuitive psychological types. In APT-IX Proceedings, Ninth Biennial International Conferences of the Association for Psychological Type, Richmond, VA, July 11–14.

Lappe, M. (1994). *Evolutionary Medicine: Rethinking the Origins of Disease*. San Francisco, CA: Sierra Club Books.

Lashley, K. (1960). The problem of serial order. In F. Beach et al. (Eds.), *The Neuropsychology of Lashley*. New York, NY: McGraw-Hill, 506–523.

Lawrence, G. (1982). *People Types and Tiger Stripes: A Practical Guide to Learning Styles*, (2nd ed.). Gainesville, FL: Center for Applications of Psychological Type.

Lawrence, G. (1984). A synthesis of learning style research. *Journal of Psychological Type, 8*, 2–15.

Laytner, R. (1985, May 20). Clue to genius locked in cells. *Calgary Herald Sunday Magazine, 13*. Report on the unpublished work of M. Diamond, University of California (Berkeley).

Lebrun, Y., C. Van Endert and H. Szliwowski (1988). Trilingual hyperlexia. In L. Obler and D. Fein (Eds.), *The Exceptional Brain: Neuropsychology of Talent and Special Abilities*. New York, NY: Guilford Press, 253–264.

Lehmann, H. (1953). *Age and Achievement*. Princeton, NJ: Princeton University Press.

Lenneberg, E. (1967). *Biological Foundations of Language*. New York, NY: Wiley.

LeShan, L. (1977). *You Can Fight for Your Life: Emotional Factors in the Causation of Cancer*. New York, NY: M. Evans & Co.

Lester, W., W. Woloschuk, B. Juschka and H. Mandin (1995). Assessing the psychological type of specialists to assist students in career choice. *Academic Medicine, 70* (10), 932–933.

Levy, J. (1976). Lateral dominance and aesthetic preference. *Neuropsychologia, 14,* 431–445.

Levy-Agresti, J. and R. Sperry (1968). Differential perceptual capacities in major and minor hemispheres. *Proceedings of the National Academy of Science, 61,* 1151 (Summary).

Ley, R. and M. Bryden (1976). Hemispheric differences in   processing emotions and faces. *Brain and Language, 7,* 127–138.

Lezak, M. (1976). *Neuropsychological Assessment.* New York, NY: Oxford University Press.

Lombroso, C. (1976). Genius and insanity. In A. Rothenberg and C. Hausman (Eds.), *The Creativity Question.* Durham, NC: Duke University Press, 79–86.

Luria, A. (1966). *Human Brain and Psychological Processes.* New York, NY: Harper and Row.

Luria, A., L. Tsvetkova and D. Futer (1965). Aphasia in a composer. *Journal of Neurological Sciences, 2,* 288–292.

Luzader, M. (1984). Chemical dependency and type. *Journal of Psychological Type, 8,* 59–64.

Maccoby, E. and C. Jacklin (1974). *The Psychology of Sex Differences.* Stanford, CA: Stanford University Press.

Maccoby, E., C. Doering, C. Jacklin and H. Kraemer (1979). Concentrations of sex hormones in umbilical-cord blood: Their relation to sex and birth order of infants. *Child Development, 50,* 632–642.

Macdaid, G., M. McCaulley and R. Kainz (1986). *Myers-Briggs Type Indicator Atlas of Type Tables.* Gainesville, FL: Center for Applications of Psychological Type.

MacKinnon, D. (1961). Creativity in architects. In *Proceedings of the Conference on "The Creative Person."* Berkeley, CA: University of California, Extension Division.

MacKinnon, D. (1970). The personality correlates of creativity: A study of American architects. In P. Vernon (Ed.), *Creativity: Selected Readings.* Harmondsworth: Penguin Books, 289–311.

Maddi, S. (1975). The strenuousness of creative life. In I. Taylor and J. Getzels (Eds.), *Perspectives in Creativity.* Chicago, IL: Aldine Publishing.

Madge, C. and B. Weinberger (1973). *Art Students Observed.* London: Faber and Faber.

Marland, S., Jr. (1971, August). *Education of the Gifted and Talented.* Vol.1. Report to the Congress of the United States by the U.S. Commissioner of Education. Washington, DC: Government Printing Office.

Maslow, A. (1967). The creative attitude. In R. Mooney and T. Razik (Eds.), *Explorations in Creativity.* New York, NY: Harper and Row.

Matthysse, S. and S. Greenberg (1988). Anomalous calculating abilities and the computer architecture of the brain. In L. Obler and D. Fein (Eds.), *The Exceptional Brain: Neuropsychology of Talent and Special Abilities.* New York, NY: Guilford Press, 427–435.

Mazziotta, J. and M. Phelps (1985). Metabolic evidence of lateralized cerebral function demonstrated by positron emission tomography in patients with neuropsychiatric disorders and normal individuals. In F. Benson and E. Zaidel (Eds.), *The Dual Brain.* New York, NY: Guilford Press, 181–192.

Mazziotta, J., M. Phelps, R. Carson and D. Kuhl (1982). Tomographic mapping of human cerebral metabolism: Auditory stimulation. *Neurology, 32* (9), 921–937.

McCaulley, M. (1981). *Jung's Theory and the Myers-Briggs Type Indicator.* Gainesville, FL: Center for Applications of Psychological Type.

McElroy, W. (1954). A sex difference in preference for shapes. *British Journal of Psychology, 45,* 209–216.

McGlone, J. and W. Davidson (1973). The relation between cerebral speech laterality and spatial ability with special reference to sex and hand preference. *Neuropsychologia, 11,* 105–113.

McGlone, J. and A. Kertese (1973). Sex differences in cerebral processing of visuospatial tasks. *Cortex, 9,* 313–320.

McMullan, W. (1976). Creative individuals: Paradoxical personages. *Journal of Creative Behavior, 10,* 265–275.

Mebert, C. and G. Michel (1980). Handedness in artists. In J. Herron (Ed.), *Neuropsychology of Left-Handedness.* New York, NY: Academic Press, 273–279.

Mednick, S. (1962). The associative basis of the creative process. *Psychological Review, 69,* 220–227.

Mellman, T. and T. Uhde (1987). Obsessive-compulsive symptoms in panic disorder. *American Journal of Psychiatry, 144,* 1573–1576.

Michaud, E., A. Feinstein et al. (1989). *Fighting Disease: The Complete Guide to Natural Immune Power.* Emmaus, PA: Rodale Press.

Miller, L. (1990). *Inner Natures: Brain, Self and Personality.* New York, NY: St. Martin's Press.

Miller, P. (1987, June). Tracking tornadoes. *National Geographic, 171* (6), 690–715.

Milner, B. (1962). Laterality effects in audition. In V. Mountcastle (Ed.), *Interhemispheric Relations and Cerebral Dominance.* Baltimore, MD: Johns Hopkins Press, 177–195.

Milner, B. (1973). Hemispheric specialization: Scope and limits. In F. Schmidt and F. Worden (Eds.) *The Neurosciences: Third Study Program. Boston,* MA: MIT Press, 75–89.

Milner, B. (1980). Complementary functional specializations of the human cerebral hemispheres: Abstract of the proceedings of the study week on nerve cells, transmitters and behavior. *Pontificiae Academiae Scientiarum Scripta Varia,* 601–625.

Morgan, M. (1994). *Mutant Message Downunder.* Vancouver, BC: Abundance Productions International.

Moscovitch, M. (1977). The development of lateralization of language functions and its relation to cognitive and linguistic development: A review and some theoretical speculations. In S. Segalowitz and F. Gruber (Eds.), *Language Development and Neurological Theory.* New York, NY: Academic Press.

Motoyama, H. and R. Brown (1978). *Science and the Evolution of Consciousness: Chakras, Ki, and Psi.* Brookline, MA: Autumn Press Inc.

Myers, I. (1980b). *Introduction to Type: A Description of the Theory and Applications of the Myers-Briggs Type Indicator.* Palo Alto, CA: Consulting Psychologists Press.

Myers, I. (1987). *Introduction to Type* (4th ed.). Palo Alto, CA: Consulting Psychologists Press.

Myers, I. with P. Myers (1980). *Gifts Differing.* Palo Alto, CA: Consulting Psychologists Press.

Myers, I. and M. McCaulley (1985). *Manual: A Guide to the Development and Use of the Myers-Briggs Type Indicator.* Palo Alto, CA: Consulting Psychologists Press.

Neiman, C. and E. Goldman (1994). *AfterLife: The Complete Guide to Life After Death.* Harmondsworth: Viking Studio Books.

Newman, J. (1989). *The Human Brain: A Frontier of Psychological Type* (Audiotape). Gainesville, FL: Center for Applications of Psychological Type.

Novoa, L., D. Fein and L. Obler (1988). Talent in foreign languages: A case study. In L. Obler and D. Fein (Eds.), *The Exceptional Brain: Neuropsychology of Talent and Special Abilities.* New York, NY: Guilford Press, 294–302.

Obler, L. and D. Fein (Eds.) (1988). *The Exceptional Brain: Neuropsychology of Talent and Special Abilities.* New York, NY: Guilford Press.

O'Leary, D. (1991). *Windows of Wonder: A Spirituality of Self-Esteem.* Mahwah, NJ: Paulist Press.

Oscar-Berman, M. (1988). Superior memory: Perspective from the neuropsychology of memory disorders. In L. Obler and D. Fein (Eds.), *The Exceptional Brain: Neuropsychology of Talent and Special Abilities.* New York, NY: Guilford Press, 212–217.

Oscar-Berman, M., S. Blumstein and D. Deluca (1974). Iconic recognition of musical symbols in lateral visual field. Paper presented at the American Psychological Association Annual Meeting, New Orleans, LA. Cited by Pribram (1982).

Osterrieth, P. (1944). Le test de copie d'une figure complexe. *Archives de Psychologie, 30,* 206–356.

Ott, J. (1973). *Health and Light: The Effects of Natural and Artificial Light on Man and Other Living Things.* Old Greenwich, CT: The Devin-Adair Company.

Peterson, J. and L. Lansky (1974). Left-handedness among architects: Some facts and speculation. *Perceptual and Motor Skills, 38,* 547–550.

Peterson, J. and L. Lansky (1977). Left-handedness among architects: Partial replication and some new data. *Perceptual and Motor Skills, 45,* 1216–1218.

Phelps, M., J. Mazziotta, R. Gerner, et al. (1983). Human cerebral glucose metabolism in affective disorders: Drug-free states and pharmacologic effects. *Journal of Cerebral Blood Flow Metabolism, 3* (Supplement 1): S7–S8.

Piazza, D. (1977). Cerebral lateralization in young children as measured by dichotic listening and finger tapping tasks. *Neuropsychologia, 45,* 417–425.

Piercy, M., H. Hecaen and J. Ajuriaguerra (1960). Constructional apraxia associated with unilateral cerebral lesions—left and right sides compared. *Brain, 83,* 225–242.

Pomeranz, B. (1978). Do endorphins mediate acupuncture analgesia? *Advances in Biochemical Psychopharmacology, 18,* 351–359.

Pribram, K. (1982). Brain mechanism in music: Prolegomena for a theory of the meaning of meaning. In M. Clynes (Ed.), *Music, Mind and Brain: The Neuropsychology of Music.* New York, NY: Plenum Press, 21–35.

Provost, J. (1993). *Applications of the Myers-Briggs Type Indicator in Counseling: A Casebook.* Gainesville, FL: Center for Applications of Psychological Type.

Provost, J. and S. Anchors (1987). *Applications of the Myers-Briggs Type Indicator in Higher Education.* Palo Alto, CA: Consulting Psychologists Press.

Quenk, N. (1993). *Beside Ourselves: Our Hidden Personality in Everyday Life.* Palo Alto, CA: Davies-Black Publishing.

Radeloff, D. (1991). Psychological types, color attributes, and color preferences of clothing, textiles, and design students. *Clothing and Textiles Research Journal, 9* (3), 59–67.

Rapoport, J. (1989). *The Boy Who Couldn't Stop Washing: The Experience and Treatment of Obsessive-Compulsive Disorder.* New York, NY: Penguin Books.

Rasmussen, T. and B. Milner (1977). The role of early left brain injury in determining lateralization of cerebral speech functions. *Annals of the New York Academy of Sciences, 299,* 355–369.

Restak, R. (1984). *The Brain.* Toronto, ON: Bantam Books.

Rimland, B. and D. Fein (1988). Special talents of autistic savants. In L. Obler and D. Fein (Eds.), *The Exceptional Brain: Neuropsychology of Talent and Special Abilities.* New York, NY: Guilford Press, 474–492.

Ritsema, R. and S. Karcher (1994). *I Ching: The Classic Chinese Oracle of Change, The First Complete Translation with Concordance.* Shaftesbury, Dorset: Element Books.

Robbins, K. and D. McAdam (1974). Interhemispheric alpha asymmetry and imagery mode. *Brain and Language, 1,* 189–193.

Roberts, E. and D. Roberts (1988). Jungian psychological traits and coronary heart disease. *Journal of Psychological Type, 15,* 3–12.

Robinson, G. and D. Solomon (1974). Rhythm is processed by the speech hemisphere. *Journal of Experimental Psychology, 102,* 508.

Roe, A. (1975). Painters and painting. In I. Taylor and J. Getzels (Eds.), *Perspectives in Creativity.* Chicago, IL: Aldine Publishing, 157–172.

Roederer, J. (1982). Physical and neuropsychological foundations of music: The basic questions. In M. Clynes (Eds.), *Music, Mind and Brain: The Neuropsychology of Music.* New York, NY: Plenum Press, 37–46.

Rosenfeld, A. (1988). New images, new insights into your brain. *Psychology Today, 22.*

Rosenblatt, E. and E. Winner (1988). Is superior visual memory a component of superior drawing ability? In L. Obler and D. Fein (Eds.), *The Exceptional Brain: Neuropsychology of Talent and Special Abilities.* New York, NY: Guilford Press, 341–363.

Rossi, E. (1986). *The Psychobiology of Mind-Body Healing: New Concepts of Therapeutic Hypnosis.* New York, NY: W.W. Norton & Co.

Rourke, B., D. Bakker, J. Fish and J. Strang (1983). *Child Neuropsychology.* New York, NY: Guilford Press.

Rovin, J. (1993). *Sports Babylon.* New York, NY: Signet.

Rubens, A. (1977). Anatomical asymmetries of human cerebral cortex. In S. Harnad et al. (Eds.), *Lateralization in the Nervous System.* New York, NY: Academic Press, 503–516.

Ruelle (1980). EKG regular before a heart attack. Cited in Goldberger et. al (1990, Feb.). Chaos and fractals in human physiology. *Scientific American, 262,* 42–49.

Sacks, O. (1985). *The Man Who Mistook His Wife for a Hat and Other Clinical Tales.* New York, NY: Simon and Schuster.

Schneiderman, E. and C. Desmarais (1988). A neuropsychological substrate for talent in second-language acquisition. In L. Obler and D. Fein (Eds.), *The Exceptional Brain: Neuropsychology of Talent and Special Abilities.* New York, NY: Guilford Press, 103–126.

Schweiger, A. (1985). Harmony of the spheres and the hemispheres: The arts and hemispheric specialization. In F. Benson and E. Zaidel (Eds.), *The Dual Brain.* New York, NY: Guilford Press, 359-373.

Schweiger, A. (1988). A portrait of the artist as a brain-damaged patient. In L. Obler and D. Fein (Eds.), *The Exceptional Brain: Neuropsychology of Talent and Special Abilities*. New York, NY: Guilford Press, 303–309.

Selfe, L. (1977). Nadia: A Case of Extraordinary Drawing Ability in an Autistic Child. New York, NY: Harcourt Brace Jovanovich.

Seltzer, B. and I. Sherwin (1983). A comparison of clinical features in early- and late-onset primary degenerative dementia. *Archives of Neurology, 40,* 143–146.

Sewell, T. (1986). *The measurement of learning style: A critique of four assessment tools.* Green Bay, WI: Wisconsin University.

Shagass, C., R. Roemer, J. Straumanis and M. Amadeo (1978). Evoked potential correlates of psychosis. *Biological Psychiatry, 13* (2).

Shapiro, B., M. Grossman and H. Gardner (1981). Selective musical processing deficits in brain damaged populations. *Neuropsychologia, 19,* 161–169.

Shapiro, R. (1968). *Creative Research Scientists.* Buffalo, NY: National Institute for Personnel Research.

Shanon, B. (1980). Lateralization effects in musical decision tasks. *Neuropsychologia, 18,* 21–31.

Sherwood, K. (1985). *The Art of Spiritual Healing.* St. Paul, MN: Llewellyn Publications.

Sidtis, J. (1980). On the nature of the cortical function underlying right hemisphere auditory perception. *Neuropsychologia, 18* (3), 321–330.

Smith, A. (1992). Time of day and performance. In A. Smith and D. Jones (Eds.), *Handbook of Human Performance: Vol. 3, State and Trait.* San Diego, CA: Academic Press.

Smith, B. (1979). *Community Health: An Epidemiological Approach.* New York, NY: Macmillan Publishing.

Smith, S. (1988). Calculating prodigies. In L. Obler and D. Fein (Eds.), *The Exceptional Brain Neuropsychology of Talent and Special Abilities.* New York, NY: Guilford Press, 19–47.

Somerville, R. and Editors of Time-Life Books (1993). *The Defending Army: Journey Through the Mind and Body.* Alexandria, VA: Time-Life Books.

Soukes, A. and H. Baruk (1930). Autopsie d'un case d'amusie (avec aphasie) chez un professeur de piano. *Revue Neurologique, 1,* 545–556. Cited by Gardner and Winner (1981).

Spencer, J., T. Carskadon and M. Thorne (1986). Type and Type A Behavior. *Journal of Psychological Type, 12,* 50–57.

Sperry, R. (1974). Lateral specialization in the surgically separated hemispheres. In F. Schmidt and F. Worden (Eds.), *The Neurosciences: Third Study Program.* Cambridge, MA: MIT Press, 5–19.

Staudenmayer, H. and M. Camazine (1989). Sensing type personality, projection, and Universal "Allergic" Reactivity. *Journal of Psychological Type, 18,* 59–62.

Stein, M. and S. Heinze (1970). A summary of Galton's Hereditary Genius. In P. Vernon (Ed.), *Creativity: Selected Readings.* Harmondsworth: Penguin Books.

Sternberg, R. and J. Powell (1982). Theories of intelligence. In R. Sternberg (Ed.), *Handbook of Human Intelligence.* New York, NY: Cambridge University Press.

Stevens, A. (1994). *Jung.* Oxford: Oxford University Press.

Storm, H. (1973). *Seven Arrows.* New York, NY: Ballantine Books.

Strauss, A. (1970). The art school and its students: A study and an interpretation. In M. Albrecht, et al. (Eds.), *The Sociology of Art and Literature.* London: G. Duckworth, 159–177.

Sunnucks, A. (1970). *The Encyclopedia of Chess.* New York: St. Martins Press.

Tanguay, P. (1985). Implications of hemispheric specialization for psychiatry. In F. Benson and E. Zaidel (Eds.), *The Dual Brain.* New York, NY: Guilford Press, 375–384.

Taylor, D. and C. Ounsted (1971). Biological mechanisms influencing the outcome of seizures in response to fever. *Epilepsia, 12,* 33–45.

Taylor, I. (1975). A retrospective view of creativity investigation. In I. Taylor and J. Getzels (Eds.), *Perspectives in Creativity.* Chicago, IL: Aldine Publishing.

Taylor, I. and J. Getzels (Eds.) (1975). *Perspectives in Creativity.* Chicago, IL: Aldine Publishing.

Taylor, D. and C. Ounsted (1971). Biological mechanisms influencing the outcome of seizures in response to fever. *Epilepsia, 12,* 33–45.

Tegano, D., V. Fu and J. Moran (1983). Divergent thinking and hemispheric dominance for language function among preschool children. *Perceptual and Motor Skills, 56,* 691–698.

TenHouten, W. (1985). Cerebral lateralization theory and the sociology of knowledge. In F. Benson and E. Zaidel (Eds.), *The Dual Brain.* New York, NY: Guilford Press, 341–358.

Terman, L. (Ed.) (1947). *Genetic Studies of Genius, Vol. 4: The Gifted Child Grows Up.* Palo Alto, CA: Stanford University Press.

Terman, L. (Ed.) (1959). *Genetic Studied of Genius, Vol. 5.* Palo Alto, CA: Stanford University Press.

Thatcher, R., R. McAlaster, M. Lester, R. Horst and D. Cantor (1983). Hemispheric EEG asymmetries related to cognitive functioning in children. In E. Perecman (Ed.), *Cognitive Processing in the Right Hemisphere.* New York, NY: Academic Press, 125–146.

*The Canadian Encyclopedia* (1985). Edmonton, AB: Hurtig Publishers.

Thomas, D. and D. Shucard (1983). Changes in patterns of hemispheric electrophysiological activity as a function of instructional set. *International Journal of Neuroscience, 18* (1–2), 11–19.

Thorne, A. and H. Gough (1991). *Portraits of Type: An MBTI Research Compendium.* Palo Alto, CA: Consulting Psychologists Press.

Tobler, J. (1993). *This Day in Rock.* London: Carlton Books.

Torrance, E. (1962). *Guiding Creative Talent.* Englewood Cliffs, NJ: Prentice Hall.

Truax, R. (1996). Personal communication on Schrödinger equations, with the Head, Department of Chemistry, The University of Calgary, Calgary, AB.

Tucker, D. (1976). Sex differences in hemispheric specialization for synthetic visuospatial functions. *Neuropsychologia, 14,* 447–454.

Tucker, D. (1981). Lateral brain function, emotion, and conceptualization. *Psychological Bulletin, 89,* 19–46.

Tucker, D., R. Roth, B. Arneson and V. Buckingham (1977). Note: Right hemisphere activation during stress. *Neuropsychologia, 15,* 697–700.

Tucker, D., C. Stenslie, R. Roth and S. Shearer (1981). Right frontal lobe activation and right hemisphere performance: Decrement during a depressed mood. *Archives of General Psychiatry, 38,* 169–174.

Vernon, P. (1970). *Creativity: Selected Readings.* Harmondsworth: Penguin Books.

Waber, D. (1976). Sex differences in cognition: A function of maturation rate? *Science, 192,* 572–573.

Waldrop, M. (1992). *Complexity: The Emerging Science at the Edge of Order and Chaos.* New York, NY: Simon & Schuster.

Wallach, M. and N. Kogan (1970). A new look at the creativity-intelligence distinction. In P. Vernon (Ed.), *Creativity: Selected Readings.* Harmondsworth: Penguin Books.

Wapner, W., T. Judd and H. Gardner (1978). Visual agnosia in an artist. *Cortex, 14,* 343–364.

Warrington, E., J. Merle and M. Kinsbourne (1966). Drawing disability in relation to laterality of cerebral lesion. *Brain, 89,* 53–82.

Waterhouse, L. (1988). Extraordinary visual memory and pattern perception in an autistic boy. In L. Obler and D. Fein (Eds.), *The Exceptional Brain: Neuropsychology of Talent and Special Abilities.* New York, NY: Guilford Press, 325–338.

Watson, J. (1968). *The Double Helix.* New York, NY: New American Library.

Webster, W. and A. Thurber (1978). Problem-solving strategies and manifest brain asymmetry. *Cortex, 14,* 474–484.

Weinstein, S. (1978). Functional cerebral hemispheric asymmetry. In M. Kinsbourne (Ed.), *Asymmetrical Function of the Brain.* Cambridge, MA: Cambridge University Press, 17–48.

Wertheim, N. and M. Botez (1961). Receptive amusia. *Brain, 84,* 19–30.

Whyte, K. (1990, January–February). Nobody's fifteen feet tall. *Saturday Night,* 23.

Wiesel, T. and D. Hubel (1963). The effects of visual deprivation on morphology and physiology of cells in the cat's lateral geniculate body. *Journal of Neurophysiology, 26,* 978–993.

Wilson, D. (1994, Winter). Looking for the light. *Second Wind, 5* (1), 6.

Wilson, M. and M. Languis (1989). Differences in brain electrical activity patterns between introverted and extraverted adults. *Journal of Psychological Type, 18,* 14–23

Winner, E. and H. Gardner (1977). The comprehension of metaphor in brain damaged patients. *Brain, 100,* 719–727.

Witelson, S. (1974). Hemispheric specialization for linguistic and nonlinguistic tactual perception using a dichotomous stimulation technique. *Cortex, 10,* 3–17.

Witelson, S. (1976). Sex and the single hemisphere: Right hemisphere processing for spatial processing. *Science, 193,* 425–427.

Witelson, S. (1977). Developmental dyslexia: Two right hemispheres and none left. *Science, 195,* 309–311.

Witelson, S. (1985). The brain connection: The corpus callosum is larger in left-handers. *Science, 229,* 665–668.

Witelson, S. and W. Pallie (1973). Left hemisphere specialization for language in the newborn: Neuro-anatomical evidence of asymmetry. *Brain, 96,* 641–646.

Witkin, J., R. Dyk, H. Faterson, D. Goodenough and S. Karp (1962). *Psychological Differentiation.* New York, NY: J. Wiley.

Wolfe, J. (1988). Where is eidetic imagery? Speculations on its psychological and neurophysiological locus. In L. Obler and D. Fein (Eds.), *The Exceptional Brain: Neuropsychology of Talent and Special Abilities.* New York, NY: Guilford Press, 242–250.

Wolff, K. (1933). The experimental study of forms of expression. *Characteristics of Personality, 68,* 377–417.

Wood, M. (1994, August). Untitled paper on applications of psychological type to traditions in native cultures, presented at Navigating Global Transformations and Inner Explorations, Third International Conference on Myers-Briggs Typology, University of Quebec, Montreal, PQ.

Zaimov, K., D. Kitov and N. Kolev (1969). Aphasie chez un peintre. *Encephale, 68,* 377–417. Cited by Gardner and Winner (1981).

Zajonc, R. (1976). Family configuration and intelligence. *Science, 192,* 227–236.

Zangwill, O. (1966). Psychological deficits associated with frontal lobe lesions. *International Journal of Neurology, 5,* 395–402.

# APPENDIX A
## TYPE TABLES OF RELEVANT VOCATIONAL GROUPS

✳ ✳ ✳

**Table 32. Law Students (n = 2248; Myers & Myers, 1980)**

| ISTJ | ISFJ | INFJ | INTJ |
|---|---|---|---|
| n = 236<br>10.50% | n = 58<br>2.58% | n = 58<br>2.58% | n = 194<br>8.63% |
| **ISTP**<br>n = 87<br>3.87% | **ISFP**<br>n = 33<br>1.47% | **INFP**<br>n = 120<br>5.34% | **INTP**<br>n = 221<br>9.83% |
| **ESTP**<br>n = 87<br>3.87% | **ESFP**<br>n = 42<br>1.87% | **ENFP**<br>n = 132<br>5.87% | **ENTP**<br>n = 245<br>10.90% |
| **ESTJ**<br>n = 295<br>13.12% | **ESFJ**<br>n = 80<br>3.56% | **ENFJ**<br>n = 75<br>3.34% | **ENTJ**<br>n = 285<br>12.68% |

**Table 33. Women Chess Players (n = 248; Kelly, 1986)**

| ISTJ | ISFJ | INFJ | INTJ |
|---|---|---|---|
| n = 39<br>15.73% | n = 11<br>4.44% | n = 7<br>2.82% | n = 30<br>12.10% |
| **ISTP**<br>n = 13<br>5.24% | **ISFP**<br>n = 7<br>2.82% | **INFP**<br>n = 19<br>7.66% | **INTP**<br>n = 25<br>10.08% |
| **ESTP**<br>n = 4<br>1.61% | **ESFP**<br>n = 9<br>3.63% | **ENFP**<br>n = 27<br>10.89% | **ENTP**<br>n = 10<br>4.03% |
| **ESTJ**<br>n = 20<br>8.06% | **ESFJ**<br>n = 5<br>2.02% | **ENFJ**<br>n = 3<br>1.21% | **ENTJ**<br>n = 19<br>7.66% |

**Table 34. Male Inc. 500 Founders (n = 133; Ginn & Sexton, 1988)**

| ISTJ | ISFJ | INFJ | INTJ |
|------|------|------|------|
| n = 19 | n = 1 | n = 1 | n = 16 |
| 14.29% | 0.75% | 0.75% | 12.03% |
| **ISTP** | **ISFP** | **INFP** | **INTP** |
| n = 6 | n = 2 | n = 6 | n = 21 |
| 4.51% | 1.50% | 4.51% | 15.79% |
| **ESTP** | **ESFP** | **ENFP** | **ENTP** |
| n = 8 | n = 2 | n = 1 | n = 14 |
| 6.02% | 1.50% | 0.75% | 10.53% |
| **ESTJ** | **ESFJ** | **ENFJ** | **ENTJ** |
| n = 12 | n = 1 | n = 4 | n = 19 |
| 9.02% | 0.75% | 3.01% | 14.29% |

**Table 35. High-Level Corporate Executives (n = 136; Macdaid et. al., 1986)**

| ISTJ | ISFJ | INFJ | INTJ |
|------|------|------|------|
| n = 33 | n = 0 | n = 1 | n = 15 |
| 24.26% | 0.00% | 0.74% | 11.03% |
| **ISTP** | **ISFP** | **INFP** | **INTP** |
| n = 6 | n = 1 | n = 3 | n = 4 |
| 4.41% | 0.74% | 2.21% | 2.94% |
| **ESTP** | **ESFP** | **ENFP** | **ENTP** |
| n = 4 | n = 4 | n = 1 | n = 11 |
| 2.94% | 2.94% | 0.74% | 8.09% |
| **ESTJ** | **ESFJ** | **ENFJ** | **ENTJ** |
| n = 27 | n = 3 | n = 1 | n = 22 |
| 19.85% | 2.21% | 0.74% | 16.18% |

**Table 36. Finance and Commerce Students (n = 488; Myers & Myers, 1980)**

| ISTJ | ISFJ | INFJ | INTJ |
|---|---|---|---|
| n = 44 | n = 19 | n = 1 | n = 13 |
| 9.02% | 3.89% | 0.20% | 2.66% |
| **ISTP** | **ISFP** | **INFP** | **INTP** |
| n = 35 | n = 7 | n = 11 | n = 15 |
| 7.17% | 1.43% | 2.25% | 3.07% |
| **ESTP** | **ESFP** | **ENFP** | **ENTP** |
| n = 63 | n = 34 | n = 30 | n = 35 |
| 12.91% | 6.97% | 6.15% | 7.17% |
| **ESTJ** | **ESFJ** | **ENFJ** | **ENTJ** |
| n = 106 | n = 43 | n = 8 | n = 24 |
| 21.72% | 8.81% | 1.64% | 4.92% |

**Table 37. Scientists (n = 226; Macdaid et. al, 1986)**

| ISTJ | ISFJ | INFJ | INTJ |
|---|---|---|---|
| n = 32 | n = 13 | n = 10 | n = 29 |
| 14.6% | 5.75% | 4.42% | 12.83% |
| **ISTP** | **ISFP** | **INFP** | **INTP** |
| n = 8 | n = 2 | n = 12 | n = 19 |
| 3.54% | 0.88% | 5.31% | 8.41% |
| **ESTP** | **ESFP** | **ENFP** | **ENTP** |
| n = 3 | n = 4 | n = 13 | n = 15 |
| 1.33% | 1.77% | 5.75% | 6.64% |
| **ESTJ** | **ESFJ** | **ENFJ** | **ENTJ** |
| n = 20 | n = 15 | n = 8 | n = 23 |
| 8.85% | 6.64% | 3.54% | 10.18% |

**Table 38. Science Students (n = 715; Myers & Myers, 1980)**

| ISTJ | ISFJ | INFJ | INTJ |
|---|---|---|---|
| n = 39<br>5.53% | n = 12<br>1.70% | n = 44<br>6.24% | n = 128<br>18.16% |
| **ISTP**<br>n = 18<br>2.55% | **ISFP**<br>n = 15<br>2.13% | **INFP**<br>n = 58<br>8.23% | **INTP**<br>n = 123<br>17.45% |
| **ESTP**<br>n = 12<br>1.70% | **ESFP**<br>n = 1<br>0.14% | **ENFP**<br>n = 55<br>7.80% | **ENTP**<br>n = 79<br>11.21% |
| **ESTJ**<br>n = 13<br>1.84% | **ESFJ**<br>n = 8<br>1.13% | **ENFJ**<br>n = 27<br>3.83% | **ENTJ**<br>n = 73<br>10.35% |

**Table 39. Actors (n = 62; Macdaid et al., 1986)**

| ISTJ | ISFJ | INFJ | INTJ |
|---|---|---|---|
| n = 3<br>4.84% | n = 1<br>1.61% | n = 1<br>1.61% | n = 6<br>9.68% |
| **ISTP**<br>n = 0<br>0.00% | **ISFP**<br>n = 0<br>0.00% | **INFP**<br>n = 7<br>11.29% | **INTP**<br>n = 5<br>8.06% |
| **ESTP**<br>n = 2<br>3.23% | **ESFP**<br>n = 3<br>4.84% | **ENFP**<br>n = 10<br>16.13% | **ENTP**<br>n = 7<br>11.29% |
| **ESTJ**<br>n = 3<br>4.84% | **ESFJ**<br>n = 0<br>0.00% | **ENFJ**<br>n = 8<br>12.90% | **ENTJ**<br>n = 6<br>9.68% |

Table 40. Coaches (n = 164; Macdaid et al., 1986)

| ISTJ | ISFJ | INFJ | INTJ |
|------|------|------|------|
| n = 25<br>15.24% | n = 17<br>10.37% | n = 3<br>1.83% | n = 6<br>3.66% |
| **ISTP**<br>n = 7<br>4.27% | **ISFP**<br>n = 6<br>3.66% | **INFP**<br>n = 5<br>3.05% | **INTP**<br>n = 6<br>3.66% |
| **ESTP**<br>n = 4<br>2.44% | **ESFP**<br>n = 13<br>7.93% | **ENFP**<br>n = 11<br>6.71% | **ENTP**<br>n = 8<br>4.88% |
| **ESTJ**<br>n = 25<br>15.24% | **ESFJ**<br>n = 19<br>11.59% | **ENFJ**<br>n = 5<br>3.05% | **ENTJ**<br>n = 4<br>2.44% |

Table 41. Lifeguards, Attendants, Recreation and Amusement (n = 211; Macdaid et al., 1986)

| ISTJ | ISFJ | INFJ | INTJ |
|------|------|------|------|
| n = 23<br>10.90% | n = 13<br>6.16% | n = 5<br>2.37% | n = 5<br>2.37% |
| **ISTP**<br>n = 6<br>2.84% | **ISFP**<br>n = 14<br>6.64% | **INFP**<br>n = 16<br>7.58% | **INTP**<br>n = 8<br>3.79% |
| **ESTP**<br>n = 10<br>4.74% | **ESFP**<br>n = 17<br>8.06% | **ENFP**<br>n = 22<br>10.43% | **ENTP**<br>n = 9<br>4.27% |
| **ESTJ**<br>n = 26<br>12.32% | **ESFJ**<br>n = 24<br>11.37% | **ENFJ**<br>n = 6<br>2.84% | **ENTJ**<br>n = 7<br>3.32% |

# APPENDIX B
## INCIDENCE OF DISEASE, BY TALENT GROUP

\* \*\* \*

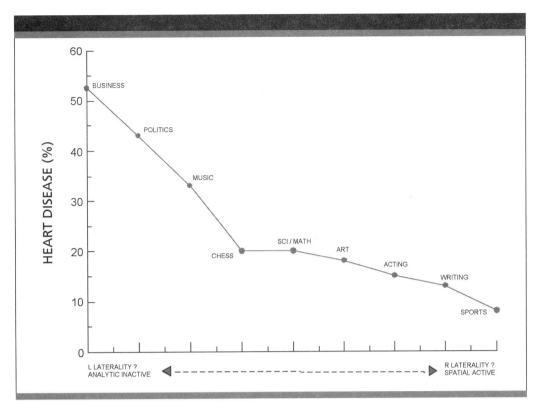

**Figure 77. Incidence of Heart Disease in Nine Talent Areas**

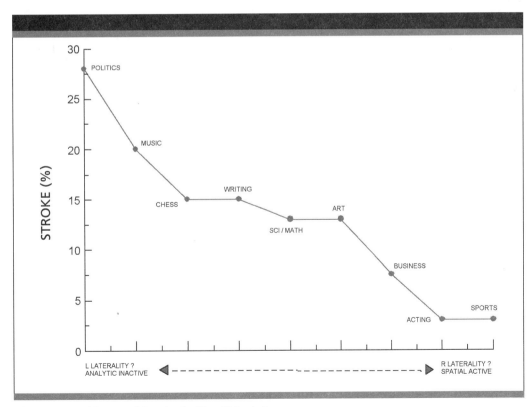

**Figure 78. Incidence of Stroke in Nine Talent Areas**

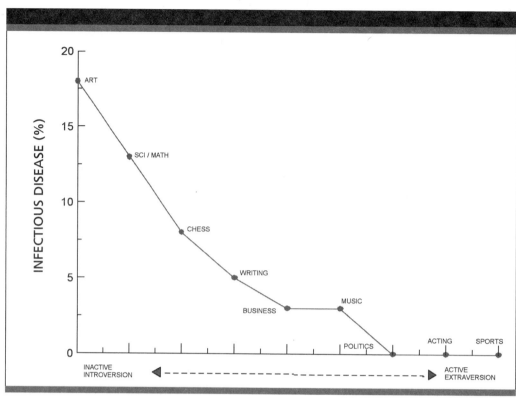

**Figure 79. Incidence of Infectious Disease (Excluding AIDS) in Nine Talent Areas**

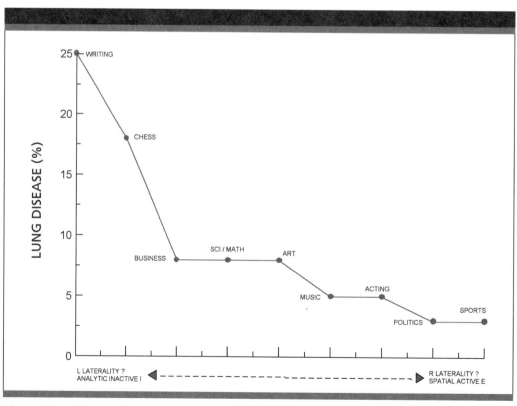

**Figure 80. Incidence of Lung Disease in Nine Talent Areas**

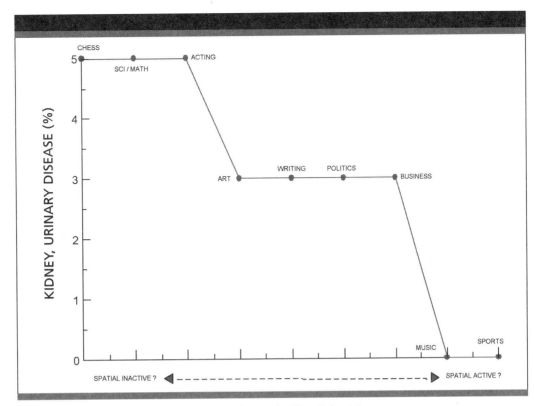

**Figure 81. Incidence of Kidney/Urinary Disease in Nine Talent Areas**

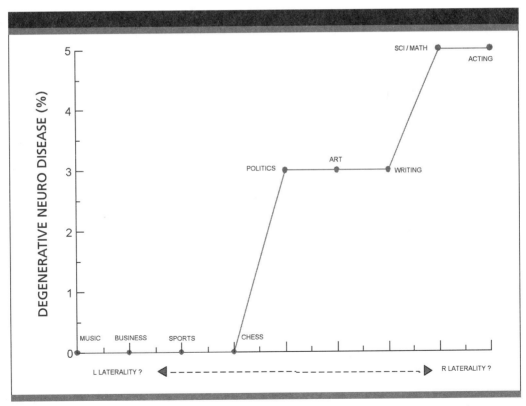

**Figure 82. Incidence of Degenerative Neurological Disease (e.g., MS, ALS) in Nine Talent Areas**

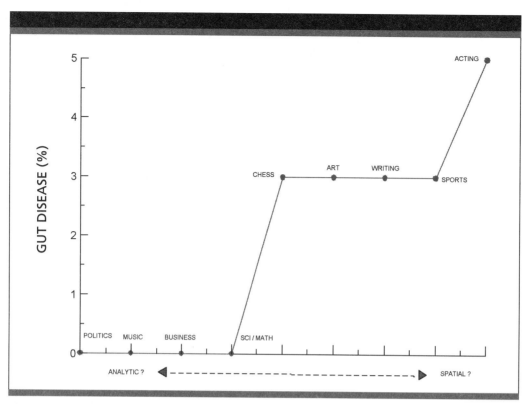

**Figure 83. Incidence of Diseases of the Gut in Nine Talent Areas**

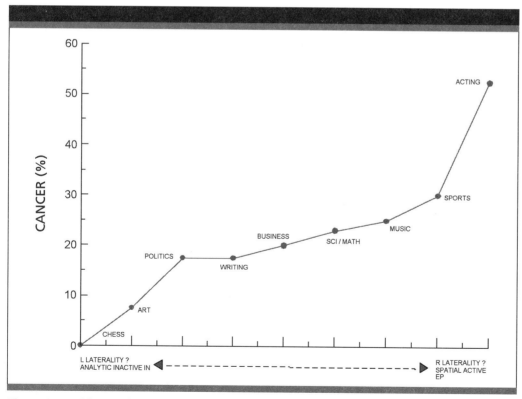

**Figure 84. Incidence of Cancer in Nine Talent Areas**

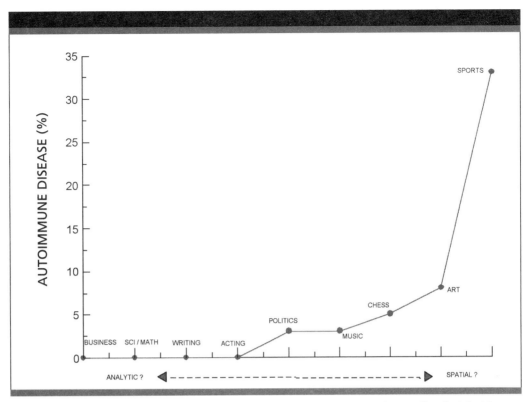

**Figure 85. Incidence of Autoimmune Disease (Arthritis, Diabetes, Asthma/Allergies) in Nine Talent Areas**

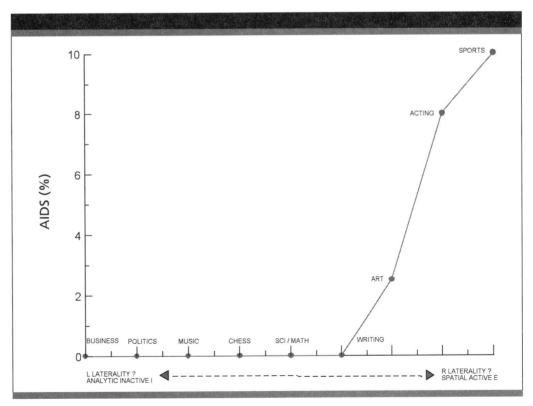

**Figure 86. Incidence of AIDS in Nine Talent Areas**

# APPENDIX C
## DISTRIBUTION OF TALENT AND DISEASE, BY MONTH OF BIRTH

✳ ✳ ✳

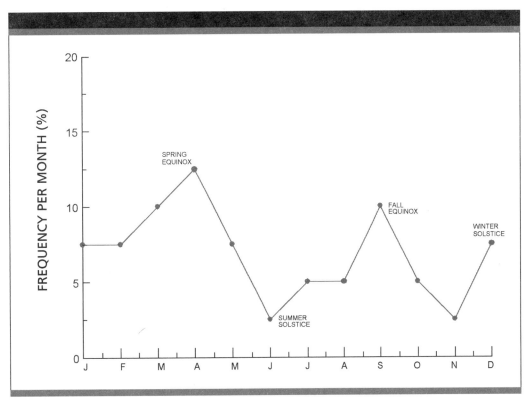

**Figure 87. Distribution of Scientists and Mathematicians by Month of Birth**

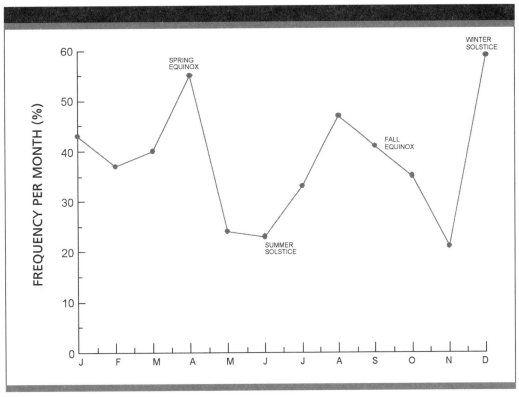

**Figure 88. Distribution of Heart Disease and Stroke by Month of Birth**

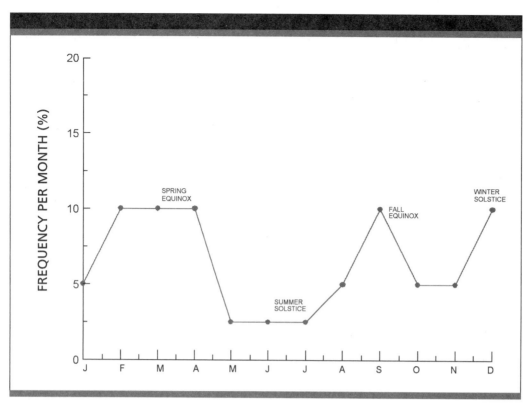

**Figure 89. Distribution of Musicians by Month of Birth**

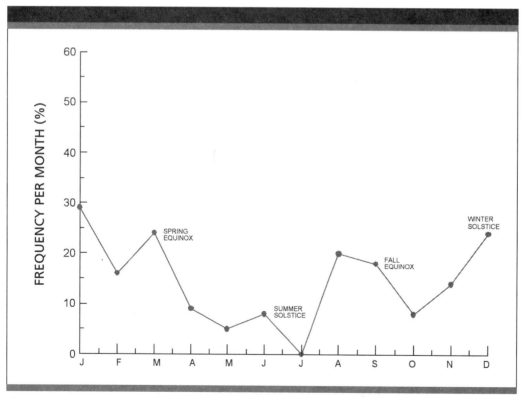

**Figure 90. Distribution of Stroke by Month of Birth**

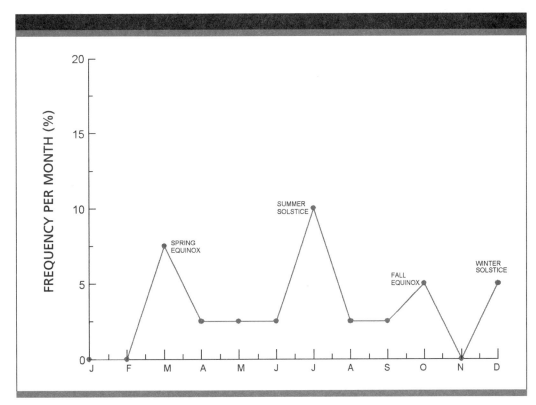

Figure 91. Distribution of Athletes by Month of Birth

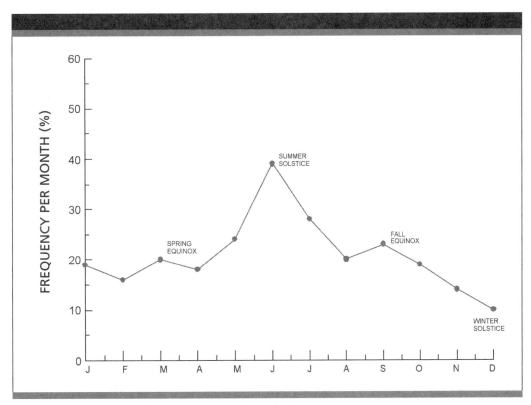

Figure 92. Distribution of Cancer by Month of Birth

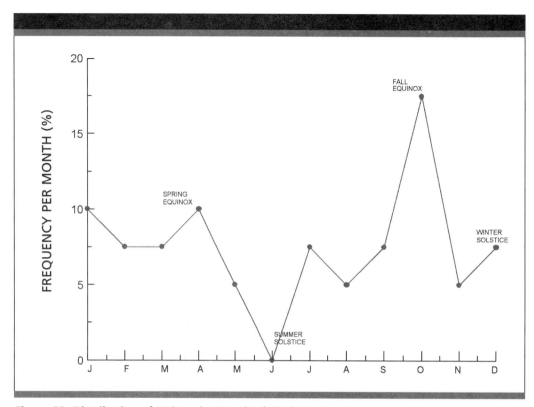

**Figure 93. Distribution of Writers by Month of Birth**

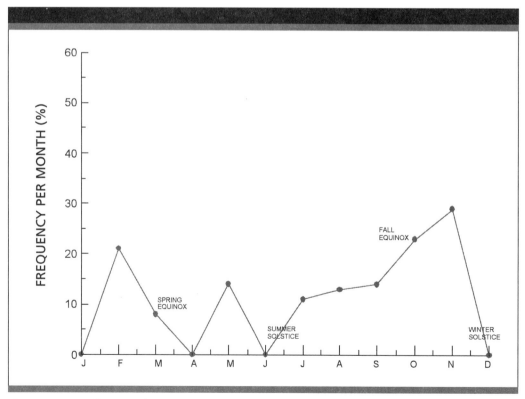

**Figure 94. Distribution of Lung Disease by Month of Birth**

# ABOUT THE AUTHOR

Dr. Barbara E. Bryden (INTJ) has worked in counseling, teaching, writing and research capacities in academic and applied settings. She is currently teaching psychology at Mount Royal College and is an adjunct professor of psychology at Athabasca University. A Canadian Certified Counselor, she is a member of the Association for Psychological Type, the Canadian Counseling Association, and the American Psychological Association.

Barb has been a Killam scholar in counseling psychology and education at the University of Calgary. In 2002, she was approved by the National Academies of Science, Washington DC, to work as a National Research Council associate with investigators at the Psychophysiological Research Laboratory, NASA Ames Research Center.

Barb lives in Calgary, and enjoys family and friends, music and art, golden retrievers, and the lakes and mountains of Canada. Of all her accomplishments, she is proudest of her three children.

# A

# B

# C

chess masters 100

Chi 169–175, 180–181, 188, 207, 212, 279

cluster disorders 83, 94, 97, 105, 123

cluster traits 83–84

cognition 1, 23, 33, 34, 37, 48, 74–76, 81, 94, 125, 130–132, 134, 137, 139–141, 145, 148–150, 153, 155, 161, 165, 167, 169, 177, 190, 197, 205, 209, 211, 219, 221–223, 227, 229, 237, 248, 255, 261, 267, 271, 274, 277

cognitive shift 17, 19, 39, 46, 48, 49, 64, 76, 125, 148, 178, 182, 217, 222, 255

color 53, 153–169, 180, 188–190, 203–204, 209, 231, 243, 254, 256–257, 273, 275

compensation 5, 16, 17, 19, 23, 34–35, 143

# D

degenerative neurological disease 135, 140, 150, 311

depotentiation 13, 34

dichotic listening 25, 45–46, 87

DNA 217, 231, 233, 234, 237, 253, 268

dominance theory 30, 33

# E

EEG 12, 25–26, 36, 55, 65–66, 68, 89, 92, 118, 141, 209, 214, 223, 227, 237, 239, 242, 248–250, 255, 268, 271, 277

Einstein-Tiller model of space-time 2, 3, 276

electromagnetic spectrum 159, 161, 255

energy 5, 8, 10–17, 33, 48, 109, 145, 153, 155–159, 161–162, 164–169, 172–173, 175–179, 191, 194–196, 200, 201, 204, 209, 211–223, 227, 236–239, 241–252, 255, 258, 262, 264, 267–268, 271, 273–279

# G

gastrointestinal disease 140, 149

Geschwind, Norman 2, 81–87, 93–96, 116, 129, 153, 166, 185, 190, 191, 200, 203

# H

handedness 7, 17, 23, 25, 37, 39, 48, 59, 62–64, 71–74, 76, 77, 79, 81–84, 95–98, 113–114, 117, 120, 123–125, 131, 141, 147, 155, 164, 165, 166, 197, 203, 205, 206, 222, 231, 237, 239, 268, 269

heart disease 81, 94, 108, 114, 129–142, 146, 147, 149–150, 164–167, 173, 180, 190–195, 198, 204–206, 217, 221, 226, 237, 270, 309, 317

cardiovascular disease 129, 134, 179–180, 203, 205, 206, 219

# I

Immune disease 144, 179, 181, 219, 222

Immune pattern 140–141, 149, 174, 180, 182, 190–194, 207–209, 237

individuation 5, 10, 17, 77, 125, 153, 185, 197, 207–208

infectious diseases 134, 180, 206, 208

intelligence 21–22, 36, 56, 64–66, 76, 86, 93–94, 103, 123–124, 141

   IQ 21–22, 65–66, 88, 92, 94, 123–124

# J

Jung, Carl 2, 5, 7, 9–19, 35, 37, 64, 66, 77, 81, 82, 113, 115, 140, 141, 153, 155, 177, 192, 196, 197, 207, 208, 227, 230, 235, 258, 262, 265, 268, 274

# K

kidney disease 176

Kirlian photography 12, 159, 239, 246–247

Krieger, Dolores 244–250, 273–274

Kundalini 158, 161, 169, 212, 216, 254, 273, 279

# L

laterality 19, 23–27, 30–34, 36, 39, 48, 49, 59, 60, 62–66, 68, 70–77, 80, 81, 83, 89, 96, 110, 113–115, 117, 122–124, 127, 131, 133–135, 137–138, 141–142, 147, 161, 174–175, 177, 180–183, 191, 193, 197–198, 200, 203–205, 208, 209, 211, 213, 216–219, 221, 223–226, 228, 236, 237, 241–242, 251, 253, 262, 265–268, 276–277

laterality hypothesis 19, 23, 30, 77, 208

left laterality 72–74, 203, 253

lesion study 23

Lorentz transformation 211, 265–267

lung disease 134–135, 137–138, 140, 149, 167, 175, 180, 216, 227, 310, 320

# M

migraine 129, 131, 143, 147, 176

# N

neuropsychology 2, 5, 19, 21–38, 39–76, 171

# O

obsession 35, 100, 102, 104, 108, 110, 123

one-sided personality 5, 10, 17, 19, 37, 77

# P

pendulum 123, 173, 176, 182, 200, 201, 216, 263

PET scan 25, 139, 159

politicians 133, 135, 192

projection 16–17, 35

psychiatric disorders 68, 133, 217

psychic energy 5, 10, 12, 17, 211, 271

# R

relativity 2, 239, 262–269, 277

right laterality 60, 72–74, 134, 203

# S

scientists and mathematicians 66, 135, 137, 191, 317

second law of thermodynamics 12

sensory impairment 139

shadow 9, 115, 118, 148, 274

sodium Amytal 24, 34, 37, 45

spirals 207, 227, 236, 258, 260, 262, 268, 271

spiritual psychology 2, 198

stroke 21, 42, 50, 59, 60, 61, 101, 114, 116, 129, 130, 131, 133–136, 138, 139, 140, 143, 144, 147, 149, 150, 165–167, 173, 174, 180, 182, 190–192, 194, 195, 216, 223, 226, 227, 237, 309, 317, 318

substance abuse  139, 204

suicide 60, 93, 113, 133, 135, 138, 166, 204

Sundial model of type, talent and disease 220, 237

# T

T'ai Chi 169, 171–172, 175, 180–181, 188, 207, 279

Tachistoscopic technique 26

talent database 180, 182, 185, 190, 192, 194, 205, 207, 237, 242 talent genera 80